The Impact of the Freeze of Kuwaiti and Iraqi Assets on Financial Institutions and Financial Transactions

International Bar Association Series

The Impact of the Freeze of Kuwaiti and Iraqi Assets on Financial Institutions and Financial Transactions

Editors

Barry R. Campbell,
Tory Tory DesLauriers & Binnington,
Toronto

and
Danforth Newcomb,
Shearman & Sterling,
New York

Graham & Trotman
A member of the Kluwer Academic Publishers Group
LONDON/DORDRECHT/BOSTON

and
International Bar Association

Graham & Trotman Limited
Sterling House
66 Wilton Road
London SW1V 1DE
UK

Kluwer Academic Publishers Group
101 Philip Drive
Assinippi Park
Norwell, MA 02061
USA

International Bar Association
2 Harewood Place
Hanover Square
London W1R 9HB
UK

British Library Cataloguing in Publication Data
The impact of the freeze of Kuwaiti and Iraqi assets on financial
    institutions and financial transactions.–
(International Bar Association series).
1. Iraq. Kuwait. International economic sanctions
 I. Campbell, Barry R. II. Newcomb, Danforth III. Series 341.75

ISBN 1-85333-558-4

Library of Congress CIP data is available

Series ISBN: 1 85333 096 5

Prelims typeset by BookEns Ltd, Baldock, Herts
Printed and bound in Great Britain by Bell & Bain Ltd., Glasgow

Contents

STOP PRESS October 19, 1990
UNITED STATES

General License No. 4 has been revoked and License Nos. 3 and 7 have been amended. The
revised texts appear on pages 184b to 184j.

About the IBA and the Section on Business Law

The International Bar Association (IBA) is the world's foremost international association of lawyers, with a membership of some 13,000 individual lawyers in 132 countries, as well as 113 Bar Associations and Law Societies. Its principal aims and objectives are:
— To encourage the discussion of problems relating to professional organisation and status.
— To promote an exchange of information between legal associations worldwide.
— To support the independence of the judiciary and the right of lawyers to practice their profession without interference.
— To keep abreast of developments in the law, and help in improving and making new laws.
Above all, though, it seeks to provide a forum in which individual lawyers can contact and exchange ideas with other lawyers.

The IBA has three Sections: the Section on Business Law, the Section on General Practice and the Section on Energy and Natural Resources Law. The largest is the Section on Business Law which has in the region of 10,000 members. Within the Section on Business Law there are 26 Committees, each specialising in a particular area of Business Law.

Section on Business Law
The Committees of the Section on Business Law aim to study and discuss the legal and practical aspects of issues relating to their particular topic from an international viewpoint.

Members are typically partners of law firms practising in national and international business matters, or in-house or corporate lawyers of companies active in international business. Members of the judiciary and academics also join and participate in the activities of the Committees.

Publisher's Note

The publisher wishes to express the importance it attaches to making these materials available under one cover as soon as possible. The format adopted attempts to respond to that urgent requirement.

While original copies of materials have been used wherever possible, many of the documents have been reproduced from copies themselves of varying degrees of quality. Every effort has been made to faithfully reproduce all the materials made available to us at short notice. Certain foreign documents have been accompanied by an English translation.

This volume consists of documents gathered for the panel on the Iraq/Kuwait sanctions, at the International Bar Association meeting held in New York, 19–23 September 1990. It includes some supplementary materials submitted to the publisher since the panel met. It does not include any of the discussions of the panel which were held in private and closed to the press.

Readers should note that in several jurisdictions specific licenses, certificates, etc. have been issued exempting certain entities and specific transactions from the freeze as implemented in those jurisdictions. Some of these exemptions are potentially significant but have not been reproduced in this volume as they are confidential.

The book is up to date to October 19, 1990.

Corrigenda to Program Agenda

Mr. Brian McDonald was unable to attend. Mr. Robert P. Briner of Schellenberg, von Segesser & Ronca, Geneva, whose name does not appear on the Program Agenda, participated as a member of the panel and spoke about the implementation of sanctions in Switzerland.

Acknowledgments

The Editors would like to express their thanks to Philip Urofsky of Shearman & Sterling for his invaluable assistance in compiling materials.

In the Canadian section and accompanying Supplementary section the source of the government material is: Privy Council Office—External Affairs and International Trade Canada. These materials are reproduced by permission of the Minister of Supply and Services Canada 1990.

In the European Community section extracts from the *Official Journal of the European Communities* are reproduced by permission of the Office for Official Publications of the European Communities.

In the UK section and accompanying Supplementary section Statutory Instruments are reproduced by permission of the Controller of Her Majesty's Stationery Office. Bank of England Notices and Press Notices are reproduced by permission of The Bank of England.

The Freeze of Kuwaiti and Iraqi Assets and its Impact on Financial Institutions and Financial Transactions

International Bar Association Program
New York, Saturday, September 22, 1990 from 2:30 - 5:00 p.m.

PROGRAM AGENDA

TIME	INTRODUCTORY REMARKS	
2:30 pm	- welcome	BARRY R. CAMPBELL Tory Tory Deslauriers & Binnington, Toronto
	- introduction of panel	
	- comments re Security Council Resolution 661 (1990), the unprecedented international response, unique aspects of the situation: financial institutions in exile, the scope of the assets involved, etc.	

	UNITED STATES	
2:45 pm	- the implementation of sanctions by the United States.	DANFORTH NEWCOMB Shearman & Sterling New York
3:00 pm	- the Government/policy perspective.	R. RICHARD NEWCOMB Director, Office of Foreign Assets Control Department of the Treasury Washington, D.C.

UNITED KINGDOM

| 3:15 pm | - | the implementation of sanctions by the United Kingdom | **GRAHAM W. H. ROWBOTHAM** Simmons & Simmons London |
| 3:30 pm | - | the Government/policy perspective | **MALCOLM GILL** Chief Cashier Bank of England |

CANADA

| 3:45 pm | - | the implementation of sanctions by Canada | **BARRY R. CAMPBELL** Tory Tory DesLauriers & Binnington, Toronto |
| 4:00 pm | - | the Government/policy perspective | **J. C. WALL** Director, Economic & Trade Law Division, Department of External Affairs, Ottawa |

EEC

4:15 pm	-	the implementation of sanctions in major European jurisdictions (Germany, Switzerland, France, Italy)	**EMMANUEL GAILLARD** Shearman & Sterling Paris
4:30 pm	-	the EEC/policy perspective	**BRIAN McDONALD** Economic Counsellor Delegation of the Commission of the European Communities to the United Nations, New York
4:45 - 5:30 pm	-	Discussion/Questions	

IBA Program — Speakers List

Robert P. Briner is the resident partner in Geneva of Schellenberg, von Segesser & Ronca. He received his law degree from the University of Geneva in 1978 and was a foreign associate at Shearman & Sterling in 1984-85. He specializes in Swiss Corporate and tax law.

BARRY R. CAMPBELL attended McGill University and McGill Law School where in 1975 he earned his Civil Law and, in 1976, his Common Law Degrees. He then attended Harvard Law School where he received his LL.M (1977). Upon completing his studies at Harvard, Mr. Campbell moved to Toronto, articled with McCarthy & McCarthy, and was called to the Ontario Bar in 1979. He then returned to McCarthy & McCarthy. In 1981, Mr. Campbell moved to Washington, D.C. to become a Legal Counsellor at The International Monetary Fund, later joining the Washington law firm of Arnold and Porter. In late 1983, he returned to Toronto to resume his corporate law practice. Mr. Campbell became a partner of McCarthy & McCarthy in 1985. In 1987 Mr. Campbell became President of a private, investment holding company with interests in the communications and high technology sectors. In 1990, he joined the Toronto firm of Tory Tory DesLauriers & Binnington.

In addition to general corporate matters, Mr. Campbell's practice has encompassed competition law and international matters including transactions on behalf of Canadian and foreign clients, trade law and international banking matters. Mr. Campbell has published articles on competition law, bilateral dispute resolution and the international debt crisis.

EMMANUEL GAILLARD has been European Counsel in Shearman & Sterling's Paris Office since 1987. Mr. Gaillard specializes in international arbitration, litigation and European Community Law. He has represented multinational corporations, government owned entities and governments in numerous international arbitration cases (including oil and gas, construction and procurement contracts).

Emmanuel Gaillard was educated at the University of Paris II, J.D. 1975; D.E.A. in Private Law, 1976; D.E.A. in Criminal Law, 1977; LL.D., 1981; and Agregation in Private Law, 1982. He has written two books and over thirty articles on international arbitration, conflicts of laws and European Community Law.

MALCOLM GILL is Chief of the Banking Department and Chief Cashier since March 1988 of the Bank of England. As Chief Cashier his signature appears on current Bank of England notes.

Malcolm Gill joined the Bank of England in 1957 after University and National Service. During his bank career, he has had secondments away from the Bank to UK Treasury Delegation in Washington, D.C. (1966-68) and to HM Treasury in London (1977-80). Before taking up his present post Mr. Gill was Head of the Bank's Foreign Exchange Division. Mr. Gill is 56 and is married with two children.

DANFORTH NEWCOMB specializes in financial services litigation in Shearman & Sterling's New York Office. He has handled major litigation for financial services clients located in Europe, the Middle East, the Far East and Latin America in addition to his North American based clients.

Mr. Newcomb has been with Shearman & Sterling since 1968 after graduating from the University of Vermont, B.A. 1965 and Columbia University Law School, J.D. 1968. He has published articles and participated in continuing legal education programs on a variety of subjects including export controls, international fraud investigations and money laundering.

R.RICHARD NEWCOMB is Director of the Office of Foreign Assets Control of the United States Treasury Department. During the period from 1981 to 1986 he held a number of posts in the United States Treasury including Director of the Office of Trade and Tariff Affairs. Prior to that time he was a policy advisor to the Assistant Secretary on criminal law matters in the Enforcement Bureau. From 1974 to 1978 he served in several positions at the Department of Justice.

Mr. Newcomb received a Bachelor of Arts degree from Kenyon College, Gambier, Ohio and a Juris Doctor degree from Case-Western Reserve University School of Law, Cleveland, Ohio.

GRAHAM W.H. ROWBOTHAM was educated at The King's School, Canterbury and St. John's College, Oxford where he took an M.S. degree in Law. He worked successively with the London offices of Arthur Andersen & Co. and Slaughter and May, before joining Simmons & Simmons in 1980, where he became a partner in 1981 and head of the firm's Banking and Capital Markets Group in 1985. He is a member of the Editorial Advisory Board of International Financial Law Review.

JAMES C. WALL, 43, is the Director of the Economic and Trade Law Division of the Department of External Affairs and International Trade Canada.

He graduated from Carleton University in 1968 with an Honours B.A., and from the University of Ottawa in 1973 with an LL.B. After his call to the bar in Ontario in 1975 he practiced in Toronto for a year with McKeown, Yoerger and Hudson before joining the federal government as a foreign service officer. He has had a two and a half year posting in New Delhi, India and a three year posting in Jakarta, Indonesia.

In his work at headquarters Mr. Wall has dealt with the settlement of private claims against other states (the People's Republic of China and Cuba), government claims (Cosmos 954 against the Soviet Union), extraterritoriality in the areas of antitrust and export controls, and trade law involving the GATT, the Canada/U.S. Free Trade Agreement and issues in the current MTN Round.

THE IMPACT OF THE FREEZE OF KUWAITI AND IRAQI ASSETS ON FINANCIAL INSTITUTIONS AND FINANCIAL TRANSACTIONS

Chairman's Remarks

Good afternoon ladies and gentlemen. I am pleased to welcome you to this special International Bar Association/Section on Business Law Program entitled "The Impact of the Freeze of Kuwaiti and Iraqi Assets on Financial Institutions and Financial Transactions".

Since August 2nd, the members of this Panel have spent considerable time dealing with issues related to the sudden freeze of Kuwaiti and Iraqi assets. It is a pleasure for all of us to have the opportunity to meet in person to discuss some of these issues with you and to have what I am sure will be a lively exchange of views.

I would like to express my personal gratitude to each member of the panel for finding the time, in a hectic schedule, to be in New York. This Panel was only conceived of two weeks ago and I am grateful for the extraordinary effort which has been made by each member of the panel to be here today.

At this point I would like to introduce the panel and with their permission I am dispensing with detailed biographical information which may be found in the materials which have been provided to you. Dan Newcomb is with Shearman & Sterling in New York. R. Richard Newcomb is the Director, Office of Foreign Assets Control, Department of the Treasury. Robert Briner is with Swiss firm of Schellenberg. von Segesser & Ronca. Emmanuel Gaillard is with Shearman & Sterling in Paris. Graham Rowbotham is with Simmons & Simmons in London. Malcolm Gill is Chief Cashier of the Bank of England. Jim Wall is Director, Economic and Trade Law Division, Department of External Affairs, Ottawa.

There are two matters which I would like to mention before we begin.

First, we have requested that this session be closed to the press. If any representatives of the press are present we would invite you to depart at this time. The decision to exclude the press will ensure that we have a full and frank discussion for the benefit of our audience. The discussion this afternoon is off the record. You are requested not to repeat anything you hear today to the press.

Second, I would like to take this opportunity to thank Dan Newcomb and Shearman & Sterling for the assistance which they have provided generally and, in particular, for their help in the preparation of the comprehensive set of materials which have been made available to participants.

The invasion of Kuwait by Iraq has been called the first crisis of the post cold war world. In this new world we see the United Nations acting decisively, little super-power rivalry and an unprecedented level of international cooperation.

Several unique features of this situation bear mention - themes that will be developed further by the Panel:

First, an extraordinary amount of assets are affected by the freeze. Publicly quoted figures place the value of off-shore Kuwaiti assets in the neighbourhood of US $125 billion.

Second, this freeze is a truly international affair. Unlike the cases of Libya, Iran or Argentina, this freeze is not being imposed unilaterally and applied extraterritorially by one state. Indeed, as a Canadian, it is refreshing to be participating in discussions about a freeze which has not been imposed upon Canadian citizens and Canadian companies by another state.

Third, unlike the case of Iran, regulators are not confronted with rival claims to the same assets. There is a Government-in-Exile, the legitimate recognized Government of Kuwait and there is no rival government. This Government-in-Exile has survived with virtually all of its financial instrumentalities and the bulk of its financial assets intact. The closest analogy is perhaps to the governments in exile in London in 1939-1940. Some have suggested, however, that what we have is not so much a government-in-exile as a financial institution-in-exile, the first truly sovereign financial institution - a non-territorial financial entity, a status envied by all international money centre banks.

Fourth, the Security Council Resolution imposing sanctions has two goals. It is <u>protective</u> of Kuwaiti assets but <u>punitive</u> with respect to Iraq. Iraq is to be denied the benefit of economic activity but Kuwaiti assets are to be protected, and assistance to the legitimate Government of Kuwait is specifically not prohibited.

Fifth, this freeze calls for, and to date had led to, an unprecedented level of international cooperation. This has been necessary to ensure the effectiveness of the freeze and to respond to the protective aspect of the Security Council Resolution.

Sixth, while states which have implemented the Security Council Resolution share a common goal, they are discovering that the various tools at their disposal to implement this dual purpose freeze are archaic and imperfect.

Seventh, lurking in the background are the imponderables, the "what ifs". What if sovereignty is restored to Kuwait but not the pre-existing government? In that situation will we see disputes emerging as to ownership of these very substantial assets?

With that background I am now pleased to turn to our panel. In most cases we will hear first from a practitioner who will describe steps taken to implement the freeze in a jurisdiction. This will be followed by a government official who will comment on the political/policy underpinnings of the freeze in particular jurisdictions. There will then be discussion among the panel and time for questions from the audience.

TEXT OF MATERIALS

United Nations

UNITED
NATIONS

Security Council

Distr.
GENERAL

*/RES/660 (1990)
2 August 1990

RESOLUTION 660 (1990)

Adopted by the Security Council at its 2932nd meeting,
on 2 August 1990

The Security Council,

Alarmed by the invasion of Kuwait on 2 August 1990 by the military forces of Iraq,

Determining that there exists a breach of international peace and security as regards the Iraqi invasion of Kuwait,

Acting under Articles 39 and 40 of the Charter of the United Nations,

1.   Condemns the Iraqi invasion of Kuwait;

2.   Demands that Iraq withdraw immediately and unconditionally all its forces to the positions in which they were located on 1 August 1990;

3.   Calls upon Iraq and Kuwait to begin immediately intensive negotiations for the resolution of their differences and supports all efforts in this regard, and especially those of the League of Arab States;

4.   Decides to meet again as necessary to consider further steps to ensure compliance with the present resolution.

UNITED NATIONS

Security Council

Distr.
GENERAL

S/RES/661 (1990)
6 August 1990

RESOLUTION 661 (1990)

Adopted by the Security Council at its 2933rd meeting on
6 August 1990

The Security Council,

Reaffirming its resolution 660 (1990) of 2 August 1990,

Deeply concerned that that resolution has not been implemented and that the invasion by Iraq of Kuwait continues with further loss of human life and material destruction,

Determined to bring the invasion and occupation of Kuwait by Iraq to an end and to restore the sovereignty, independence and territorial integrity of Kuwait,

Noting that the legitimate Government of Kuwait has expressed its readiness to comply with resolution 660 (1990),

Mindful of its responsibilities under the Charter of the United Nations for the maintenance of international peace and security,

Affirming the inherent right of individual or collective self-defence, in response to the armed attack by Iraq against Kuwait, in accordance with Article 51 of the Charter,

Acting under Chapter VII of the Charter of the United Nations,

1.   Determines that Iraq so far has failed to comply with paragraph 2 of resolution 660 (1990) and has usurped the authority of the legitimate Government of Kuwait;

2.   Decides, as a consequence, to take the following measures to secure compliance of Iraq with paragraph 2 of resolution 660 (1990) and to restore the authority of the legitimate Government of Kuwait;

3.   Decides that all States shall prevent:

(a) The import into their territories of all commodities and products originating in Iraq or Kuwait exported therefrom after the date of the present resolution;

(b) Any activities by their nationals or in their territories which would promote or are calculated to promote the export or trans-shipment of any commodities or products from Iraq or Kuwait; and any dealings by their nationals or their flag vessels or in their territories in any commodities or products originating in Iraq or Kuwait and exported therefrom after the date of the present resolution, including in particular any transfer of funds to Iraq or Kuwait for the purposes of such activities or dealings;

(c) The sale or supply by their nationals or from their territories or using their flag vessels of any commodities or products, including weapons or any other military equipment, whether or not originating in their territories but not including supplies intended strictly for medical purposes, and, in humanitarian circumstances, foodstuffs, to any person or body in Iraq or Kuwait or to any person or body for the purposes of any business carried on in or operated from Iraq or Kuwait, and any activities by their nationals or in their territories which promote or are calculated to promote such sale or supply of such commodities or products;

4. Decides that all States shall not make available to the Government of Iraq or to any commercial, industrial or public utility undertaking in Iraq or Kuwait, any funds or any other financial or economic resources and shall prevent their nationals and any persons within their territories from removing from their territories or otherwise making available to that Government or to any such undertaking any such funds or resources and from remitting any other funds to persons or bodies within Iraq or Kuwait, except payments exclusively for strictly medical or humanitarian purposes and, in humanitarian circumstances, foodstuffs;

5. Calls upon all States, including States non-members of the United Nations, to act strictly in accordance with the provisions of the present resolution notwithstanding any contract entered into or licence granted before the date of the present resolution;

6. Decides to establish, in accordance with rule 28 of the provisional rules of procedure of the Security Council, a Committee of the Security Council consisting of all the members of the Council, to undertake the following tasks and to report on its work to the Council with its observations and recommendations:

(a) To examine the reports on the progress of the implementation of the present resolution which will be submitted by the Secretary-General;

(b) To seek from all States further information regarding the action taken by them concerning the effective implementation of the provisions laid down in the present resolution;

7. Calls upon all States to co-operate fully with the Committee in the fulfilment of its task, including supplying such information as may be sought by the Committee in pursuance of the present resolution;

8. _Requests_ the Secretary-General to provide all necessary assistance to the Committee and to make the necessary arrangements in the Secretariat for the purpose;

9. _Decides_ that, notwithstanding paragraphs 4 through 8 above, nothing in the present resolution shall prohibit assistance to the legitimate Government of Kuwait, and _calls upon_ all States:

(a) To take appropriate measures to protect assets of the legitimate Government of Kuwait and its agencies;

(b) Not to recognize any régime set up by the occupying Power;

10. _Requests_ the Secretary-General to report to the Council on the progress of the implementation of the present resolution, the first report to be submitted within thirty days;

11. _Decides_ to keep this item on its agenda and to continue its efforts to put an early end to the invasion by Iraq.

UNITED
NATIONS

Security Council

Distr.
GENERAL

S/RES/662 (1990)
9 August 1990

RESOLUTION 662 (1990)

Adopted by the Security Council at its 2934th meeting,
on 9 August 1990

The Security Council,

Recalling its resolutions 660 (1990) and 661 (1990),

Gravely alarmed by the declaration by Iraq of a "comprehensive and eternal merger" with Kuwait,

Demanding, once again, that Iraq withdraw immediately and unconditionally all its forces to the positions in which they were located on 1 August 1990,

Determined to bring the occupation of Kuwait by Iraq to an end and to restore the sovereignty, independence and territorial integrity of Kuwait,

Determined also to restore the authority of the legitimate Government of Kuwait,

1.   Decides that annexation of Kuwait by Iraq under any form and whatever pretext has no legal validity, and is considered null and void;

2.   Calls upon all States, international organizations and specialized agencies not to recognize that annexation, and to refrain from any action or dealing that might be interpreted as an indirect recognition of the annexation;

3.   Further demands that Iraq rescind its actions purporting to annex Kuwait;

4.   Decides to keep this item on its agenda and to continue its efforts to put an early end to the occupation.

UNITED NATIONS

Security Council

S

Distr.
GENERAL

S/RES/664 (1990)
18 August 1990

RESOLUTION 664 (1990)

Adopted by the Security Council at its 2937th meeting
on 18 August 1990

The Security Council,

Recalling the Iraqi invasion and purported annexation of Kuwait and resolutions 660, 661 and 662,

Deeply concerned for the safety and well being of third state nationals in Iraq and Kuwait,

Recalling the obligations of Iraq in this regard under international law,

Welcoming the efforts of the Secretary-General to pursue urgent consultations with the Government of Iraq following the concern and anxiety expressed by the members of the Council on 17 August 1990,

Acting under Chapter VII of the United Nations Charter:

1. Demands that Iraq permit and facilitate the immediate departure from Kuwait and Iraq of the nationals of third countries and grant immediate and continuing access of consular officials to such nationals;

2. Further demands that Iraq take no action to jeopardise the safety, security or health of such nationals;

3. Reaffirms its decision in resolution 662 (1990) that annexation of Kuwait by Iraq is null and void, and therefore demands that the government of Iraq rescind its orders for the closure of diplomatic and consular missions in Kuwait and the withdrawal of the immunity of their personnel, and refrain from any such actions in the future;

4. Requests the Secretary-General to report to the Council on compliance with this resolution at the earliest possible time.

UNITED NATIONS

Security Council

Distr.
GENERAL

S/RES/665 (1990)
25 August 1990

S

RESOLUTION 665 (1990)

Adopted by the Security Council at its 2938th meeting.
on 25 August 1990

The Security Council,

Recalling its resolutions 660 (1990), 661 (1990), 662 (1990) and 664 (1990) and demanding their full and immediate implementation,

Having decided in resolution 661 (1990) to impose economic sanctions under Chapter VII of the Charter of the United Nations,

Determined to bring an end to the occupation of Kuwait by Iraq which imperils the existence of a Member State and to restore the legitimate authority, and the sovereignty, independence and territorial integrity of Kuwait which requires the speedy implementation of the above resolutions,

Deploring the loss of innocent life stemming from the Iraqi invasion of Kuwait and determined to prevent further such losses,

Gravely alarmed that Iraq continues to refuse to comply with resolutions 660 (1990), 661 (1990), 662 (1990) and 664 (1990) and in particular at the conduct of the Government of Iraq in using Iraqi flag vessels to export oil,

1. Calls upon those Member States co-operating with the Government of Kuwait which are deploying maritime forces to the area to use such measures commensurate to the specific circumstances as may be necessary under the authority of the Security Council to halt all inward and outward maritime shipping in order to inspect and verify their cargoes and destinations and to ensure strict implementation of the provisions related to such shipping laid down in resolution 661 (1990);

2. Invites Member States accordingly to co-operate as may be necessary to ensure compliance with the provisions of resolution 661 (1990) with maximum use of political and diplomatic measures, in accordance with paragraph 1 above;

B

3.   Requests all States to provide in accordance with the Charter such assistance as may be required by the States referred to in paragraph 1 of this resolution;

4.   Further requests the States concerned to co-ordinate their actions in pursuit of the above paragraphs of this resolution using as appropriate mechanisms of the Military Staff Committee and after consultation with the Secretary-General to submit reports to the Security Council and its Committee established under resolution 661 (1990) to facilitate the monitoring of the implementation of this resolution;

5.   Decides to remain actively seised of the matter.

UNITED NATIONS

Security Council

Distr.
GENERAL

S/RES/666 (1990)
13 September 1990

RESOLUTION 666 (1990)

Adopted by the Security Council at its 2939th meeting
on 13 September 1990

The Security Council,

Recalling its resolution 661 (1990), paragraphs 3 (c) and 4 of which apply, except in humanitarian circumstances, to foodstuffs,

Recognizing that circumstances may arise in which it will be necessary for foodstuffs to be supplied to the civilian population in Iraq or Kuwait in order to relieve human suffering,

Noting that in this respect the Committee established under paragraph 6 of that resolution has received communications from several Member States,

Emphasizing that it is for the Security Council, alone or acting through the Committee, to determine whether humanitarian circumstances have arisen,

Deeply concerned that Iraq has failed to comply with its obligations under Security Council resolution 664 (1990) in respect of the safety and well-being of third State nationals, and reaffirming that Iraq retains full responsibility in this regard under international humanitarian law including, where applicable, the Fourth Geneva Convention,

Acting under Chapter VII of the Charter of the United Nations,

1.   Decides that in order to make the necessary determination whether or not for the purposes of paragraph 3 (c) and paragraph 4 of resolution 661 (1990) humanitarian circumstances have arisen, the Committee shall keep the situation regarding foodstuffs in Iraq and Kuwait under constant review;

2.   Expects Iraq to comply with its obligations under Security Council resolution 664 (1990) in respect of third State nationals and reaffirms that Iraq remains fully responsible for their safety and well-being in accordance with international humanitarian law including, where applicable, the Fourth Geneva Convention;

3.   __Requests__, for the purposes of paragraphs 1 and 2 of this resolution, that the Secretary-General seek urgently, and on a continuing basis, information from relevant United Nations and other appropriate humanitarian agencies and all other sources on the availability of food in Iraq and Kuwait, such information to be communicated by the Secretary-General to the Committee regularly;

4.   __Requests further__ that in seeking and supplying such information particular attention will be paid to such categories of persons who might suffer specially, such as children under 15 years of age, expectant mothers, maternity cases, the sick and the elderly;

5.   __Decides__ that if the Committee, after receiving the reports from the Secretary-General, determines that circumstances have arisen in which there is an urgent humanitarian need to supply foodstuffs to Iraq or Kuwait in order to relieve human suffering, it will report promptly to the Council its decision as to how such need should be met;

6.   __Directs__ the Committee that in formulating its decisions it should bear in mind that foodstuffs should be provided through the United Nations in co-operation with the International Committee of the Red Cross or other appropriate humanitarian agencies and distributed by them or under their supervision in order to ensure that they reach the intended beneficiaries;

7.   __Requests__ the Secretary-General to use his good offices to facilitate the delivery and distribution of foodstuffs to Kuwait and Iraq in accordance with the provisions of this and other relevant resolutions;

8.   __Recalls__ that resolution 661 (1990) does not apply to supplies intended strictly for medical purposes, but in this connection recommends that medical supplies should be exported under the strict supervision of the Government of the exporting State or by appropriate humanitarian agencies.

UNITED NATIONS

 S

Security Council

Distr.
GENERAL

S/RES/667 (1990)
16 September 1990

RESOLUTION 667 (1990)

Adopted by the Security Council at its 2940th meeting,
on 16 September 1990

The Security Council,

Reaffirming its resolutions 660 (1990), 661 (1990), 662 (1990), 664 (1990), 665 (1990) and 666 (1990),

Recalling the Vienna Conventions of 18 April 1961 on diplomatic relations and of 24 April 1963 on consular relations, to both of which Iraq is a party,

Considering that the decision of Iraq to order the closure of diplomatic and consular missions in Kuwait and to withdraw the immunity and privileges of these missions and their personnel is contrary to the decisions of the Security Council, the international Conventions mentioned above and international law,

Deeply concerned that Iraq, notwithstanding the decisions of the Security Council and the provisions of the Conventions mentioned above, has committed acts of violence against diplomatic missions and their personnel in Kuwait,

Outraged at recent violations by Iraq of diplomatic premises in Kuwait and at the abduction of personnel enjoying diplomatic immunity and foreign nationals who were present in these premises,

Considering that the above actions by Iraq constitute aggressive acts and a flagrant violation of its international obligations which strike at the root of the conduct of international relations in accordance with the Charter of the United Nations,

Recalling that Iraq is fully responsible for any use of violence against foreign nationals or against any diplomatic or consular mission in Kuwait or its personnel,

Determined to ensure respect for its decisions and for Article 25 of the Charter of the United Nations,

Further considering that the grave nature of Iraq's actions, which constitute a new escalation of its violations of international law, obliges the Council not only to express its immediate reaction but also to consult urgently to take further concrete measures to ensure Iraq's compliance with the Council's resolutions,

Acting under Chapter VII of the Charter of the United Nations,

1.   Strongly condemns aggressive acts perpetrated by Iraq against diplomatic premises and personnel in Kuwait, including the abduction of foreign nationals who were present in those premises;

2.   Demands the immediate release of those foreign nationals as well as all nationals mentioned in resolution 664 (1990);

3.   Further demands that Iraq immediately and fully comply with its international obligations under resolutions 660 (1990), 662 (1990) and 664 (1990) of the Security Council, the Vienna Conventions on diplomatic and consular relations and international law;

4.   Further demands that Iraq immediately protect the safety and well-being of diplomatic and consular personnel and premises in Kuwait and in Iraq and take no action to hinder the diplomatic and consular missions in the performance of their functions, including access to their nationals and the protection of their person and interests;

5.   Reminds all States that they are obliged to observe strictly resolutions 661 (1990), 662 (1990), 664 (1990), 665 (1990) and 666 (1990);

6.   Decides to consult urgently to take further concrete measures as soon as possible, under Chapter VII of the Charter, in response to Iraq's continued violation of the Charter, of resolutions of the Council and of international law.

Supplementary Material: UN

**UNITED
NATIONS**

Security Council

Distr.
GENERAL

S/RES/670 (1990)
25 September 1990

RESOLUTION 670 (1990)

<u>Adopted by the Security Council at its 2943rd meeting,
on 25 September 1990</u>

<u>The Security Council</u>,

<u>Reaffirming</u> its resolutions 660 (1990), 661 (1990), 662 (1990), 664 (1990), 665 (1990), 666 (1990), and 667 (1990),

<u>Condemning</u> Iraq's continued occupation of Kuwait, its failure to rescind its actions and end its purported annexation and its holding of third State nationals against their will, in flagrant violation of resolutions 660 (1990), 662 (1990), 664 (1990) and 667 (1990) and of international humanitarian law,

<u>Condemning further</u> the treatment by Iraqi forces of Kuwaiti nationals, including measures to force them to leave their own country and mistreatment of persons and property in Kuwait in violation of international law,

<u>Noting with grave concern</u> the persistent attempts to evade the measures laid down in resolution 661 (1990),

<u>Further noting</u> that a number of States have limited the number of Iraqi diplomatic and consular officials in their countries and that others are planning to do so,

<u>Determined</u> to ensure by all necessary means the strict and complete application of the measures laid down in resolution 661 (1990),

<u>Determined</u> to ensure respect for its decisions and the provisions of Articles 25 and 48 of the Charter of the United Nations,

<u>Affirming</u> that any acts of the Government of Iraq which are contrary to the above-mentioned resolutions or to Articles 25 or 48 of the Charter of the United Nations, such as Decree No. 377 of the Revolution Command Council of Iraq of 16 September 1990, are null and void,

Reaffirming its determination to ensure compliance with Security Council resolutions by maximum use of political and diplomatic means,

Welcoming the Secretary-General's use of his good offices to advance a peaceful solution based on the relevant Security Council resolutions and noting with appreciation his continuing efforts to this end,

Underlining to the Government of Iraq that its continued failure to comply with the terms of resolutions 660 (1990), 661 (1990), 662 (1990), 664 (1990), 666 (1990) and 667 (1990) could lead to further serious action by the Council under the Charter of the United Nations, including under Chapter VII,

Recalling the provisions of Article 103 of the Charter of the United Nations,

Acting under Chapter VII of the Charter of the United Nations,

1.   Calls upon all States to carry out their obligations to ensure strict and complete compliance with resolution 661 (1990) and in particular paragraphs 3, 4 and 5 thereof;

2.   Confirms that resolution 661 (1990) applies to all means of transport, including aircraft;

3.   Decides that all States, notwithstanding the existence of any rights or obligations conferred or imposed by any international agreement or any contract entered into or any licence or permit granted before the date of the present resolution, shall deny permission to any aircraft to take off from their territory if the aircraft would carry any cargo to or from Iraq or Kuwait other than food in humanitarian circumstances, subject to authorization by the Council or the Committee established by resolution 661 (1990) and in accordance with resolution 666 (1990), or supplies intended strictly for medical purposes or solely for UNIIMOG;

4.   Decides further that all States shall deny permission to any aircraft destined to land in Iraq or Kuwait, whatever its State of registration, to overfly its territory unless:

(a)   The aircraft lands at an airfield designated by that State outside Iraq or Kuwait in order to permit its inspection to ensure that there is no cargo on board in violation of resolution 661 (1990) or the present resolution, and for this purpose the aircraft may be detained for as long as necessary; or

(b)   The particular flight has been approved by the Committee established by resolution 661 (1990); or

(c)   The flight is certified by the United Nations as solely for the purposes of UNIIMOG;

5.   Decides that each State shall take all necessary measures to ensure that any aircraft registered in its territory or operated by an operator who has his

principal place of business or permanent residence in its territory complies with the provisions of resolution 661 (1990) and the present resolution;

6.   Decides further that all States shall notify in a timely fashion the Committee established by resolution 661 (1990) of any flight between its territory and Iraq or Kuwait to which the requirement to land in paragraph 4 above does not apply, and the purpose for such a flight;

7.   Calls upon all States to co-operate in taking such measures as may be necessary, consistent with international law, including the Chicago Convention, to ensure the effective implementation of the provisions of resolution 661 (1990) or the present resolution;

8.   Calls upon all States to detain any ships of Iraqi registry which enter their ports and which are being or have been used in violation of resolution 661 (1990), or to deny such ships entrance to their ports except in circumstances recognized under international law as necessary to safeguard human life;

9.   Reminds all States of their obligations under resolution 661 (1990) with regard to the freezing of Iraqi assets, and the protection of the assets of the legitimate Government of Kuwait and its agencies, located within their territory and to report to the Committee established under resolution 661 (1990) regarding those assets;

10.   Calls upon all States to provide to the Committee established by resolution 661 (1990) information regarding the action taken by them to implement the provisions laid down in the present resolution;

11.   Affirms that the United Nations Organization, the specialized agencies and other international organizations in the United Nations system are required to take such measures as may be necessary to give effect to the terms of resolution 661 (1990) and this resolution;

12.   Decides to consider, in the event of evasion of the provisions of resolution 661 (1990) or of the present resolution by a State or its nationals or through its territory, measures directed at the State in question to prevent such evasion;

13.   Reaffirms that the Fourth Geneva Convention applies to Kuwait and that as a High Contracting Party to the Convention Iraq is bound to comply fully with all its terms and in particular is liable under the Convention in respect of the grave breaches committed by it, as are individuals who commit or order the commission of grave breaches.

United States

SHEARMAN & STERLING

CITICORP CENTER
153 EAST 53RD STREET
NEW YORK, N.Y. 10022
212 848-4000

FAX: 212-848-5255
212-848-5252
TELEX: 668769 WUI

WRITER'S DIRECT DIAL NUMBER:

SAN FRANCISCO
LOS ANGELES
WASHINGTON, D.C.
TORONTO
LONDON
PARIS
TOKYO
ABU DHABI

OLD TOOLS FOR A NEW JOB
U.S. SANCTIONS AGAINST IRAQ

At 5:00 a.m. on August 2, in the wake of the Iraqi invasion of Kuwait, President Bush issued two executive orders freezing all Iraqi and Kuwaiti governmental assets. After the initial flurry of activity surrounding the news of the invasion and transmission of the freeze order to key personnel died down, U.S. banks and other financial institutions settled back into business-as-usual relatively quickly considering the breadth of the order and the magnitude of assets affected -- after all, this is the third freeze order these entities have been ordered to implement in the last five years.

The current freeze orders are based on a long series of such orders that date back to World War I, when Congress enacted the Trading With the Enemy Act. That act authorized the president to issue orders affecting property under the control of enemy governments during wars and national emergencies. U.S. presidents have since used this power to block assets and to regulate transactions involving the property of Germany, China, Cuba and Vietnam, to name just a few.

In 1977, as financial markets became increasingly global in nature, Congress enacted IEEPA, the International Emergency Economic Powers Act. This statute replaced the Trading with the Enemy Act and expanded the scope of the president's authority to block assets. IEEPA allows the president to act in response to "any unusual and extraordinary threat, which has its source in whole or substantial part outside the United States, to the national security, foreign policy, or economy of the United States . . . ." IEEPA gives the president broad authority to take unilateral action to protect American interests. But, given the global nature of financial markets, any action to protect American interests will inevitably cause a substantial impact on the world's markets.

The impact of IEEPA freezes on the international financial markets was demonstrated the very first time IEEPA was used. In 1979, President Carter, responding to the Iranian hostage crisis, froze all property of the government of Iran subject to the jurisdiction of the U.S. or within the control of any person subject to U.S. jurisdiction. By a simple three-paragraph statement, the president temporarily threw the world's financial markets into chaos. Since all dollar transactions clear through New York, the president's freeze order affected all dollar transactions with Iran, regardless of where the transactions occurred. Although regulations were subsequently issued to implement the president's freeze order, bankers and their legal advisors were initially confronted with conflicting demands and had to step warily to avoid incurring liability.

From the perspective of U.S. banks, in contrast with the Iran experience, the Iraq and Kuwait freeze orders have been implemented with relatively little pain. Although the regulations for Iraq and Kuwait have not yet been issued, U.S. banks have developed a drill for dealing with freeze orders and can consult the three sets of regulations that have been issued to implement previous IEEPA freeze orders -- Iran, Libya and Panama. In fact, we understand that the Office of Foreign Asset Controls (OFAC) considers the Iran and Libyan regulations to be good guides to follow in giving advice on the Iraq and Kuwait freeze orders and this may explain, to some extent, why no regulations implementing the current freeze orders have yet beem promulgated. The Iranian regulations were issued the day after the freeze order was issued. In contrast, under the current freeze orders, the U.S. government has appeared to focus on the specific disputes created by freezing Kuwaiti and Iraqi assets and has issued general licenses to resolve these disputes first, leaving the formal regulations for later.

From an international perspective, the most obvious difference between the U.S. sanctions against Iraq and the three previous instances in which the U.S. imposed sanctions is that this time we are not alone. This one fact has eliminated many of the conflicts that arose in connection with the Iran and Libya sanctions. For example, we do not have the conflict between English law and U.S. law over the extraterritoriality of U.S. sanctions by their application to branches of U.S. banks. This conflict was raised by the Iran sanctions and finally litigated in connection with the Libyan sanctions.[*] Now, however, those countries that objected to

---

[*] See Libyan Arab Foreign Bank v. Bankers Trust Co., [1989] 1 Q. B. 728 (2 Sept. 1987).

the extraterritorial application of U.S. sanctions against Iraq and Libya have adopted their own extraterritorial sanctions against Iraq. Perhaps, a norm of customary international law has been created that recognizes the validity of extraterritoriality in such circumstances.

A second major difference between the Iraq/Kuwait situation and the previous cases in which the U.S. has imposed sanctions is that, to date, the frozen assets have not been subject to conflicting claims of ownership. Although Iraq now claims that it or its puppet government rules Kuwait, it has not made any claims to the vast overseas assets of Kuwaiti entities. The Kuwaitis who run these entities quickly set up offices outside Kuwait, informed their counterparties that the entities were still in existence, and designated which individuals had the authority to act on behalf of these entities. Thus, in the absence of any decree from Iraq purporting to rescind this authority, U.S. banks have managed to resolve disputes caused by the freeze orders promptly. As time passes and commercial practice solidifies, Iraq will have to surmount increasingly substantial barriers against any attempt to upset such resolutions and to assert claims to these overseas Kuwaiti assets.

A related difference between this situation and the Iran experience is that the Kuwaiti royal family has not claimed that vast amounts of the overseas Kuwaiti assets are personal assets of the royal family. This, too, has decreased the amount of conflict caused by the freeze orders.

Finally, unlike previous occasions, the U.S. freeze is not only part of a nearly worldwide set of economic sanctions, but it is also backed up by an international military blockade of Iraq. The combination of worldwide sanctions and a blockade should make U.S. sanctions against Iraq far more effective than previous U.S. sanctions against countries such as Cuba, Iran or Libya.

This changed environment suggests that the legal issues will be different this time. No longer should U.S. banks face the problem of conflicting legal mandates as occurred with the U.S. sanctions against Iran and Libya. This time the key issue will be to minimize the restriction on Kuwaiti external assets so that they may be used to aid in efforts to oust Iraq while not letting those assets fall under the control of Iraq. Moreover, because the blockade cuts off trade with Iraq, restrictions on financial transactions will be less central to the policy makers' efforts. Without a blockade, financial transactions are often used as a substitute for a blockage to indirectly impede the flow of goods. In this instance, the blockade provides that function directly. Restrictions on financial transactions are only an adjunct.

The response to the Iraq and Kuwait freeze orders demonstrates that U.S. banks and foreign governments believe that such orders are here to stay, despite the initial resistance to them. U.S. banks have developed procedures to implement these freezes quickly and strategies to deal with disputes caused by the orders. Moreover, these orders protect the banks against the uncertainties caused by unstable international situations by keeping the assets of the perpetrators within the jurisdiction of the U.S. without the risks and costs associated with attachment and restraining orders. Perhaps these practical benefits are the reason why the old tools of economic sanctions used so often in the past by the U.S. are being used by so many countries this time.

SHEARMAN & STERLING

FAX: 212-848-5255
212-848-5252
TELEX: 668769 WUI

CITICORP CENTER
153 EAST 53RD STREET
NEW YORK, N.Y. 10022
212 848-4000

SAN FRANCISCO
LOS ANGELES
WASHINGTON, D.C.
TORONTO
LONDON
PARIS
TOKYO
ABU DHABI

WRITER'S DIRECT DIAL NUMBER:

Memorandum to: Danforth Newcomb

From: Philip Urofsky

Date: September 21, 1990

U.S. Sanctions Against Iraq

You have asked me to summarize the U.S. sanctions against Iraq arising out of the Iraqi invasion of Kuwait on August 2, 1990. Since August 2, President Bush has issued four executive orders and the U.S. Treasury's Office of Foreign Assets Control (OFAC) has issued eleven general licenses as well as several letters to the Federal Reserve Bank of New York and countless special licenses. I have summarized the sanctions and general licenses authorizing particular classes of transactions.

Scope of Coverage

The initial executive orders, issued by President Bush on August 2, 1990, effectively banned all transactions with Iraq but only froze Kuwaiti assets. Following U.N. Security Council resolution 661, the president issued two new executive orders on August 9 bringing the U.S. sanctions into line with the U.N. resolution and making those sanctions identical with respect to Iraq and Kuwait. These orders apply to all "U.S. persons," a terms that is defined to include "any United States citizen, permanent resident alien, juridical person organized under the laws of the United States (including foreign branches), or any person in the United States, and vessels of U.S. registration." Although neither the orders nor subsequent licenses explicitly reach foreign subsidiaries, they are very clear in their extraterritorial effect with respect to foreign branches of U.S. companies. Definitions in the later licenses defined "U.S. financial institutions" as "any U.S. person (including foreign branches) that is engaged in the business of accepting deposits or making, granting, transferring, holding or brokering loans or credits, or of purchasing or selling

foreign exchange or commodities or procuring purchasers and
sellers thereof, as principal or agent."

The executive orders seek to reach property of the
governments of Iraq or Kuwait (or any entity purporting to be
the government of Kuwait), the agencies, instrumentalities
and controlled entities of such governments, and the Central
Banks of Iraq and Kuwait. The initial definition was later
expanded and clarified in the general licenses, and the
uniform definition used in the more recent licenses reads:

The term "Goverment of Kuwait" shall mean

a) the state and the Government of Kuwait, or
any entity purporting to be the Government of
Kuwait, any political subdivision, agency, or
instrumentality thereof, including the Central Bank
of Kuwait;

b) Any partnership, association, corporation,
or other organization owned or controlled by the
foregoing;

c) Any person to the extent that such person
is, or has been, or to the extent that there is
reasonable cause to believe such person is, or has
been, since the effective date, acting or purporting
to act, directly or indirectly on behalf of any of
the foregoing, and

d) Any other person determined by the Secretary
of the Treasury to be included within this section.

A similar definition has been developed for the Goverment of
Iraq and its instrumentalities.

Since the freeze order went into effect, OFAC has
also identified specific entities that are or are not
considered to be controlled by the Government of Kuwait.
Some of these, such as the Kuwait Investment Office, have
been handled through special licenses. Others, such as many
Persian Gulf and Swiss banks, have been handled by letters
from OFAC to the Federal Reserve Banks. (See attached list
of frozen and not-frozen banks.)

Blocked Property and Prohibited Transactions

The August 9 executive orders blocked all property
interests in property belonging to the Iraqi and Kuwaiti
governments that are in the United States, that later come

within the United States, and that are within or come within
the control of United States persons <u>including their overseas
branches</u>. They also prohibited importation of goods of
Kuwaiti and Iraqi origin into the United States and the
exportation of goods to Iraq or Kuwait or to any entity
operated from Iraq or Kuwait or owned or controlled by Iraq
or Kuwait. Thus, exporting goods to European companies that
are substantially owned by Kuwait is banned by the U.S.
orders. In addition, U.S. persons are prohibited from
performing under any contract, including a financing
contract, that supports any projects within Iraq or Kuwait.
Finally, of course, the orders prohibit any commitment or
transfer of funds to the governments of Kuwait or Iraq <u>or any
person in Kuwait or Iraq</u>.

General Licenses Permitting Certain Transactions

<u>Securities Transactions</u>. On the day the first
orders were issued, OFAC issued General License No. 1 that
permitted financial institutions to complete transactions
involving the sale or loan of securities held for the account
of the Government of Kuwait provided proceeds were paid into
blocked accounts.

<u>Oil Contracts</u>. Oil in which the governments of
Kuwait or Iraq have an interest may be imported into the
United States under General License No. 2 if the oil was
loaded onto a tanker and the bill of lading issued prior to
August 2, 1990 and it arrives in the United States prior to
October 1. Any payment to the Government of Iraq or the
Government of Kuwait for the oil must be into a blocked
account, and the transaction must be reported to OFAC.

<u>Investment of Blocked Funds</u>. Financial institutions
may invest or reinvest blocked funds held for the account of
the government of Kuwait under General License No. 3 provided
the proceeds are credited to a blocked account held in the
same name and the transaction is registered with OFAC.

<u>Transactions by Kuwaiti-Controlled Entities</u>. A U.S.
financial institution is authorized under General License
No. 4 to accept payments or transfers into blocked accounts
held in the name of Kuwaiti-controlled entities or to make
payments or transfers from such a blocked account provided
that no benefit accrues to the Government of Iraq. Entities
that wish to take advantage of this license must register
with OFAC and financial institutions must obtain evidence of
such registration before making any transfers.

Foreign Exchange and Commodities Transactions. U.S. financial institutions are authorized under General License No. 5 may perform under foreign exchange or commodities contracts entered into with the Government of Kuwait or to close out, offset or liquidate, individually or on a net basis, such contracts. Such contracts must have been entered into prior to August 2, 1990, and all payments for the Government of Kuwait must be paid into blocked accounts in the United States or in another country that has enacted satisfactory blocking legislation.

Telecommunciations. Payments by U.S. common carriers with respect to telecommunications involving Iraq or Kuwait are permitted under General License No. 6 provided they are paid into blocked accounts.

Goods Exported Prior to August 2, 1990. General License No. 7 provides that specific licenses allowing payment from a blocked account or other account for goods shipped directly or indirectly to Iraq or Kuwait prior to August 2 may be granted if the exporter presents evidence that the export occurred prior to August 2 and that the exporter exercised due diligence to divert the shipment to a non-prohibited destination or to prevent performance of services in Iraq or Kuwait.

Mail. Payment and transfers to common carriers incident to the transmission of mail between the U.S. and Iraq or Kuwait are permitted under General License No. 8 provided the mail is limited to items not exceeding twelve ounces.

Export Transactions Initiated Prior to August 2. Under General License No. 9, an exporter may regain possession of goods originally bound for Iraq or Kuwait that were seized by the U.S. Customs Service under the executive orders. The exporter must file a declaration explaining the circumstances of the export contract, providing a bill of lading, agreeing to place all amounts received from the Government of Kuwait or the Government of Iraq into a blocked account, and agreeing to indemnify the U.S. Government for claims arising from the nondelivery of the goods.

Bankers Acceptances. General License No. 10 provides that a bankers acceptance accepted or a deferred payment obligation incurred prior to August 2, 1990 that involves the importation or exportation of goods to or from Iraq or involving an interest of the Government of Iraq or the Government of Kuwait may be honored and persons other than the government of Iraq or Kuwait may buy, sell, and satisfy obligations with respect to such acceptances and obligations.

Importation of Household and Personal Effects. A person arriving directly or indirectly from Iraq or Kuwait is authorized under General License No. 11 to import household and personal effects of Kuwaiti origin provided they were actually used by that person and are not intended for sale to other persons.

Special Licenses

In addition to the general licenses, OFAC has issued numerous special licenses permitting specific entities to continue to do business or to participate in specific transactions. The most notable of these are the special licenses issued to Santa Fe Corporation, the Kuwait Investment Agency, and the Kuwait Investment Office. The terms and even the existence of these licenses are considered confidential by OFAC and may be disclosed only with the consent of the licensee.

BLOCKED STATUS OF KUWAITI BANKS

Category I: ENTITIES BLOCKED

Bahrain Arab International Bank
Bank of Kuwait & Middle East
Burgan Bank
Central Bank of Kuwait
Crédit des Bargues
Kuwait Finance House
Savings and Credit Bank

Category II: ENTITIES NOT BLOCKED

Arab African International Bank
Arab Banking Corporation
Arab Hellenic Bank
Arab Turkish Bank
Bahrain Middle East Bank
Banco Arabe Espanol
Banco Atlantico
Bank of Bahrain and Kuwait
Dao Hong Bank
Gulf International Bank B.S.C.
Kuwait and Bahrain Bank
Kuwait French Bank
National Bank of Kuwait
Swiss Kuwaiti Bank
UBAF Arab American Bank
United Bank of Kuwait

Category III: ENTITIES SUBJECT TO FURTHER DETERMINATION

(None at this time)

Category IV: ENTITIES BLOCKED *(as "de facto" controlled)*

Al-Ahlie Bank of Kuwait
Commercial Bank of Kuwait
Industrial Bank of Kuwait
Kuwait Real Estate Bank
The Gulf Bank

Source: Office of Foreign Assets Control Releases dated Aug. 2, 5, 12, 15, 19, 21, 24, 1990.

Federal Register

Vol. 55, No. 156

Monday, August 13, 1990

Presidential Documents

Title 3—

The President

Executive Order 12724 of August 9, 1990

Blocking Iraqi Government Property and Prohibiting Transactions With Iraq

By the authority vested in me as President by the Constitution and laws of the United States of America, including the International Emergency Economic Powers Act (50 U.S.C. 1701 *et seq.*), the National Emergencies Act (50 U.S.C. 1601 *et seq.*), section 301 of title 3 of the United States Code, and the United Nations Participation Act (22 U.S.C. 287c), in view of United Nations Security Council Resolution No. 661 of August 6, 1990, and in order to take additional steps with respect to Iraq's invasion of Kuwait and the national emergency declared in Executive Order No. 12722,

I, GEORGE BUSH, President of the United States of America, hereby order:

Section 1. Except to the extent provided in regulations that may hereafter be issued pursuant to this order, all property and interests in property of the Government of Iraq that are in the United States, that hereafter come within the United States, or that are or hereafter come within the possession or control of United States persons, including their overseas branches, are hereby blocked.

Sec. 2. The following are prohibited, except to the extent provided in regulations that may hereafter be issued pursuant to this order:

(a) The importation into the United States of any goods or services of Iraqi origin, or any activity that promotes or is intended to promote such importation;

(b) The exportation to Iraq, or to any entity operated from Iraq, or owned or controlled by the Government of Iraq, directly or indirectly, of any goods, technology (including technical data or other information), or services either (i) from the United States, or (ii) requiring the issuance of a license by a Federal agency, or any activity that promotes or is intended to promote such exportation, except donations of articles intended to relieve human suffering, such as food and supplies intended strictly for medical purposes;

(c) Any dealing by a United States person related to property of Iraqi origin exported from Iraq after August 6, 1990, or property intended for exportation from Iraq to any country, or exportation to Iraq from any country, or any activity of any kind that promotes or is intended to promote such dealing;

(d) Any transaction by a United States person relating to travel by any United States citizen or permanent resident alien to Iraq, or to activities by any such person within Iraq, after the date of this order, other than transactions necessary to effect (i) such person's departure from Iraq, (ii) travel and activities for the conduct of the official business of the Federal Government or the United Nations, or (iii) travel for journalistic activity by persons regularly employed in such capacity by a news-gathering organization;

(e) Any transaction by a United States person relating to transportation to or from Iraq; the provision of transportation to or from the United States by any Iraqi person or any vessel or aircraft of Iraqi registration; or the sale in the United States by any person holding authority under the Federal Aviation Act of 1958, as amended (49 U.S.C. 1301 *et seq.*), of any transportation by air that includes any stop in Iraq;

(f) The performance by any United States person of any contract, including a financing contract, in support of an industrial, commercial, public utility, or governmental project in Iraq;

(g) Except as otherwise authorized herein, any commitment or transfer, direct or indirect, of funds, or other financial or economic resources by any United States person to the Government of Iraq or any other person in Iraq;

(h) Any transaction by any United States person that evades or avoids, or has the purpose of evading or avoiding, any of the prohibitions set forth in this order.

Sec. 3. For purposes of this order:

(a) the term "United States person" means any United States citizen, permanent resident alien, juridical person organized under the laws of the United States (including foreign branches), or any person in the United States, and vessels of U.S. registration.

(b) the term "Government of Iraq" includes the Government of Iraq, its agencies, instrumentalities and controlled entities, and the Central Bank of Iraq.

Sec. 4. This order is effective immediately.

Sec. 5. The Secretary of the Treasury, in consultation with the Secretary of State, is hereby authorized to take such actions, including the promulgation of rules and regulations, as may be necessary to carry out the purposes of this order. Such actions may include prohibiting or regulating payments or transfers of any property or any transactions involving the transfer of anything of economic value by any United States person to the Government of Iraq, or to any Iraqi national or entity owned or controlled, directly or indirectly, by the Government of Iraq or Iraqi nationals. The Secretary of the Treasury may redelegate any of these functions to other officers and agencies of the Federal Government. All agencies of the Federal Government are directed to take all appropriate measures within their authority to carry out the provisions of this order, including the suspension or termination of licenses or other authorizations in effect as of the date of this order.

Sec. 6. Executive Order No. 12722 of August 2, 1990, is hereby revoked to the extent inconsistent with this order. All delegations, rules, regulations, orders, licenses, and other forms of administrative action made, issued, or otherwise taken under Executive Order No. 12722 and not revoked administratively shall remain in full force and effect under this order until amended, modified, or terminated by proper authority. The revocation of any provision of Executive Order No. 12722 pursuant to this section shall not affect any violation of any rules, regulations, orders, licenses, or other forms of administrative action under that order during the period that such provision cf that order was in effect.

This order shall be transmitted to the Congress and published in the **Federal Register**.

THE WHITE HOUSE,
August 9, 1990.

[FR Doc. 90-19151
Filed 8-10-90; 10:35 am]
Billing code 3195-01-m

Editorial note: For the President's message to the Congress on the blockage of Iraqi Government property, see the *Weekly Compilation of Presidential Documents* (vol. 26, no. 32).

Presidential Documents

Executive Order 12725 of August 9, 1990

Blocking Kuwaiti Government Property and Prohibiting Transactions With Kuwait

By the authority vested in me as President by the Constitution and laws of the United States of America, including the International Emergency Economic Powers Act (50 U.S.C. 1701 *et seq.*), the National Emergencies Act (50 U.S.C. 1601 *et seq.*), section 301 of title 3 of the United States Code, and the United Nations Participation Act (22 U.S.C. 287c), in view of United Nations Security Council Resolution No. 661 of August 6, 1990, and in order to take additional steps with respect to Iraq's invasion of Kuwait and the national emergency declared in Executive Order No. 12722,

I, GEORGE BUSH, President of the United States of America, hereby order:

Section 1. Except to the extent provided in regulations that may hereafter be issued pursuant to this order, all property and interests in property of the Government of Kuwait that are in the United States, that hereafter come within the United States, or that are or hereafter come within the possession or control of United States persons, including their overseas branches, are blocked.

Sec. 2. The following are prohibited, except to the extent provided in regulations that may hereafter be issued pursuant to this order:

(a) The importation into the United States of any goods or services of Kuwaiti origin, or any activity that promotes or is intended to promote such importation;

(b) The exportation to Kuwait, or to any entity operated from Kuwait or owned or controlled by the Government of Kuwait, directly or indirectly, of any goods, technology (including technical data or other information), or services either (i) from the United States, or (ii) requiring the issuance of a license by a Federal agency, or any activity that promotes or is intended to promote such exportation, except donations of articles intended to relieve human suffering, such as food and supplies intended strictly for medical purposes;

(c) Any dealing by a United States person related to property of Kuwaiti origin exported from Kuwait after August 6, 1990, or property intended for exportation from Kuwait to any country or exportation to Kuwait from any country, or any activity of any kind that promotes or is intended to promote such dealing;

(d) Any transaction by a United States person relating to travel by any United States citizen or permanent resident alien to Kuwait, or to activities by any such person within Kuwait, after the date of this order, other than transactions necessary to effect (i) such person's departure from Kuwait, (ii) travel and activities for the conduct of the official business of the Federal Government or the United Nations, or (iii) travel for journalistic activity by persons regularly employed in such capacity by a news-gathering organization;

(e) Any transaction by a United States person relating to transportation to or from Kuwait; the provision of transportation to or from the United States by any Kuwaiti person or any vessel or aircraft of Kuwaiti registration; or the sale in the United States by any person holding authority under the Federal Aviation Act of 1958, as amended (49 U.S.C. 1301 *et seq.*), of any transportation by air that includes any stop in Kuwait;

(f) The **performance by any United States** person of any contract, including a financing contract, in support of an industrial, commercial, public utility, or governmental project in Kuwait;

(g) Except as otherwise authorized herein, any commitment or transfer, direct or indirect, of funds, or other financial or economic resources by any United States person to the Government of Kuwait or any other person in Kuwait;

(h) Any transaction by any United States person that evades or avoids, or has the purpose of evading or avoiding, any of the prohibitions set forth in this order.

Sec. 3. For purposes of this order:

(a) the term "United States person" means any United States citizen, permanent resident alien, juridical person organized under the laws of the United States (including foreign branches), or any person in the United States, and vessels of U.S. registration.

(b) the term "Government of Kuwait" includes the Government of Kuwait or any entity purporting to be the Government of Kuwait, its agencies, instrumentalities and controlled entities, and the Central Bank of Kuwait.

Sec. 4. This order is effective immediately.

Sec. 5. The Secretary of the Treasury, in consultation with the Secretary of State, is hereby authorized to take such actions, including the promulgation of rules and regulations, as may be necessary to carry out the purposes of this order. Such actions may include prohibiting or regulating payments or transfers of any property or any transactions involving the transfer of anything of economic value by any United States person to the Government of Kuwait, or to any Kuwaiti national or entity owned or controlled, directly or indirectly, by the Government of Kuwait or Kuwaiti nationals. The Secretary of the Treasury may redelegate any of these functions to other officers and agencies of the Federal Government. All agencies of the Federal Government are directed to take all appropriate measures within their authority to carry out the provisions of this order, including the suspension or termination of licenses or other authorizations in effect as of the date of this order.

Sec. 6. Executive Order No. 12723 of August 2, 1990, is hereby revoked to the extent inconsistent with this order. All delegations, rules, regulations, orders, licenses, and other forms of administrative action made, issued, or otherwise taken under Executive Order No. 12723 and not revoked administratively shall remain in full force and effect under this order until amended, modified, or terminated by proper authority. The revocation of any provision of Executive Order No. 12723 pursuant to this section shall not affect any violation of any rules, regulations, orders, licenses, or other forms of administrative action under that order during the period that such provision of that order was in effect.

This order shall be transmitted to the Congress and published in the Federal Register.

THE WHITE HOUSE,
August 9, 1990.

[FR Doc. 90-19158
Filed 8-10-90; 10:41 am]
Billing code 3195-01-M

Editorial note: For the President's message to the Congress on the blockage of Kuwaiti Government property, see the *Weekly Compilation of Presidential Documents* (vol. 26, no. 32).

Federal Register
Vol. 55, No. 150
Friday, August 3, 1990

Presidential Documents

Title 3—

The President

Executive Order 12722 of August 2, 1990

Blocking Iraqi Government Property and Prohibiting Transactions With Iraq

By the authority vested in me as President by the Constitution and laws of the United States of America, including the International Emergency Economic Powers Act (50 U.S.C. 1701 *et seq.*), the National Emergencies Act (50 U.S.C. 1601 *et seq.*), and section 301 of title 3 of the United States Code.

I, GEORGE BUSH, President of the United States of America, find that the policies and actions of the Government of Iraq constitute an unusual and extraordinary threat to the national security and foreign policy of the United States and hereby declare a national emergency to deal with that threat.

I hereby order:

Section 1. All property and interests in property of the Government of Iraq, its agencies, instrumentalities and controlled entities and the Central Bank of Iraq that are in the United States, that hereafter come within the United States or that are or hereafter come within the possession or control of United States persons, including their overseas branches, are hereby blocked.

Section 2. The following are prohibited, except to the extent provided in regulations which may hereafter be issued pursuant to this Order:

(a) The import into the United States of any goods or services of Iraqi origin, other than publications and other informational materials;

(b) The export to Iraq of any goods, technology (including technical data or other information controlled for export pursuant to Section 5 of the Export Administration Act (50 U.S.C. App. 2404)) or services from the United States, except publications and other informational materials, and donations of articles intended to relieve human suffering, such as food, clothing, medicine and medical supplies intended strictly for medical purposes;

(c) Any transaction by a United States person relating to transportation to or from Iraq; the provision of transportation to or from the United States by any Iraqi person or any vessel or aircraft of Iraqi registration; or the sale in the United States by any person holding authority under the Federal Aviation Act of 1958, as amended (49 U.S.C. 1514), of any transportation by air which includes any stop in Iraq;

(d) The purchase by any United States person of goods for export from Iraq to any country;

(e) The performance by any United States person of any contract in support of an industrial or other commercial or governmental project in Iraq;

(f) The grant or extension of credits or loans by any United States person to the Government of Iraq, its instrumentalities and controlled entities;

(g) Any transaction by a United States person relating to travel by any United States citizen or permanent resident alien to Iraq, or to activities by any such person within Iraq, after the date of this Order, other than transactions necessary to effect such person's departure from Iraq, or travel for journalistic activity by persons regularly employed in such capacity by a newsgathering organization; and

(h) Any transaction by any United States person which evades or avoids, or has the purpose of evading or avoiding, any of the prohibitions set forth in this Order.

For purposes of this Order, the term "United States person" means any United States citizen, permanent resident alien, juridical person organized under the laws of the United States, or any person in the United States.

Section 3. This Order is effective immediately.

Section 4. The Secretary of the Treasury, in consultation with the Secretary of State, is hereby authorized to take such actions, including the promulgation of rules and regulations, as may be necessary to carry out the purposes of this Order. Such actions may include prohibiting or regulating payments or transfers of any property or any transactions involving the transfer of anything of economic value by any United States person to the Government of Iraq, its instrumentalities and controlled entities, or to any Iraqi national or entity owned or controlled, directly or indirectly, by Iraq or Iraqi nationals. The Secretary may redelegate any of these functions to other officers and agencies of the Federal government. All agencies of the United States government are directed to take all appropriate measures within their authority to carry out the provisions of this Order, including the suspension or termination of licenses or other authorizations in effect as of the date of this Order.

This Order shall be transmitted to the Congress and published in the Federal Register.

THE WHITE HOUSE,
August 2, 1990.

[FR Doc. 90-18381

Filed 8-2-90; 9:44 am]

Billing code 3195-01-M

Editorial note: For a statement by Deputy Press Secretary Popadiuk on the blockage of Iraqi and Kuwaiti property, see the *Weekly Compilation of Presidential Documents* (vol. 26, no. 31).

Presidential Documents

Executive Order 12723 of August 2, 1990

Blocking Kuwaiti Government Property

By the authority vested in me as President by the Constitution and laws of the United States of America, including the International Emergency Economic Powers Act (50 U.S.C. 1701 *et seq.*), the National Emergencies Act (50 U.S.C. 1601 *et seq.*), and 3 U.S.C. 301.

I, GEORGE BUSH, President of the United States, find that the situation caused by the invasion of Kuwait by Iraq constitutes an unusual and extraordinary threat to the national security, foreign policy and economy of the United States and have declared a national emergency to deal with that threat.

I hereby order blocked all property and interests in property of the Government of Kuwait or any entity purporting to be the Government of Kuwait, its agencies, instrumentalities and controlled entities and the Central Bank of Kuwait that are in the United States, that hereafter come within the United States or that are or hereafter come within the possession or control of United States persons, including their overseas branches.

For purposes of this Order, the term "United States person" means any United States citizen, permanent resident alien, juridical person organized under the laws of the United States or any person in the United States.

The Secretary of the Treasury is authorized to employ all powers granted to me by the International Emergency Economic Powers Act to carry out the provisions of this Order.

This Order is effective immediately and shall be transmitted to the Congress and published in the **Federal Register**.

THE WHITE HOUSE,
August 2, 1990.

[FR Doc. 90-18382
Filed 8-3-90; 9:45 am]
Billing code 3195-01-M

Editorial note: For a statement by Deputy Press Secretary Popadiuk on the blockage of Iraqi and Kuwaiti property, see the *Weekly Compilation of Presidential Documents* (vol. 26, no. 31).

DEPARTMENT OF THE TREASURY
WASHINGTON

OFFICE OF FOREIGN ASSETS CONTROL
KUWAIT ASSETS CONTROL REGULATIONS
GENERAL LICENSE NO. 1. AMENDED

Completion of Certain Securities Transactions.

(a) U.S. financial institutions are authorized to complete transactions entered into prior to the effective date, involving securities purchased, sold, lent, or borrowed for the account of the Government of Kuwait, provided the following terms and conditions are complied with, respectively:

(1) The proceeds of such sale by, or return of funds to, the Government of Kuwait are credited to a blocked account in a U.S. financial institution in the name of the Government of Kuwait entity for whose account such sale or return was made; and

(2) The securities so purchased by, or lent or returned to, the Government of Kuwait are held in a U.S. financial institution in the name of the person for whose account the purchase, borrowing, or loan was made.

(b) This section does not authorize the crediting of the proceeds of, or funds received with respect to, Government of Kuwait securities held in a blocked account or a sub-account, or securities returned with respect to funds held in a blocked account or sub account, to a blocked account or sub-account under any name or designation which differs from the name or designation of the specific blocked account or sub-account in which such funds or securities were held.

(c) Terms used in this license are defined as follows:

(1) The term "Government of Kuwait" shall mean

a) The state and the Government of Kuwait, or any entity purporting to be the Government of Kuwait, any political subdivision, agency, or instrumentality thereof, including the Central Bank of Kuwait;

b) Any partnership, association, corporation, or other organization owned or controlled by the foregoing;

c) Any person to the extent that such person is, or has been, or to the extent that there is reasonable cause to believe such person is, or has been, since the effective date, acting or purporting to act, directly or indirectly on behalf of any of the foregoing, and

d) Any other person determined by the Secretary of the Treasury to be included within this section.

(2) The term "effective date" shall mean 5:00 a.m. Eastern Daylight Time, August 2, 1990.

(3) The term "blocked account" shall mean an account in a U.S. financial institution with respect to which account payments, transfers or withdrawals or other dealings may not be made or effected except pursuant to an authorization or license from the Office of Foreign Assets Control authorizing such action.

(4) The term "U.S. financial institution" shall mean any U.S. person (including foreign branches) that is engaged in the business of accepting deposits or making, granting, transferring, holding, or brokering loans or credits, or of

purchasing or selling foreign exchange or commodities or procuring purchasers and sellers thereof, as principal or agent, including, but not limited to, banks, savings banks, trust companies, securities brokers and dealers, clearing houses, securities depositories, commodities brokers and dealers, investment companies, employee benefit plans, and U.S. holding companies, U.S. affiliates, and U.S. subsidiaries of any of the foregoing.

Issued: August 15, 1990

R. Richard Newcomb
Director
Office of Foreign Assets Control

DEPARTMENT OF THE TREASURY
WASHINGTON

OFFICE OF FOREIGN ASSETS CONTROL
KUWAIT ASSETS CONTROL REGULATIONS
GENERAL LICENSE NO. 2

Oil Under Contract Entered Into Prior to August 2, 1990 And En
Route To The United States.

(a) Oil of Iraqi origin or oil in which the Government of
Kuwait or the Government of Iraq has an interest may be
imported into the United States only if:

(1) prior to the effective date, the oil was loaded
for ultimate delivery to the United States on board a vessel in
Iraq, Kuwait, or a third country,

(2) the oil is imported into the United States
before 11:59 p.m. Eastern Daylight Time, October 1, 1990, and

(3) the bill of lading accompanying the oil was
issued prior to the effective date.

(b) Any payment owed or balance not paid to or for the
benefit of the Government of Iraq or the Government of Kuwait
prior to the effective date for oil imported pursuant to
section (a) must be paid into a blocked account in a U.S.
financial institution.

(c) Transactions conducted pursuant to this section must
be reported in writing to the Office of Foreign Assets Control,
Blocked Assets Section within ten (10) days of the date of
importation.

(d) Terms used in this license are defined as follows:

(1) The term "oil of Iraqi origin" shall mean oil
extracted, processed or refined in Iraq.

(2) The term "Government of Iraq" includes:

a) The state and the Government of Iraq, as well as any political subdivision, agency, or instrumentality thereof, including the Central Bank of Iraq;

b) Any partnership, association, corporation, or other organization substantially owned or controlled by the foregoing;

c) Any person to the extent that such person is, or has been, or to the extent that there is reasonable cause to believe such person is, or has been, since the effective date, acting or purporting to act, directly or indirectly on behalf of any of the foregoing;

d) Any other person or organization determined by the Secretary of the Treasury to be included within section (1).

(3) The term "Government of Kuwait" shall mean

a) The state and the Government of Kuwait, as well as any political subdivision, agency, or instrumentality thereof, including the Central Bank of Kuwait;

b) Any partnership, association, corporation, or other organization substantially owned or controlled by the foregoing;

c) Any person to the extent that such person is, or has been, or to the extent that there is reasonable cause to believe such person is, or has been, since the effective date, acting or purporting to act, directly or indirectly on behalf of any of the foregoing, and

d) Any other person or organization determined by the Secretary of the Treasury to be included within section (1).

(4) The term "effective date" shall mean 5:00 a.m. Eastern Daylight Time, August 2, 1990.

(5) The term "blocked account" shall mean an account in a financial institution with respect to which account payments, transfers or withdrawals or other dealings may not be made or effected except pursuant to an authorization or license from the Office of Foreign Assets Control authorizing such action.

(6) The term "U.S. financial institution" shall mean any U.S. person engaged in the business of accepting deposits or making, granting, transferring, holding, or brokering loans or credits, or of purchasing or selling foreign exchange or commodities or procuring purchasers and sellers thereof, as principal or agent, including, but not limited to, banks, savings banks, trust companies, securities brokers and dealers,

commodities brokers, investment companies, employee pension plans, and holding companies or subsidiaries of any of the foregoing.

Issued: August 8, 1990

R. Richard Newcomb

Director

Office of Foreign Assets Control

DEPARTMENT OF THE TREASURY
WASHINGTON

OFFICE OF FOREIGN ASSETS CONTROL
KUWAIT ASSETS CONTROL REGULATIONS
GENERAL LICENSE NO. 3

<u>Investment of Government of Kuwait Funds Held in Blocked
Accounts</u>.

(a) U.S. financial institutions are hereby authorized
to invest and reinvest funds held in blocked accounts in the
name of the Government of Kuwait, subject to the following
conditions:

(1) The proceeds of such investments and
reinvestments are credited to a blocked account or
sub-account which is in the name of the Government of Kuwait
and which is subject to the jurisdiction of the United
States;

(2) The proceeds of such investments and
reinvestments are not credited to a blocked account or
sub-account under any name or designation which differs from
the name or designation of the specific blocked account or
sub-account in which such funds or securities were held; and

(3) no financial or economic benefit accrues to
the Government of Iraq as a result of the transaction.

(b)(1) U.S. persons seeking to avail themselves of this
authorization must register with the Office of Foreign
Assets Control, Blocked Assets Section.

(2) Transactions conducted pursuant to this
section must be reported to the Office of Foreign Assets
Control, Blocked Assets Section within ten (10) days of
completion of the transaction.

(d) Terms used in this license are defined as follows:

(1) The term "Government of Iraq" includes:

a) The state and the Government of Iraq, as well as any political subdivision, agency, or instrumentality thereof, including the Central Bank of Iraq;

b) Any partnership, association, corporation, or other organization substantially owned or controlled by the foregoing;

c) Any person to the extent that such person is, or has been, or to the extent that there is reasonable cause to believe such person is, or has been, since the effective date, acting or purporting to act, directly or indirectly on behalf of any of the foregoing;

d) Any other person or organization determined by the Secretary of the Treasury to be included within section (1).

(2) The term "Government of Kuwait" shall mean

a) The state and the Government of Kuwait, as well as any political subdivision, agency, or instrumentality thereof, including the Central Bank of Kuwait;

b) Any partnership, association, corporation, or other organization substantially owned or controlled by the foregoing;

c) Any person to the extent that such person is, or has been, or to the extent that there is reasonable cause to believe such person is, or has been, since the effective date, acting or purporting to act, directly or indirectly on behalf of any of the foregoing, and

d) Any other person or organization determined by the Secretary of the Treasury to be included within section (1).

(3) The term "blocked account" shall mean an account in the United States with respect to which account payments, transfers or withdrawals or other dealings may not be made or effected except pursuant to an authorization or license from the Office of Foreign Assets Control authorizing such action.

(4) The term "U.S. financial institution" shall mean any U.S. person engaged in the business of accepting deposits or making, granting, transferring, holding, or brokering loans or credits, or of purchasing or selling foreign exchange or commodities or procuring purchasers and sellers thereof, as principal or agent, including, but not limited to, banks, savings banks, trust companies,

securities brokers and dealers, commodities brokers, investment companies, employee pension plans, and holding companies or subsidiaries of any of the foregoing.

Issued: August 8, 1990

R. Richard Newcomb

Director

Office of Foreign Assets Control

DEPARTMENT OF THE TREASURY
WASHINGTON

OFFICE OF FOREIGN ASSETS CONTROL
KUWAIT ASSETS CONTROL REGULATIONS
GENERAL LICENSE NO. 4 ·

<u>Transactions by U.S. Entities Owned or Controlled by the
Government of Kuwait</u>.

(a) The following transactions by a U.S. financial
institution that is not owned or controlled by the
Government of Kuwait are hereby authorized with respect to
blocked accounts held in the name of entities owned or
controlled by the Government of Kuwait that are located
within the United States:

(1) Any payment or transfer, including any payment
or transfer from outside the United States, into such
blocked accounts;

(2) Any payment or transfer from such blocked
accounts, provided that no benefit accrues to the Government
of Iraq from such transactions.

(b)(1) Entities owned or controlled by the Government
of Kuwait, seeking to avail themselves of this
authorization, must register with the Office of Foreign
Assets Control, Blocked Assets Section.

(2) Financial institutions must require evidence
of such registration before undertaking any transaction
pursuant to this license.

(c) Terms used in this license are defined as follows:

(1) The term "Government of Iraq" includes:

a) The state and the Government of Iraq, as well as any political subdivision, agency, or instrumentality thereof, including the Central Bank of Iraq;

b) Any partnership, association, corporation, or other organization substantially owned or controlled by the foregoing;

c) Any person to the extent that such person is, or has been, or to the extent that there is reasonable cause to believe such person is, or has been, since the effective date, acting or purporting to act, directly or indirectly on behalf of any of the foregoing;

d) Any other person or organization determined by the Secretary of the Treasury to be included within section (1).

(2) The term "Government of Kuwait" shall mean

a) The state and the Government of Kuwait, as well as any political subdivision, agency, or instrumentality thereof, including the Central Bank of Kuwait;

b) Any partnership, association, corporation, or other organization substantially owned or controlled by the foregoing;

c) Any person to the extent that such person is, or has been, or to the extent that there is reasonable cause to believe such person is, or has been, since the effective date, acting or purporting to act, directly or indirectly on behalf of any of the foregoing, and

d) Any other person or organization determined by the Secretary of the Treasury to be included within section (1).

(3) The term "blocked account" shall mean an account in a financial institution with respect to which account payments, transfers, or withdrawals or other dealings may not be made or effected except pursuant to an authorization or license from the Office of Foreign Assets Control authorizing such action.

(4) The term "U.S. financial institution" shall mean any U.S. person engaged in the business of accepting deposits or making, granting, transferring, holding, or brokering loans or credits, or of purchasing or selling foreign exchange or commodities or procuring purchasers and sellers thereof, as principal or agent, including, but not limited to, banks, savings banks, trust companies, securities brokers and dealers, commodities brokers, investment companies, employee pension plans, and holding companies or subsidiaries of any of the foregoing.

Issued August 8, 1990

R. Richard Newcomb

Director

Office of Foreign Assets Control

DEPARTMENT OF THE TREASURY
WASHINGTON

OFFICE OF FOREIGN ASSETS CONTROL
KUWAIT ASSETS CONTROL REGULATIONS
GENERAL LICENSE NO. 5

Completion of Certain Foreign Exchange and Commodities
Transactions.

(a) U.S. financial institutions are authorized to
perform and complete in accordance with its terms or, in
agreement with the Government of Kuwait, to close out, offset,
or liquidate, individually or on a net basis, any contract
with or on behalf of the Government of Kuwait for (i) foreign
exchange, currency, and interest rate transactions (including,
without limitation, spot, forward, option, swap, and futures
transactions), and (ii) commodity option, swap, and futures
transactions (including the posting or payment of margin or
settlement variation with respect to transactions described in
subparagraphs (i) and (ii)), provided the contract was entered
into prior to the effective date and any of the following
requirements is met:

(1) Any funds, currency, securities, or other assets
to be paid or delivered to the Government of Kuwait are
credited to a blocked account in the name of the entity of the
Government of Kuwait with which, or on whose behalf, the
transaction was executed; or

(2) Any funds, currency, securities, or other assets
to be paid or delivered to the Government of Kuwait are
credited to a blocked or restricted account in the name of the
Government of Kuwait in the financial institution and location
designated in the original payment instructions or terms of

settlement or delivery for that contract; provided that the country in which payment, settlement, or delivery occurs has in place an arrangement satisfactory to the Office of Foreign Assets Control for ensuring that Government of Kuwait assets in such accounts are blocked or restricted; or

(3) All funds, currency, securities, or other assets due to the Government of Kuwait in connection with such transaction were paid or delivered to the Government of Kuwait prior to the effective date.

(b) All transactions by U.S. persons incidental to the transactions authorized in paragraph (a) are also authorized.

(c) This license does not authorize the crediting of the funds, currency, securities, or other assets received by, or for the benefit of, the Government of Kuwait in a transaction authorized in paragraph (a) to a blocked account or sub-account for the Government of Kuwait under any name or designation which differs from the name or designation of the specific blocked account or sub-account in which the assets utilized by, or on behalf of, the Government of Kuwait in such transaction were held.

(d) The following terms are defined as follows for purposes of this license:

(1) The term "Government of Kuwait" includes

(A) The state and the Government of Kuwait, as well as any political subdivision, agency, or instrumentality thereof, including the Central Bank of Kuwait;

(B) Any partnership, association, corporation, or other organization owned or controlled by the foregoing;

(C) Any person to the extent that such person is, or has been, or to the extent that there is reasonable cause to believe such person is, or has been, since the effective date, acting or purporting to act, directly or indirectly on behalf of any of the foregoing, and

(D) Any other person determined by the Secretary of the Treasury to be included within this section.

(2) The term "effective date" shall mean 5:00 a.m. Eastern Daylight Time, August 2, 1990.

(3) The term "blocked account" shall mean an account in a U.S. financial institution with respect to which account payments, transfers, withdrawals, or other dealings may not be made or effected except pursuant to an authorization or license from the Office of Foreign Assets Control authorizing such action.

(4) The term "U.S. financial institution" shall mean any U.S. person (including foreign branches) that is engaged in the business of accepting deposits or making, granting, transferring, holding, or brokering loans or credits, or of purchasing or selling foreign exchange, commodity futures or options, or procuring purchasers and sellers thereof, as principal or agent, including, but not limited to, banks, savings banks, trust companies, securities brokers and dealers, commodity futures and options brokers and dealers, forward contract and foreign exchange merchants,

securities and commodities exchanges, clearing corporations, investment companies, employee benefit plans, and U.S. holding companies, U.S. affiliates, or U.S. subsidiaries of any of the foregoing.

Issued: August 13, 1990

R. Richard Newcomb

Director

Office of Foreign Assets Control

DEPARTMENT OF THE TREASURY

WASHINGTON

OFFICE OF FOREIGN ASSETS CONTROL
KUWAIT ASSETS CONTROL REGULATIONS
GENERAL LICENSE NO. 6

<u>Telecommunications Payments</u>.

(a) All transactions of U.S. common carriers with respect to the receipt and transmission of telecommunications involving Kuwait and Iraq are authorized, provided any payment owed to the Government of Kuwait, the Government of Iraq, or persons in Kuwait or Iraq is paid into a blocked account in a U.S. bank.

(b) Terms used in this license are defined as follows:

(1) The term "Government of Kuwait" shall mean

a) The state and the Government of Kuwait, or any entity purporting to be the Government of Kuwait, as well as any political subdivision, agency, or instrumentality thereof, including the Central Bank of Kuwait;

b) Any partnership, association, corporation, or other organization owned or controlled by the foregoing;

c) Any person to the extent that such person is, or has been, or to the extent that there is reasonable cause to believe such person is, or has been, since the effective date, acting or purporting to act, directly or indirectly on behalf of any of the foregoing, and

d) Any other person or organization determined by the Secretary of the Treasury to be included within this section.

(2) The term "Government of Iraq" shall mean

a) The state and the Government of Iraq, as well as any political subdivision, agency, or instrumentality thereof, including the Central Bank of Iraq;

b) Any partnership, association, corporation, or other organization owned or controlled by the foregoing;

c) Any person to the extent that such person is, or has been, or to the extent that there is reasonable cause to believe such person is, or has been, since the effective date, acting or purporting to act, directly or indirectly on behalf of any of the foregoing, and

d) Any other person or organization determined by the Secretary of the Treasury to be included within this section.

(3) The term "blocked account" shall mean an account with respect to which account payments, transfers or withdrawals or other dealings may not be made or effected except pursuant to an authorization or license from the Office of Foreign Assets Control authorizing such action.

(4) The term "telecommunications" shall mean telephone, telex, and telegraph transmissions, and transmissions for newsgathering purposes.

Issued: August 15, 1990

R. Richard Newcomb
Director
Office of Foreign Assets Control

DEPARTMENT OF THE TREASURY

WASHINGTON

OFFICE OF FOREIGN ASSETS CONTROL
KUWAIT ASSETS CONTROL REGULATIONS
IRAQI SANCTIONS REGULATIONS
GENERAL LICENSE NO. 7

Payment For Goods or Services Exported Prior to Effective Date to Iraq or Kuwait or to the Government of Iraq or Government of Kuwait.

(a) Specific licenses may be issued on a case-by-case basis to permit payment, from a blocked account or otherwise, of amounts owed to or for the benefit of a U.S. person for goods or services exported by a U.S. person or from the United States prior to the effective date directly or indirectly to Iraq or Kuwait, or to third countries for the benefit of the Government of Iraq or the Government of Kuwait, where the exporter's license application presents evidence satisfactory to the Office of Foreign Assets Control that:

(1) the exportation occurred prior to the effective date (such evidence may include, e.g., bill of lading, air waybill, the purchaser's written confirmation of completed services, customs documents, insurance documents), and

(2) if delivery or performance occurred after the effective date, due diligence was exercised to divert delivery of the goods from Iraq or Kuwait and to effect final delivery of the goods to a non-prohibited destination, or to prevent performance of the services.

(b) This section does not authorize exportations or the performance of services after the effective date pursuant to a contract entered into or partially performed prior to the effective date.

(c)   Transactions conducted under specific licenses granted pursuant to this section must be reported in writing to the Office of Foreign Assets Control, Blocked Assets Section within ten (10) days of the date of payment.

(d)   Separate criteria may be applied to the issuance of licenses authorizing payment from an account held in a blocked U.S. bank.

(e)   Terms used in this license are defined as follows:

(1)   The term "U.S. person" shall mean any United States citizen, permanent resident alien, juridical person organized under the laws of the United States (including foreign branches), or any person in the United States, and vessels of U.S. registration.

(2)   The term "effective date" shall mean (A) 5:00 a.m. Eastern Daylight Time, August 2, 1990, in the case of exportations to or for the benefit of the Government of Iraq or the Government of Kuwait; or (B) 8:55 p.m. Eastern Daylight Time, August 9, 1990, in the case of exportations to Iraq or Kuwait, or to a non-governmental business in a third country operated from Iraq or Kuwait.

(3) The term "Government of Iraq" shall mean

a) The state and the Government of Iraq, as well as any political subdivision, agency, or instrumentality thereof, including the Central Bank of Iraq;

b) Any partnership, association, corporation, or other organization owned or controlled by the foregoing;

c) Any person to the extent that such person is, or has been, or to the extent that there is reasonable cause to believe such person is, or has been, since the effective date, acting or purporting to act, directly or indirectly on behalf of any of the foregoing, and

d) Any other person or organization determined by the Secretary of the Treasury to be included within this section.

(4) The term "Government of Kuwait" shall mean

a) The state and the Government of Kuwait, any entity purporting to be the Government of Kuwait, as well as any political subdivision, agency, or instrumentality thereof, including the Central Bank of Kuwait;

b) Any partnership, association, corporation, or other organization owned or controlled by the foregoing;

c) Any person to the extent that such person is, or has been, or to the extent that there is reasonable cause to believe such person is, or has been, since the effective date, acting or purporting to act, directly or indirectly on behalf of any of the foregoing, and

d) Any other person or organization determined by the Secretary of the Treasury to be included within this section.

(5) The term "blocked account" shall mean an account in a U.S. financial institution with respect to which account payments, transfers or withdrawals or other dealings may not be made or effected except pursuant to an authorization or license

from the Office of Foreign Assets Control authorizing such action.

(6) The term "exportation" shall mean (A) the actual departure of goods from the territorial jurisdiction of the country from which exported, or (B) the performance by a U.S. person of services that are intended to result in a benefit to the Government of Iraq, the Government of Kuwait, a person in Iraq or Kuwait, or an entity operated from Iraq or Kuwait.

Issued: August 15, 1990

R. Richard Newcomb
Director
Office of Foreign Assets Control

DEPARTMENT OF THE TREASURY

WASHINGTON

OFFICE OF FOREIGN ASSETS CONTROL
KUWAITI ASSETS CONTROL REGULATIONS
IRAQI SANCTIONS REGULATIONS
GENERAL LICENSE NO. 8

Transactions Related to Mail Service

All transactions by U.S. persons including payment and transfers to common carriers incident to the receipt or transmission of mail between the United States and Kuwait and between the United States and Iraq are authorized, provided mail is limited to items not exceeding twelve (12) ounces.

Issued: August 23, 1990

R. Richard Newcomb
Director
Office of Foreign Assets Control

DEPARTMENT OF THE TREASURY
WASHINGTON

OFFICE OF FOREIGN ASSETS CONTROL
KUWAITI ASSETS CONTROL REGULATIONS
IRAQI SANCTIONS REGULATIONS

GENERAL LICENSE NO. 9

<u>Export Transactions Initiated Prior to Effective Date.</u>

(a) Goods awaiting exportation to Iraq or Kuwait on the effective date and seized or detained by the U.S. Customs Service on the effective date or thereafter pursuant to Executive Orders 12722 or 12723 or Executive Orders 12724 or 12725, may be released to the exporter provided the following documents are filed with Customs officials at the port where such goods are located:

(1) A copy of the contract governing the exportation (sale or other transfer) of the goods to Iraq or Kuwait or, if no contract exists, a written explanation of the circumstances of exportation, including in either case a description of the manner and terms of payment received or to be received by the exporter (or other person) for, or by reason of, the exportation of the goods;

(2) An invoice, bill of lading, or other documentation fully describing the goods; and

(3) A statement by the exporter substantially in the following form:

Any amount received from or on behalf of the Government of Iraq or the Government of Kuwait by reason of the attempted exportation of the goods released to [name of exporter] by the U.S. Customs Service on [date], and fully described in the attached documents, has been or will be placed into a blocked account in a U.S. banking institution and the Office of Foreign Assets Control, Blocked Assets

Section, will be immediately notified. [Name of exporter] agrees to fully indemnify the U.S. Government for any amount ultimately determined by a court of competent jurisdiction to be due or payable to or for the benefit of any person by reason of the failure of [name of exporter] to properly pay into a blocked account any amount received for the goods from or on behalf of the Government of Iraq or the Government of Kuwait. [Name of exporter] also agrees to waive all claims (1) against any payments received and placed into a blocked account, except as may be later authorized by law, regulations, or license, and (2) against the U.S. Government with regard to the disposition of the amounts placed into a blocked account.

The statement should be dated and signed by the exporter or by a person authorized to sign on the exporter's behalf. The Customs Service may release the goods to the exporter upon receipt of the documentation and statement described above, provided it is satisfied that all Customs laws and regulations have been complied with, including the execution of such hold harmless assurances as it shall determine to be appropriate. The documentation and statement received by Customs will be forwarded to the Office of Foreign Assets Control for review and appropriate action.

(c) Terms used in this license are defined as follows:

(1) The term "effective date" shall mean (A) 5:00 a.m., Eastern Daylight Time (EDT), August 2, 1990, in the case of exportations to Iraq or to or for the benefit of the Government of Iraq or the Government of Kuwait; or (B) 8:55 p.m., EDT, August 9, 1990, in the case of other exportations to Kuwait, or to a nongovernmental business in a third country operated from Iraq or Kuwait.

(2) The term "Government of Iraq" shall mean

(A) The state and the Government of Iraq, as well as any political subdivision, agency, or instrumentality thereof, including the Central Bank of Iraq;

(B) Any partnership, association, corporation, or other organization owned or controlled by the foregoing;

(C) Any person to the extent such person is, or has been, or to the extent there is reasonable cause to believe such person is, or has been, since the effective date, acting or purporting to act, directly or indirectly on behalf of any of the foregoing; and

(D) Any other person or organization determined by the Secretary of the Treasury to be included within this section.

(3) The term "Government of Kuwait" shall mean

(A) The state and Government of Kuwait or any entity purporting to be the Government of Kuwait, as well as any political subdivision, agency, or instrumentality thereof, including the Central Bank of Kuwait;

(B) Any partnership, association, corporation, or other organization owned or controlled by any of the foregoing;

(C) Any person to the extent that such person is, or has been, or to the extent that there is reasonable cause to believe such person is, or has been, since the effective date, acting or purporting to act, directly or indirectly, on behalf of any of the foregoing; and

(D) Any other person or organization determined by the Secretary of the Treasury to be included within this section.

(4) The term "blocked account" shall mean an account in a U.S. banking institution with respect to which account payments, transfers or withdrawals or other dealings may not be made or effected except pursuant to an authorization or license from the Office of Foreign Assets Control.

(5) The term "U.S. banking institution" shall mean any U.S. person (including foreign branches) that is engaged in the business of accepting deposits or making, granting, transferring, holding, or brokering loans or credits, including but not limited to, banks, savings banks, and trust companies.

(6) The term "U.S. person" shall mean any United States citizen, permanent resident alien, juridical person organized under the laws of the United States (including foreign branches), or any person in the United States.

Issued: August 27, 1990

R. Richard Newcomb
Director, Office of Foreign Assets Control

DEPARTMENT OF THE TREASURY
WASHINGTON

OFFICE OF FOREIGN ASSETS CONTROL
KUWAIT ASSETS CONTROL REGULATIONS
GENERAL LICENSE NO. 10

Completion of Certain Transactions Involving Bankers
Acceptances and Other Irrevocable Undertakings.

(a)   Persons other than the Government of Iraq and the
Government of Kuwait are authorized to buy, sell and satisfy
obligations with respect to bankers acceptances, and to pay
under deferred payment undertakings, involving the
importation or exportation of goods to or from Iraq or
involving an interest of the Government of Iraq or the
Government of Kuwait, as long as the bankers acceptance was
accepted or the deferred payment obligation was incurred
prior to 5:00 a.m. Eastern Daylight Time ("EDT"), August 2,
1990.

(b)   Persons other than the Government of Iraq and the
Government of Kuwait are authorized to buy, sell and satisfy
obligations with respect to bankers acceptances, and to pay
under deferred payment undertakings, involving the
importation or exportation of goods to or from Kuwait that
do not involve an interest of the Government of Iraq or the
Government of Kuwait, as long as the bankers acceptance was
accepted or the deferred payment obligation was incurred
prior to 8:55 p.m. EDT, August 9, 1990.

(c)   Nothing in this license shall authorize or permit
a debit to a blocked account. Specific licenses for the
debiting of a blocked account may be issued on a case-by-
case basis.

(d)   Terms used in this license are defined as follows:

(1) The term "Government of Iraq" shall mean:

(A) The state and the Government of Iraq, as well as any political subdivision, agency, or instrumentality thereof, including the Central Bank of Iraq;

(B) Any partnership, association, corporation, or other organization substantially owned or controlled by the foregoing;

(C) Any person to the extent that such person is, or has been, or to the extent that there is reasonable cause to believe such person is, or has been, since the effective date, acting or purporting to act, directly or indirectly on behalf of any of the foregoing, and

(D) Any other person or organization determined by the Secretary of the Treasury to be included within this section.

(2) The term "Government of Kuwait" shall mean:

(A) The state and the Government of Kuwait or any entity purporting to be the Government of Kuwait, as well as any political subdivision, agency, or instrumentality thereof, including the Central Bank of Kuwait;

(B) Any partnership, association, corporation, or other organization substantially owned or controlled by the foregoing;

(C) Any person to the extent that such person is, or has been, or to the extent that there is reasonable cause to believe such person is, or has been, since the effective date, acting or purporting to act, directly or indirectly on behalf of any of the foregoing, and

(D) Any other person or organization determined by the Secretary of the Treasury to be included within this section.

(3) The term "deferred payment" shall mean a payment to be made under a letter of credit at a maturity date specified by or determinable from the wording of the credit, but not involving the acceptance of a tenor draft, and is as used in the Uniform Customs and Practice for Documentary Credits, 1983 Revision, ICC Publication No. 400.

Issued: August 30, 1990

R. Richard Newcomb
Director
Office of Foreign Assets Control

DEPARTMENT OF THE TREASURY
WASHINGTON

OFFICE OF FOREIGN ASSETS CONTROL
KUWAITI ASSETS CONTROL REGULATIONS
IRAQI SANCTIONS REGULATIONS

GENERAL LICENSE NO. 11

Importation of Household and Personal Effects from Iraq or Kuwait.

The importation of the household and personal effects of
Iraqi or Kuwaiti origin, including baggage and articles for
family use, of a person arriving in the United States directly
or indirectly from Iraq or Kuwait is authorized. Articles
included in such effects may be imported without limitation
provided they were actually used by such person or family abroad,
are not intended for any other person or for sale, and are not
otherwise prohibited from importation.

Issued: _September 1, 1990_

R. Richard Newcomb

R. Richard Newcomb

Director

Office of Foreign Assets Control

§ 2349aa-7. Coordination of all United States anti-terrorism assistance to foreign countries

(a) Responsibility

The Secretary of State shall be responsible for coordinating all assistance related to international terrorism which is provided by the United States Government to foreign countries.

(b) Reports

Not later than February 1 each year, the Secretary of State, in consultation with appropriate United States Government agencies, shall report to the appropriate committees of the Congress on the assistance related to international terrorism which was provided by the United States Government during the preceding fiscal year. Such reports may be provided on a classified basis to the extent necessary, and shall specify the amount and nature of the assistance provided.

(c) Rule of construction

Nothing contained in this section shall be construed to limit or impair the authority or responsibility of any other Federal agency with respect to law enforcement, domestic security operations, or intelligence activities as defined in Executive Order 12333.

(Pub.L. 99-83, Title V, § 502, Aug. 8, 1985, 99 Stat. 220, amended Pub. L. 99-399, Title V, § 503, Aug. 27, 1986, 100 Stat. 871.)

References in Text. Executive Order 12333, referred to in subsec. (c), is Ex. Ord. No. 12333, Dec. 4, 1981, 46 F.R. 59941, which is set out as a note under section 401 of Title 50, War and National Defense.

Codification. Section was enacted as part of the International Security and Development Cooperation Act of 1985, and not as part of the Foreign Assistance Act of 1961 which comprises this chapter.

1986 Amendment. Heading. Pub.L. 99-399, § 503(1), substituted "terrorism-related" for "anti-terrorism".

Subsec. (a). Pub.L. 99-399, § 503(2), substituted "assistance related to international terrorism which is provided by the United States Government to foreign countries" for "anti-terrorism assistance to foreign countries provided by the United States Government".

Subsec. (b). Pub.L. 99-399, § 503(3), substituted "assistance related to international terrorism which was" for "anti-terrorism assistance".

Subsec. (c). Pub.L. 99-399, § 503(4), added subsec. (c).

Effective Date. Section effective Oct. 1, 1985, see section 1301 of Pub.L. 99-83, set out as a note under section 2151-1 of this title.

Legislative History. For legislative history and purpose of Pub.L. 99-83, see 1985 U.S. Code Cong. and Adm. News, p. 158. See, also, Pub. L. 99-399, 1986 U.S. Code Cong. and Adm. News, p. 1865.

§ 2349aa-8. Prohibition on imports from and exports to Libya

(a) Prohibition on imports

Notwithstanding any other provision of law, the President may prohibit any article grown, produced, extracted, or manufactured in Libya from being imported into the United States.

(b) Prohibition on exports

Notwithstanding any other provision of law, the President may prohibit any goods or technology, including technical data or other information, subject to the jurisdiction of the United States or exported by any person subject to the jurisdiction of the United States, from being exported to Libya.

(c) Definition

For purposes of this section, the term "United States", when used in a geographical sense, includes territories and possessions of the United States.

(Pub.L. 99-83, Title V, § 504, Aug. 8, 1985, 99 Stat. 221.)

Effective Date. Section effective Oct. 1, 1985, see section 1301 of Pub.L. 99-83, set out as a note under section 2151-1 of this title.

Delegation of Functions. For provisions relating to delegation and reservation of functions conferred on the President by this section, see Ex.Ord. No. 12163, Sept. 29, 1979, 44 F.R. 56673, as amended, set out as a note under section 2381 of this title.

Legislative History. For legislative history and purpose of Pub.L. 99-83, see 1985 U.S. Code Cong. and Adm. News, p. 158.

Library References
    Commerce ⚖=73.
    C.J.S. Commerce §§ 13 et seq., 135.

§ 2349aa-9. Ban on importing goods and services from countries supporting terrorism

(a) Authority

The President may ban the importation into the United States of any good or service from any country which supports terrorism or terrorist organizations or harbors terrorists or terrorist organizations.

(b) Consultation

The President, in every possible instance, shall consult with the Congress before exercising the authority granted by this section and shall consult regularly with the Congress so long as that authority is being exercised.

(c) Reports

Whenever the President exercises the authority granted by this section, he shall immediately transmit to the Congress a report specifying—

(1) the country with respect to which the authority is to be exercised and the imports to be prohibited;

(2) the circumstances which necessitate the exercise of such authority;

(3) why the President believes those circumstances justify the exercise of such authority; and

(4) why the President believes the prohibitions are necessary to deal with those circumstances.

At least once during each succeeding 6-month period after transmitting a report pursuant to this subsection, the President shall report to the Congress with respect to the actions taken, since the last such report, pursuant to this section and with respect to any changes which have occurred concerning any information previously furnished pursuant to this subsection.

(d) Definition

For purposes of this section, the term "United States" includes territories and possessions of the United States.

(Pub.L. 99-83, Title V, § 505, Aug. 8, 1985, 99 Stat. 221.)

Codification. Section was enacted as part of the International Security and Development Cooperation Act of 1985, and not as part of the Foreign Assistance Act of 1961 which comprises this chapter.

Effective Date. Section effective Oct. 1, 1985, see section 1301 of Pub.L. 99-83, set out as a note under section 2151-1 of this title.

Delegation of Functions. For provisions relating to delegation and reservation of functions conferred on the President by this section, see Ex.Ord. No. 12163, Sept. 29, 1979, 44 F.R. 56673, as amended, set out as a note under section 2381 of this title.

Legislative History. For legislative history and purpose of Pub.L. 99-83, see 1985 U.S. Code Cong. and Adm. News, p. 158.

Library References
    Commerce ⚖=73.
    C.J.S. Commerce §§ 13 et seq., 135.

SUBCHAPTER III—GENERAL AND ADMINISTRATIVE PROVISIONS

PART I—GENERAL PROVISIONS

§ 2351. Encouragement of free enterprise and private participation

Transcribed From Foreign Relations 22 § 2349 aa-8
_____

§2349aa-8 Prohibition on imports from exports to Libya

(a) Prohibition on imports

Notwithstanding any other provision of law, the President may
prohibit any article grown, produced, extracted, or manufactured in
Libya from being imported into the United States.

(b) Prohibition on exports

Notwithstanding any other provision of law, the President may
prohibit any goods or technology, including technical data or other
information, subject to the jurisdiction of the United States or
exported by any person subject to the jurisdiction of the United
States, from being exported to Libya.

(c) Definition

For purposes of this section, the term "United States", when used in
a geographical sense, includes territories and possessions of the
United States.

Effective Data. Section effective Oct 1, 1985, see section 1301 of
Pub.L. 99-83, set out as a note under section 2151-1 of this title.

Delegation of Functions. For provisions relating to delegation and
reservation of functions conferred on the President by this section, see
Ex.Ord. No. 12163, Sept. 29, 1979, 44 F.R. 56673, as ammended, set out
as a note under section 2381 of this title.

Legislative History. For legislative history and purpose of Pub.L.
99-83, see 1985 U.S. Code Cong. and Adm. News, p.158.

Library References
Commerce - 75.
C.J.S. Commerce   13 et seq., 135.

(b) The Commodity Control List (Supplement No. 1 to § 799.1) indicates that a validated license is required for export to Canada.

[46 FR 870, Jan. 5, 1981, as amended at 46 FR 38349, July 27, 1981; 53 FR 12669, Apr. 15, 1988. Redesignated at 53 FR 37751, Sept. 28, 1988]

§ 785.7 Country Group S; Libya.

As authorized by section 6 of the Export Administration Act of 1979, the following special policies and procedures for commodities and technical data are in effect for Libya for foreign policy purposes.

NOTE: The Libyan Sanctions regulations (31 CFR Part 550) administered by the Department of the Treasury restrict exports from the United States to Libya. As reflected in the General Order contained in § 790.7, effective February 1, 1986, a license issued under the Treasury regulations will constitute an authorization under the Export Administration regulations for an export from the United States. No license application need be filed with Commerce. Shipments to Libya from foreign countries that are subject to the provisions of 15 CFR Part 774, §§ 776.12 and 779.8 and this section and are not subject to the Libyan Sanctions regulations continue to require authorization under the Export Administration regulations.

(a) Except as stated below, a validated license or reexport authorization is required for all U.S.-orgin commodities or technical data, as well as foreign produced products of U.S. technical data exported from the United States after March 12, 1982 subject to national security controls for which written assurances against shipments to Libya are required under § 779.4 of the Export Administration Regulations. Excepted from this licensing requirement are medicines and medical supplies, food and other agricultural commodities, and commodities and data exported pursuant to special general licenses described in Parts 771 and 779.

(1) Licenses will generally be denied for:

(i) Items controlled for national security purposes and related technical data, including controlled foreign produced products of U.S. technical data exported from the United States after March 12, 1982; and

(ii) Oil and gas equipment and technical data, if determined by the Export Administration not to be readily available from sources outside the United States; and

(iii) Goods and technical data destined for the petrochemical processing complex at Ras Lanuf, where such items would contribute directly to the development or construction of that complex. Items destined for the township at Ras Lanuf, or for the public utilities or harbor facilities associated with that township, generally will *not* be regarded as making such a contribution where their functions will be primarily related to the township, utilities or harbor.

(2) Notwithstanding the presumptions of denial in paragraph (a)(1) of this section:

(i) Licenses and authorizations generally will be issued when the transaction involves:

(A) The export or reexport of commodities or technical data under a contract in effect prior to March 12, 1982, where failure to obtain a license would not excuse performance under the contract;

(B) Reexport of goods or technical data not controlled for national security purposes that had been exported from the United States prior to March 12, 1982, or exports of foreign products incorporating such items as components; or

(C) Use of U.S. origin parts, components, or materials in foreign origin products destined for Libya, where the U.S. content is 20 percent or less by value.

(ii) Licenses and authorizations will generally be considered favorably on a case-by-case basis when the transaction involves:

(A) Reexports of goods or technical data subject to national security controls that were exported prior to March 12, 1982 and exports of foreign products incorporating such U.S.-origin components, where the particular authorization would not be contrary to specific foreign policy objectives of the United States; or

(B) Items destined for use in the development or construction of the petrochemical processing complex at Ras Lanuf, where the transaction could be approved but for the general policy of denial set out in paragraph (a)(1)(iii) of this section, and where either:

(1) The transaction involves a contract in effect before December 20, 1983 that requires export or reexport of the goods or technical data in question; or

(2) The goods or technical data had been exported from the U.S. before that date.

(C) Other unusual situations such as transactions involving firms with contractual commitments in effect before March 12, 1982.

(3) All other exports and reexports will generally be approved, subject to any other licensing policies applicable to a particular transaction.

(b) Libya has been designated by the Secretary of State as a nation repeatedly supporting acts of international terrorism. For licensing requirements relating to Anti-Terrorism Controls see 15 CFR 785.4(d).

(c) A validated license is required for the export to Libya of off-highway wheel tractors of carriage capacity of 10 tons or more, as defined in CCL entry 6490F. Applications for validated licenses will generally be considered favorably on a case-by-case basis for the export of such tractors in reasonable quantities if for civil use.

(d) A validated license is required for foreign policy purposes for the export or reexport to Libya of any aircraft (including helicopters) and any parts and accessories controlled under ECCNs 1460A, 2460A, 4460B, 5460F, 6460F, 1485A, and 1501A(a), (b)(1) and (c)(1). This control includes any such aircraft parts intended for use in the manufacture, overhaul, or rehabilitation in any third country of aircraft that will be exported or reexported to Libya or Libyan nationals. Applications for validated licenses will generally be approved on a case-by-case basis for aircraft unlikely to be diverted to military use because they are destined to a priority civil use. Applications will generally be denied for exports that would constitute a high risk of increasing Libyan capabilities to carry military cargo or troops or to conduct military reconnaissance or observation missions.

(e) In appropriate cases, applications for licenses and requests for extensions of licenses under paragraph (a) of this section must be accompanied by a certified true copy of a contract entered into prior to March 12, 1982. Where the custom in an industry is to rely upon agreements other than contracts, substitute documentation will be considered on a case-by-case basis. Requests for authorization to reexport must be accompanied by shipping documents establishing the date of export from the United States.

(f) Commodities and technical data subject to more than one type of control (e.g., national security, anti-terrorism, regional stability, nuclear nonproliferation) will be reviewed under all applicable standards. The most restrictive standard will be applied.

[47 FR 11249, Mar. 16, 1982, as amended at 49 FR 10248, Mar. 20, 1984; 50 FR 3743, Jan. 28, 1985; 51 FR 2354, Jan. 16, 1986; 51 FR 8485, Mar. 12, 1986; 51 FR 9649, Mar. 20, 1986. Redesignated at 53 FR 37751, Sept. 28, 1988 and amended at 53 FR 40411, Oct. 17, 1988]

SUPPLEMENT NO. 1—SOUTH AFRICA
ENTITIES ENFORCING APARTHEID

The following have been identified as South African entities that enforce apartheid. Exporters should be aware that this list cannot be all-inclusive because names of agencies are subject to change, and because agencies may assume apartheid enforcing activities in the future. Before making commitments to export, exporters may wish to seek guidance from the Office of Southern African Affairs (AF/S), Department of State, Washington, DC 20520, to ascertain whether or not a potential customer is an "agency enforcing apartheid."

Ministry of Justice

Ministry of Home Affairs and National Education

Ministry of Constitutional Development and Planning

Ministry of Law and Order

Ministry of Manpower

Department of Public Works and Land Affairs

Ministry of Education and Development Aid, including the Development Boards and the Rural Development Boards (formerly known as the Ministry of Cooperation, Development and Education), but excluding the Department of National Education and Training.

Other agencies enforcing apartheid, including local, regional and "Homeland" agencies, e.g., those that regulate employment, classification, or residence of non-whites.

NOTE: The Department of State has determined that the following agencies are not considered to be apartheid enforcing entities:

Ministry of Communication and Public Works (This includes post and telecommunication agencies)
Ministry of Agricultural Economics and Water Affairs
Ministry of Mineral and Energy Affairs
Ministry of Finance
Department of Transportation

[50 FR 47366, Nov. 17, 1985, as amended at 52 FR 27798, July 24, 1987. Redesignated at 53 FR 37751, Sept. 28, 1988]

SUPPLEMENT NO. 2—INTERPRETATIONS

1. The Department has received inquiries as to whether certain entities in the Republic of South Africa and Namibia are considered police or military entities and hence subject to the embargo policy set forth in § 785.4.

(a) In addition to the military and police of South Africa and Namibia, the following are considered to be police or military entities:

ARMSCOR (Armaments Development and Production Corporation) and its subsidiaries (Nimrod, Atlas Aircraft Corporation, Eloptro (Pty) Ltd., Kentron (Pty) Ltd., Infoplan Ltd., Lyttleton Engineering Works (Pty) Ltd., Naschem (Pty) Ltd., Pretoria Metal Pressing (P.M.P.) (Pty) Ltd., Somchem (Pty) Ltd., Swartklip Products (Pty) Ltd., Telecast (Pty) Ltd., and Musgrave Manufacturers and Distributors)
Department of Prisons
"Homeland" Police and Armed Forces
National Institute for Aeronautics & Systems Technology (NIAST) of the Council for Scientific & Industrial Research (CSIR)
National Intelligence Services
South African Railways Police Force
Weapons research activities of the Council for Scientific and Industrial Research (CSIR)

(b) It is also the Department's position that certain municipal and provincial law enforcement officials, such as traffic inspectors and highway patrolmen, although separate from the South African police, are police entities because they have functions that are performed by the police in the United States. Other law enforcement entities and officials that do not have functions performed by the police in the United States, such as the Department of Customs,

Department of Justice, health inspectors and licensing authorities, are not considered police entities.

[43 FR 43450, Sept. 26, 1978, as amended at 47 FR 40540, Sept. 15, 1982; 48 FR 3361, Jan. 25, 1983; 50 FR 47366, Nov. 18, 1985; 52 FR 2107, Jan. 20, 1987. Redesignated at 53 FR 37751, Sept. 28, 1988]

PART 786—EXPORT CLEARANCE

Sec.
786.1 General export clearance requirements.
786.2 Use of validated license.
786.3 Shipper's export declaration.
786.4 Conformity of documents for validated license shipments.
786.5 General destination control requirements.
786.6 Destination control statements.
786.7 Shipping tolerance.
786.8 Authority of custom offices and postmasters in clearing shipments.
786.9 Return or unloading of cargo at direction of U.S. Department of Commerce.
786.10 Other applicable laws and regulations.

SUPPLEMENT NO. 1

AUTHORITY: Pub. L. 96-72, 93 Stat. 503 (50 U.S.C. app. 2401 *et seq.*), as amended by Pub. L. 97-145 of December 29, 1981, by Pub. L. 100-418 of August 23, 1988, and by Pub. L. 99-64 of July 12, 1985; E.O. 12525 of July 12, 1985 (50 FR 28757, July 16, 1985); Pub. L. 95-223 of December 28, 1977 (50 U.S.C. 1701 *et seq.*); E.O. 12532 of September 9, 1985 (50 FR 36861, September 10, 1985) as affected by notice of September 4, 1986 (51 FR 31925, September 8, 1986); Pub. L. 99-440 of October 2, 1986 (22 U.S.C. 5001 *et seq.*); and E.O. 12571 of October 27, 1986 (51 FR 39505, October 29, 1986).

SOURCE: 13th Gen. Rev. of Export Regs., 37 FR 12222, June 21, 1972, unless otherwise noted. Redesignated at 53 FR 37751, Sept. 28, 1988.

§ 786.1 General export clearance requirements.

(a) *Responsibility of licensee and agent.* Under the Export Administration regulations, the exporter to whom a validated license is issued or who undertakes to export under a general license is legally responsible for the proper use of that license and for the due performance of all its terms and provisions. This responsibility continues even when he acts through a

[37 FR 12222, June 21, 1972, as amended at 40 FR 23994, June 4, 1975; 48 FR 17582, Apr. 25, 1983; 51 FR 12840, Apr. 16, 1986; 51 FR 30632, Aug. 28, 1986. Redesignated at 53 FR 37751, Sept. 28, 1988]

§ 786.9 Return or unloading of cargo at direction of U.S. Department of Commerce.

(a) *Exporting carrier.* As used in this section, the term "exporting carrier" includes a connecting or on-forwarding carrier, as well as the owner, charterer, agent, master, or any other person in charge of the vessel, aircraft, or other kind of carrier, whether such person is located in the United States or in a foreign country.

(b) *Ordering return or unloading of shipment.* Where there are reasonable grounds to believe that a violation of the Export Administration regulations has occurred or will occur with respect to a particular export from the United States, the Office of Export Licensing or any U.S. customs officer may order any person in possession or control of such shipment, including the exporting carrier, to return or unload the shipment. Such person shall, as ordered, either:

(1) Return the shipment to the United States or cause it to be returned, or (2) unload the shipment at a port of call and take steps to assure that it is placed in custody under bond or other guaranty not to enter the commerce of any foreign country without prior approval of the Office of Export Licensing. For the purpose of this section, the furnishing of a copy of the order to any person included within the definition of exporting carrier shall be sufficient notice of the order to the exporting carrier.

(c) *Requirements regarding shipment to be unloaded.* The provisions of § 786.5(b), relating to reporting, notification to the Office of Export Licensing, and the prohibition against unauthorized delivery or entry of the commodity or technical data into a foreign country, shall apply also to commodities or technical data directed to be unloaded at a port of call, as provided in this section.

(d) *Notification.* Upon discovery by any person included within the term "exporting carrier," as defined in this section, that a violation of the Export Administration Regulations has occurred or will occur with respect to a shipment on board, or otherwise in the possession or control of the carrier, such person shall immediately notify both (1) Office of Export Enforcement, P.O. Box 7138, Washington, DC 20044; and (2) the person in actual possession or control of the shipment.

[13th Gen. Rev. of Export Regs., 37 FR 12222, June 21, 1972, as amended at 47 FR 15115, Apr. 8, 1982; 48 FR 17583, Apr. 25, 1983. Redesignated at 53 FR 37751, Sept. 28, 1988]

§ 786.10 Other applicable laws and regulations.

The Export Control Regulations contained in this part apply only to exports regulated by the Export Administration, U.S. Department of Commerce. Nothing contained in this Part 786 shall relieve any person from complying with any other law of the United States or rules and regulations issued thereunder, including those governing declarations and manifests, or any applicable rules and regulations of the Bureau of Customs.

SUPPLEMENT No. 1 TO PART 786

SUBPART D—EXEMPTIONS FROM THE REQUIREMENTS FOR THE FILING OF SHIPPER'S EXPORT DECLARATIONS—OF THE FOREIGN TRADE STATISTICS REGULATIONS OF THE BUREAU OF THE CENSUS (15 CFR 30.50-30.57)

NOTE: This Supplement references regulations regarding exemptions from Shipper's Export Declaration filing requirements, which are issued by the Bureau of the Census. These regulations are referenced in the Export Administration Regulations (EAR) for an informational purpose and are codified in the *Code of Federal Regulations* under Title 15, Part 30, Subpart D. The looseleaf version of the EAR contains the text of these regulations reprinted in full.

[52 FR 6139, Mar. 2, 1987. Redesignated at 53 FR 37751, Sept. 28, 1988]

PART 787—ENFORCEMENT

Sec.
787.1 Sanctions.
787.2 Causing, aiding, and abetting a violation.
787.3 Solicitation, attempt, and conspiracy.

AUTHORITY: Pub. L. 96–72, 93 Stat. 503 (50 U.S.C. app. 2401 *et seq.*), as amended by Pub. L. 97–145 of December 29, 1981, by Pub. L. 100–418 of August 23, 1988, and by Pub. L. 99–64 of July 12, 1985; E.O. 12525 of July 12, 1985 (50 FR 28757, July 16, 1985); Pub. L. 95–223 of December 28, 1977 (50 U.S.C. 1701 *et seq.*); E.O. 12532 of September 9, 1985 (50 FR 36861, September 10, 1985) as affected by notice of September 4, 1986 (51 FR 31925, September 8, 1986); Pub. L. 99–440 of October 2, 1986 (22 U.S.C. 5001 *et seq.*); and E.O. 12571 of October 27, 1986 (51 FR 39505, October 29, 1986).

SOURCE: 50 FR 53131, Dec. 30, 1985, unless otherwise noted. Redesignated at 53 FR 37751, Sept. 28, 1988.

§ 787.1 Sanctions.

(a) Criminal—(1) *Violations of Export Administration Act*—(i) *General.* Except as provided in paragraph (a)(1)(ii) of this section, whoever knowingly violates or conspires to or attempts to violate the Export Administration Act ("the Act") or any regulation, order, or license issued under the Act is punishable for each violation by a fine of not more than five times the value of the exports involved or $50,000, whichever is greater, or by imprisonment for not more than five years, or both.

(ii) *Willful violations.* (A) Whoever willfully violates or conspires to or attempts to violate any provision of this Act or any regulation, order, license issued thereunder, with knowledge that the exports involved will be used for the benefit of or that the destination or intended destination of the goods or technology involved is any controlled country or any country to which exports are controlled for foreign policy purposes, except in the case of an individual, shall be fined not more than five times the value of the export involved or $1,000,000 whichever is greater; and in the case of an individual, shall be fined not more than $250,000, or imprisoned not more than 10 years, or both.

(B) Any person who is issued a validated license under this Act for the export of any goods or technology to a controlled country and who, with the knowledge that such export is being used by such controlled country for military or intelligence gathering purposes contrary to the conditions under which the license was issued, willfully fails to report such use to the Secretary of Defense, except in the case of an individual, shall be fined not more than five times the value of the exports involved or $1,000,000, whichever is greater; and in the case of an individual, shall be fined not more than $250,000, or imprisoned not more than five years, or both.

(C) Any person who possesses any goods or technology with the intent to export such goods or technology in violation of an export control imposed under section 5 or 6 of the Act or any regulation, order, or license issued with respect to such control, or knowing or having reason to believe that the goods or technology would be so exported, shall, in the case of a violation of an export control imposed under section 5 of the Act (or any regulation, order, or license issued with respect to such control), be subject to the penalties set forth in paragraph (a)(1)(ii)(A) of this section and shall, in the case of a violation of an export control imposed under section 6 of the Act (or any regulation, order, or license issued with respect to such control), be subject to the penalties set forth in paragraph (a)(1)(i) of this section.

(D) Any person who takes any action with the intent to evade the provisions of this Act or any regulation, order, or license issued under this Act shall be subject to the penalties set forth in paragraph (a)(1)(i) of this section, except that in the case of an evasion of an export control imposed under section 5 or 6 of the Act (or any regulation, order, or license issued with respect to such control), such person shall be subject to the penalties set forth in paragraph (a)(1)(ii)(A) of this section.

(2) *Violations of False Statements Act.* The submission of false or misleading information or the concealment of material facts, whether in connection with license applications, boycott reports, Shipper's Export Declarations, investigations, compliance proceedings, appeals, or otherwise, is also punishable by a fine of not more than $10,000 or by imprisonment for not more than five years, or both, for each violation (18 U.S.C. 1001).

(b) *Administrative* [1]—(1) *Denial of export privileges.* Whoever violates any law, regulation, order, or license relating to export controls or restrictive trade practices and boycotts is also subject to administrative action which may result in suspension, revocation, or denial of export privileges conferred under the Export Administration Act (*see* § 788.3 *et seq*).

(2) *Exclusion from practice.* Whoever violates any law, regulation, order, or license relating to export controls or restrictive trade practices and boycotts is further subject to administrative action which may result in exclusion from practice before the International Trade Administration (*see* § 790.2(a)).

(3) *Civil penalty.* A civil penalty may be imposed for each violation of the Export Administration Act or any regulation, order or license issued under the Act either in addition to, or instead of, any other liability or penalty which may be imposed. The civil penalty may not exceed $10,000 for each

---

[1] Violations of the Act or regulations, or any order or license issued under the Act, may result in the imposition of administrative sanctions, and also or alternatively of a fine or imprisonment as described in paragraph (a) of this section, seizure or forfeiture of property under section 11(g) of this Act or 22 U.S.C. 401, or any other liability or penalty imposed by law. The U.S. Department of Commerce may compromise and settle any administrative proceeding brought with respect to such violations.

violation except that the civil penalty for each violation involving national security controls imposed under section 5 of the Act may not exceed $100,000. The payment of such penalty may be deferred or suspended, in whole or in part, for a period of time that may exceed one year. Deferral or suspension shall not operate as a bar in the collection of the penalty in the event that the conditions of the suspension or deferral are not fulfilled. When any person fails to pay a penalty imposed under this paragraph (b)(3), civil action for the recovery of the penalty may be brought in the name of the United States, in which action the court shall determine *de novo* all issues necessary to establish liability. Once a penalty has been paid, no action for its refund may be maintained in any court.[2]

(4) *Seizure.* Commodities or technical data which have been, are being, or are intended to be, exported or shipped from or taken out of the United States in violation of the Export Administration Act or of any regulation, order, or license issued under the Act are subject to being seized and detained, as are the vessels, vehicles, and aircraft carrying such commodities or technical data. Seized commodities or technical data are subject to forfeiture (50 U.S.C. app. 2411(g)) (22 U.S.C. 401, *see* § 786.8(b)(6)).

§ 787.2 Causing, aiding, and abetting a violation.

No person may cause, or aid, abet, counsel, command, induce, procure, or permit the doing of any act prohibited, or the omission of any act required, by the Export Administration Act or any regulation, order, or license issued under the Act.

§ 787.3 Solicitation, attempt, and conspiracy.

(a) *Solicitation and attempt.* No person may do any act that solicits the commission of, or that constitutes an

---

[2] The U.S. Department of Commerce may refund the penalty at any time within two years of payment if it is found that there was a material error of fact or of law.

attempt to bring about, a violation of the Export Administration Act or any regulation, order, or license issued under the Act.

(b) *Conspiracy.* No person may conspire or act in concert with one or more persons in any manner or for any purpose to bring about or to do any act that constitutes a violation of the Export Administration Act or any regulation, order, or license issued under the Act.

§ 787.4 **Acting with knowledge of a violation; possession with intent to export illegally.**

(a) No person may order, buy, receive, conceal, store, use, sell, loan, dispose of, transfer, transport, finance, forward, or otherwise service, in whole or in part, any commodity or technical data exported or to be exported from the United States or which is otherwise subject to the Export Administration Regulations, with knowledge or reason to know that a violation of the Export Administration Act or any regulation, order, or license has occurred, is about to occur, or is intended to occur with respect to any transaction.

(b) No person may possess any commodities or technical data, controlled for national security or foreign policy reasons under section 5 or 6 of the Act:

(1) With the intent to export such commodities or technical data in violation of the Export Administration Act or any regulation, order, license or other authorization under the Act, or

(2) Knowing or having reason to believe that the commodities or technical data would be so exported.

§ 787.5 **Misrepresentation and concealment of facts; evasion.**

(a)(1) *Misrepresentation and concealment.* No person may make any false or misleading representation, statement, or certification, or falsify or conceal any material fact, whether directly to the Office of Export Licensing, the Office of Export Enforcement,[3] the Office of Antiboycott Com-

pliance, any customs office, or an official of any other United States agency, or indirectly to any of the foregoing through any other person or foreign government agency or official:

(i) In the course of an investigation or other action instituted under the authority of the Export Administration Act;

(ii) In connection with the preparation, submission, issuance, use, or maintenance of any export control document, as defined in § 770.2, or restrictive trade practice or boycott request report, as defined in § 769.6;

(iii) For the purpose of or in connection with effecting an export from the United States, or the reexport, transshipment, or diversion of any such export.

(2) *Scope.* Paragraph (a)(1) of this section applies to all representations, statements, and certifications made to, and material facts concealed from, the Office of Export Licensing, the Office of Export Enforcement, the Office of Antiboycott Compliance, and the U.S. Customs Service, or other agencies with respect to matters within the jurisdiction of these agencies under the statutes, Executive Orders, and regulations relating to export control, restrictive trade practices or boycotts, and orders or licenses issued or established under the Act.

(3) *Representations to be continuing in effect; notification.* All representations, statements, and certifications made by any person are deemed to be continuing in effect. Every person who has made any representation, statement, or certification must notify, in writing, the Office of Export Licensing, the Office of Export Enforcement, or the Office of Antiboycott Compliance, as well as any other cognizant agency(ies), of any change of any material fact or intention from that previously represented, stated, or certified. Such notification shall be made immediately upon receipt of any information which would lead a reasonably prudent person to believe that a change of material fact or intention

---

[3] For purposes of Part 787, the Office of Export Enforcement enforces the Export Administration Regulations relating to short supply controls imposed under section

7 of the Act. Such controls are otherwise the responsibility of the Office of Industrial Resource Administration.

has occurred or may occur in the future.

(b) *Evasion.* No person may engage in any transaction or take any other action, either independently or through any other person, with intent to evade the provisions of the Act, or any regulation, order, license or other authorization issued under the Act.

§ 787.6 Export, diversion, reexport, transshipment.

Except as specifically authorized by the Office of Export Licensing, in consultation with the Office of Export Enforcement, no person may export, dispose of, divert, direct, mail or otherwise ship, transship, or reexport commodities or technical data to any person or destination or for any use in violation of or contrary to the terms, provisions, or conditions of any export control document, any prior representation, any form of notification of prohibition against such action, or any provision of the Export Administration Act or any regulation, order, or license issued under the Act.

§ 787.7 Failure to comply with reporting requirements.

No person may fail or refuse to comply with reporting requirements in violation of the Export Administration Act or of any order, regulation or license issued under the Act. *See,* for example, §§ 769.6, 772.9(e) and 779.6(b).

§ 787.8 Failure to answer interrogatories or respond to requests for admission or to produce documents.

(a) *Interrogatories and requests for admission or to produce documents.* Whenever the Office of Export Enforcement or the Office of Antiboycott Compliance finds it impracticable, during the course of an investigation, other proceeding or action, to subpoena a person, or books, writings, records, or other tangible things bearing upon the matter being investigated, the Office of Export Enforcement or the Office of Antiboycott Compliance may serve upon such person interrogatories, requests for admission of facts, requests for the production of books, records and other writings, or requests to produce or make available other tangible things for inspection,

including commodities or technical data exported from the United States, as therein specifically set forth. If a person, within 20 days after receiving interrogatories or requests, fails or refuses to:

(1) Furnish responsive answers to such interrogatories or requests for admissions;

(2) Produce the requested books, records and other writings; or

(3) Produce or make available for inspection other tangible things requested, including commodities or technical data exported from the United States, which are in that person's possession, custody or control, without good cause being shown, an order may be issued as provided in § 788.3(a)(2), denying export privileges to such person. This order shall remain in effect for five years or until such person responds to the interrogatories or requests or gives adequate reasons for failure or refusal to so respond.

(b) *Service.* Interrogatories or requests shall be served in the same manner as provided in § 788.4 (b) and (c) for service of a charging letter.

(c) *Enforcement procedures.* The procedure regarding applications for denial orders under § 787.8(a) and motions to vacate or modify such orders shall conform substantially to that provided for temporary denial orders by § 788.19.

§ 787.9 Licensee accountable for use of license.

The person to whom a license is issued becomes the licensee and will be held strictly accountable for use of the license. The licensee may not, without prior written approval of the Office of Export Licensing, in consultation with the Office of Export Enforcement, permit any other person to facilitate or effect the export of any commodity or technical data described in the license, except under this direction and responsibility as his true agent in fact. No term of sale or export or other agreement between the licensee or the order party and the purchaser or ultimate consignee of such commodity or technical data may provide otherwise.

§ 787.10 **Unauthorized use and alterations of export control documents.**

Except as otherwise specifically authorized in the Export Administration regulations or in writing by the Office of Export Licensing, in consultation with the Office of Export Enforcement, no licensee or other person, may obtain, use, alter, or assist in or permit the use or alteration of, any export control document, for the purpose of or in connection with facilitating or effecting any export or reexport other than that set forth in such document and in accordance with all the terms, provisions, and conditions thereof.

§ 787.11 **Trafficking and advertising export control documents.**

(a) *Unlawful practices.* Without prior written approval of the Office of Export Licensing, in consultation with the Office of Export Enforcement, no person may do any of the following with respect to any export or reexport under any export control document:

(1) *Transfers or changes of authority.* Effect any transfer of, or other change of the authority granted in such document, whether by sale, grant, gift, loan or otherwise, to any person; or permit any person to use the same other than for the true account of and as true agent in fact for the licensee; or, if that person is not the licensee, to receive or accept a transfer or other change of the authority granted in, or otherwise use an export control document except for the true account of and as true agent in fact for the licensee.

(2) *Change in named parties.* Effect any change of, substitution for, or addition to, the parties named in an export control document; or transfer, obtain, purchase, or create any interest or participation in the transaction described in any export control document.

(3) *Unlawful advertising or soliciting.* Offer or solicit by advertisement, circular, or other communication any transfer or change of an export control document or any interest therein prohibited above. Such communication shall be deemed unlawful:

(i) Even though coupled with a condition requiring approval by the Office of Export Licensing of a new consign-or or consignee or other change in the export license, by way of transfer, amendment or otherwise;

(ii) Where, in offering or soliciting the sale for export of any commodities or technical data, the communication indicates that the proposed seller of such commodities or technical data holds or will furnish a license or other export control document for the export of such commodities or technical data;

(iii) Where, in offering or soliciting the purchase for export of any commodities or technical data, that communication is addressed by the proposed buyer directly or indirectly to any person on the condition that such person as a seller then holds or will furnish a license or other export control document for the export of those commodities or technical data.

(4) *Other unlawful practices.* Sections 787.10, 787.11, and 787.12, among other things, make it unlawful:

(i) For a licensee or other person holding an export control document to sell or offer to sell, or for any person to purchase or to offer to purchase, the commodities or technical data described in such document with the understanding that the document may be used by or for the benefit of the purchaser to effect export of those commodities or technical data;

(ii) For any person to effect the export of the commodities referred to in paragraph (a)(4)(i) of this section for the benefit of or "for the account" of any person other than the licensee, regardless of the device, means, or fiction employed;

(iii) For the licensee to act fictitiously as principal or agent of another person who actually is effecting the export, or for such other person to act fictitiously as the licensee's principal or agent for the same purpose;

(iv) For the named consignee to act "for the account" of a new unlicensed consignee; or

(v) For any person to use a license, originally issued for a specified transaction which was not effected, for any other transaction without the specific written authorization of the Office of Export Licensing.

(b) *Transfer of dock receipts, bills of lading, or liens—(1) Use of certain export control documents.* Section 787.12(a) is not to be construed as affecting the transfer and other use of dock receipts, bills of lading, or other commercial documents necessary to complete a transaction authorized by the export license, or impairing the validity of liens or other security titles or interests created in good faith with respect to commodities or technical data or documents in the course of financing, warehousing, forwarding, or transporting commodities or technical data.

(2) *Disposition of export.* A person who is entitled to foreclose on any lien or other security title or interest, or who may exercise any rights as holder of the lien or other security title or interest, or who contemplates an export under the license by someone other than the licensee or to someone other than the purchaser or ultimate consignee designated in the license, must apply for a new license in accordance with the provisions of Part 772.

§ 787.12 Transactions with persons subject to denial orders.

(a) *Prohibited activities.* Without prior disclosure of the facts to and specific authorization of the Office of Export Licensing, in consultation with the Office of Export Enforcement, no person may directly or indirectly, in any manner or capacity:

(1) Apply for, obtain, or use any license, Shipper's Export Declaration, bill of lading, or other export control document relating to an export or reexport of commodities or technical data by, to, or for another person then subject to an order revoking or denying his export privileges or then excluded from practice before the International Trade Administration; or

(2) Order, buy, receive, use, sell, deliver, store, dispose of, forward, transport, finance, or otherwise service or participate:

(i) In any transaction which may involve any commodity or technical data exported or to be exported from the United States;

(ii) In any reexport thereof; or

(iii) In any other transaction which is subject to the Export Administration Regulations, if the person denied export privileges may obtain any benefit or have any interest in, directly or indirectly, any of these transactions.

(b) *Definition of "person denied export privileges".* For the purpose of this section the term "person denied export privileges" means:

(1) Any person, firm, corporation, or other business organization whose export privileges are revoked or denied by any order or who is excluded by such order from practice before the International Trade Administration; and

(2) Any other person, firm, corporation, or other business organization also denied export privileges or excluded from practice before the International Trade Administration because of a relationship to any person denied export privileges through affiliation, ownership, control, position of responsibility, or other connection in the conduct of trade or related services during the period of such order.

(c) *Applicability of orders.* Orders which revoke or deny the export privileges of any person or which exclude any person from practice before the International Trade Administration may provide that the terms and prohibitions of such orders apply not only to the persons expressly named therein but also, for the purpose of preventing evasion, to any other person, firm corporation, or other business organization with which that person may then or thereafter (during the term of the order) be related by affiliation, ownership, control, position of responsibility, or other connection in the conduct of trade or related services. The Table of Denial Orders (*See* Supplement No. 1 to Part 788 and §§ 788.3 and 790.2) contains all orders which currently deny export privileges in whole or in part. The table also lists the names and addresses of such persons, the effective and expiration dates of the orders, a brief summary of the export privileges affected, and the citations to the volumes and pages of the FEDERAL REGISTER where complete texts of the orders are published. The publication of such orders in the FEDERAL REGISTER constitutes legal notice of the terms thereof to all persons.

§ 787.13 Recordkeeping.

(a) *Transactions subject to this regulation.* This section applies to—(1) transactions involving restrictive trade practice or boycott requirements or requests, (2) exports of commodities or technical data from the United States and any known reexports, transshipments, or diversions of commodities or technical data originally exported from the United States, or (3) any other transactions subject to these Regulations, regardless of whether the export or reexport is made, or proposed to be made, by any person with or without authorization by a validated license, a general license, or any other export authorization. This section also applies to all negotiations connected with those transactions, except that for export control matters a mere preliminary inquiry or offer to do business and negative response thereto shall not constitute negotiations, unless the inquiry or offer to do business proposes a transaction which a reasonably prudent exporter would believe likely to lead to a violation of export orders or regulations. It also applies to any exports to Canada, if, at any stage in the transaction, it appears that a person in a country other than the United States or Canada has an interest therein or that the commodity or technical data involved is to be reexported, transshipped, or diverted from Canada to another foreign country.

(b) *Persons subject to this regulation.* Any person subject to the jurisdiction of the United States who, as principal or agent (including a forwarding agent), participates in any transaction described in paragraph (a) of this section, and any person in the United States or abroad who is required to make and keep records under any provisions of the Export Administration regulations, shall keep all the records described in paragraph (c) of this section, which are made or obtained by that person, and shall produce them in the manner provided in paragraph (f) of this section.

(c) *Records to be kept.* The records to be kept under this section shall include export control documents, as defined in § 770.2, memoranda, notes, correspondence, contracts, invitations to bid, books of account, financial records, restrictive trade practice or boycott documents and reports, and other written matter pertaining to the transactions described in paragraph (a) of this section, which are made or obtained by a person described in paragraph (b) of this section. In addition to the records required to be kept by this section, other sections of the Regulations require the retention of records, including but not limited to §§ 768.2, 769.6, 771.9, 771.10, 771.12, 771.17, 771.19, 771.22, 772.1, 772.4, 772.5, 772.6, 772.7, 772.8, 772.10, 772.11, 772.13, 773.2, 773.3, 773.7, 773.8, 774.7, 775.2, 775.3, 775.4, 775.5, 775.7, 776.4, 776.6, 776.7, 776.8, 776.9, 776.10, 776.11, 776.12, 778.6, 778.7, 779.4, 779.8, 779.9, 786.2, 786.5, 786.3, 786.6 and 791.2. The revocation or revision of any provision of the Export Administration Regulations which requires the making and keeping of records shall not be retroactive in effect unless specifically provided and shall not affect the original requirement to keep these records for the prescribed period.

(d) *Reproduction of records*—(1) *Definition.* "Reproduction" for the purpose of this paragraph (d) is defined to include any photographic, photostatic, micrographic, miniature photographic or other process which completely, accurately and durably reproduces the original record.

(2) *Use of reproductions.* Reproductions may not be substituted for original documents with respect to all categories of records required to be retained under any provisions of the Export Administration Regulations or of any order, until all of the following conditions are met:

(i) The original documents have been retained for twelve months after the beginning of the retention period set forth in paragraph (e) of this section or an exception has been granted under the provisions of paragraph (g) of this section.

(ii) All significant information, marks and/or other characteristics on the original document must be clearly visible and legibly reproduced.

(iii) Appropriate facilities must be provided and maintained for the preservation of the reproduced records during the retention period and for the ready location and inspection of the records, including a projector for viewing films, if needed.

(e) *Period of retention.* (1) Except for records relating to restrictive trade practice or boycott requests, which must be kept for three years (*see* § 769.6(b)(8)), records required under this section shall be kept for a period of two years from the latest of the following times:

(i) The export from the United States; or

(ii) Any known reexport, transshipment, or diversion; or

(iii) Any other termination of the transaction, whether formally in writing or by any other means. It may be advisable to maintain records longer than the mandatory two-year retention period because the statute of limitations for criminal actions brought under the Export Administration Act of 1979 and its predecessor Acts is five years (18 U.S.C. 3282). The statute for administrative compliance proceedings is also five years (28 U.S.C. 2462).

(2) If the Department of Commerce or any other Government agency makes a formal or informal request for a certain record or records, such record or records may not be destroyed or disposed of without the written authorization of the agency concerned.

(f) *Producing and inspecting records.* (1) Persons within the United States may be requested to produce records which are required to be kept by any provision of the Export Administration Regulations or by any order, and to make them available for inspection and copying by any authorized agent, official or employee of the International Trade Administration, the U.S. Customs Service, or the U.S. Government, without any charge or expense to such agent, official or employee. The Office of Export Enforcement and the Office of Antiboycott Compliance encourage voluntary cooperation with such requests. When voluntary cooperation is not forthcoming, the Office of Export Enforcement and the Office of Antiboycott Compliance are authorized to issue subpoenas for books, records, and other writings. In instances where a person does not comply with a subpoena, the Depart-

ment of Commerce may petition a district court to have the subpoena enforced.

(2) Every person abroad, required to keep records by any provision of the Export Administration Regulations or by any order, shall produce all records or reproductions of records required to be kept, and make them available for inspection and copying upon request by an authorized agent, official, or employee of the International Trade Administration, the U.S. Customs Service, or a U.S. Foreign Service post, or by any other accredited representative of the U.S. Government, without any charge or expense to such agent, official or employee. Persons located outside the United States who fail to comply with certain requests, including requests to produce documents, may be subject to orders denying export privileges. (*See* § 787.8.)

(g) *Requests for exceptions to recordkeeping requirements*—(1) *Effect of exception.* Recordkeeping entities (as defined in paragraph (b) of this section) wishing to maintain records on micrographic systems prior to the second year of the retention period may request an exception to the recordkeeping requirements. An exception, if granted, permits the recordkeeping entity or substitute micrographic records for original documents for the full retention period.

(2) *Basis for consideration.* When reviewing requests for exceptions, the Office of Export Licensing, in consultation with the Office of Export Enforcement or the Office of Antiboycott Compliance, will take into consideration the requestor's previous performance with respect to general export control matters and antiboycott matters, respectively.

(3) *Guidelines for micrographic systems.* To maintain records under this exception, a micrographic system shall have the following minimum requirements:

(i) The system shall provide commercial permanence of all records.

(ii) The system shall provide for frequent quality control inspection to ensure readability of all records.

(iii) Micrographed records must have a degree of legibility and readability, when displayed on a viewer and when reproduced on paper, equal to that of the original records. (*See* section 5 of IRS Revenue Procedure No. 81–46, 1981–40 C.B. 6 concerning technical standards of micrographed records.)

(iv) A detailed index of all micrographic data shall be maintained, and arranged in such a manner as to permit the immediate location of any particular record, location of all documents relating to a given transaction, and determination of disposition of corresponding original documents.

(4) *Submission of requests for exception.* (i) The recordkeeping entity shall submit requests for exceptions involving general export matters to: Office of Export Licensing, International Trade Administration, U.S. Department of Commerce, P.O. Box 273, Washington, DC 20044.

(ii) The recordkeeping entity shall submit requests for exceptions involving antiboycott matters to: Office of Antiboycott Compliance, International Trade Administration, U.S. Department of Commerce, 14th Street and Constitution Ave., NW., Room H3886, Washington, DC 20230.

(iii) The requesting firm shall include in the request:

(A) Data on the proposed micrographic system, including specific information as to how the system conforms to requirements set forth in paragraph (g)(3) of this section;

(B) A statement concerning intended disposition of corresponding original documents; and

(C) Samples of records to be kept on the system.

(5) *Micrographing records under an exception.* Upon receiving written notice that an exception has been granted under this paragraph (g), the recordkeeping entity may substitute micrographic reproductions for only those records *already* in the retention period and approved under the exception. Originals of records that have not entered the retention period must be kept until the retention period begins (as set forth in §769.6(b)(8) and paragraph (e) of this section) and micrographed records may then be substituted for the originals.

(6) *Disposition of original documents.* The recordkeeping entity shall include with micrographed records a signed document indicating final disposition of original documents, and the date of final disposition.

(7) *Revocation of exception.* The Department of Commerce may revoke an individual exception at any time if it determines that the firm has acted improperly, or for other good cause. A decision to revoke this exception may be appealed under the provisions of Part 789 of these regulations.

(h) *Records exempt from recordkeeping requirements.* The following kinds of records have been determined to be exempt from recordkeeping requirements:

Export Information Page;
Special Export Price List;
Vessel Log from Freight Forwarder;
Inspection Certificate;
Warranty Certificate;
Guarantee Certificate;
Packing Material Certificate;
Goods Quality Certificate;
Notification to Customer of Advance Mailings;
Letter of Indemnity;
Financial Release Form;
Financial Hold Form;
Export Parts Shipment Problem Form;
Draft Number Log;
Expense Invoice Mailing Log;
Financial Status Report;
Bank Release of Guarantees;
Cash Sheet;
Commission Payment Back-up;
Commissions Payable Worksheet;
Commissions Payable Control;
Check Request Forms;
Accounts Receivable Correction Form;
Check Request Register;
Commission Payment Printout;
Engineering Fees Invoice;
Foreign Tax Receipt;
Individual Customer Credit Status;
Request for Export Customers Code Forms;
Acknowledgement for Receipt of Funds;
Escalation Development Form;
Summary Quote;
Purchase Order Review Form;
Proposal Extensions;
Financial Proposal to Export Customers;
Sales Summaries

(The information collection requirements in paragraph (a)(1) were approved by the Office of Management and Budget under control no. 0625–0036; the information collection requirements in paragraph (a)(2) were approved under control nos. 0625–0052 and 0625–0104.)

[50 FR 53131, Dec. 30, 1985, as amended at 52 FR 48809, Dec. 28, 1987. Redesignated at 53 FR 37751, Sept. 28, 1988]

§ 787.14   Where to report violations.

(a) *Notification.* The Office of Export Enforcement has the primary responsibility for enforcing these Regulations except that the Office of Antiboycott Compliance has the responsibility for enforcing the Restrictive Trade Practices or Boycott Regulations in particular.

(1) If a person obtains knowledge that a violation of these Regulations has occurred or will occur, that person may notify:

Office of Export Enforcement, International Trade Administration, U.S. Department of Commerce, P.O. Box 7138, Washington, DC 20044, Telephone (202) 377–4608, or

Office of Antiboycott Compliance, U.S. Department of Commerce, International Trade Administration, 14th Street and Constitution Avenue, NW., Room H3886, Washington, DC (202) 377–2381,

as appropriate

(2) Any Federal, State, or local government agency obtaining knowledge of a potential violation under these Regulations should immediately report such potential violation to:

Office of Export Enforcement, P.O. Box 7138, Washington, DC 20044, Telephone (202) 377–4608, and

Office of Antiboycott Compliance, U.S. Department of Commerce, 14th Street and Constitution Avenue NW. Room 3886, Washington, DC 20230, Telephone (202) 377–2381.

Failure to report such potential violations may result in the unwarranted issuance of validated export licenses or unlicensed exports to the deteriment of national security, foreign policy or short supply interests of the United States.

(b) *Reporting requirement distinguished.* The notification provisions set forth in paragraph (a) of this section are not "reporting requirements" within the meaning of § 787.7.

PART 788—ADMINISTRATIVE PROCEEDINGS

Sec.
788.1   Purpose and limitations.
788.2   Definitions.
788.3   Denial of export privileges and imposition of civil penalties.
788.4   Institution of administrative proceedings.
788.5   Representation.
788.6   Filing and service of papers other than charging letter.
788.7   Answer and demand for hearing.
788.8   Default.
788.9   Discovery.
788.10   Subpoenas.
788.11   Matter protected against disclosure.
788.12   Prehearing conference.
788.13   Hearings.
788.14   Proceeding without a hearing.
788.15   Procedural stipulations extension of time.
788.16   Decision of the administrative law judge.
788.17   Consent proceedings.
788.18   Reopening.
788.19   Temporary denials.
788.20   Record for decision and availability of documents.
788.21   Consolidation of proceedings.
788.22   Appeals.
788.23   Review by Assistant Secretary.

SUPPLEMENT 1—TABLE OF DENIAL ORDERS CURRENTLY IN EFFECT

SUPPLEMENT 2—GEOGRAPHICAL LISTING OF PARTIES SUBJECT TO DENIAL ORDER [NOTE]

AUTHORITY: Pub. L. 96–72, 93 Stat. 503 (50 U.S.C. app. 2401 *et seq.*), as amended by Pub. L. 97–145, of December 29, 1981 and by Pub. L. 99–64, of July 12, 1985; E.O. 12525 of July 12, 1985 (50 FR 28757, July 16, 1985).

SOURCE: 50 FR 53137, Dec. 30, 1985, unless otherwise noted. Redesignated at 53 FR 37751, Sept. 28, 1988.

§ 788.1   Purpose and limitations.

The regulations in this part set forth the procedures for imposing administrative sanctions for violation of the Export Administration Act of 1979 (50 U.S.C. app. 2401–2420 (1982), as amended by the Export Administration Amendments Act of 1985 (Pub. L. 99–64, 99 Stat. 120)) (Act), the regulations, or any order, license or other authorization issued under the Act. An administrative law judge shall conduct the proceedings, except for purposes

§ 789.3 **Request to issue, amend or revoke a regulation.**

Requests to issue, amend or revoke a regulation are not subject to the appeals process, but may be submitted to the Department at any time.

[45 FR 85448, Dec. 29, 1980. Redesignated at 53 FR 37751, Sept. 28, 1988]

PART 790—GENERAL ORDERS

Sec.
790.1 Advisory committees.
790.2 Conduct of business and practice in connection with export control matters.
790.3 Export control authority to be exercised by U.S. Department of Commerce Field Office Directors in the event of enemy attack on the United States.
790.4 Disclosure of license issuance and other information.
790.5 General order extending outstanding individual validated licenses for commodities.
790.6 General order preventing the use of special licensing procedures for aircraft controlled by Iran.
790.7 General order on exports involving Libya.

AUTHORITY: Pub. L. 96-72, 93 Stat. 503 (50 U.S.C. app. 2401 *et seq.*), as amended by Pub. L. 97-145 of December 29, 1981, by Pub. L. 100-418 of August 23, 1988, and by Pub. L. 99-64 of July 12, 1985; E.O. 12525 of July 12, 1985 (50 FR 28757, July 16, 1985); Pub. L. 95-223 of December 28, 1977 (50 U.S.C. 1701 *et seq.*); E.O. 12543 of January 7, 1986 (51 FR 875, January 9, 1986).

SOURCE: 13th Gen. Rev. of Export Regs., 35 FR 9206, June 12, 1970. Redesignated at 53 FR 37751, Sept. 28, 1988, unless otherwise noted.

§ 790.1 Advisory committees.

(a) *Purpose.* The purpose of this section is to set forth the procedures and criteria for the establishment and operation of technical advisory committees under the provisions of section 5(h) of the Export Administration Act of 1979.

(b) *Technical Advisory Committees.* Any producer of articles, materials, or supplies including technical data and other information which are subject to export controls, or are being considered for such controls because of their significance to the national security of the United States, may request the Secretary of Commerce to establish a technical advisory committee, under the provisions of section 5(h) of the Export Administration Act of 1979, to advise and assist the Department of Commerce and other appropriate U.S. Government agencies or officials with respect to questions involving: technical matters, worldwide availability and actual utilization of production technology, licensing procedures which affect the level of export controls applicable to a clearly defined grouping of articles, materials, or supplies, including technical data or other information, and exports subject to multilateral controls in which the United States participates including proposed revisions of any such multilateral controls. If producers of articles, materials, or supplies, including technical data, or other information which are subject to export controls because of their significance to the national security of the United States, wish a trade association or other representative to submit a written request on their behalf for the appointment of a technical advisory committee, such request shall be submitted in accordance with the provisions of paragraph (b)(4) of this section.

(1) *Form and substance of requests.* Each request for the appointment of a technical advisory committee shall be submitted in writing to—Director, Office of Technology and Policy Analysis, P.O. Box 273, Washington, DC 20044. The request shall include:

(i) A description of the articles, materials, or supplies including technical data, in terms of a clear, cohesive grouping (citing the applicable Export Control Commodity Numbers where practicable);

(ii) A statement of the reasons for requesting the appointment of a technical advisory committee; and

(iii) Any information in support of any contention that may be made that the request meets the criteria set forth in paragraph (b)(2) of this section.

(2) *Consideration of request for establishment of a technical Advisory Committee.* The Department of Commerce will review all requests for the establishment of a technical advisory committee to determine if the following criteria are met: (i) That a sub-

stantial segment of the industry producing the specified articles, materials or supplies including technical data desires such a committee and (ii) that the evaluation of such articles, materials or supplies including technical data, for export control purposes is difficult because of questions involving technical matters, worldwide availability and actual utilization of production and technology, or licensing procedures.

(3) *Determination of substantial segment of an industry.* In determining whether a substantial segment of any industry has requested the appointment of a technical advisory committee, the Department of Commerce will consider:

(i) The number of persons or firms requesting the establishment of a technical advisory committee for a particular grouping of commodities in relation to the total number of U.S. producers of such commodities; and

(ii) The volume of annual production by such persons or firms of each commodity and all technical data in the grouping in relation to the total U.S. production. Generally, a substantial segment of an industry (for purposes of paragraph (b)) shall consist of:

(A) Not less than 30 percent of the total number of U.S. producers of the commodities or technical data concerned; or

(B) Three or more U.S. producers who produce a combined total of not less than 30 percent of the total U.S. annual production, by dollar value of the commodities or technical data concerned; or

(C) Not less than 20 percent of the total number of U.S. producers of the commodities or technical data concerned; provided that the total of their annual production thereof is not less than 20 percent of the total U.S. annual production, by dollar value.

If it is determined that a substantial segment of the industry concerned has requested the establishment of a technical advisory committee concerning a specific grouping of commodities or technical data that the Department of Commerce determines difficult to evaluate for export control purposes, the Department of Commerce will es-

tablish and utilize the technical advisory committee requested.

(4) *Requests from trade associations or other representatives.* Requests from trade associations or other representatives of U.S. producers for the establishment of a Technical Advisory Committee must comply with the provisions of paragraphs (b) (1) through (3). In addition, in order to assist the Department in determining whether the criteria set forth in paragraph (b)(3) of this section have been met, a trade association or other representative submitting a request for the establishment of a technical advisory committee should include the following information: (i) The total number of firms in the particular industry, (ii) the total number of firms in the industry that have authorized the trade association or other representative to act in their behalf in this matter, (iii) the approximate amount of total U.S. annual production by dollar value of the commodities or technical data concerned produced by those firms that have authorized the trade association or other representative to act in their behalf, and (iv) a description of the method by which authorization to act on behalf of these producers was obtained.

(5) *Nominations for membership on Technical Advisory Committee.* When the Department of Commerce determines that the establishment of a technical advisory committee is warranted, it will request nominations for membership on the committee among the producers of the commodities and from any other sources that may be able to suggest well-qualified nominees.

(6) *Selection of industry members of Committee.* Industry members of a technical advisory committee will be selected by the Department of Commerce from a list of the nominees who have indicated their availability for service on the committee. To the extent feasible, the Department of Commerce will select a committee balanced to represent all significant facets of the industry involved, taking into consideration such factors as the size of the firms, their geographical distribution, and their product lines. No industry representative shall serve

on such committee for more than four consecutive years. The membership of a member who is absent from four consecutive committee meetings shall be terminated automatically.

(7) *Government members.* Government members of a technical advisory committee will be selected by the Department of Commerce from the agencies having an interest in the subject matter concerned.

(8) *Invitation to serve on committee.* Invitations to serve on a technical advisory committee will be sent by letter to the selected nominees. Acceptance or declination should also be conveyed by letter.

(9) *Election of chairman.* The Chairman of each technical advisory committee shall be elected by a vote of a majority of the members of the committee present and voting.

(c) *Charter.* (1) No technical advisory committee established pursuant to paragraph (b) of this section shall meet or take any action until an advisory committee charter has been filed with the Assistant Secretary for Administration of the Department of Commerce and with the standing committees of the Senate and of the House of Representatives having legislative jurisdiction of the Department. Such charter shall contain the following information:

(i) The committee's official designation;

(ii) The committee's objectives and the scope of its activity;

(iii) The period of time necessary for the committee to carry out its purposes;

(iv) The agency or official to whom the committee reports;

(v) The agency responsible for providing the necessary support for the committee;

(vi) A description of the duties for which the committee is responsible, and, if such duties are not solely advisory, a specification of the authority for such functions;

(vii) The estimated annual operating costs in dollars and man-years for such committee;

(viii) The estimated number and frequency of committee meetings;

(ix) The committee's termination date, if less than two years from the

date of the committee's establishment; and

(x) The date the charter is filed.

(2) A copy of any such charter shall also be furnished to the Library of Congress, Exchange and Gift Division, Federal Advisory Committee Desk, Washington, DC 20540.

(d) *Meetings.* (1) Each technical advisory committee established under the provisions of the Export Administration Act, as amended, and § 790.1(b) of this part shall meet at least once every three months at the call of its chairman unless it is specifically determined by the Chairman, in consultation with other members of the committee, that a particular meeting is not necessary.

(2) No technical advisory committee may meet except at the call of its Chairman.

(3) Each meeting of a technical advisory committee shall be conducted in accordance with an agenda approved by a designated Federal employee.

(4) No technical advisory committee shall conduct a meeting in the absence of a designated Federal employee who shall be authorized to adjourn any advisory committee meeting, whenever he determines adjournment to be in the public interest.

(e) *Public notice.* Notice to the public of each meeting of a technical advisory committee shall be issued at least twenty days in advance and shall be published in the FEDERAL REGISTER. The notice shall include the time and place of the meeting and its agenda.

(f) *Public attendance and participation.* (1) Any member of the public who wishes to do so may file a written statement with any technical advisory committee before or after any meeting of a committee.

(2) A request for an opportunity to deliver an oral tatement relevant to matters on the agenda of a meeting of a technical advisory committee will be granted to the extent that the time available for the meeting permits. A committee may establish procedures requiring such persons to obtain advance approval for such participation.

(3) Attendance at meetings of technical advisory committees will be open to the public unless it is determined pursuant to section 10(d) of the Feder-

al Advisory Committee Act to be necessary to close all, or some portion, of the meeting to the public. A determination that a meeting or portion thereof be closed to the public may be made if all or a specific portion of a meeting of a technical advisory committee is concerned with matters set forth in section 552(b) of Title 5, U.S. Code.

(4) Participation by members of the public in open technical advisory committee meetings or questioning of committee members or other participants shall not be permitted except in accordance with procedures established by the committee.

(5) All persons wishing to attend an open technical advisory committee meeting should submit a written request for admission to the meeting in advance of the announced date of the meeting. Every effort will be made to accommodate all members of the public who wish to attend. Where limitations of space prevent the attendance of everyone who has requested admittance, members of the public will be admitted in the order in which their requests are received.

(g) *Minutes.* (1) Detailed minutes of each meeting of each technical advisory committee shall be kept and shall contain a record of the persons present, a complete and accurate description of the matters discussed and conclusions reached, and copies of all reports received, issued or approved by the advisory committee.

(2) The accuracy of all minutes shall be certified to by the chairman of the advisory committee.

(h) *Records.* (1) Subject to section 552 of Title 5, U.S. Code and Department of Commerce Administrative Order 205-12, "Public Information," and "Public Information" regulations issued by the Department of Commerce that are contained in 15 CFR Part 4, Subtitle A, the records, reports, transcripts, minutes, appendixes, working papers, drafts, studies, agenda, or other documents that were made available to or prepared for or by each technical advisory committee shall be available for public inspection and copying.

(2) Each technical advisory committee shall prepare at least once each year a report describing its membership, functions, activities and such related matters as would be informative to the public consistent with the policy of section 552(b) of Title 5, U.S. Code.

(3) Requests for records should be addressed to: International Trade Administration Freedom of Information Officer, Records Inspection Facility, Room 4001B, U.S. Department of Commerce, 14th Street and Pennsylvania Avenue, NW., Washington, DC 20230. Telephone 202-377-3031. Rules concerning the use of the Records Inspection Facility are contained in 15 CFR Part 4, Subtitle A, or may be obtained from the facility.

(i) *Compensation.* If the Department of Commerce deems it appropriate, a member of a technical advisory committee, upon request, may be reimbursed for travel, subsistence, and other necessary expenses incurred by him in connection with his duties as a member.

(j) *Scope of advisory committee functions.* All technical advisory committees are limited to the functions set forth in their charters.

(k) *Duration of committees.* Each technical advisory committee shall terminate at the end of two years from the date the committee was established or two years from the effective date of its most recent extension, whichever is later. Committees may be continued only for successive two-year periods by appropriate action taken by the authorized officer of the Department of Commerce prior to the date on which such advisory committee would otherwise terminate. Technical advisory committees may be extended or terminated only after consultation with the committee.

(l) *Miscellaneous.* (1) Technical advisory committees established pursuant to paragraph (b) of this section, in addition to conforming to the provisions of this part, shall also conform to the provisions of the Federal Advisory Committee Act (Pub. L. 92-463), Office of Management and Budget (OMB) Circular A-63 and OMB/Department of Justice Memorandum, "Advisory Committee Management," Department of Commerce Administrative Order 205-12, "Public Information," the applicable provisions of the Export Administrative Act of 1979, as amended, and any other applicable Department of Commerce regulations or procedures affecting the establishment or operation of advisory committees.

(2) Whenever the Department of Commerce desires the advice or assistance of a particular segment of an industry with respect to any export control problem for which the service of a technical advisory committee, as described in paragraph (b) of this section, is either unavailable or impracticable, an advisory committee may be established pursuant to the provisions of section 9 of the Federal Advisory Committee Act. Such committees will be subject to the requirements of the Federal Advisory Committee Act, Office of Management and Budget (OMB) Circular A–63 and OMB/Department of Justice Memorandum "Advisory Committee Management," Department of Commerce Administrative Order 205–12, "Public Information," and any other applicable Department of Commerce regulations or procedures affecting the establishment or operation of advisory committees.

(3) Nothing in the provisions of this § 790.1 shall be construed to restrict in any manner the right of any person or firm to discuss any export control matter with the Department of Commerce or to offer advice or information on export control matters. Similarly, nothing in these provisions shall be construed to restrict the Department of Commerce in consulting any person or firm relative to any export control matters.

[13th Gen. Rev., Export Regs., Amdt. 66, 38 FR 20332, July 31, 1973, as amended at 42 FR 54530, Oct. 7, 1977; 45 FR 46067, July 9, 1980; 45 FR 59301, Sept. 9, 1980; 47 FR 15115, Apr. 8, 1982; 48 FR 20044, May 4, 1983; 51 FR 30632, Aug. 28, 1986. Redesignated at 53 FR 37751, Sept. 28, 1988]

§ 790.2 Conduct of business and practice in connection with export control matters.

(a) *Exclusion of persons guilty of unethical conduct or not possessing required integrity and ethical standards*—(1) *Who may be excluded.* Any person, whether acting on his own behalf or on behalf of another, who shall be found guilty of engaging in any unethical activity or who shall be demonstrated not to possess the required integrity and ethical standards, may be excluded from (denied) export privileges on his own behalf, or may be excluded from practice before the International Trade Administration of the U.S. Department of Commerce on behalf of another, in connection with any export control matter, or both, as provided in Part 788 of this subchapter.

(2) *Grounds for exclusion.* Among the grounds for exclusion are the following:

(i) Inducing or attempting to induce by gifts, promises, bribes, or otherwise, any officer or employee of the International Trade Administration of the U.S. Department of Commerce or any customs or post office official, to take any action with respect to the issuance of licenses or any other aspects of the administration of the Export Administration Act, whether or not in violation of any regulation;

(ii) Offering or making gifts or promises thereof to any such officer or employee for any other reason;

(iii) Soliciting by advertisement or otherwise the handling of business before the International Trade Administration on the representation, express or implied, that such person, through personal acquaintance or otherwise, possesses special influence over any officer or employee of the International Trade Administration.

(iv) Charging, or proposing to charge, for any service performed in connection with the issuance of any license, any fee wholly contingent upon the granting of such license and the amount or value thereof. This provision will not be construed to prohibit the charge of any fee agreed to by the parties; provided that the out-of-pocket expenditures and the reasonable value of the services performed, whether or not the license is issued and regardless of the amount thereof, are fairly compensated; and

(v) Knowingly violating or participating in the violation of, or an attempt to violate, any regulation with respect to the export of commodities or technical data, including the making of or inducing another to make any false representations to facilitate any export in violation of the Export Administration Act or any order or regulation issued thereunder.

(3) *Definition.* As used in this section, the terms "practice before the International Trade Administration" and "appear before the International Trade Administration" include:

(i) The submission on behalf of another of applications for export licenses or other documents required to be filed with the International Trade Administration, or the execution of the same;

(ii) Conferences or other communications on behalf of another with officers or employees of the International Trade Administration for the purpose of soliciting or expediting approval by the International Trade Administration of applications for export licenses or other documents, or with respect to quotas, allocations, requirements or other export control actions, pertaining to matters within the jurisdiction of the International Trade Administration;

(iii) Participation on behalf of another in any proceeding pending before the International Trade Administration; and

(iv) The submission to a customs official on behalf of another of a license or Shipper's Export Declaration or other export control document.

(4) *Proceedings.* All proceedings under this section shall be conducted in the same manner as provided in Part 388 of this subchapter.

(b) *Employees and former employees.* Persons who are or at any time have been employed on a full-time or part-time, compensated or uncompensated, basis by the U.S. Government are subject to the provisions of Title 18, United States Code, sections 203, 205 and 207 (Pub. L. 87–849, 87th Congress) in connection with representing a private party or interest before the U.S. Department of Commerce in connection with any export control matter.

[13th Gen. Rev. of Export Regs., 35 FR 9206, June 12, 1970, as amended at 45 FR 59301, Sept. 9, 1980. Redesignated at 53 FR 37751, Sept. 28, 1988]

§ **790.3 Export control authority to be exercised by U.S. Department of Commerce Field Office Directors in the event of enemy attack on the United States.**

(a) *Delegation to field office director.* In the event of an enemy attack on the United States, each Director of a U.S. Department of Commerce field office is authorized to exercise control over exports from the area assigned to him for purposes of this regulation.

(b) *Areas for which field office directors may control exports.* The area of jurisdiction assigned to each Director will be his area of jurisdiction at the time of an attack.

(c) *Orders from U.S. Department of Commerce.* The authorization set forth in paragraph (a) of this section shall be subject to any orders or directives transmitted from the U.S. Department of Commerce.

§ **790.4 Disclosure of license issuance and other information.**

As provided by section 12(c) of the Export Administration Act of 1979, as amended, information obtained for the purpose of considering license applications and other information obtained by the U.S. Department of Commerce concerning license applications will not be made available to the public without the approval of the Secretary of Commerce. Shippers' Export Declarations also are exempt from public disclosure, except with the approval of the Secretary of Commerce, in accordance with section 12(c) of the Export Administration Act of 1979 and section 301(g) of Title 13, United States Code.

[53 FR 20834, June 7, 1988. Redesignated at 53 FR 37751, Sept. 28, 1988]

§ **790.5 General order extending outstanding individual validated licenses for commodities.**

Effective November 5, 1986 all outstanding individual validated licenses that were initially issued for one-year validity periods, except for short supply licenses issued under 15 CFR Part 777, are extended for 12 months from their original expiration dates. Also effective November 5, 1986 all re-export authorizations that were initially granted with one-year validity periods, except for reexport authorizations under 15 CFR Part 777, are extended for 12 months from their original expiration dates.

[51 FR 40159, Nov. 5, 1986. Redesignated at 53 FR 37751, Sept. 28, 1988]

§ 790.6 General order preventing the use of special licensing procedures for aircraft controlled by Iran.

Effective September 28, 1984, the special licensing procedures (including outstanding or future authorizations) described in Part 773 may not be used to provide aircraft parts and accessories (Export Control Commodity Numbers 1460, 4460, 5460, 6460, 1485, and 1501 (a), (b)(1) and (c)(1)) intended for aircraft (wherever located) owned, operated, or controlled by, or under charter or lease to Iran, or any of its nationals; except that for regularly scheduled civilian airlines, such procedures may be used up to (two weeks after publication). Except as stated above, effective (publication date), such procedures (including outstanding and future authorizations) may not be used for any shipments to Iran.

[49 FR 39155, Oct. 4, 1984. Redesignated at 53 FR 37751, Sept. 28, 1988]

§ 790.7 General order on exports involving Libya.

(a) Effective September 24, 1981 bulk licenses described in Part 373 may not be used to provide aircraft parts and accessories (Export Control Commodity Numbers 1460, 4460, 1485, 1501(a), (b)(1) and (c)(1)) to aircraft owned, operated, or controlled by, or under charter or lease to Libya or any of its nationals.

(b) Effective 12:01 a.m. Eastern Standard Time February 1, 1986, any authorization to export directly or indirectly from the United States to Libya contained in a validated export license (including both individual and special licenses) if the export is prohibited by the Libyan Sanctions regulations (31 CFR Part 550) is hereby revoked. Authorizations not revoked hereby continue in effect. Pursuant to § 772.9(f) of the Export Administration regulations, revoked licenses must be returned immediately upon revocation to Export Administration. Original licenses need not be returned where they include both authorizations that are revoked and those that continue in effect. In such cases, a copy of the license must be returned.

(c) Effective February 1, 1986, the Libyan Sanctions regulations issued by the Department of the Treasury impose restrictions on exports from the United States to Libya (31 CFR Part 550). To avoid duplication in licensing procedures, the Department of Commerce will not require exporters to obtain a separate license for exports from the United States to Libya subject to the Libyan Sanctions Regulations that are licensed by the Office of Foreign Assets Control of the Department of the Treasury. Effective February 1, the issuance of such license by the Department of the Treasury shall also constitute an authorization under the Export Administration regulations. Shipments to Libya from foreign countries that are subject to the provisions of 15 CFR Part 774 and §§ 776.12, 779.8 and 785.7 of the Export Administration regulations and that are not subject to the Libyan Sanctions regulations continue to require authorization from the Department of Commerce.

[46 FR 47067, Sept. 24, 1981, as amended at 51 FR 2354, Jan. 16, 1986. Redesignated at 53 FR 37751, Sept. 28, 1988]

PART 791—FOREIGN AVAILABILITY PROCEDURES AND CRITERIA

AUTHORITY: Pub. L. 96–72, 93 Stat. 503 (50 U.S.C. app. 2401 et seq.), as amended by Pub. L. 97–145 of December 29, 1981, by Pub. L. 100–418 of August 23, 1988, and by Pub. L. 99–64 of July 12, 1985; E.O. 12525 of July 12, 1985 (50 FR 28757, July 16, 1985).

SOURCE: 50 FR 52914, Dec. 27, 1985, unless otherwise noted. Redesignated at 53 FR 37751, Sept. 28, 1988.

§ 791.1 **Definitions.**

(a) *Available-in-fact.* As used in this part, "available-in-fact" means that a non-U.S. origin item may be obtained by one or more of the proscribed countries.

(b) *Proscribed countries.* As used in this part, "proscribed countries" means Country Groups Q, W, and Y and Afghanistan. These countries are: The USSR, Albania, Bulgaria, Afghanistan, Czechoslovakia, the German Democratic Republic (including East Berlin), Hungary, Laos, the Mongolian People's Republic, Poland and Romania. Country Group Z (North Korea, Vietnam, Kampuchea, and Cuba) is not included since these countries are subject to a virtual embargo notwithstanding any foreign availability.

(c) *Foreign availability.* "Foreign availability" for a national security-controlled item exists when the Secretary of Commerce determines that a non-U.S. origin item of comparable quality is available-in-fact to proscribed countries in quantities sufficient to satisfy their needs so that U.S. exports of such an item would not make a significant contribution to the military potential of such countries.

(d) *Foreign Availability Submission.* A "Foreign Availability Submission" (FAS) is a written claim submitted by an applicant requesting a foreign availability assessment for items controlled for national security purposes in accordance with the requirements contained in § 791.2 of this part.

(e) *Item.* An "item," as used in this part, may be a commodity or technical data.

(f) *Non-U.S. origin.* A commodity or technical data is of "non-U.S. origin" when it is not subject to U.S. export or re-export controls.

§ 791.2 **Foreign Availability Submission.**

(a) *General requirements.* Foreign Availability Submissions (FASs) must be in writing and refer to specific items controlled for national security purposes (reasons for control are noted in each Commodity Control List entry of Supplement No. 1 to § 799.1). A FAS must relate to either (1) a validated license or (2) decontrol.

(b) *Validated licenses.* A claim of foreign availability may be made in connection with an application for a validated license or a request for re-export authorization for exports to any destination (except Country Group Z). A foreign availability claim consists of a Foreign Availability Submission (FAS), which is part of the license application. An assessment of foreign availability, however, will be initiated only on items in applications that have been denied on national security grounds. A FAS may be submitted at the time an export license application or request for re-export authorization is filed, or at any time up to 90 days after the date of a denial.

(c) *Decontrol.* (1) A FAS may also be submitted for the purpose of removing commodities or technical data from national security controls. FASs involving similar items may be consolidated. The Office of Foreign Availability, in consultation with the Department of Defense and other appropriate Government agencies, has responsibility for reviewing and consolidating FASs for action to determine appropriate levels of control.

(2) Any person, including a trade association or a Department of Commerce Technical Advisory Committee, may submit a decontrol FAS. The Department may also begin foreign availability assessments on its own initiative to determine whether national security controls should be maintained on specific items.

(d) *Submission requirements.* (1) A FAS should contain at least the following elements:

(i) Names of sources outside the U.S. and their overseas business addresses;

(ii) Product names and model designations of both the U.S. commodities or technical data and their non-U.S. origin counterparts;

(iii) Available technical information, including known performance attributes and quality considerations needed for comparison of U.S. and non-U.S. origin commodities or technical data; and

(iv) Information on production and demand, including quantities of known trade in such commodities to proscribed countries.

(2) *Supporting evidence.* (i) A submission should be accompanied by the best available supporting evidence.

The Department may request more information from the applicant if necessary or if it appears that the claim is lacking in substance.

(ii) Information on foreign availability provided in the FAS will be reviewed in conjunction with any other pertinent information available to the Department of Commerce. Such information may include data received from other sources, including the Department of Defense and other appropriate governmental agencies. A detailed description of foreign availability sources, including any supporting information available to the applicant, will greatly assist in a timely and complete assessment.

(iii) Supporting information may include such items as foreign manufacturers' catalogs, brochures, operation or maintenance manuals, articles from reputable trade publications, photographs, depositions based on eyewitness accounts, and other credible data. Foreign availability assessment criteria outlined in section 791.3 of this part should be considered when assembling data in support of a FAS. (See Supplement No. 1 for examples of evidence.)

(3) FASs that do not accompany a license application must be addressed to:

Office of Foreign Availability, Room 2606, U.S. Department of Commerce, 14th & Pennsylvania Ave., NW, Washington, DC 20230

(The information collection requirements in paragraph (d)(3) have been approved by the Office of Management and Budget under control number 0625-0150.)

[50 FR 52914, Dec. 27, 1985, as amended at 53 FR 36008, Sept. 16, 1988. Redesignated at 53 FR 37751, Sept. 28, 1988]

§ 791.3   Criteria for determination.

(a) *Non-U.S. origin.* Only information pertaining to availability of non-U.S. origin commodities or technical data (as defined in § 791.1 of this part) will be considered in support of foreign availability claims. Notwithstanding the foregoing, the Department welcomes the submission at any time of specific information concerning the availability of U.S. origin commodities or technical data to proscribed destinations so that appropriate measures can be taken to make U.S. controls more effective.

(b) *Availability-in-fact.* Only non-U.S. origin commodities or technical data that are available-in-fact to the proscribed countries will be considered in establishing foreign availability.

(c) *Standards of comparison for commodities.* All of the following tests must be met in determining the comparability and quantitative sufficiency of U.S. and non-U.S. origin commodities:

(1) *Comparable quality.* U.S. and non-U.S. origin commodities must be substantially similar in:

(i) Function;

(ii) Technological approach;

(iii) Performance thresholds;

(iv) Maintainability and service life or any other attributes relevant to the purposes for which controls were placed on that commodity.

(2) *Sufficient quantity.* For all submissions, comparable non-U.S. origin commodities must be available-in-fact to the proscribed countries in quantities sufficient to satisfy their needs so that U.S. exports would not make a significant contribution to the military potential of such countries.

(d) *Standards of comparison for technical data.* Non-U.S. origin technical data submitted as evidence of foreign availability must meet the following standards of comparison as to comparable quality:

(1) Non-U.S. origin technical data is or can be used or adapted for use in ways and with results similar to those of its U.S. counterparts; and

(2) End products of the use of non-U.S. origin technical data are substantially similar to end products resulting from the use of its U.S. counterparts.

(e) *Evidence.* The Department of Commerce may consider evidence from any source in determining foreign availability. A claim of foreign availability for an item supported by reasonable evidence shall be accepted unless contradicted by reliable evidence available to the Department. To the extent consistent with the national security and foreign policy interests of the United States and with the protection of proprietary information, the Department of Commerce will inform the claimant of information contradicting the representations and supporting information where such evidence is the basis for a negative determination of foreign availability. The Department of Commerce will normally rely upon its own and other governmental sources for evidence bearing on the needs of proscribed countries and will determine whether the denial of a license or continuation of controls would be ineffective in achieving the national security purposes of the controls.

§ 791.4 **Procedures.**

(a) *Claims associated with license applications.* (1) Assessments of foreign availability for items included in a validated license application (or request for reexport authorization) will be initiated only when all the following conditions are met:

(i) A license has been denied based only on national security grounds, and

(ii) An FAS is received no later than 90 days from the date of the license denial.

(2) If a complete FAS has been submitted prior to the license denial, the applicant will be notified that an assessment of foreign availability has been initiated at the time of license denial. The Department of Commerce will seek to complete its evaluation of the claim within 90 days of the date of denial.

(3) If an incomplete FAS was submitted, the applicant will be informed that a foreign availability assessment will be initiated upon the Department's receipt of a timely and complete FAS. The Department of Commerce will seek to complete its evaluation of the claim within 90 days of the submission of a completed FAS.

(4) Formal notice of both positive and negative determinations will be published in the FEDERAL REGISTER within thirty days of their completion, to the extent consistent with U.S. national security and foreign policy interests and with the protection of proprietary information. Such notice will include a description of the relevant item and the results (positive or negative) of the evaluation. Information permitting the identification of the claimant will not appear in the notice. Except as provided in paragraph (c)(5)

of this section, if a positive determination is made, a validated license will be forwarded to the applicant; if a positive determination is not made, to the extent consistent with the U.S. national security and foreign policy interests, a negative foreign availability determination notice will inform the applicant of the reasons for denial.

(5) Despite a positive determination of foreign availability, the Secretary of Commerce, in consultation with the Secretary of Defense, may determine that approval of a validated license would be detrimental to national security. In such cases, no approval will occur, and the applicant will be so informed. The Department shall publish that determination in the FEDERAL REGISTER with a concise statement of its basis. Negotiations provided in § 791.6 will then be pursued.

(6) In cases where a positive determination of foreign availability has been made and a validated license issued, the Office of Foreign Availability will decide whether to initiate a foreign availability assessment to determine whether national security controls should be maintained on such items.

(b) *Review of decontrol submissions.* (1) The Office of Foreign Availability will collect and evaluate all foreign availability information for decontrol purposes and initiate appropriate assessments. Such assessments will refer to generic equipment categories or characteristics or will propose changes to the Commodity Control List. Standards outlined in § 791.3 of this part shall be use to make the assessments. When appropriate, preliminary findings will be forwarded to the Department of Defense, other relevant U.S. Government agencies, and/or the Department of Commerce's Technical Advisory Committee (TACs) for review and comment. Notice of both positive and negative foreign availability findings will be published in the FEDERAL REGISTER within thirty days of their completion to the extent consistent with U.S. national security and foreign policy interests and with the protection of proprietary information. Except as provided in paragraphs (b)(1) through (5) of this section, in cases where the Department of Commerce determines the existence of foreign availability, action ot decontrol the relevant commodities or technical data will be taken and notice of such action will be published in the FEDERAL REGISTER.

(2) Information used to arrive at final determinations may come from any source, Government or non-Government, deemed appropriate by the Department of Commerce.

(3) In cases where a decontrol submission consists of a TAC certification, the Department will seek to complete its evaluation within 90 days.

(4) Despite positive foreign availability determinations, the President may determine that decontrol would be detrimental to the national security. In such cases, no decontrol will occur.

(5) Where such a determination has been made, the Department will publish that determination in the FEDERAL REGISTER with a concise statement of its basis and the estimated economic impact of the decision. In addition, negotiations will be initiated to eliminate sources of foreign availability on such items pursuant to § 791.6 of this part.

(6) When the Department of Commerce determines that conditions under which a positive determination of foreign availability were made have changed so as to cast doubt on the continued existence of foreign availability, a review of the original decontrol action will be undertaken.

(7) If foreign availability is determined no longer to exist, controls may be re-imposed. Appropriate notice will be published in the FEDERAL REGISTER.

§ 791.5 Appeals.

Appeals of negative foreign availability determinations must be received by the Office of the Assistant Secretary for Trade Administration, International Trade Administration, 14th Street and Pennsylvania Ave. NW., Room 3898B, U.S. Department of Commerce, Washington, DC 20230 no later than 45 days after the date appearing on the negative foreign availability assessment notice. Appeals will be conducted according to standards and procedures outlined in 15 CFR Part 789. A decision to deny a license or continue controls notwithstanding a determination of foreign availability shall not be subject to appeal.

§ 791.6 Negotiations to end foreign availability.

In any case in which national security export controls are maintained notwithstanding foreign availability, negotiations will be actively pursued with the governments of the appropriate foreign countries for the purpose of eliminating such availability. If such negotiations have not resulted in the elimination of foreign availability within 6 months of the publication of the finding of foreign availability in the FEDERAL REGISTER, the item in question will be removed from the Commodity Control List. The President may extend this 6 month period for an additional 12 months if he certifies to the Congress that the negotiations are progressing and that the absence of the export control involved would be detrimental to the national security.

SUPPLEMENT No. 1 to PART 791

EVIDENCE OF FOREIGN AVAILABILITY

Below is a list of examples of evidence that the Office of Foreign Availability has found useful in conducting assessments of foreign availability. A claimant submitting evidence supporting a claim of foreign availability may want to review this list for suggestions as evidence is collected.

This list is not all inclusive. Acceptable evidence is not limited to these examples. A foreign availability submission should include as much reasonable evidence as possible on *all four* of the criteria listed below. A combination of several types of evidence will usually be required. The list is representative of the types of evidence OFA has found useful in its assessments. The Office of Foreign Availability will combine this evidence with the evidence it collects from other government and public sources. The Office of Foreign Availability will evaluate carefully and fully the evidence, taking into account factors that may include, but are not limited to: information concerning the source of the evidence; corroborative or contradictory indications; and experience concerning the reliability or reasonableness of such evidence. OFA will assess whether the four criteria are met.

From time to time, as OFA identifies new examples of evidence that would enhance assessment submissions, we will amend this informational list.

EXAMPLES OF EVIDENCE OF FOREIGN
AVAILABILITY

The Export Administration Act of 1979, as amended, requires that four criteria be met to prove foreign availability. The four criteria are: available-in-fact, from a non-U.S. source, in sufficient quantity and of comparable quality.

Available-In-Fact

—Evidence of marketing of a comparable foreign product in a proscribed country (e.g., an advertisement in the media of the proscribed country that the commodity is for sale);
—Copies of sales receipts demonstrating sales to proscribed countries;
—The terms of a contract under which the commodity has been or is being sold to a proscribed country;
—Information from a named foreign government official that it will not deny the sale of an item it produces to a proscribed country in accordance with its laws and regulations;
—Information from a named company official that the company legally can and would sell an item it produces to a proscribed country;
—Evidence of actual shipments of the product to proscribed countries (e.g., shipping documents, photographs, news reports);
—An eyewitness report of such items in operation in a proscribed country;
—Evidence of sales or technical service personnel in a proscribed country;
—Evidence of production within a proscribed country;
—Evidence of the item being exhibited at a trade fair in a proscribed country;
—A copy of the export control laws or regulations of the source country which shows that the product is not controlled.

Non-U.S. Source

—A list of non-U.S. (COCOM, non-COCOM, or proscribed countries) manufacturers of the item;
—A report from a reputable source of information on Commercial relationships that a foreign manufacturer is not linked financially or administratively with a U.S. company;
—A list of the components in the U.S. and non-U.S. items indicating model numbers and their sources;
—A schematic of the non-U.S. item identifying the components and their sources;
—Evidence that the commodity is a direct product of non-U.S. technology (e.g., a patent law suit lost by a U.S. producer, a foreign patent);
—A list of producers of a similar commodity and evidence of indigenous technology, production facilities, the capabilities at those facilities, and/or distribution of the commodity;
—Evidence that the parts and components of the item are of non-U.S. origin or are exempt from U.S. export licensing requirements by the Parts and Components provision (Section 776.12).

Sufficient Quantity

—Evidence that non-U.S. sources have the item in serial production;
—Evidence that the item or its manufacture is used in civilian applications in proscribed countries;
—Evidence that a proscribed country is marketing in the West a comparable product of its manufacture;
—Evidence of excess capacity in a proscribed country's production facility;
—Evidence that proscribed countries have not targeted the commodity or are not seeking to purchase it in the West;
—A proscribed country's official or a knowledgeable source's estimate of the proscribed country's needs;
—A trade paper anlaysis of the worldwide market (i.e., demand, production rate for the commodity for various manufacturers, plant capacities, installed tooling, monthly production rates, orders, sales and cumulative sales over 5-6 years).

Comparable Quality

—A sample of the non-U.S. product;
—Operation or maintenance manuals;
—Records or a statement from a user of the non-U.S. product;
—A comprehensive evaluation of the U.S. and non-U.S. product by a western producer or purchaser of the product, a recognized expert, trade publication, or independent laboratory;
—A comparative list identifying, by manufacturer and model numbers, the key performance components and the material used in the product that qualitatively affect the performance of the U.S. and non-U.S. products;
—Evidence of the interchangeability of the U.S. and non-U.S. products;
—Published specifications for the U.S. and non-U.S. products;
—Evidence of the competitiveness of the non-U.S. product in the world market (e.g., sales contracts, repeat purchases, orders);
—Patent descriptions for the U.S. and non-U.S. products;
—Evidence that the U.S. and non-U.S. items meet a published industry or universal standard;
—A report or eyewitness account, by deposition or otherwise, of the non-U.S. product's operation;

er, or furskins, classifiable under Schedule 1, Part 5, "Hide, Skins, and Leather; Furskins" (including TSUS numbers 120.11 through 120.50, 121.10 through 121.65, 123.00 through 123.50, and 124.10 through 124.80), of animals that are taken from the wild in South Africa, and that are not cultivated, ranched, or otherwise the product of animal husbandry, the following signed certificate shall be filed with the U.S. Customs Service upon making an entry of such goods from South Africa:

These _____ [hides, skins, leather, or furskins], classifiable under TSUS number(s) _____ [from Schedule 1, Part 5, "Hide, Skins, and Leather; Furskins" (including TSUS numbers 120.11 through 120.50, 121.10 through 121.65, 123.00 through 123.50, and 124.10 through 124.80)], are from _____ [type of animal] that were taken from the wild in South Africa, and that were not cultivated, ranched, or otherwise the product of animal husbandry. The requirements of Title 50 of the Code of Federal Regulations (Wildlife and Fisheries), including those relating to endangered species, have been fully complied with in removing these articles from South Africa, and all applicable import certificates required pursuant to Title 50 are presented with this entry.

[52 FR 7855, Mar. 13, 1987]

Subpart I—Miscellaneous

§ 545.901 Paperwork Reduction Act notice.

The information collection requirements in §§ 545.503, 545.504, 545.601, and 545.602 have been approved by the Office of Management and Budget (OMB) and have been assigned control number 1505-0091. The information collection requirements of § 545.807 have been approved by OMB and assigned control number 1505-0097. The information collection requirements of §§ 545.603 and 545.604 have been approved by OMB and assigned control number 1505-0098.

[52 FR 7274, Mar. 10, 1987]

PART 550—LIBYAN SANCTIONS REGULATIONS

Sec.

AUTHORITY: 50 U.S.C. 1701 et seq.; E.O. 12543, 51 FR 875, Jan. 9, 1986; E.O. 12544, 51 FR 1235, Jan. 10, 1986.

SOURCE: 51 FR 1354, Jan. 10, 1986, unless otherwise noted.

Subpart A—Relation of this Part to Other Laws and Regulations

§ 550.101 Relation of this part to other laws and regulations.

(a) This part is independent of Parts 500, 505, 515, 520, 535, 540, and 545 of this chapter. Those parts do not relate to Libya. No license or authorization contained in or issued pursuant to those other parts authorizes any transaction prohibited by this part. In addition, licenses or authorizations contained in or issued pursuant to any other provision of law or regulations do not authorize any transaction prohibited by this part.

(b) No license or authorization contained in or issued pursuant to this part relieves the involved parties from complying with any other applicable laws or regulations. In particular, no license or authorization contained in or issued pursuant to this part authorizes the importation of petroleum products which would be banned by Presidential Proclamation 5141 of December 22, 1983 or Executive Order 12538 of November 15, 1985.

Subpart B—Prohibitions

§ 550.201 Prohibited imports of goods or services from Libya.

Except as authorized, no goods or services of Libyan origin, other than publications and materials imported for news publication or news broadcast dissemination, may be imported into the United States.

§ 550.202 Prohibited exports of goods, technology or services to Libya.

Except as authorized, no goods, technology (including technical data or other information) or services may be exported to Libya from the United States, except publications and donated articles intended to relieve human suffering, such as food, clothing, medicine and medical supplies intended strictly for medical purposes.

§ 550.203 Prohibited transportation-related transactions.

Except as authorized, the following are prohibited:

(a) Any transaction by a United States person relating to transportation to or from Libya;

(b) The provision of transportation to or from the United States by any Libyan person or any vessel or aircraft of Libyan registration; or

(c) The sale in the United States by any person holding authority under the Federal Aviation Act of any transportation by air which includes any stop in Libya.

§ 550.204 Prohibited purchases of goods from Libya.

Except as authorized, no U.S. person may purchase goods for export from Libya to any other country.

§ 550.205 Prohibited engagement in contracts.

Except as authorized, no U.S. person may perform any contract in support of an industrial or other commercial or governmental project in Libya.

§ 550.206 Prohibited grants or extensions of credits or loans.

Except as authorized, no U.S. person may grant or extend credits or loans to the Government of Libya.

§ 550.207 Prohibited transactions relating to travel to Libya or to activities within Libya.

Except as authorized, no U.S. person may engage in any transaction relating to travel by any U.S. citizen or permanent resident alien to Libya, or to activities by any U.S. citizen or permanent resident alien within Libya, after the effective date, other than transactions:

(a) Necessary to effect the departure of a U.S. citizen or permanent resident alien from Libya;

(b) Relating to travel to, from, or within Libya prior to February 1, 1986 to perform acts prohibited by §§ 550.201, 550.202, 550.203, 550.204, or 550.205 after that date; or

(c) Relating to journalistic activity by persons regularly employed in such capacity by a newsgathering organization.

This section prohibits the unauthorized payment by a U.S. person of his own travel or living expenses to or within Libya.

§ 550.208 Evasions.

Any transaction for the purpose of, or which has the effect of, evading or avoiding any of the prohibitions set forth in this subpart is hereby prohibited.

§ 550.209 Prohibited transactions involving property in which the Government of Libya has an interest; transactions with respect to securities.

(a) Except as authorized by regulations, rulings, instructions, licenses, or otherwise, no property or interests in property of the Government of Libya that are in the United States that hereafter come within the United States or that are or hearafter come within the possession or control of U.S. persons, including their overseas branches, may be transferred, paid, exported, withdrawn or otherwise dealt in.

(b) Unless authorized by a license expressly referring to this section, the acquisition, transfer (including the transfer on the books of any issuer or agent thereof), disposition, transportation, importation, exportation, or withdrawal of, or the endorsement or guaranty of signatures on or otherwise dealing in any security (or evidence thereof) registered or inscribed in the name of the Government of Libya is prohibited irrespective of the fact that at any time (either prior to, on, or subsequent to 4:10 p.m. e.s.t., January 8, 1986) the registered or inscribed owner thereof may have, or appears to have, assigned, transferred or otherwise disposed of any such security.

[51 FR 2462, Jan. 16, 1986]

§ 550.210 Effect of transfers violating the provisions of this part.

(a) Any transfer after 4:10 p.m. e.s.t., January 8, 1986, which is in violation of any provision of this part or of any regulation, ruling, instruction, license, or other direction or authorization thereunder and involves any property in which the Government of Libya has or has had an interest since such date is null and void and shall not be the basis for the assertion or recognition of any interest in or right, remedy, power or privilege with respect to such property.

(b) No transfer before 4:10 p.m. e.s.t., January 8, 1986, shall be the basis for the assertion or recognition of any right, remedy, power, or privilege with respect to, or interest in, any property in which the Government of Libya has or has had an interest since such date,

unless the person with whom such property is held or maintained had written notice of the transfer or by any written evidence had recognized such transfer prior to such date.

(c) Unless otherwise provided, an appropriate license or other authorization issued by or pursuant to the direction or authorization of the Secretary of the Treasury before, during or after a transfer shall validate such transfer or render it enforceable to the same extent as it would be valid or enforceable but for the provisions of the International Emergency Economic Powers Act and this part and any ruling, order, regulation, direction or instruction issued hereunder.

(d) Transfers of property which otherwise would be null and void or unenforceable, by virtue of the provisions of this section, shall not be deemed to be null and void or unenforceable pursuant to such provisions, as to any person with whom such property was held or maintained (and as to such person only) in cases in which such person is able to establish each of the following:

(1) Such transfer did not represent a willfull violation of the provisions of this part by the person with whom such property was held or maintained:

(2) The person with whom such property was held or maintained did not have reasonable cause to know or suspect, in view of all the facts and circumstances known or available to such person, that such transfer required a license or authorization by or pursuant to this part and was not so licensed or authorized, or if a license or authorization did purport to cover the transfer, that such license or authorization had been obtained by misrepresentation or the withholding of material facts or was otherwise fraudulently obtained; and

(3) Promptly upon discovery that: (i) Such transfer was in violation of the provisions of this part or any regulation, ruling, instruction, license or other direction or authorization thereunder, or (ii) such transfer was not licensed or authorized by the Secretary of the Treasury, or (iii) if a license did purport to cover the transfer, such license had been obtained by misrepresentation or the withholding of mate-

rial facts or was otherwise fraudulently obtained; the person with whom such property was held or maintained filed with the Treasury Department, Washington, D.C., a report in triplicate setting forth in full the circumstances relating to such transfer. The filing of a report in accordance with the provisions of this paragraph shall not be deemed to be compliance or evidence of compliance with paragraphs (d)(1) and (2) of this section.

(e) Unless licensed or authorized pursuant to this part, any attachment, judgment, decree, lien, execution, garnishment or other judicial process is null and void with respect to any property in which on or since 4:10 p.m. e.s.t., January 8, 1986, there existed an interest of the Government of Libya.

[51 FR 2462, Jan. 16, 1986]

Subpart C—Definitions

§ 550.301 Effective date.

The "effective date" means:

(a) 12:01 a.m. Eastern Standard Time (e.s.t.), February 1, 1986, with respect to the transactions prohibited by §§ 550.201, 550.202, 550.203, 550.204, and 550.205;

(b) 8:06 p.m. Eastern Standard Time (e.s.t.), January 7, 1986, with respect to transactions prohibited by §§ 550.206 and 550.207; and

(c) 4:10 p.m. Eastern Standard Time (e.s.t.), January 8, 1986, with respect to transactions prohibited by §550.209.

[51 FR 2463, Jan. 16, 1986]

§ 550.302 Libya; Libyan.

The term "Libya" means the country of Libya and any Libyan territory, dependency, colony, protectorate, mandate, dominion, possession, or place subject to the jurisdiction thereof. The term "Libyan" means pertaining to Libya as defined in this section.

§ 550.303 Libyan origin.

The term "goods or services of Libyan origin" includes:

(a) Goods produced, manufactured, grown, or processed within Libya;

(b) Goods which have entered into Libyan commerce;

(c) Services performed in Libya or by a Libyan national who is acting as an agent, employee, or contractor of the Government of Libya, or of a business entity located in Libya. Services of Libyan origin are not imported into the United States when such services are provided in the United States by a Libyan national who, during indefinite residency in the United States, works as, for example, a teacher, athlete, restaurant or domestic worker, or a person employed in any other regular occupation.

§ 550.304 Government of Libya.

(a) The "Government of Libya" includes:

(1) The state and the Government of Libya, as well as any political subdivision, agency, or instrumentality thereof, including the Central Bank of Libya;

(2) Any partnership, association, corporation, or other organization substantially owned or controlled by the foregoing;

(3) Any person to the extent that such person is, or has been, or to the extent that there is reasonable cause to believe that such person is, or has been, since the effective date, acting or purporting to act directly or indirectly on behalf of any of the foregoing;

(4) Any other person or organization determined by the Secretary of the Treasury to be included within paragraph (a) of this section.

(b) A person specified in paragraph (a)(2) of this section shall not be deemed to fall within the definition of Government of Libya solely by reason of being located in, organized under the laws of, or having its principal place of business in, Libya.

[51 FR 2463, Jan. 16, 1986, as amended at 53 FR 5571, Feb. 25, 1988]

§ 550.305 Libyan person.

The term "Libyan person" means any Libyan citizen, any juridical person organized under the laws of Libya, or any juridical person owned or controlled, directly or indirectly, by a Libyan citizen or the Government of Libya.

§ 550.306 Person.

The term "person" means an individual, partnership, association, corporation, or other organization.

§ 550.307 United States.

The term "United States" means the United States and all areas under the jurisdiction or authority thereof.

§ 550.308 United States person.

The term "United States person" or, as abbreviated, "U.S. person," means any United States citizen, permanent resident alien, juridical person organized under the laws of the United States, or any person in the United States.

§ 550.309 License.

Except as otherwise specified, the term "license" shall mean any license or authorization contained in or issued pursuant to this part.

§ 550.310 General license.

A general license is any license or authorization the terms of which are set forth in this part.

§ 550.311 Specific license.

A specific license is any license or authorization issued purusant to this part but not set forth in this part.

§ 550.312 Credits or loans.

The term "credits" or "loans" means any transfer or extension of funds or credit on the basis of an obligation to repay, or any assumption or guarantee of the obligation of another to repay an extension of funds or credit. The term "credits" or "loans" includes, but is not limited to: overdrafts; currency swaps; purchases of debt securities issued by the Government of Libya after January 7, 1986; purchases of a loan made by another person; sales of financial assets subject to an agreement to repurchase; renewals or refinancings whereby funds or credits are transferred to or extended to the Government of Libya; and draw-downs on existing lines of credit.

§ 550.313 Transfer.

The term "transfer" shall mean any actual or purported act or transaction, whether or not evidenced by writing, and whether or not done or performed within the United States, the purpose, intent or effect of which is to create, surrender, release, transfer, or alter, directly or indirectly, any right, remedy, power, privilege, or interest with respect to any property and, without limitation upon the foregoing, shall include the making, execution, or delivery of any assignment, power, conveyance, check, declaration, deed, deed of trust, power of attorney, power of appointment, bill of sale, mortgage, receipt, agreement, contract, certificate, gift, sale, affidavit, or statement; the appointment of any agent, trustee, or fiduciary; the creation or transfer of any lien; the issuance, docketing, filing, or the levy of or under any judgment, decree, attachment, injunction, execution, or other judicial or administrative process or order, or the service of any garnishment; the acquisition of any interest of any nature whatsoever by reason of a judgment or decree of any foreign country; the fulfillment of any condition, or the exercise of any power of appointment, power of attorney, or other power.

[51 FR 2463, Jan. 16, 1986]

§ 550.314 Property; property interests.

The terms "property" and "property interest" or "property interests" shall include, but not by way of limitation, money, checks, drafts, bullion, bank deposits, savings accounts, debts, indebtedness, obligations, notes, debentures, stocks, bonds, coupons, any other financial securities, bankers' acceptances, mortgages, pledges, liens or other rights in the nature of security, warehouse receipts, bills of lading, trust receipts, bills of sale, any other evidences of title, ownership or indebtedness, letters of credit and any documents relating to any rights or obligations thereunder, powers of attorney, goods, wares, merchandise, chattels, stocks on hand, ships, goods on ships, real estate mortgages, deeds of trust, vendors' sales agreements, land contracts, real estate and any interest therein, leaseholds, ground rents, options, negotiable instruments, trade acceptances, royalties, book accounts,

accounts payable, judgments, patents, trademarks or copyrights, insurance policies, safe deposit boxes and their contents, annuities, pooling agreements, contracts of any nature whatsoever, and any other property, real, personal, or mixed, tangible or intangible, or interest or interests therein, present, future or contingent.

[51 FR 2463, Jan. 16, 1986]

§ 550.315 Interest.

Except as otherwise provided in this part, the term "interest" when used with respect to property shall mean an interest of any nature whatsoever, direct or indirect.

[51 FR 2464, Jan. 16, 1986]

§ 550.316 Blocked account; blocked property.

The terms "blocked account" and "blocked property" shall mean any account or property in which the Government of Libya has an interest, with respect to which payments, transfers or withdrawals or other dealings may not be made or effected except pursuant to an authorization or license authorizing such action.

[51 FR 2464, Jan. 16, 1986]

§ 550.317 Domestic bank.

(a) The term "domestic bank" shall mean any branch or office within the United States of any of the following which is not a Libyan entity: Any bank or trust company incorporated under the banking laws of the United States or of any state, territory, or district of the United States, or any private bank or banker subject to supervision and examination under the banking laws of the United States or of any state, territory or district of the United States. The Secretary of the Treasury may also authorize any other banking institution to be treated as a "domestic bank" for the purpose of this definition or for the purpose of any or all sections of this part.

(b) The term "domestic bank" includes any branch or office within the United States of a foreign bank that is not a Libyan entity.

[51 FR 2464, Jan. 16, 1986]

§ 550.318 Entity.

The term "entity" includes a corporation, partnership, association, or other organization.

[51 FR 2464, Jan. 16, 1986]

§ 550.319 Entity of the Government of Libya; Libyan entity.

The terms "entity of the Government of Libya" and "Libyan entity" include:

(a) Any corporation, partnership, association, or other entity in which the Government of Libya owns a majority or controlling interest, any entity substantially managed or funded by that government, and any entity which is otherwise controlled by that government;

(b) Any agency or instrumentality of the Government of Libya, including the Central Bank of Libya.

[51 FR 2464, Jan. 16, 1986]

§ 550.320 Banking institution.

The term "banking institution" shall include any person engaged primarily or incidentally in the business of banking, of granting or transferring credits, or of purchasing or selling foreign exchange or procuring purchasers and sellers thereof, as principal or agent, or any person holding credits for others as a direct or incidental part of its business, or any broker; and each principal, agent, home office, branch or correspondent of any person so engaged shall be regarded as a separate "banking institution."

[51 FR 2464, Jan. 16, 1986]

Subpart D—Interpretations

§ 550.401 Reference to amended sections.

Reference to any section of this part or to any regulation, ruling, order, instruction, direction or license issued pursuant to this part shall be deemed to refer to the same as currently amended unless otherwise so specified.

§ 550.402 Effect of amendment of sections of this part or of other orders, etc.

Any amendment, modification, or revocation of any section of this part or of any order, regulation, ruling, instruction, or license issued by or under the direction of the Secretary of the Treasury pursuant to section 203 of the International Emergency Economic Powers Act shall not, unless otherwise specifically provided, be deemed to affect any act done or omitted to be done, or any suit or proceeding had or commenced in any civil or criminal case prior to such amendment, modification, or revocation, and all penalties, forfeitures, and liabilities under any such order, regulation, ruling, instruction or license shall continue and may be enforced as if such amendment, modification, or revocation had not been made.

§ 550.403 Extensions of credits or loans to Libya.

(a) The prohibition in § 550.205 applies to the unlicensed renewal of credits or loans in existence on the effective date.

(b) The prohibition in § 550.205 applies to credits or loans extended in any currency.

§ 550.404 Import and export of goods in transit before the effective date.

(a) Section 550.201 does not apply to goods:

(1) If imported by vessel, where the vessel arrives within the limits of a port in the United States prior to the effective date with the intent to unlade such goods; or

(2) If imported other than by vessel, where the goods arrive within the Customs territory of the United States before the effective date.

(b) Section 550.202 does not apply to goods:

(1) If exported by vessel or airline, where the goods are laden on board before the effective date; or

(2) If exported other than by vessel or airplane, where the goods have left the United States before the effective date.

[51 FR 1354, Jan. 10, 1986, as amended at 51 FR 2464, Jan. 16, 1986]

§ 550.405 Payments in connection with certain authorized transactions.

Payments are authorized in connection with transactions authorized under Subpart E.

§ 550.406 Offshore transactions.

(a) The provisions contained in §§ 550.209 and 550.210 apply to transactions by U.S. persons in locations outside the United States with respect to property in which the U.S. person knows, or has reason to know, that the Government of Libya has or has had any interest since 4:10 p.m. EST, January 8, 1986, including:

(1) Importation into such locations of, or

(2) Dealings within such locations in, goods or services of Libyan origin.

(b) Example. A U.S. person may not, within the United States or abroad, purchase, sell, finance, insure, transport, act as a broker for the sale or transport of, or otherwise deal in, Libyan crude oil or petroleum products refined in Libya.

(c) Note. Exports or reexports of goods and technical data, or of the direct products of technical data (regardless of U.S. content), not prohibited by this part may require authorization from the U.S. Department of Commerce pursuant to the Export Administration Act of 1979, as amended, 50 U.S.C. App. 2401 *et seq.*, and the Export Administration Regulations implementing that Act, 15 CFR Parts 368–399.

[53 FR 5572, Feb. 25, 1988]

§ 550.407 Transshipment through the United States prohibited.

(a) The prohibitions in § 550.202 apply to the import into the United States, for transshipment or transit, of goods which are intended or destined for Libya.

(b) The prohibitions in § 550.201 apply to the import into the United States, for transshipment or transit, of goods of Libyan origin which are intended or destined for third countries.

§ 550.408 Imports from third countries; transshipments.

(a) Imports into the United States from third countries of goods containing raw materials or components of Libyan origin are not prohibited if those raw materials or components have been incorporated into manufactured products or otherwise substantially transformed in a third country.

(b) Imports into the United States of goods of Libyan origin which have been transshipped through a third country without being incorporated into manufactured products or otherwise substantially transformed in a third country are prohibited.

§ 550.409 Exports to third countries; transshipment.

(a) Exports of goods or technology (including technical data and other information) from the United States to third countries are prohibited if the exporter knows, or has reason to know, that:

(1) The goods or technology are intended for transshipment to Libya (including passage through, or storage in, intermediate destinations) without coming to rest in a third country and without being substantially transformed or incorporated into manufactured products in a third country, or

(2) The exported goods are intended specifically for substantial transformation or incorporation in a third country into products to be used in Libya in the petroleum or petrochemical industry, or

(3) The exported technology is intended specifically for use in a third country in the manufacture of, or for incorporation into, products to be used in Libya in the petroleum or petrochemical industry.

(b) For the purposes of paragraph (a) of this section:

(1) The scope of activities encompassed by the petroleum and petrochemical industries shall include, but not be limited to, the following activities: Oil, natural gas, natural gas liquids, or other hydrocarbon exploration (including geophysical and geological assessment activity), extraction, production, refining, distillation, cracking, coking, blending, manufacturing, and transportation; petrochemical production, processing, manufacturing, and transportation;

(2) Exports subject to the prohibition in paragraph (a) of this section, include not only goods and technology for use in third-country products uniquely suited for use in the petroleum or petrochemical industry, such as oilfield services equipment, but also goods and technology for use in products, such as computers, office equipment, construction equipment, or building materials, which are suitable for use in other industries, but which are intended specifically for use in the petroleum or petrochemical industry; and

(3) Goods and technology are intended specifically for a third-country product to be used in Libya if the particular product is being specifically manufactured to fill a Libyan order or if the manufacturer's sales of the particular product are predominantly to Libya.

(c) Specific licenses may be issued to authorize exports to third countries otherwise prohibited by paragraph (a)(2) of this section in appropriate cases, such as those involving extreme hardship or where the resulting third-country products will have insubstantial U.S. content.

(d) Exports of goods or technology from the United States to third countries are not prohibited where the exporter has reasonable cause to believe that:

(1) Except as otherwise provided in paragraph (a) of this section, the goods will be substantially transformed or incorporated into manufactured products before export to Libya, or

(2) The goods will come to rest in a third country for purposes other than reexport to Libya, e.g., for purposes of restocking the inventory of a distributor whose sales of the particular goods are not predominantly to Libya, or

(3) The technology will come to rest in a third country for purposes other than reexport to Libya.

(e) *Note:* Exports or reexports of goods and technical data, or of the direct products of technical data (regardless of U.S. content), not prohibited by this part may require authorization from the U.S. Department of Commerce pursuant to the Export Administration Act of 1979, as amended, 50 U.S.C. App. 2401 *et seq.*, and the Export Administration Regulations Implementing that Act, 15 CFR Parts 368 through 399.

[51 FR 22803, June 23, 1986; 51 FR 25635, July 15, 1986]

§ 550.410 **Release from bonded warehouse or foreign trade zone.**

Section 550.201 does not prohibit the release from a bonded warehouse or a foreign trade zone of goods of Libyan origin imported into a bonded warehouse or a foreign trade zone prior to the effective date.

§ 550.411 **Publications.**

For purposes of this part, publications include books, newspapers, magazines, films, phonograph records, tape recordings, photographs, microfilm, microfiche, and posters, including items described in the following:

(a) 15 CFR 399.1, Control List, Group 5, CL No. 7599I: microfilm that reproduces the content of certain publications, and similar materials.

(b) 15 CFR 399.1, Control List, Group 9, CL No. 7999I: certain publications and related materials.

§ 550.412 **Termination and acquisition of an interest of the Government of Libya.**

(a) Whenever a transaction licensed or authorized by or pursuant to this part results in the transfer of property (including any property interest) away from the Government of Libya, such property shall no longer be deemed to be property in which the Government of Libya has or has had an interest unless there exists in the property another such interest the transfer of which has not been effected pursuant to license or other authorization.

(b) Unless otherwise specifically provided in a license or authorization issued pursuant to this part, if property (including any property interest) is transferred to the Government of Libya, such property shall be deemed to be property in which there exists an interest of the Government of Libya.

[51 FR 2464, Jan. 16, 1986]

§ 550.413 **Payments to Libya prohibited.**

The prohibition of transfers of property or interests in property to the Government of Libya in § 550.209 applies to payments and transfers of any kind whatsoever, including payment of debt obligations, fees, taxes, and royalties owed to the Government of Libya, and also including payment or transfer of dividend checks, interest payments, and other periodic payments. Such payments may be made into blocked accounts as provided in § 550.511.

[51 FR 2464, Jan. 16, 1986]

§ 550.414 **Exports of Libyan-titled goods.**

(a) The prohibitions contained in § 550.209 shall apply to any goods in the possession or control of a U.S. person if the Government of Libya had title to such property as of 4:10 p.m. e.s.t., on January 8, 1986, or acquired title after such time.

(b) Section 550.209 does not prohibit the export to Libya of the goods described in paragraph (a) of this section if such export is either not prohibited by § 550.202 or permitted by an authorization or license issued pursuant to this part.

(c) If the goods described in paragraph (a) of this section are not exported as described in paragraph (b) of this section, the property shall remain blocked and no change in title or other transaction regarding such property is permitted, except pursuant to an authorization or license issued pursuant to this part.

[51 FR 2464, Jan. 16, 1986]

§ 550.415 **Advance payments.**

The prohibitions contained in § 550.209 do not apply to goods manufactured, consigned, or destined for export to Libya, if the Government of Libya did not have title to such goods on or at any time after 4:10 p.m. e.s.t., January 8, 1986. However, if such goods are not exported to Libya prior to 12:01 p.m. e.s.t., February 1, 1986, then any advance payment received in connection with such property is subject to the prohibitions contained in § 550.209.

[51 FR 2464, Jan. 16, 1986]

§ 550.416 **Imports of Libyan goods and purchases of goods from Libya.**

The prohibitions contained in § 550.209 shall not apply to the goods described in §§ 550.201 and 550.204 if the importation or purchase of such goods is either not prohibited by §§ 550.201 and 550.204 or permitted by an authorization or license issued pursuant to this part. However, any payments in connection with such imports or purchases are subject to the prohibitions contained in § 550.209.

[51 FR 2464, Jan. 16, 1986]

§ 550.417 Letters of credit.

(a) Q. Prior to 4:10 p.m. e.s.t., January 8, 1986, a bank that is a U.S. person has issued or confirmed a documentary letter of credit for the Government of Libya as account party in favor of a U.S. person. The bank does not hold funds for the Government of Libya out of which it could reimburse itself for payment under the letter of credit. The U.S. person presents documentary drafts for exports to Libya made after 4:10 p.m. e.s.t., January 8, 1986. May the bank pay the U.S. exporter against the drafts?

A. No. Such a payment is prohibited by §§ 550.206 and 550.209, as an extension of credit to the Government of Libya and a transfer of property in which there is an interest of the Government of Libya.

(b) Q. On the same facts as in paragraph (a), the bank holds deposits for the Government of Libya. May it pay on the letter of credit and debit the blocked funds for reimbursement?

A. No. A debit to a blocked account is prohibited by § 550.209 except as licensed.

(c) Q. On the same facts as in paragraph (a), the Government of Libya, after 4:10 p.m. e.s.t., January 8, 1986, transfers funds to the bank to collateralize the letter of credit for purposes of honoring the obligation to the U.S. exporter. Is the transfer authorized and may the bank pay against the draft?

A. Yes. In accordance with § 550.515, the transfer by the Government of Libya to the bank is licensed. The funds are not blocked and the bank is authorized to pay under the letter of credit and reimburse itself from the funds.

(d) Q. Prior to 4:10 p.m. e.s.t., January 8, 1986, a foreign bank confirms a documentary letter of credit issued by its U.S. agency or branch for a non-Libyan account party in favor of a Libyan entity. Can the U.S. agency or branch of the foreign bank transfer funds to that foreign bank in connection with that foreign bank's payment under the letter of credit?

A. No, the payment of the U.S. agency or branch is blocked, unless the foreign bank made payment to the Libyan entity prior to 4:10 p.m. e.s.t., January 8, 1986.

[51 FR 2465, Jan. 16, 1986]

§ 550.418 Payments from blocked accounts for U.S. exporters and other obligations prohibited.

No debits may be made to a blocked account to pay obligations to U.S. persons or other persons, including payment for goods, technology or services exported prior to 12:01 a.m. e.s.t., February 1, 1986, except as authorized pursuant to this part.

[51 FR 2465, Jan. 16, 1986]

§ 550.419 Acquisition of instruments, including bankers' acceptances.

Section 550.209 prohibits the acquisition by any U.S. person of any obligation, including bankers' acceptances, in which the documents evidencing the obligation indicate, or the U.S. person has actual knowledge, that the transaction being financed covers property in which, on or after 4:10 p.m. e.s.t., January 8, 1986, the Government of Libya has an interest of any nature whatsoever.

[51 FR 2465, Jan. 16, 1986]

§ 550.420 Indirect payments to the Government of Libya.

The prohibition in § 550.209 on payments or transfers to the Government of Libya applies to indirect payments (including reimbursement of a non-U.S. person for payment, as, for example, on a guarantee) made after 4:10 p.m. e.s.t., January 8, 1986.

[51 FR 2465, Jan. 16, 1986]

§ 550.421 Setoffs prohibited.

A setoff against a blocked account, whether by a bank or other U.S. person, is a prohibited transfer under § 550.209 if effected after 4:10 p.m. e.s.t., January 8, 1986.

[51 FR 2465, Jan. 16, 1986]

Subpart E—Licenses, Authorizations, and Statements of Licensing Policy

§ 550.501 Effect of license or authorization.

(a) No license or other authorization contained in this part, or otherwise issued by or under the direction of the Secretary of the Treasury pursuant to section 203 of the International Emergency Economic Powers Act, shall be deemed to authorize or validate any transaction effected prior to the issuance of the license, unless such license or other authorization specifically so provides.

(b) No regulation, ruling, instruction, or license authorizes a transaction prohibited under this part unless the regulation, ruling, instruction, or license is issued by the Treasury Department and specifically refers to this part. No regulation, ruling, instruction, or license referring to this part shall be deemed to authorize any transactions prohibited by any provision of Parts 500, 505, 515, 520, 535, 540, or 545 of this chapter unless the regulation, ruling, instruction or license specifically refers to such provision.

(c) Any regulation, ruling, instruction, or license authorizing a transaction otherwise prohibited under this part has the effect of removing a prohibition or prohibitions in Subpart B from the transaction, but only to the extent specifically stated by its terms. Unless the regulation, ruling, instruction, or license otherwise specifies, such an authorization does not create any right, duty, obligation, claim, or interest in, or with respect to, any property which would not otherwise exist under ordinary principles of law.

§ 550.502 Exclusion from licenses and authorizations.

The Secretary of the Treasury reserves the right to exclude any person or property from the operation of any license or to restrict the applicability thereof to any person or property. Such action shall be binding upon all persons receiving actual or constructive notice thereof.

§ 550.503 Imports pursuant to Executive Order 12538.

Petroleum products loaded aboard maritime vessels at any time prior to November 17, 1985 may be imported into the United States if such importation would be permitted pursuant to Executive Order 12538 of November 15, 1985 (50 FR 47527).

§ 550.504 Certain exports authorized.

All transactions ordinarily incident to the exportation of any item, commodity, or product from the United States to or destined for Libya are authorized if such exports are authorized under one or more of the following regulations administered by the Department of Commerce:

(a) 15 CFR 371.6, General license BAGGAGE: accompanied and unaccompanied baggage;

(b) 15 CFR 371.13, General license GUS: shipments to personnel and agencies of the U.S. Government;

(c) 15 CFR 371.18, General license GIFT: shipments of gift parcels;

(d) 15 CFR 379.3, General license GTDA: technical data available to all destinations.

§ 550.505 Certain imports for diplomatic or official personnel authorized.

All transactions ordinarily incident to the importation of any goods or services into the United States from Libya are authorized if such imports are destined for official or personal use by personnel employed by Libyan missions to international organizations located in the United States, and such imports are not for resale.

§ 550.506 Certain services relating to participation in various events authorized.

The importation of services of Libyan origin into the United States is authorized where a Libyan national enters the United States on a visa issued by the State Department for the purpose of participating in a public conference, performance, exhibition or similar event.

§ 550.507 Import of publications authorized.

The importation into the United States is authorized of all Libyan publications as defined in § 550.411.

§ 550.508 Import of certain gifts authorized.

The importation into the United States is authorized for goods of Libyan origin sent as gifts to persons in the United States where the value of the gift is not more than $100.

§ 550.509 Import of accompanied baggage authorized.

Persons entering the United States directly or indirectly from Libya are authorized to import into the United States personal accompanied baggage normally incident to travel.

§ 550.510 Telecommunications and mail transactions authorized.

All transactions of common carriers incident to the receipt or transmission of telecommunications and mail between the United States and Libya are authorized.

§ 550.511 Payments to blocked accounts in domestic banks.

(a) Any payment or transfer of credit, including any payment or transfer by any U.S. person outside the United States, to a blocked account in a domestic bank in the name of the Government of Libya is hereby authorized, provided that such payment or transfer shall not be made from any blocked account if such payment or transfer represents, directly or indirectly, a transfer of any interest of the Government of Libya to any other country or person.

(b) This section does not authorize any transfer from a blocked account within the United States to an account held by any bank outside the United States. This section only authorizes payment into a blocked account held by a domestic bank as defined in § 550.317.

(c) This section does not authorize:

(1) Any payment or transfer to any blocked account held in a name other than that of the Government of Libya where such government is the ultimate beneficiary of such payment or transfer; or

(2) Any foreign exchange transaction in the United States including, but not by way of limitation, any transfer of credit, or payment of an obligation, expressed in terms of the currency of any foreign country.

(d) This section does not authorize any payment or transfer of credit comprising an integral part of a transaction which cannot be effected without the subsequent issuance of a further license.

(e) This section does not authorize the crediting of the proceeds of the sale of securities held in a blocked account or a sub-account thereof, or the income derived from such securities to a blocked account or sub-account under any name or designation which differs from the name or designation of the specific blocked account or sub-account in which such securities were held.

(f) This section does not authorize any payment or transfer from a blocked account in a domestic bank to a blocked account held under any name or designation which differs from the name or designation of the specified blocked account or sub-account from which the payment or transfer is made.

(g) The authorization in paragraph (a) of this section is subject to the condition that written notification from the domestic bank receiving an authorized payment or transfer is furnished by the transferor to the Office of Foreign Assets Control confirming that the payment or transfer has been deposited in a blocked account under the regulations in this part and providing the account number, the name and address of the Libyan entity in whose name the account is held, and the name and address of the domestic bank.

(h) This section authorizes transfer of a blocked demand deposit account to a blocked interest-bearing account in the name of the same person at the instruction of the depositor at any time. If such transfer is to a blocked account in a different domestic bank, such bank must furnish notification as described in paragraph (g) of this section.

[51 FR 2465, Jan. 16, 1986]

§ 550.512 **Payment of certain checks and drafts and documentary letters of credit.**

(a) A bank which is a U.S. person is hereby authorized to make payments from blocked accounts within such bank of checks and drafts drawn or issued prior to 4:10 p.m. e.s.t., January 8, 1986, provided that:

(1) The amount involved in any one payment, acceptance, or debit does not exceed $5,000; or

(2) The check or draft was in process of collection by a bank which is a U.S. person on or prior to such date and does not exceed $50,000; or

(3) The check or draft is in payment for goods furnished or services rendered by a non-Libyan entity prior to 4:10 p.m. e.s.t., January 8, 1986.

(4) The authorization contained in paragraph (a) of this section, shall expire at 12:01 a.m., February 17, 1986.

(b) Payments are authorized from blocked accounts of documentary drafts drawn under irrevocable letters of credit issued or confirmed in favor of a non-Libyan entity by a bank which is a U.S. person prior to 4:10 p.m. e.s.t., January 8, 1986, provided that (1) the goods that are the subject of the payment under the letter of credit have been exported prior to 4:10 p.m. e.s.t., January 8, 1986; and (2) payment under the letter of credit is made by 12:01 a.m. e.s.t., February 17, 1986.

(c) Paragraphs (a) and (b) of this section, do not authorize any payment to a Libyan entity except payments into a blocked account in a domestic bank in accordance with § 550.511.

[51 FR 2465, Jan. 16, 1986]

§ 550.513 **Completion of certain securities transactions.**

(a) Banking institutions within the United States are hereby authorized to complete, on or before January 21, 1986, purchases and sales made prior to 4:10 p.m. e.s.t., January 8, 1986, of securities purchased or sold for the account of the Government of Libya provided the following terms and conditions are complied with, respectively:

(1) The proceeds of such sale are credited to a blocked account in a banking institution within the United States in the name of the person for whose account the sale was made; and

(2) The securities so purchased are held in a blocked account in a banking institution within the United States in the name of the person for whose account the purchase was made.

(b) This section does not authorize the crediting of the proceeds of the sale of securities held in a blocked account or a sub-account thereof, to a blocked account or sub-account under any name or designation which differs from the name or designation of the specific blocked account or sub-account in which such securities were held.

[51 FR 2466, Jan. 16, 1986]

§ 550.514 **Transfers between accounts located in the United States for credit to Government of Libya.**

Transfers are authorized by order of a foreign bank which is not a Libyan entity from its account in a domestic bank (directly or through a foreign branch or subsidiary of a domestic bank) to an account held by a domestic bank (directly or through a foreign branch or subsidiary) for a second foreign bank which is not a Libyan entity and which in turn credits an account held by it abroad for the Government of Libya. For purposes of this section, "foreign bank" includes a foreign subsidiary, but not a foreign branch, of a domestic bank.

[51 FR 2466, Jan. 16, 1986]

§ 550.515 **Payment by the Government of Libya of obligations to persons within the United States.**

(a) The transfer of funds after 4:10 p.m. e.s.t., January 8, 1986, by, through, or to any banking institution or other person within the United States solely for purposes of payment of obligations owed by the Government of Libya to persons within the United States is authorized, provided that there is no debit to a blocked account. Property is not blocked by virtue of being transferred or received pursuant to this section.

(b) A person receiving payment under this section may distribute all or part of that payment to anyone, provided that any such payment to the Government of Libya must be to a blocked account in a domestic bank.

[51 FR 2466, Jan. 16, 1986]

§ 550.516 Unblocking of foreign currency deposits held by U.S. persons overseas.

Deposits in currencies other than U.S. dollars held abroad by U.S. persons are unblocked, provided, however, that conversions of blocked dollar deposits into foreign currencies are not authorized.

[51 FR 2466, Jan. 16, 1986]

§ 550.560 Transactions related to travel to, and residence within, Libya by immediate family members of Libyan nationals.

(a) *General License.* Subject to compliance with the registration requirements set forth in paragraph (d) of this section, the following transactions are authorized in connection with travel to, from and within Libya and residence within Libya by U.S. citizens and permanent resident aliens who are immediate family members of Libyan nationals:

(1) All transportation-related transactions ordinarily incident to travel to, from and within Libya.

(2) All transactions ordinarily incident to residence within Libya, including payment of living expenses and the acquisition in Libya of goods for personal use or consumption there.

(3) All transactions incident to the processing and payment of checks, drafts, traveler's checks, and similar instruments negotiated in Libya by any person licensed under this section.

(4) The purchase within Libya and importation as accompanied baggage of items for noncommercial use, provided that the aggregate value of such purchases imported into the United States conforms to limitations established by the United States Customs Service.

(b) *Definition.* For purposes of this section, the term "immediate family member" means a spouse, child, parent, mother-in-law, father-in-law, son-in-law or daughter-in-law.

(c) *Specific Licenses.* Specific licenses authorizing the transactions set forth in paragraph (a) of this section may be issued in appropriate cases to persons similarly situated to the persons described in paragraph (b) of this section where such specific licenses are necessary to preserve the integrity of established family units.

(d) *Registration.* (1) The general license set forth in this section is available only to those U.S. citizens and permanent resident aliens who register their eligibility in writing with either of the following:

Embassy of Belgium, Ali Obeydah St., Ibn El Jarah No. 1, Immeuble Chirlando, Tripoli, Libya, Telephone: 37797

or

Licensing Section, Office of Foreign Assets Control, Department of the Treasury, Washington, DC 20220, Telephone: (202) 376–0236.

Registration under this paragraph is deemed complete upon receipt at one of the above addresses of a letter, signed by or on behalf of each eligible U.S. citizen or permanent resident alien being registered, containing the following information:

(i) The name and the date and place of birth of the U.S. citizen(s) or permanent resident alien(s) registering (the "registrant"), including the name on which the registrant's most recent U.S. passport or Alien Registration Receipt Card was issued, if different;

(ii) If applicable, the place and date of the registrant's naturalization as a U.S. citizen, and the number of the registrant's naturalization certificate, *or,* for permanent resident aliens, the Alien Registration Number of the registrant's Alien Registration Receipt Card;

(iii) The name, relationship, and address of the Libyan national with whom the registrant resides as an immediate family member and whose relationship forms the basis for the registrants's eligibility under this general license; and

(iv) The number and issue date of the registrant's current U.S. passport, and the most recent date on which the passport was validated by the U.S. Department of State for travel to Libya; *or,* if the registrant does not hold a current U.S. passport, the country, issue date, and number of the registrant's current passport or other travel document, if any.

(2) The lack of validation of a registrant's U.S. passport for travel to Libya does not affect eligibility for the benefits of the general license set forth in this section for persons who otherwise qualify. Current information on travel document status as requested in paragraph (d)(1) of this section must, however, be furnished to register a registrant's eligibility for this license.

(e) *Other Requirements.* The general license set forth in this section shall not operate to relieve any person licensed hereunder from compliance with any other U.S. legal requirements applicable to the transactions authorized pursuant to paragraph (a) of this section.

[51 FR 19752, June 2, 1986]

§ 550.568 Certain standby letters of credit and performance bonds.

(a) Notwithstanding any other provision of law, payment into a blocked account in a domestic bank by an issuing or confirming bank under a standby letter of credit in favor of a Libyan entity is prohibited by § 550.209 and not authorized, notwithstanding the provisions of § 550.511, if either (1) a specific license has been issued pursuant to the provisions of paragraph (b) of this section or (2) ten business days have not expired after notice to the account party pursuant to paragraph (b) of this section.

(b) Whenever an issuing or confirming bank shall receive such demand for payment under such a standby letter of credit, it shall promptly notify the account party. The account party may then apply within five business days for a specific license authorizing the account party to establish a blocked account on its books in the name of the Libyan entity in the amount payable under the credit, in lieu of payment by the issuing or confirming bank into a blocked account and reimbursement therefor by the account party. Nothing in this section relieves any such bank or such account party from giving any notice of defense against payment or reimbursement that is required by applicable law.

(c) Where there is outstanding a demand for payment under a standby letter of credit, and the issuing or confirming bank has been enjoined from making payment, upon removal of the injunction, the account party may apply for a specific license for the same purpose and in the same manner as that set forth in paragraph (b) of this section. The issuing or confirming bank shall not make payment under the standby letter of credit unless (1) ten business days have expired since the bank has received notice of the removal of the injunction and (2) a specific license issued to the account party pursuant to the provisions of this paragraph has not been presented to the bank.

(d) If necessary to assure the availability of the funds blocked, the Secretary may at any time require the payment of the amounts due under any letter of credit described in paragraph (a) of this section into a blocked account in a domestic bank or the supplying of any form of security deemed necessary.

(e) Nothing in this section precludes the account party on any standby letter of credit or any other person from at any time contesting the legality of the demand from Libyan entity or from raising any other legal defense to payment under the standby letter of credit.

(f) This section does not affect the obligation of the various parties of the instruments covered by this section if the instruments and payments thereunder are subsequently unblocked.

(g) For the purposes of this section, (1) the term "standby letter of credit" shall mean a letter of credit securing performance of, or repayment of any advance payments or deposits under, a contract with the Government of Libya, or any similar obligation in the nature of a performance bond; and (2) the term "account party" shall mean the person for whose account the standby letter of credit is opened.

(h) The regulations do not authorize any U.S. person to reimburse a non-U.S. bank for payment to the Government of Libya under a standby letter of credit, except by payments into a blocked account in accordance with

§ 550.511 or paragraph (b) or (c) of this section.

(i) A person receiving a specific license under paragraph (b) or (c) of this section shall certify to the Office of Foreign Assets Control within five business days after receipt of that license that it has established the blocked account on its books as provided for in those paragraphs. However, in appropriate cases, this time period may be extended upon application to the Office of Foreign Assets Control when the account party has filed a petition with an appropriate court seeking a judicial order barring payment by the issuing or confirming bank.

(j) The extension or renewal of a standby letter of credit is authorized.

[51 FR 2466, Jan. 16, 1986]

Subpart F—Reports

§ 550.601 Required records.

Every person engaging in any transaction subject to this part shall keep a full and accurate record of each transaction in which he engages, including any transaction effected pursuant to license or otherwise, and such records shall be available for examination for at least two years after the date of such transaction.

§ 550.602 Reports to be furnished on demand.

Every person is required to furnish under oath, in the form of reports or otherwise, at any time as may be required, complete information relative to any transaction subject to this part, regardless of whether such transaction is effected pursuant to license or otherwise. Such reports may be required to include the production of any books of account, contracts, letters, and other papers connected with any transaction in the custody or control of the persons required to make such reports. Reports with respect to transactions may be required either before or after such transactions are completed. The Secretary of the Treasury may, through any person or agency, conduct investigations, hold hearings, administer oaths, examine witnesses, receive evidence, take depositions, and require by subpoena the attendance and testimony of witnesses and the production of all books, papers, and documents relating to any matter under investigation.

[51 FR 1354, Jan. 10, 1986, as amended at 51 FR 2467, Jan. 16, 1986]

§ 550.605 Reports of U.S. persons with foreign affiliates that engage in Libyan transactions.

(a) *Requirement for reports.* Reports are required to be filed on or before August 15, 1986, in the manner prescribed in this section, with respect to all foreign affiliates that engaged in Libyan transactions at any time between July 1, 1985 and June 30, 1986.

(b) *Who must report.* A report must be filed by each U.S. person owning or controlling any foreign affiliate that engaged in Libyan transactions at any time between July 1, 1985 and June 30, 1986. A single U.S. person within a consolidated or affiliated group may be designated to report on each foreign affiliate of the U.S. members of the group. Such centralized reporting may be done by the U.S. person who owns or controls, or has been delegated authority to file on behalf of, the remaining U.S. persons in the group.

(1) *Reporting exemption.* A U.S. person is exempt from the filing requirements of this section if the Libyan transactions of all foreign affiliates of such person, and of such person's consolidated or affiliated group, for the period from July 1, 1985, through June 30, 1986, had an aggregate value not exceeding $50,000.

(2) *U.S. branches of foreign entities.* The Libyan transactions of an entity organized or located outside the United States, and which is not owned or controlled by U.S. persons, are not subject to the reporting requirements of this section merely because such foreign entity has a U.S. branch, office, or agency that constitutes a U.S. person pursuant to § 550.308.

(c) *Contents of report.* The following information shall be provided concerning each foreign affiliate that engaged in Libyan transactions during the Reporting Period (with responses numbered to correspond with the numbers used below):

(1) Identification of reporting U.S. person.

(i) Name;

(ii) Address (indicate both street and mailing address, if different);

(iii) Name and telephone number of individual to contact (indicate title or position, if applicable);

(iv) Relationship to foreign affiliate and percentage of direct and/or indirect ownership.

(2) Identification of foreign affiliate.

(i) Full entity name;

(ii) Address (street and mailing addresses);

(iii) Country in which organized or incorporated, and entity type (corporation, partnership, limited liability company, etc.).

(3) Information on Libyan transactions of each foreign affiliate. (Data provided in response to paragraphs (c)(3) (i), (ii), (iii), and (iv) of this section shall be separately stated for Periods I and II, as defined in paragraph (e)(3) of this section, with aggregate data in response to paragraphs (c)(3) (i), (iii), and (v) of this section further segregated between sales and purchase transactions.)

(i) Brief but complete description of the nature of goods or technology sold or purchased, or of services rendered or purchased, by the foreign affiliate in Libyan transactions during the Reporting Period, and, for each type of transaction, identification of the Libyan end-user(s) or vendor(s) of the goods, technology, or services;

(ii) Number of employees involved in Libyan transactions to the extent of at least 25% of their time during Period I or Period II, categorized by nationality and location (example: Five [nationality] employees in Libya);

(iii) Approximate amount (in U.S. dollars) of revenue from, or expense for, Libyan transactions of the foreign affiliate during the Reporting Period;

(iv) Approximate amount (in U.S. dollars) of (A) taxes, (B) rents, and (C) royalties (state each separately) paid to the Government of Libya or Libyan entities (as defined in §§ 550.304 and 550.319) during the Reporting Period;

(v) Anticipated revenue from, or expense for, Libyan transactions of the foreign affiliate (in U.S. dollars) for the period from July 1, 1986 through June 30, 1987;

(vi) Anticipated number of employees involved in Libyan transactions to the extent of at least 25% of their time for the period from July 1, 1986 through June 30, 1987.

(d) *Where to report.* Reports should be prepared in triplicate, two copies of which are to be filed with the Census Section, Unit 605, Office of Foreign Assets Control, Department of the Treasury, Washington, DC 20220. The third copy shall be retained for the reporter's business records.

(e) *Definitions.* For the purposes of this section, the following terms have the meanings indicated below:

(1) "Foreign affiliate" means an entity (other than a U.S. person as defined in § 550.308) which is organized or located outside the United States, and which is owned or controlled by a U.S. person or persons.

(2) "Libyan transactions" means (i) sales of goods or technology, or the provision of services (including brokerage and financial services), to, or for the benefit of, the Government of Libya, persons within Libya, or Libyan entities wherever located, or (ii) purchases of goods, technology, or services from the Government of Libya, persons within Libya, or Libyan entities wherever located.

(3) "Reporting Period" means the 12-month period from July 1, 1985, through June 30, 1986. The Reporting Period is divided into two six-month periods: "Period I" consists of the six-month period ended December 31, 1985; "Period II" consists of the six-month period ending June 30, 1986.

[51 FR 25634, July 15, 1986; 51 FR 26687, July 25, 1986]

§ 550.630 Reports on Form TFR–630 (TDF 90–22.32).

(a) *Requirement for reports.* Reports on Form TFR–630 (TDF 90–22.32) are hereby required to be filed on or before November 20, 1987, in the manner prescribed herein, with respect to all property held by any United States person at any time between 4:10 p.m. e.s.t., January 8, 1986, and June 30, 1987, in which property the Government of Libya or any

Libyan entity has or has had any interest.

(b) *Who must report.* Reports on Form TFR-630 (TDF 90-22.32) must be filed by each of the following:

(1) Any U.S. person, or his successor, who at 4:10 p.m. e.s.t., January 8, 1986, or any subsequent date up to and including June 30, 1987, had in his custody, possession or control, directly or indirectly, in trust or otherwise, property in which there was, within such period, any direct or indirect interest of the Government of Libya or any Libyan entity, whether or not such property continued to be held by that person on June 30, 1987; and

(2) Any business or non-business entity in the United States in which the Government of Libya or any Libyan entity held any financial interest on January 8, 1986, or any subsequent date up to and including June 30, 1987.

(c) *Property not required to be reported.* A report on Form TFR-630 (TDF 90-22.32) is not required with respect to:

(1) Property of a private Libyan national; and

(2) Patents, copyrights, trademarks and inventions, but this exemption shall not constitute a waiver of any reporting requirement with respect to royalties due and unpaid.

(d) *Filing Form TFR-630 (TDF 90-22.32).* Reports on Form TFR-630 (TDF 90-22.32) shall be prepared in triplicate. On or before November 20, 1987, two copies shall be sent in a set to Unit 630, Office of Foreign Assets Control, Department of the Treasury, Washington, DC 20220. The third copy must be retained with the reporter's records.

(e) *Certification.* Every report on Form TFR-630 (TDF 90-22.32) shall contain the certification required in Part E of the form. Failure to complete the certification shall render the report ineffective, and the submission of such a report shall not constitute compliance with this section.

(f) *Confidentiality of reports.* Reports on Form TFR-630 (TDF 90-22.32) are regarded as privileged and confidential.

(Approved by the Office of Management and Budget under control number 1505-0102)

[52 FR 35548, Sept. 22, 1987]

§ 550.635 **Reports on Form TFR-635 (TDF 90-22.33).**

(a) *Requirement for reports.* Reports on Form TFR-635 (TDF 90-22.33) are hereby required to be filed on or before November 20, 1987, in the manner prescribed herein, with respect to claims for losses due to expropriation, nationalization, or other taking of property or businesses in Libya, including any special measures such as Libyan exchange controls directed against such property or businesses; claims for debt defaults, for damages for breach of contract or similar damages; and personal claims for salaries or for injury to person or property.

(b) *Who must report.* Reports on Form TFR-635 (TDF 90-22.33) must be filed by every U.S. person who had a claim outstanding against the Government of Libya or any Libyan entity which arose before June 30, 1987. No report is to be submitted by a U.S. branch of a foreign firm not owned or controlled by a U.S. person.

(c) *Filing Form TFR-635 (TDF 90-22.33).* Reports on Form TFR-635 (TDF 90-22.33) shall be prepared in triplicate. On or before November 20, 1987, two copies shall be sent in a set to Unit 635, Office of Foreign Assets Control, Department of the Treasury, Washington, DC 20220. The third copy must be retained with the reporter's record.

(d) *Certification.* Every report on Form TFR-635 (TDF 90-22.33) shall contain the certification required on Part C of the form. Failure to complete the certification shall render the report ineffective, and the submission of such a report shall not constitute compliance with this section.

(e) *Confidentiality of reports.* Reports on Form TFR-635 (TDF 90-22.33) are regarded as privileged and confidential.

(Approved by the Office of Management and Budget under control number 1505-0103)

[52 FR 35549, Sept. 22, 1987]

Subpart G—Penalties

§ 550.701 Penalties.

(a) Attention is directed to section 206 of the International Emergency Economic Powers Act, 50 U.S.C. 1705, which provides in part:

A civil penalty of not to exceed $10,000 may be imposed on any person who violates any license, order, or regulation issued under this title.

Whoever willfully violates any license, order, or regulation issued under this title shall, upon conviction, be fined not more than $50,000, or, if a natural person, may be imprisoned for not more than ten years, or both; and any officer, director, or agent of any corporation who knowingly participates in such violation may be punished by a like fine, imprisonment, or both.

This section of the International Emergency Economic Powers Act is applicable to violations of any provision of this part and to violations of the provisions of any license, ruling, regulation, order, direction, or instruction issued by or pursuant to the direction or authorization of the Secretary of the Treasury pursuant to this part or otherwise under the International Emergency Economic Powers Act.

(b) Attention is also directed to 18 U.S.C. 1001, which provides:

Whoever, in any matter within the jurisdiction of any department or agency of the United States knowingly and willfully falsifies, conceals or covers up by any trick, scheme, or device a material fact, or makes any false, fictitious or fraudulent statements or representation or makes or uses any false writing or document knowing the same to contain any false, fictitious or fraudulent statement or entry, shall be fined not more than $10,000 or imprisoned not more than five years, or both.

(c) Violations of this part may also be subject to relevant provisions of the Customs laws and other applicable laws.

§ 550.702 Detention of shipments.

Import shipments into the United States of goods of Libyan origin in violation of § 550.201 and export shipments from the United States of goods destined for Libya in violation of § 550.202 shall be detained. No such import or export shall be permitted to proceed, except as specifically authorized by the Secretary of the Treasury. Such shipments shall be subject to licensing, penalties or forfeiture action, under the Customs laws or other applicable provision of law, depending on the circumstances.

§ 550.703 Prepenalty notice.

(a) *When required.* If the Director of the Office of Foreign Assets Control (hereinafter "Director) has reasonable cause to believe that there has occurred a violation of any provision of this part or a violation of the provisions of any license, ruling, regulation, order, direction or instruction issued by or pursuant to the direction or authorization of the Secretary of the Treasury pursuant to this part or otherwise under the International Emergency Economic Powers Act, and the Director determines that further proceedings are warranted, he shall issue to the person concerned a notice of his intent to impose a monetary penalty. The prepenalty notice shall be issued whether or not another agency has taken any action with respect to this matter.

(b) *Contents*—(1) *Facts of violation.* The prepenalty notice shall:

(i) Describe the violation.

(ii) Specify the laws and regulations allegedly violated.

(iii) State the amount of the proposed monetary penalty.

(2) *Right to make presentations.* The prepenalty notice also shall inform the person of his right to make a written presentation within thirty (30) days of mailing of the notice as to why a monetary penalty should not be imposed, or, if imposed, why it should be in a lesser amount than proposed.

[53 FR 7357, Mar. 8, 1988]

§ 550.704 Presentation responding to prepenalty notice.

(a) *Time within which to respond.* The named person shall have 30 days from the date of mailing of the prepenalty notice to make a written presentation to the Director.

(b) *Form and contents of written presentation.* The written presentation need not be in any particular form, but shall contain information sufficient to indicate that it is in response to the prepenalty notice. It should contain responses to the allegations in the prepenalty notice and set forth the reasons why the person believes the penalty should not be imposed or, if imposed, why it should be in a lesser amount than proposed.

[53 FR 7357, Mar. 8, 1988]

§ 550.705 Penalty notice.

(a) *No violation.* If, after considering any presentations made in response to the prepenalty notice, the Director determines that there was no violation by the person named in the prepenalty notice, he promptly shall notify the person in writing of that determination and that no monetary penalty will be imposed.

(b) *Violation.* If, after considering any presentations made in response to the prepenalty notice, the Director determines that there was a violation by the person named in the prepenalty notice, he promptly shall issue a written notice of the imposition of the monetary penalty to that person.

[53 FR 7358, Mar. 8, 1988]

§ 550.706 Referral to United States Department of Justice.

In the event that the person named does not pay the penalty imposed pursuant to this subpart or make payment arrangements acceptable to the Director within thirty days of the mailing of the written notice of the imposition of the penalty, the matter shall be referred to the United States Department of Justice for appropriate action to recover the penalty in a civil suit in a Federal district court.

[53 FR 7358, Mar. 8, 1988]

Subpart H—Procedures

§ 550.801 Licensing.

(a) *General licenses.* General licenses have been issued authorizing under appropriate terms and conditions certain types of transactions which are subject to the prohibitions contained in Subpart B of this part. All such licenses are set forth in Subpart E of this part. It is the policy of the Office of Foreign Assets Control not to grant applications for specific licenses authorizing transactions to which the provisions of an outstanding general license are applicable. Persons availing themselves of certain general licenses may be required to file reports and statements in accordance with the instructions specified in those licenses.

(b) *Specific licenses*—(1) *General course of procedure.* Transactions subject to the prohibitions contained in Subpart B of this part which are not authorized by general license may be effected only under specific licenses. The specific licensing activities of the Office of Foreign Assets Control are performed by its Washington office and by the Foreign Assets Control Division of the Federal Reserve Bank of New York.

(2) *Applications for specific licenses.* Applications for specific licenses to engage in any transaction prohibited under this part are to be filed in duplicate with the Federal Reserve Bank of New York, Foreign Assets Control Division, 33 Liberty Street, New York, NY 10045. Any person having an interest in a transaction or proposed transaction may file an application for a license authorizing such transaction, and there is no requirement that any other person having an interest in such transaction shall or should join in making or filing such application.

(3) *Information to be supplied.* The applicant must supply all information specified by the respective forms and instructions. Such documents as may be relevant shall be attached to each application except that documents previously filed with the Office of Foreign Assets Control may, where appropriate, be incorporated by reference. Applicants may be required to furnish such further information as is deemed necessary to a proper determination by the Office of Foreign Assets Control. Failure to furnish necessary information will not be excused because of any provision of Libyan law. If an applicant or other party in interest desires to present additional information or discuss or argue the application, he may do so at any time before or after decision. Arrangements for oral presentation should be made with the Office of Foreign Assets Control.

(4) *Effect of denial.* The denial of a license does not preclude the reopening of an application or the filing of a

further application. The applicant or any other party in interest may at any time request explanation of the reasons for a denial by correspondence or personal interview.

(5) *Reports under specific licenses.* As a condition of the issuance of any license, the licensee may be required to file reports with respect to the transaction covered by the license, in such form and at such times and places as may be prescribed in the license or otherwise.

(6) *Issuance of license.* Licenses will be issued by the Office of Foreign Assets Control acting on behalf of the Secretary of the Treasury or by the Federal Reserve Bank of New York, acting in accordance with such regulations, rulings, and instructions as the Secretary of the Treasury or the Office of Foreign Assets Control may from time to time prescribe, or licenses may be issued by the Secretary of the Treasury acting directly or through a designated person, agency, or instrumentality.

§ 550.802 Decisions.

The Office of Foreign Assets Control or the Federal Reserve Bank of New York will advise each applicant of the decision respecting filed applications. The decision of the Office of Foreign Assets Control with respect to an application shall constitute a final agency action.

§ 550.803 Amendment, modification, or revocation.

The provisions of this part and any rulings, licenses, authorizations, instructions, orders or forms issued hereunder may be amended, modified, or revoked at any time.

§ 550.804 Rulemaking.

(a) All rules and other public documents are issued by the Secretary of the Treasury upon recommendation of the Director of the Office of Foreign Assets Control. Except to the extent that there is involved any military, naval, or foreign affairs function of the United States or any matter relating to agency management or personnel or to public property, loans, grants, benefits, or contracts, and except when interpretive rules, general statements of policy, or rules of agency organization, practice, or procedure are involved, or when notice and public procedure are impracticable, unnecessary, or contrary to the public interest, interested persons will be afforded an opportunity to participate in rulemaking through the submission of written data, views, or arguments, with oral presentation at the discretion of the Director. In general, rulemaking by the Office of Foreign Assets Control involves foreign affairs functions of the United States. Wherever possible, however, it is the practice to hold informal consultations with interested groups or persons before the issuance of any rule or other public document.

(b) Any interested person may petition the Director of the Office of Foreign Assets Control in writing for the issuance, amendment or revocation of any rule.

§ 550.805 Delegation by the Secretary of the Treasury.

Any action which the Secretary of the Treasury is authorized to take pursuant to Executive Order 12543 may be taken by the Director of the Office of Foreign Assets Control, or by any other person to whom the Secretary of the Treasury has delegated authority so to act.

§ 550.806 Rules governing availability of information.

(a) The records of the Office of Foreign Assets Control which are required by 5 U.S.C. 552 to be made available to the public shall be made available in accordance with the definitions, procedures, payment of fees, and other provisions of the regulations on the disclosure of records of the Office of the Secretary and of other bureaus and offices of the Department issued under 5 U.S.C. 552 and published as Part 1 of this Title 31 of the Code of Federal Regulations.

(b) Any form issued for use in connection with this part may be obtained in person from or by writing to the Office of Foreign Assets Control, Treasury Department, Washington, DC 20220, or the Foreign Assets Control Division, Federal Reserve Bank of

New York, 33 Liberty Street, New York, NY 10045.

§ 550.807 Customs procedures: Merchandise specified in § 550.201.

(a) With respect to merchandise specified in § 550. 201, appropriate Customs officers shall not accept or allow any:

(1) Entry for consumption or warehousing (including any appraisement entry, any entry of goods imported in the mails, regardless of value, and any informal entry);

(2) Entry for immediate exportation;

(3) Entry for transportation and exportation;

(4) Entry for immediate transportation;

(5) Withdrawal from warehouse;

(6) Entry, transfer or withdrawal from a foreign trade zone; or

(7) Manipulation or manufacture in a warehouse or in a foreign trade zone, unless:

(i) The merchandise was imported prior to 12:01 a.m., Eastern Standard Time, February 1, 1986, or

(ii) A specific license pursuant to this part is presented, or

(iii) Instructions from the Office of Foreign Assets Control, either directly or through the Federal Reserve Bank of New York, authorizing the transactions are received.

(b) Whenever a specific license is presented to an appropriate Customs officer in accordance with this section, one additional legible copy of the entry, withdrawal or other appropriate document with respect to the merchandise involved shall be filed with the appropriate Customs officers at the port where the transaction is to take place. Each copy of any such entry, withdrawal or other appropriate document, including the additional copy, shall bear plainly on its face the number of the license pursuant to which it is filed. The original copy of the specific license shall be presented to the appropriate Customs officers in respect of each such transactions and shall bear a notation in ink by the licensee or person presenting the license showing the description, quantity and value of the merchandise to be entered, withdrawn or otherwise dealt with. This notation shall be so placed and so written that there will exist no possibility of confusing it with anything placed on the license at the time of its issuance. If the license in fact authorizes the entry, withdrawal or other transactions with regard to the merchandise, the appropriate Customs officer, or other authorized Customs employee, shall verify the notation by signing or initialing it after first assuring himself that it accurately describes the merchandise it purports to represent. The license shall thereafter be returned to the person presenting it and the additional copy of the entry, withdrawal or other appropriate document shall be forwarded by the appropriate Customs officer to the Office of Foreign Assets Control.

(c) If it is unclear whether an entry, withdrawal or other action affected by this section requires a specific Foreign Assets Control license, the appropriate Customs officer shall withhold action thereon and shall advise such person to communicate directly with the Federal Reserve Bank of New York, Foreign Assets Control Division, 33 Liberty Street, New York, New York 10045 to request that instructions be sent to the Customs officer to authorize him to take action with regard thereto.

Subpart I—Miscellaneous

§ 550.901 Paperwork Reduction Act notice.

The information collection requirements in §§ 550.210(d), 550.511 (g) and (h), 550.568 (b), (c), and (i), 550.601, 550.602, and 550.801(b) (2), (3), and (5) have been approved by the Office of Management and Budget and assigned control number 1505-0092. The information collection requirements in §§ 550.560 (c) and (d) and 550.605 have been approved by the Office of Management and Budget and assigned control number 1505-0093.

[51 FR 28933, Aug. 13, 1986]

Subpart G—Penalties

§ 530.701 Penalties.

(a) Attention is directed to section 5(b) of the United Nations Participation Act of 1945 (22 U.S.C. 287(c)), which provides in part:

Any person who willfully violates or evades or attempts to violate or evade any order, rule, or regulation issued by the President pursuant to subsection (a) of this section shall, upon conviction be fined not more than $10,000, or, if a natural person, be imprisoned for not more than 10 years, or both; and the officer, director, or agent of any corporation who knowingly participates in such violation or evasion shall be punished by a like fine, imprisonment, or both, and any property, funds, securities, papers, or other articles or documents, or any vessel, together with her tackle, apparel, furniture, and equipment, or vehicle, or aircraft, concerned in such violation shall be forfeited to the United States. (Dec. 20, 1945, ch. 583, sec. 5, 59 Stat. 620; Oct. 10, 1949, ch. 660, sec. 3, 63 Stat. 735.)

This section of the United Nations Participation Act of 1945 is applicable to violations of any provisions of this part and to violations of the provisions of any license, ruling, regulation, order, direction or instruction issued pursuant to this part or otherwise under section 5 of the United Nations Participation Act, Executive Order 11322, and Executive Order 11419.

(b) Attention is also directed to 18 U.S.C. 1001 which provides:

Whoever, in any matter within the jurisdiction of any department or agency of the United States knowingly and willfully falsifies, conceals, or covers up by any trick, scheme, or device a material fact, or makes any false, fictitious or fraudulent statements or representations, or makes or uses any false writing or document knowing the same to contain any false, fictitious or fraudulent statement or entry, shall be fined not more than $10,000 or imprisoned not more than 5 years, or both.

PART 535—IRANIAN ASSETS CONTROL REGULATIONS

Subpart A—Relation of This Part to Other Laws and Regulations

AUTHORITY: Secs. 201–207, 91 Stat. 1626; 50 U.S.C. 1701–1706; E.O. 12170, 44 FR 65729; E.O. 12205, 45 FR 24099; E.O. 12211, 45 FR 26685.

SOURCE: 44 FR 65956, Nov. 15, 1979, unless otherwise noted.

Subpart A—Relation of This Part to Other Laws and Regulations

§ 535.101 Relation of this part to other laws and regulations.

(a) This part is independent of Parts 500, 505, 515, 520 and 530 of this chapter. Those parts do not relate to Iran. No license or authorization contained in or issued pursuant to such parts shall be deemed to authorize any transaction prohibited by this part, nor shall any license or authorization issued pursuant to any other provision of law (except this part) be deemed to authorize any transaction so prohibited.

(b) No license or authorization contained in or issued pursuant to this part shall be deemed to authorize any transaction to the extent that it is prohibited by reason of the provisions of any law or any statute other than the International Emergency Economic Powers Act, as amended, or any proclamation order or regulation other than those contained in or issued pursuant to this part.

Subpart B—Prohibitions

§ 535.201 Transactions involving property in which Iran or Iranian entities have an interest.

No property subject to the jurisdiction of the United States or which is in the possession of or control of persons subject to the jurisdiction of the United States in which on or after the effective date Iran has any interest of any nature whatsoever may be transferred, paid, exported, withdrawn or otherwise dealt in except as authorized.

[45 FR 24432, Apr. 9, 1980]

§ 535.202 Transactions with respect to securities registered or inscribed in the name of Iran.

Unless authorized by a license expressly referring to this section, the acquisition, transfer (including the transfer on the books of any issuer or agent thereof), disposition, transportation, importation, exportation, or withdrawal of, or the endorsement or guaranty of signatures on or otherwise dealing in any security (or evidence thereof) registered or inscribed in the name of any Iranian entity is prohibited irrespective of the fact that at any time (either prior to, on, or subsequent to the effective date) the registered or inscribed owner thereof may have, or appears to have, assigned, transferred or otherwise disposed of any such security.

§ 535.203 Effect of transfers violating the provisions of this part.

(a) Any transfer after the effective date which is in violation of any provision of this part or of any regulation, ruling, instruction, license, or other direction or authorization thereunder and involves any property in which Iran has or has had an interest since such effective date is null and void and shall not be the basis for the assertion or recognition of any interest in or right, remedy, power or privilege with respect to such property.

(b) No transfer before the effective date shall be the basis for the assertion or recognition of any right, remedy, power, or privilege with respect to, or interest in, any property in which Iran has or has had an interest since the effective date unless the person with whom such property is held or maintained had written notice of the transfer or by any written evidence had recognized such transfer prior to such effective date.

(c) Unless otherwise provided, an appropriate license or other authorization issued by or pursuant to the direction or authorization of the Secretary of the Treasury before, during or after a transfer shall validate such transfer or render it enforceable to the same extent as it would be valid or enforceable but for the provisions of the International Emergency Economic Powers

Act and this part and any ruling, order, regulation, direction or instruction issued hereunder.

(d) Transfers of property which otherwise would be null and void, or unenforceable by virtue of the provisions of this section shall not be deemed to be null and void, or unenforceable pursuant to such provisions, as to any person with whom such property was held or maintained (and as to such person only) in cases in which such person is able to establish each of the following:

(1) Such transfer did not represent a willful violation of the provisions of this part by the person with whom such property was held or maintained;

(2) The person with whom such property was held or maintained did not have reasonable cause to know or suspect, in view of all the facts and circumstances known or availabe to such person, that such transfer required a license or authorization by or pursuant to the provision of this part and was not so licensed or authorized or if a license or authorization did purport to cover the transfer, that such license or authorization had been obtained by misrepresentation or the withholding of material facts or was otherwise fraudulently obtained; and

(3) Promptly upon discovery that:

(i) Such transfer was in violation of the provisions of this part or any regulation, ruling, instruction, license or other direction or authorization thereunder, or

(ii) Such transfer was not licensed or authorized by the Secretary of the Treasury, or

(iii) If a license did purport to cover the transfer, such license had been obtained by misrepresentation or the withholding of material facts or was otherwise fraudulently obtained; the person with whom such property was held or maintained filed with the Treasury Department, Washington, D.C., a report in triplicate setting forth in full the circumstances relating to such transfer. The filing of a report in accordance with the provisions of this paragraph shall not be deemed to be compliance or evidence of compliance with paragraphs (d) (1) and (2) of this section.

(e) Unless licensed or authorized pursuant to this part any attachment, judgment, decree, lien, execution, garnishment, or other judicial process is null and void with respect to any property in which on or since the effective date there existed an interest of Iran.

(f) For the purpose of this section the term "property" includes gold, silver, bullion, currency, coin, credit, securities (as that term is defined in section 2(1) of the Securities Act of 1933, as amended), bills of exchange, notes, drafts, acceptances, checks, letters of credit, book credits, debts, claims, contracts, negotiable documents of title, mortgages, liens, annuities, insurance policies, options and futures in commodities, and evidences of any of the foregoing. The term "property" shall not, except to the extent indicated, be deemed to include chattels or real property.

[44 FR 65956, Nov. 15, 1979, as amended at 45 FR 24432, Apr. 9, 1980]

§ 535.208   Evasions; effective date.

(a) Any transaction for the purpose of, or which has the effect of, evading or avoiding any of the prohibitions set forth in this subpart is hereby prohibited.

(b) The term "effective date" means, with respect to transactions prohibited in § 535.201, 8:10 a.m. eastern standard time, November 14, 1979, and with respect to the transactions prohibited in §§ 535.206 and 535.207, 4:19 p.m. eastern standard time, April 7, 1980.

(c) With respect to any amendments of the foregoing sections or any other amendments to this part the term "effective date" shall mean the date of filing with the FEDERAL REGISTER.

[45 FR 24433, Apr. 9, 1980, as amended at 45 FR 26940, Apr. 21, 1980]

§ 535.210   Direction for establishing an escrow agreement.

(a) The Federal Reserve Bank of New York, as fiscal agent of the United States, is licensed, authorized, directed and compelled to enter into escrow and related agreements under which certain money and other assets shall be credited to escrow accounts by the Bank of England or the N.V. Settlement Bank of the Netherlands.

(b) The Federal Reserve Bank of New York is licensed, authorized, directed and compelled, as fiscal agent of the United States, to receive certain money and other assets in which Iran or its agencies, instrumentalities or controlled entities have an interest and to hold or transfer such money and other assets, and any earnings or interest payable thereon, in such manner and at such times as the Secretary of the Treasury deems necessary to fulfill the rights and obligations of the United States under the Declaration of the government of the Democratic and Popular Republic of Algeria dated January 19, 1981, and the Undertakings of the Government of the United States of America and the Government of Islamic Republic of Iran with respect to the Declaration of the Government of the Democratic and Popular Republic of Algeria, and the escrow and related agreements described in paragraph (a) of this section. Such money and other assets may be invested, or not, at the discretion of the Federal Reserve Bank of New York, as fiscal agent of the United States.

(Secs. 201–207, 91 Stat. 1626, 50 U.S.C. 1701–1706; E.O. 12170, 44 FR 65729; E.O. 12205, 45 FR 24099; E.O. 12211, 45 FR 26685; E.O. 12276, 46 FR 7913; E.O. 12279, 46 FR 7919; E.O. 12280, 46 FR 7921; E.O. 12281, 46 FR 7923; E.O. 12282, 46 FR 7925; E.O. 12283, 46 FR 7927, and E.O. 12294, 46 FR 14111)

[46 FR 14333, Feb. 26, 1981, as amended at 46 FR 42063, Aug. 19, 1981]

§ 535.211 Direction involving transfers by the Federal Reserve Bank concerning certain Iranian property.

The Federal Reserve Bank of New York is licensed, authorized, directed and compelled to transfer to its account at the Bank of England, and subsequently to transfer to accounts in the name of the Central Bank of Algeria as Escrow Agent at the Bank of England that are established pursuant to an escrow and related agreements approved by the Secretary of the Treasury, all gold bullion, together with all other assets in its custody (or the cash equivalent thereof), of Iran or its agencies, instrumentalities or controlled entities. Such transfers, and whatever further related transactions

are deemed appropriate by the Secretary of the Treasury, shall be executed when and in the manner directed by the Secretary of the Treasury.

(Secs. 201–207, 91 Stat. 1626, 50 U.S.C. 1701–1706; E.O. 12170, 44 FR 65729; E.O. 12205, 45 FR 24099; E.O. 12211, 45 FR 26685; E.O. 12276, 46 FR 7913; E.O. 12279, 46 FR 7919; E.O. 12280, 46 FR 7921; E.O. 12281, 46 FR 7923; E.O. 12282, 46 FR 7925; E.O. 12283, 46 FR 7927, and E.O. 12294, 46 FR 14111)

[46 FR 14333, Feb. 26, 1981]

§ 535.212 Direction to transfer property in which Iran or an Iranian entity has an interest by branches and offices of United States banks located outside the United States.

(a) Any branch or office of a United States bank or subsidiary thereof, which branch, office or subsidiary is located outside the territory of the United States, and which, on or after 8:10 a.m., e.s.t., on November 14, 1979:

(1) Has been or is in possession of funds or securities legally or beneficially owned by the Government of Iran or its agencies, instrumentalities, or controlled entities, or (2) has carried or is carrying on its books deposits standing to the credit of or beneficially owned by such government, its agencies, instrumentalities or controlled entities, is licensed, authorized, directed and compelled to transfer such funds, securities and deposits, held on January 19, 1981, including interest from November 14, 1979, at commercially reasonable rates, to the account of the Federal Reserve Bank of New York, as fiscal agent of the U.S., at the Bank of England, to be held or transferred as directed by the Secretary of the Treasury. The funds, securities and deposits described in this section shall be further transferred as provided for in the Declarations of the Government of the Democratic and Popular Republic of Algeria and the Undertakings of the Government of the United States of America and the Government of the Islamic Republic of Iran with respect to the Declaration.

(b) Any banking institution subject to the jurisdiction of the United States that has executed a set-off on or after 8:10 a.m., e.s.t., November 14, 1979, against Iranian funds, securities or deposits referred to in paragraph (a) of this section is hereby licensed, authorized, directed and compelled to cancel such set-off and to transfer all funds, securities and deposits which have been subject to such set-off, including interest from November 14, 1979, at commercially reasonable rates, pursuant to the provisions of paragraph (a) of this section.

(Secs. 201-207, 91 Stat. 1626, 50 U.S.C. 1701-1706; E.O. 12170, 44 FR 65729; E.O. 12205, 45 FR 24099; E.O. 12211, 45 FR 26685; E.O. 12276, 46 FR 7913; E.O. 12279, 46 FR 7919; E.O. 12280, 46 FR 7921; E.O. 12281, 46 FR 7923; E.O. 12282, 46 FR 7925; E.O. 12283, 46 FR 7927, and E.O. 12294, 46 FR 14111)

[46 FR 14333, Feb. 26, 1981]

§ 535.213 Direction involving property held by offices of banks in the United States in which Iran or an Iranian entity has an interest.

(a) Any branch or office of a bank, which branch or office is located within the United States and is, on the effective date of this section, either:

(1) In possession of funds or securities legally or beneficially owned by the Government of Iran or its agencies, instrumentalities or controlled entities, or (2) carrying on its books deposits standing to the credit of or beneficially owned by such government or its agencies, instrumentalities or controlled entities, is licensed, authorized, directed and compelled to transfer such funds, securities and deposits, held on January 19, 1981, including interest from November 14, 1979, at commercially reasonable rates, to the Federal Reserve Bank of New York, as fiscal agent of the U.S., to be held or transferred as directed by the Secretary of the Treasury.

(b) Transfer of funds, securities or deposits under paragraph (a) of this section shall be in accordance with the provisions of § 535.221 of this part, and such funds, securities or deposits, plus interest at commercially reasonable rates from November 14, 1979, to the transfer date, shall be received by the Federal Reserve Bank of New York by 11 a.m., E.D.T., July 10, 1981. For periods for which rates are to be determined in the future, whether by agreement between Iran and the bank or otherwise (see § 535.440), interest for such periods shall be transferred to the Federal Reserve Bank of New York promptly upon such determination. Such interest shall include interest at commercially reasonable rates from July 19, 1981, on the interest which would have accrued by July 19, 1981.

(c) Any funds, securities or deposits subject to a valid attachment, injunction or other like proceeding or process not affected by § 535.218 need not be transferred as otherwise required by this section.

(d) The transfers of securities required by this section shall be made notwithstanding § 535.202.

(Secs. 201-207, 91 Stat. 1626, 50 U.S.C. 1701-1706; E.O. 12170, 44 FR 65729; E.O. 12205, 45 FR 24099; E.O. 12211, 45 FR 26685; E.O. 12276, 46 FR 7913; E.O. 12279, 46 FR 7919; E.O. 12280, 46 FR 7921; E.O. 12281, 46 FR 7923; E.O. 12282, 46 FR 7925; E.O. 12283, 46 FR 7927, and E.O. 12294, 46 FR 14111)

[46 FR 26477, May 13, 1981, as amended at 46 FR 30341, June 8, 1981; 46 FR 35106, July 7, 1981; 48 FR 253, Jan. 4, 1983]

§ 535.214 Direction involving other financial assets in which Iran or an Iranian entity has an interest held by any person subject to the jurisdiction of the United States.

(a) Any person subject to the jurisdiction of the United States which is not a banking institution and is on January 19, 1981, in possession or control of funds or securities of Iran or its agencies, instrumentalities or controlled entities is licensed, authorized, directed and compelled to transfer such funds or securities to the Federal Reserve Bank of New York, as fiscal agent of the U.S. to be held or transferred as directed by the Secretary of the Treasury. However, such funds and securities need not be transferred until any disputes (not relating to any attachment, injunction or similar order) as to the entitlement of Iran and its entities to them are resolved.

(b) Transfers of funds and securities under paragraph (a) of this section shall be in accordance with the provisions of § 535.221 of this part, and such funds and securities shall be received by the Federal Reserve Bank of New York by 11 a.m., E.D.T., July 10, 1981.

(c) Any funds, securities or deposits subject to a valid attachment, injunction or other like proceeding or process not affected by § 535.218 need not be transferred as otherwise required by this section.

(d) The transfers of securities required by this section shall be made notwithstanding § 535.202.

(Secs. 201-207, 91 Stat. 1626, 50 U.S.C. 1701-1706; E.O. 12170, 44 FR 65729; E.O. 12205, 45 FR 24099; E.O. 12211, 45 FR 26685; E.O. 12276, 46 FR 7913; E.O. 12279, 46 FR 7919; E.O. 12280, 46 FR 7921; E.O. 12281, 46 FR 7923; E.O. 12282, 46 FR 7925; E.O. 12283, 46 FR 7927, and E.O. 12294, 46 FR 14111)

[46 FR 26447, May 13, 1981, as amended at 46 FR 30341, June 8, 1981; 46 FR 35107, July 7, 1981]

§ 535.215 Direction involving other properties in which Iran or an Iranian entity has an interest held by any person subject to the jurisdiction of the United States.

(a) Except as provided in paragraphs (b) and (c) of this section, all persons subject to the jurisdiction of the United States in possession or control of properties, as defined in § 535.333 of this part, not including funds and securities owned by Iran or its agencies, instrumentalities or controlled entities are licensed, authorized, directed and compelled to transfer such properties held on January 19, 1981 as directed after that date by the Government of Iran, acting through its authorized agent. Except where specifically stated, this license, authorization and direction does not relieve persons subject to the jurisdiction of the United States from existing legal requirements other than those based upon the International Emergency Economic Powers Act.

(b) Any properties subject to a valid attachment, injunction or other like proceeding or process not affected by § 535.218 need not be transferred as otherwise required by this section.

(c) Notwithstanding paragraph (a) of this section, persons subject to the jurisdiction of the United States, including agencies, instrumentalities and entities controlled by the Government of Iran, who have possession, custody or control of blocked tangible property covered by § 535.201, shall not transfer such property without a specific Treasury license, if the export of such property requires a specific license or authorization pursuant to the provisions of any of the following acts, as amended, or regulations in force with respect to them: the Export Administration Act, 50 U.S.C. App. 2403, *et seq.,* the Arms Export Control Act, 22 U.S.C. 2751, *et seq.,* the Atomic Energy Act, 42 U.S.C. 2011, *et seq.,* or any other act prohibiting the export of such property, except as licensed.

(Secs. 201-207, 91 Stat. 1626, 50 U.S.C. 1701-1706; E.O. 12170, 44 FR 65729; E.O. 12205, 45 FR 24099; E.O. 12211, 45 FR 26685; E.O. 12276, 46 FR 7913; E.O. 12279, 46 FR 7919; E.O. 12280, 46 FR 7921; E.O. 12281, 46 FR 7923; E.O. 12282, 46 FR 7925; E.O. 12283, 46 FR 7927, and E.O. 12294, 46 FR 14111)

[46 FR 14334, Feb. 26, 1981, as amended at 46 FR 26477, May 13, 1981; 49 FR 21322, May 21, 1984]

§ 535.216 Prohibition against prosecution of certain claims.

(a) Persons subject to the jurisdiction of the United States are prohibited from prosecuting in any court within the United States or elsewhere, whether or not litigation was commenced before or after January 19, 1981, any claim against the Government of Iran arising out of events occurring before January 19, 1981 relating to:

(1) The seizure of the hostages on November 4, 1979;

(2) The subsequent detention of such hostages;

(3) Injury to United States property or property of United States nationals within the United States Embassy compound in Tehran after November 3, 1979; or

(4) Injury to United States nationals or their property as a result of popular movements in the course of the Islamic Revolution in Iran which were not an act of the Government of Iran.

(b) Any persons who are not United States nationals are prohibited from prosecuting any claim described in paragraph (a) of this section in any court within the United States.

(c) No further action, measure or process shall be taken after the effective date of this section in any judicial proceeding instituted before the effective date of this section which is based upon any claim described in paragraph (a) of this section, and all such proceedings shall be terminated.

(d) No judicial order issued in the course of the proceedings described in paragraph (c) of this section shall be enforced in any way.

(Secs. 201-207, 91 Stat. 1626, 50 U.S.C. 1701–1706; E.O. 12170, 44 FR 65729; E.O. 12205, 45 FR 24099; E.O. 12211, 45 FR 26685; E.O. 12276, 46 FR 7913; E.O. 12279, 46 FR 7919; E.O. 12280, 46 FR 7921; E.O. 12281, 46 FR 7923; E.O. 12282, 46 FR 7925; E.O. 12283, 46 FR 7927, and E.O. 12294, 46 FR 14111)

[46 FR 14334, Feb. 26, 1981]

§ 535.217 Blocking of property of the former Shah of Iran and of certain other Iranian nationals.

(a) For the purpose of protecting the rights of litigants in courts within the United States, all property and assets located in the United States in the control of the estate of Mohammad Reza Pahlavi, the former Shah of Iran, or any close relative of the former Shah served as a defendant in litigation in such courts brought by Iran seeking the return of property alleged to belong to Iran, is blocked as to each such estate or person, until all such litigation against such estate or person is finally terminated. This provision shall apply only to such estate or persons as to which Iran has furnished proof of service to the Office of Foreign Assets Control and which the Office has identified in paragraph (b) of this section.

(b) Ashraf Pahlavi, sister of Mohammad Reza Pahlavi, the former Shah of Iran May 11, 1981.

(c) The effective date of this section is January 19, 1981, except as otherwise specified after the name of a person identified in paragraph (b) of this section.

(Secs. 201-207, 91 Stat. 1626, 50 U.S.C. 1701–1706; E.O. 12170, 44 FR 65729; E.O. 12205, 45 FR 24099; E.O. 12211, 45 FR 26685; E.O. 12276, 46 FR 7913; E.O. 12279, 46 FR 7919; E.O. 12280, 46 FR 7921; E.O. 12281, 46 FR 7923; E.O. 12282, 46 FR 7925; E.O. 12283, 46 FR 7927, and E.O. 12294, 46 FR 14111)

[46 FR 26478, May 13, 1981]

§ 535.218 Prohibitions and nullifications with respect to property described in §§ 535.211, 535.212, 535.213, 535.214 and 535.215 and standby letters of credit.

(a) All licenses and authorizations for acquiring or exercising any right, power or privilege, by court order, attachment, or otherwise, including the license contained in § 535.504, with respect to the property described in §§ 535.211, 535.212, 535.213, 535.214 and 535.215 are revoked and withdrawn.

(b) All rights, powers and privileges relating to the property described in §§ 535.211, 535.212, 535.213, 535.214 and 535.215 and which derive from any attachment, injunction, other like proceedings or process, or other action in any litigation after November 14, 1979, at 8:10 a.m., e.s.t., including those derived from § 535.504, other than rights, powers and privileges of the Government of Iran and its agencies, instrumentalities and controlled entities, whether acquired by court order or otherwise, are nullified, and all persons claiming any such right, power or privilege are hereafter barred from exercising the same.

(c) All persons subject to the jurisdiction of the United States are prohibited from acquiring or exercising any right, power or privilege, whether by court order or otherwise, with respect to property (and any income earned thereon) referred to in §§ 535.211, 535.212, 535.213, 535.214 and 535.215.

(d) The prohibitions contained in paragraph (c) of this section shall not apply to Iran, its agencies, instrumentalities or controlled entities.

(e) Paragraph (a) of this section does not revoke or withdraw specific licenses authorizing the operation of blocked accounts which were issued prior to January 19, 1981, and which do not relate to litigation. Such licenses shall be deemed to be revoked as of May 31, 1981, unless extended by general or specific license issued subsequent to February 26, 1981.

(f) The provisions of paragraphs (a), (b) and (c) of this section shall apply to contested and contingent liabilities and property interests of the Government of Iran, its agencies, instrumentalities or controlled entities, including debts.

(g) All existing attachments on standby letters of credit, performance bonds and similar obligations and on substitute blocked accounts established under § 535.568 relating to standby letters of credit, performance bonds and similar obligations are nullified and all future attachments on them are hereafter prohibited. All rights, powers and privileges relating to such attachments are nullified and all persons hereafter are barred from asserting or exercising any rights, powers or privileges derived therefrom.

(Secs. 201–207, 91 Stat. 1626, 50 U.S.C. 1701–1706; E.O. 12170, 44 FR 65729; E.O. 12205, 45 FR 24099; E.O. 12211, 45 FR 26685; E.O. 12276, 46 FR 7913; E.O. 12279, 46 FR 7919; E.O. 12280, 46 FR 7921; E.O. 12281, 46 FR 7923; E.O. 12282, 46 FR 7925; E.O. 12283, 46 FR 7927, and E.O. 12294, 46 FR 14111)

[46 FR 14334, Feb. 26, 1981, as amended at 46 FR 26477, May 13, 1981]

§ 535.219 Discharge of obligation by compliance with this part.

Compliance with §§ 535.210, 535.211, 535.212, 535.213, 535.214 and 535.215, or any other orders, regulations, instructions or directions issued pursuant to this part licensing, authorizing, directing or compelling the transfer of the assets described in those sections, shall, to the extent thereof, be a full acquittance and discharge for all purposes of the obligation of the person making the same. No person shall be held liable in any court for or with respect to anything done or omitted in good faith in connection with the administration of, or pursuant to and in reliance on, such orders, regulations, instructions or directions.

(Secs. 201–207, 91 Stat. 1626, 50 U.S.C. 1701–1706; E.O. 12170, 44 FR 65729; E.O. 12205, 45 FR 24099; E.O. 12211, 45 FR 26685; E.O. 12276, 46 FR 7913; E.O. 12279, 46 FR 7919; E.O. 12280, 46 FR 7921; E.O. 12281, 46 FR 7923; E.O. 12282, 46 FR 7925; E.O. 12283, 46 FR 7927, and E.O. 12294, 46 FR 14111)

[46 FR 14334, Feb. 26, 1981]

§ 535.220 Timing of transfers required by § 535.212.

Transfers required by § 535.212 to the account of the Federal Reserve Bank of New York, as fiscal agent of the U.S., at the Bank of England shall be executed no later than 6 a.m., e.s.t., January 20, 1981, when the banking institution had knowledge of the terms of Executive Order 12278 of January 19, 1981.

(Secs. 201–207, 91 Stat. 1626, 50 U.S.C. 1701–1706; E.O. 12170, 44 FR 65729; E.O. 12205, 45 FR 24099; E.O. 12211, 45 FR 26685; E.O. 12276, 46 FR 7913; E.O. 12279, 46 FR 7919; E.O. 12280, 46 FR 7921; E.O. 12281, 46 FR 7923; E.O. 12282, 46 FR 7925; E.O. 12283, 46 FR 7927, and E.O. 12294, 46 FR 14111)

[46 FR 14335, Feb. 26, 1981]

§ 535.221 Compliance with directive provisions.

(a) Transfers of deposits or funds required by §§ 535.213 and 535.214 of this part shall be effected by means of wire transfer to the Federal Reserve Bank of New York for credit to the following accounts: with respect to transfers required by § 535.213, to the Federal Reserve Bank of New York, as fiscal agent of the United States, Special Deposit Account A, and with respect to transfers required by § 535.214, to the Federal Reserve Bank of New York, as fiscal agent of the United States, Special Deposit Account B.

(b) Securities to be transferred as required by §§ 535.213 and 535.214 of this part that are not presently registered in the name of Iran or an Iranian entity shall be delivered to the Federal Reserve Bank of New York in fully transferable form (bearer or endorsed in blank), accompanied by all necessary transfer documentation, *e.g.*, stock or bond powers or powers of attorney. All securities transferred, including those presently registered in the name of Iran or an Iranian entity, shall be accompanied by instructions to deposit such securities to the following accounts: with respect to transfers required by § 535.213, to the Federal Reserve Bank of New York, as fiscal agent of the United States, Special Custody Account A, and with respect to transfers required by § 535.214, to the Federal Reserve Bank of New York, as fiscal agent of the United States, Special Custody Account B.

(1) Securities which are in book-entry form shall be transferred by wire transfer to the Federal Reserve Bank of New York to the appropriate account named in this paragraph.

(2) Definitive securities which are in bearer or registered form shall be hand delivered or forwarded by registered mail, insured, to the Federal Reserve Bank of New York, Safekeeping Department, to the appropriate account named in this paragraph.

(c) If a security in which Iran or an Iranian entity has an interest is evidenced by a depositary receipt or other evidence of a security, the legal owner of such security shall arrange to have the security placed in fully transferable form (bearer or endorsed in blank) as provided in paragraph (b) of this section, and transferred pursuant to paragraph (b)(2) of this section.

(d) Any person delivering a security or securities to the Federal Reserve Bank of New York under paragraph (b) of this section, shall provide the Bank at least 2 business days prior written notice of such delivery, specifically identifying the sending person, the face or par amount and type of security, and whether the security is in bearer, registered or book-entry form.

(Secs. 201-207, 91 Stat. 1626, 50 U.S.C. 1701-1706; E.O. 12170, 44 FR 65729; E.O. 12205, 45 FR 24099; E.O. 12211, 45 FR 26685; E.O. 12276, 46 FR 7913; E.O. 12279, 46 FR 7919; E.O. 12280, 46 FR 7921; E.O. 12281, 46 FR 7923; E.O. 12282, 46 FR 7925; E.O. 12283, 46 FR 7927, and E.O. 12294, 46 FR 14111)

[46 FR 30341, June 8, 1981]

§ 535.222 Suspension of claims eligible for Claims Tribunal.

(a) All claims which may be presented to the Iran-United States Claims Tribunal under the terms of Article II of the Declaration of the Government of the Democratic and Popular Republic of Algeria Concerning the Settlement of Claims by the Government of the United States of America and the Government of the Islamic Republic of Iran, dated January 19, 1981, and all claims for equitable or other judicial relief in connection with such claims, are hereby suspended, except as they may be presented to the Tribunal. During the period of this suspension, all such claims shall have no

legal effect in any action now pending in any court in the United States, including the courts of any state and any locality thereof, the District of Columbia and Puerto Rico, or in any action commenced in any such court after the effective date of this section.

(b) Nothing in paragraph (a) of this section shall prohibit the assertion of a defense, set-off or counterclaim in any pending or subsequent judicial proceeding commenced by the Government of Iran, any political subdivision of Iran, or any agency, instrumentality or entity controlled by the Government of Iran or any political subdivision thereof.

(c) Nothing in this section precludes the commencement of an action after the effective date of this section for the purpose of tolling the period of limitations for commencement of such action.

(d) Nothing in this section shall require dismissal of any action for want of prosecution.

(e) Suspension under this section of a claim or a portion thereof submitted to the Iran-United States Claims Tribunal for adjudication shall terminate upon a determination by the Tribunal that it does not have jurisdiction over such claim or portion thereof.

(f) A determination by the Iran-United States Claims Tribunal on the merits that a claimant is not entitled to recover on a claim or part thereof shall operate as a final resolution and discharge of such claim or part thereof for all purposes. A determination by the Tribunal that a claimant shall have recovery on a claim or part thereof in a specified amount shall operate as a final resolution and discharge of such claim or part thereof for all purposes upon payment to the claimant of the full amount of the award including any interest awarded by the Tribunal.

(g) Nothing in this section shall apply to any claim concerning the validity or payment of a standby letter of credit, performance or payment bond or other similar instrument. However, assertion of such a claim through judicial proceedings is governed by the general license in § 535.504.

(h) The effective date of this section is February 24, 1981.

(Secs. 201-207, 91 Stat. 1626, 50 U.S.C. 1701-1706; E.O. 12170, 44 FR 65729; E.O. 12205, 45 FR 24099; E.O. 12211, 45 FR 26685; E.O. 12276, 46 FR 7913; E.O. 12279, 46 FR 7919; E.O. 12280, 46 FR 7921; E.O. 12281, 46 FR 7923; E.O. 12282, 46 FR 7925; E.O. 12283, 46 FR 7927, and E.O. 12294, 46 FR 14111)

[46 FR 14335, Feb. 26, 1981, as amended at 47 FR 29529, July 7, 1982]

Subpart C—General Definitions

§ 535.301   Iran; Iranian Entity.

(a) The term "Iran" and "Iranian Entity" includes:

(1) The state and the Government of Iran as well as any political subdivision, agency, or instrumentality thereof or any territory, dependency, colony, protectorate, mandate, dominion, possession or place subject to the jurisdiction thereof;

(2) Any partnership, association, corporation, or other organization substantially owned or controlled by any of the foregoing;

(3) Any person to the extent that such person is, or has been, or to the extent that there is reasonable cause to believe that such person is, or has been, since the effective date acting or purporting to act directly or indirectly on behalf of any of the foregoing;

(4) Any territory which on or since the effective date is controlled or occupied by the military, naval or police forces or other authority of Iran; and

(5) Any other person or organization determined by the Secretary of the Treasury to be included within paragraph (a) of this section.

(b) A person specified in paragraph (a)(2) of this section shall not be deemed to fall within the definition of Iran solely by reason of being located in, organized under the laws of, or having its principal place of business in, Iran.

§ 535.308   Person.

The term "person" means an individual, partnership, association, corporation or other organization.

[45 FR 24433, Apr. 9, 1980]

§ 535.310   Transfer.

The term "transfer" shall mean any actual or purported act or transaction, whether or not evidenced by writing, and whether or not done or performed within the United States, the purpose, intent or effect of which is to create, surrender, release, transfer, or alter, directly or indirectly, any right, remedy, power, privilege, or interest with respect to any property and, without limitation upon the foregoing, shall include the making, execution, or delivery of any assignment, power, conveyance, check, declaration, deed, deed of trust, power of attorney, power of appointment, bill of sale, mortgage, receipt, agreement, contract, certificate, gift, sale, affidavit, or statement; the appointment of any agent, trustee, or fiduciary; the creation or transfer of any lien; the issuance, docketing, filing, or the levy of or under any judgement, decree, attachment, execution, or other judicial or administrative process or order, or the service of any garnishment; the acquisition of any interest of any nature whatsoever by reason of a judgment or decree of any foreign country; the fulfillment of any condition, or the exercise of any power of appointment, power of attorney, or other power.

[44 FR 75352, Dec. 19, 1979]

§ 535.311   Property; property interests.

Except as defined in § 535.203(f) for the purposes of that section, the terms "property" and "property interest" or "property interests" shall include, but not by way of limitation, money, checks, drafts, bullion, bank deposits, savings accounts, debts, indebtedness, obligations, notes, debentures, stocks, bonds, coupons, any other financial securities, bankers' acceptances, mortgages, pledges, liens or other rights in the nature of security, warehouse receipts, bills of lading, trust receipts, bills of sale, any other evidences of title, ownership or indebtedness, powers of attorney, goods, wares, merchandise, chattels, stocks on hand, ships, goods on ships, real estate mortgages, deeds of trust, vendors' sales agreements, land contracts, real estate and any interest therein, leaseholds, grounds rents, options, negotiable instruments, trade acceptances, royalties, book accounts, accounts payable, judgments, patents, trademarks or copyrights, insurance policies, safe deposit boxes and their contents, annuities, pooling agreements, contracts of any nature whatsoever, and any other property, real, personal, or mixed, tangible or intangible, or interest or interests therein, present, future or contingent.

§ 535.312 Interest.

Except as otherwise provided in this part, the term "interest" when used with respect to property shall mean an interest of any nature whatsoever, direct or indirect.

[44 FR 75352, Dec. 19, 1979]

§ 535.316 License.

Except as otherwise specified, the term "license" shall mean any license or authorization contained in or issued pursuant to this part.

[44 FR 66832, Nov. 21, 1979]

§ 535.317 General license.

A general license is any license or authorization the terms of which are set forth in this part.

[44 FR 66832, Nov. 21, 1979]

§ 535.318 Specific license.

A specific license is any license or authorization issued pursuant to this part but not set forth in this part.

[44 FR 66832, Nov. 21, 1979]

§ 535.320 Domestic bank.

(a) The term "domestic bank" shall mean any branch or office within the United States of any of the following which is not Iran or an Iranian entity: any bank or trust company incorporated under the banking laws of the United States or of any state, territory, or district of the United States, or any private bank or banker subject to supervision and examination under the banking laws of the United States or of any state, territory or district of the United States. The Secretary of the Treasury may also authorize any other banking institution to be treated as a "domestic bank" for the purpose of this definition or for the purpose of any or all sections of this part.

(b) For purposes of §§ 535.413, 535.508, 535.531 and 535.901, the term "domestic bank" includes any branch or office within the United States of a non-Iranian foreign bank.

[44 FR 66832, Nov. 21, 1979]

§ 535.321 United States; continental United States.

The term "United States" means the United States and all areas under the jurisdiction or authority thereof including the Trust Territory of the Pacific Islands. The term "continental United States" means the states of the United States and the District of Columbia.

[44 FR 66833, Nov. 21, 1979]

§ 535.329 Person subject to the jurisdiction of the United States.

The term "person subject to the jurisdiction of the United States" includes:

(a) Any person wheresoever located who is a citizen or resident of the United States;

(b) Any person actually within the United States;

(c) Any corporation organized under the laws of the United States or of any state, territory, possession, or district of the United States; and

(d) Any partnership, association, corporation, or other organization wheresoever organized or doing business which is owned or controlled by persons specified in paragraph (a), (b), or (c) of this section.

§ 535.333 Properties.

(a) The term "properties" as used in § 535.215 includes all uncontested and non-contingent liabilities and property interests of the Government of Iran, its agencies, instrumentalities or controlled entities, including debts. It does not include bank deposits or funds and securities. It also does not include obligations under standby letters of credit or similar instruments in the nature of performance bonds, including accounts established pursuant to § 535.568.

(b) Properties are not Iranian properties or owned by Iran unless all necessary obligations, charges and fees relating to such properties are paid and liens against such properties (not including attachments, injunctions and similar orders) are discharged.

(c) Liabilities and property interests may be considered contested if the holder thereof reasonably believes that a court would not require the holder, under applicable law to transfer the asset by virtue of the existence of a defense, counterclaim, set-off or similar reason. For purposes of this paragraph, the term "holder" shall include any person who possesses the property, or who, although not in physical possession of the property, has, by contract or otherwise, control over a third party who does in fact have physical possession of the property. A person is not a "holder" by virtue of being the beneficiary of an attachment, injunction or similar order.

(d) Liabilities and property interests shall not be deemed to be contested solely because they are subject to an attachment, injunction or other similar order.

(Secs. 201-207, 91 Stat. 1626, 50 U.S.C. 1701-1706; E.O. 12170, 44 FR 65729; E.O. 12205, 45 FR 24099; E.O. 12211, 45 FR 26685; E.O. 12276, 46 FR 7913; E.O. 12279, 46 FR 7919; E.O. 12280, 46 FR 7921; E.O. 12281, 46 FR 7923; E.O. 12282, 46 FR 7925; E.O. 12283, 46 FR 7927, and E.O. 12294, 46 FR 14111)

[46 FR 14335, Feb. 26, 1981]

§ 535.334 Act of the Government of Iran.

For purposes of § 535.216, an act of the Government of Iran, includes any acts ordered, authorized, allowed, approved, or ratified by the Government of Iran, its agencies, instrumentalities or controlled entities.

(Secs. 201-207, 91 Stat. 1626, 50 U.S.C. 1701-1706; E.O. 12170, 44 FR 65729; E.O. 12205, 45 FR 24099; E.O. 12211, 45 FR 26685; E.O. 12276, 46 FR 7913; E.O. 12279, 46 FR 7919; E.O. 12280, 46 FR 7921; E.O. 12281, 46 FR 7923; E.O. 12282, 46 FR 7925; E.O. 12283, 46 FR 7927, and E.O. 12294, 46 FR 14111)

[46 FR 14336, Feb. 26, 1981]

§ 535.335 Claim arising out of events in Iran.

For purposes of § 535.216, a claim is one "arising out of events" of the type specified only if such event is the specific act that is the basis of the claim.

(Secs. 201-207, 91 Stat. 1626, 50 U.S.C. 1701-1706; E.O. 12170, 44 FR 65729; E.O. 12205, 45 FR 24099; E.O. 12211, 45 FR 26685; E.O. 12276, 46 FR 7913; E.O. 12279, 46 FR 7919; E.O. 12280, 46 FR 7921; E.O. 12281, 46 FR 7923; E.O. 12282, 46 FR 7925; E.O. 12283, 46 FR 7927, and E.O. 12294, 46 FR 14111)

[46 FR 14336, Feb. 26, 1981]

§ 535.337 Funds.

For purposes of this part, the term "funds" shall mean monies in trust, escrow and similar special funds held by non-banking institutions, currency and coins. It does not include accounts created under § 535.568.

(Secs. 201-207, 91 Stat. 1626, 50 U.S.C. 1701-1706; E.O. 12170, 44 FR 65729; E.O. 12205, 45 FR 24099; E.O. 12211, 45 FR 26685; E.O. 12276, 46 FR 7913; E.O. 12279, 46 FR 7919; E.O. 12280, 46 FR 7921; E.O. 12281, 46 FR 7923; E.O. 12282, 46 FR 7925; E.O. 12283, 46 FR 7927, and E.O. 12294, 46 FR 14111)

[46 FR 30341, June 8, 1981]

Subpart D—Interpretations

§ 535.401 Reference to amended sections.

Reference to any section of this part or to any regulation, ruling, order, instruction, direction or license issued pursuant to this part shall be deemed to refer to the same as currently amended unless otherwise so specified.

[45 FR 24433, Apr. 9, 1980]

§ 535.402 Effect of amendment of sections of this part or of other orders, etc.

Any amendment, modification, or revocation of any section of this part or of any order, regulation, ruling, instruction, or license issued by or under the direction of the Secretary of the Treasury pursuant to section 203 of the International Emergency Economic Powers Act shall not, unless otherwise specifically provided, be deemed to affect any act done or omitted to be done, or any suit or proceeding had or commenced in any civil or criminal case, prior to such amendment, modifi-

F

cation, or revocation and all penalties, forfeitures, and liabilities under any such order, regulation, ruling, instruction or license shall continue and may be enforced as if such amendment, modification, or revocation had not been made.

[45 FR 24433, Apr. 9, 1980]

§ 535.403 Termination and acquisition of an interest of Iran or an Iranian entity.

(a) Whenever a transaction licensed or authorized by or pursuant to this part results in the transfer of property (including any property interest) away from Iran or an Iranian entity, such property shall no longer be deemed to be property in which Iran or an Iranian entity has or has had an interest, unless there exists in the property another such interest the transfer of which has not been effected pursuant to license or other authorization.

(b) Unless otherwise specifically provided in a license or authorization contained in or issued pursuant to this part, if property (including any property interest) is transferred to Iran or an Iranian interest, such property shall be deemed to be property in which there exists an interest of Iran or an Iranian entity.

[45 FR 24433, Apr. 9, 1980]

§ 535.413 Transfers between dollar accounts held for foreign banks.

Transfers authorized by § 535.901 include transfers by order of a non-Iranian foreign bank from its account in a domestic bank (directly or through a foreign branch or subsidiary of a domestic bank) to an account held by a domestic bank (directly or through a foreign branch or subsidiary) for a second non-Iranian foreign bank which in turn credits an account held by it abroad for Iran. For the purposes of this section, a non-Iranian foreign bank means a bank which is not a person subject to the jurisdiction of the United States.

[44 FR 66833, Nov. 21, 1979]

§ 535.414 Payments to blocked accounts under § 535.508.

(a) Section 535.508 does not authorize any transfer from a blocked account within the United States to an account held by any bank outside the United States or any other payment into a blocked account outside the United States.

(b) Section 535.508 only authorizes payment into a blocked account held by a domestic bank as defined by § 535.320.

[44 FR 67617, Nov. 26, 1979]

§ 535.415 Payment by Iranian entities of obligations to persons within the United States.

A person receiving payment under § 535.904 may distribute all or part of that payment to anyone: *Provided,* That any such payment to Iran or an Iranian entity must be to a blocked account in a domestic bank.

[44 FR 67617, Nov. 26, 1979]

§ 535.416 Letters of credit.

(a) *Q.* Prior to the effective date, a bank subject to the jurisdiction of the United States has issued or confirmed a documentary letter of credit for a non-Iranian account party in favor of an Iranian entity. Can payment be made upon presentation of documentary drafts?

A. Yes, provided payment is made into a blocked account in a domestic bank.

(b) *Q.* Prior to the effective date, a domestic branch of a bank organized or incorporated under the laws of the United States has issued or confirmed a documentary letter of credit for a non-Iranian account party in favor of an Iranian entity. Payment is to be made through a foreign branch of the bank. Can payment be made upon presentation of documentary drafts?

A. Yes, provided payment is made into a blocked account in a domestic bank.

(c) *Q.* Prior to the effective date, a foreign bank confirms a documentary letter of credit issued by its U.S. agency or branch for a non-Iranian account party in favor of an Iranian entity. Can the U.S. agency or branch of the foreign bank transfer funds to the foreign bank in connection with that foreign bank's payment under the letter of credit?

A. No, the U.S. agency's payment is blocked, unless the foreign bank made payment to the Iranian entity prior to the effective date.

(d) *Q.* Prior to the effective date, a bank subject to the jurisdiction of the United States has issued or confirmed a documentary letter of credit for a non-Iranian account party in favor of an Iranian entity. The Iranian entity presents documentry drafts which are deficient in some detail. May the non-Iranian account party waive the documentary deficiency and authorize the bank to make payment?

A. Yes, provided payment is made into a blocked account in a domestic bank. However, the non-Iranian account party is not obligated by these Regulations to exercise a waiver of documentary deficiencies. In cases where such a waiver is not exercised, the bank's payment obligation, if any, under the letter of credit remains blocked, as does any obligation, contingent or otherwise, of the account party. The documents are also blocked.

(e) *Q.* Prior to the effective date, a bank subject to the jurisdiction of the United States has issued or confirmed a documentary letter of credit for a non-Iranian account party in favor of an Iranian entity. The Iranian entity does not make timely, complete, or proper presentation of documents, and the letter of credit expires. Does there remain a blocked payment obligation held by the bank?

A. No, but any documents held by the bank continue to be blocked. It is also possible that the account party still has a related obligation to the Iranian entity and any such obligation would be blocked.

(f) *Q.* A bank subject to the jurisdiction of the United States has issued a letter of credit for a U.S. account party in favor of an Iranian entity. The letter of credit is confirmed by a foreign bank. Prior to or after the effective date, the Iranian entity presents documents to the U.S. issuing bank. Payment is deferred. After the effective date, the Iranian entity requests that the issuing bank either return the documents to the Iranian entity or transfer them to the confirming bank. Can the issuing bank do so?

A. No. The U.S. issuing bank can neither return nor transfer the documents without a license. The documents constitute blocked property under the Regulations.

(g) *Q.* Prior to the effective date, a bank subject to the jurisdiction of the United States has issued or confirmed a documentary letter of credit for a non-Iranian account party in favor of an Iranian entity. The Iranian entity presents documentary drafts which are deficient in some detail. May the non-Iranian account party waive the documentary deficiency and make payment?

A. Yes, provided payment is made into a blocked account in a domestic bank. However, the non-Iranian account party is not obligated by these Regulations to exercise a waiver of documentary deficiencies. In cases where such a waiver is not exercised, the amount of the payment held by the account party is blocked.

[44 FR 69287, Dec. 3, 1979, as amended at 44 FR 75353, Dec. 19, 1979]

§ 535.420 Transfers of accounts under § 535.508 from demand to interest-bearing status.

Section 535.508 authorizes transfer of a blocked demand deposit account to interest-bearing status at the instruction of the Iranian depositor at any time.

[44 FR 76784, Dec. 28, 1979]

§ 535.421 Prior contractual commitments not a basis for licensing.

Specific licenses are not issued on the basis that an unlicensed firm commitment or payment has been made in connection with a transaction prohibited by this part. Contractual commitments to engage in transactions subject to the prohibitions of this part should not be made, unless the contract specifically states that the transaction is authorized by general license or that it is subject to the issuance of a specific license.

[45 FR 24433, Apr. 9, 1980]

§ 535.433 Central Bank of Iran.

The Central Bank of Iran (Bank Markazi Iran) is an agency, instrumentality and controlled entity of the Government of Iran for all purposes under this part.

(Secs. 201–207, 91 Stat. 1626, 50 U.S.C. 1701–1706; E.O. 12170, 44 FR 65729; E.O. 12205, 45 FR 24099; E.O. 12211, 45 FR 26685; E.O. 12276, 46 FR 7913; E.O. 12279, 46 FR 7919; E.O. 12280, 46 FR 7921; E.O. 12281, 46 FR 7923; E.O. 12282, 46 FR 7925; E.O. 12283, 46 FR 7927, and E.O. 12294, 46 FR 14111)

[46 FR 14336, Feb. 26, 1981]

§ 535.437 Effect on other authorities.

Nothing in this part in any way relieves any persons subject to the jurisdiction of the United States from securing licenses or other authorizations as required from the Secretary of State, the Secretary of Commerce or other relevant agency prior to executing the transactions authorized or directed by this part. This includes licenses for transactions involving military equipment.

(Secs. 201–207, 91 Stat. 1626, 50 U.S.C. 1701–1706; E.O. 12170, 44 FR 65729; E.O. 12205, 45 FR 24099; E.O. 12211, 45 FR 26685; E.O. 12276, 46 FR 7913; E.O. 12279, 46 FR 7919; E.O. 12280, 46 FR 7921; E.O. 12281, 46 FR 7923; E.O. 12282, 46 FR 7925; E.O. 12283, 46 FR 7927, and E.O. 12294, 46 FR 14111)

[46 FR 14336, Feb. 26, 1981]

§ 535.438 Standby letters of credit, performance or payment bonds and similar obligations.

(a) Nothing contained in §§ 535.212, 535.213 and 535.214 or in any other provision or revocation or amendment of any provision in this part affects the prohibition in § 535.201 and the licensing procedure in § 535.568 relating to certain standby letters of credit, performance bonds and similar obligations. The term "funds and securities" as used in this part does not include substitute blocked accounts established under section 535.568 relating to standby letters of credit, performance or payment bonds and similar obligations.

(b) No transfer requirement under § 535.213 or § 535.214 shall be deemed to authorize or compel any payment or transfer of any obligation under a standby letter of credit, performance bond or similar obligation as to which a blocked account has been established pursuant to § 535.568 or as to which payment is prohibited under an injunction obtained by the account party.

(Secs. 201–207, 91 Stat. 1626, 50 U.S.C. 1701–1706; E.O. 12170, 44 FR 65729; E.O. 12205, 45 FR 24099; E.O. 12211, 45 FR 26685; E.O. 12276, 46 FR 7913; E.O. 12279, 46 FR 7919; E.O. 12280, 46 FR 7921; E.O. 12281, 46 FR 7923; E.O. 12282, 46 FR 7925; E.O. 12283, 46 FR 7927, and E.O. 12294, 46 FR 14111)

[46 FR 14336, Feb. 26, 1981, as amended at 46 FR 30341, June 8, 1981]

§ 535.440 Commercially reasonable interest rates.

(a) For purposes of §§ 535.212 and 535.213, what is meant by "commercially reasonable rates" depends on the particular circumstances. In the case of time or savings deposits, the "commercially reasonable rate" is that rate provided for by the deposit agreement or applicable law. With respect to other obligations where the rate remains to be determined, it is presently expected that the "commercially reasonable rate" will be the rate agreed upon by the bank and Iran. However, where a deposit has in fact operated as a demand account under Treasury license, it would be appropriate to treat the deposit for purposes of §§ 535.212 and 535.213 as a non-interest bearing account. Furthermore, in the event that the Iran-U.S Claims Tribunal (the "Tribunal") determines that interest additional to that agreed upon between the bank and Iran, or compensation or damages in lieu of interest, is due Iran, then that amount determined by the Tribunal to be owing to Iran shall be transferred as, or as part of, the interest at "commercially reasonable rates" required to be transferred pursuant to §§ 535.212 and 535.213, regardless of any settlement between the bank and Iran or any release or discharge that Iran may have given the bank.

(b) The contingent interest of Iran in any liability for further or additional interest, or compensation or damages in lieu of interest, that may be claimed in, and determined by the Tribunal, constitutes an interest of Iran in property for purposes of this part, and no agreement between Iran and any person subject to the jurisdiction of the United States is effective to extinguish such Iranian interest in property unless so specifically licensed by the Treasury Department.

(c) For deposits held as time deposits, no penalty shall be imposed for early withdrawal. (In this connection, the Board of Governors of the Federal Reserve System has determined that application of the penalty for early withdrawal of time deposits transferred before maturity, pursuant to § 535.213 is not required.)

(Secs. 201-207, 91 Stat. 1626, 50 U.S.C. 1701-1706; E.O. 12170, 44 FR 65729; E.O. 12205; 45 FR 24099; E.O. 12211, 45 FR 26605; E.O. 12276, 46 FR 7913; E.O. 12277, 46 FR 7915; E.O. 12278, 46 FR 7917; E.O. 12279, 46 FR 7919; E.O. 12280, 46 FR 7921; E.O. 12281, 46 FR 7923; E.O. 12282, 46 FR 7925; and E.O. 12294, 46 FR 14111)

[48 FR 253, Jan. 4, 1983]

Subpart E—Licenses, Authorizations and Statements of Licensing Policy

§ 535.502 Effect of license or authorization.

(a) No license or other authorization contained in this part or otherwise issued by or under the direction of the Secretary of the Treasury pursuant to section 203 of the International Emergency Economic Powers Act, shall be deemed to authorize or validate any transaction effected prior to the issuance thereof, unless such license or other authorization specifically so provides.

(b) No regulation, ruling, instruction, or license authorizes a transaction prohibited under this part unless the regulation, ruling, instruction, or license is issued by the Treasury Department and specifically refers to this part. No regulation, ruling, instruction or license referring to this part shall be deemed to authorize any transaction prohibited by any provision of Parts 500, 505, 515, 520 or 530 of this chapter unless the regulation, ruling, instruction or license specifically refers to such provision.

(c) Any regulation, ruling, instruction or license authorizing a transaction otherwise prohibited under this part has the effect of removing a pro-

hibition or prohibitions in Subpart B from the transaction, but only to the extent specifically stated by its terms. Unless the regulation, ruling, instruction or license otherwise specifies, such an authorization does not create any right, duty, obligation, claim, or interest in, or with respect to, any property which would not otherwise exist under ordinary principles of law.

[44 FR 66833, Nov. 21, 1979, as amended at 44 FR 75353, Dec. 19, 1979]

§ 535.503 Exclusion from licenses and authorizations.

The Secretary of the Treasury reserves the right to exclude any person from the operation of any license or from the privileges therein conferred or to restrict the applicability thereof with respect to particular persons, transactions or property or classes thereof. Such action shall be binding upon all persons receiving actual notice or constructive notice thereof.

[44 FR 66833, Nov. 21, 1979]

§ 535.504 Certain judicial proceedings with respect to property of Iran or Iranian entities.

(a) Subject to the limitations of paragraphs (b) and (c) of this section and § 535.222, judicial proceedings are authorized with respect to property in which on or after 8:10 a.m., e.s.t., November 14, 1979, there has existed an interest of Iran or an Iranian entity.

(b) This section does not authorize:

(1) Any pre-judgment attachment or any other proceeding of similar or analogous effect pertaining to any property (and any income earned thereon) subject to the provisions of §§ 535.211, 535.212, 535.213, 535.214 or 535.215 on January 19, 1981, including, but not limited to, a temporary restraining order or preliminary injunction, which operates as a restraint on property, for purposes of holding it within the jurisdiction of a court, or otherwise;

(2) Any payment or delivery out of a blocked account based upon a judicial proceeding, pertaining to any property subject to the provisions of §§ 535.211, 535.212, 535.213, 535.214 or 535.215 on January 19, 1981;

(3)(i) Any final judicial judgment or order (A) permanently enjoining, (B) terminating or nullifying, or (C) otherwise permanently disposing of any interest of Iran in any standby letter of credit, performance bond or similar obligation. Any license authorizing such action is hereby revoked and withdrawn. This revocation and withdrawal of prior licenses prohibits judgments or orders that are within the terms of this paragraph (b)(3)(i), including any such judgments or orders which may have been previously entered but which had not become final by July 2, 1982, through the conclusion of appellate proceedings or the expiration of the time for appeal.

(ii) Nothing in this paragraph (b)(3) shall prohibit the assertion of any defense, set-off or counterclaim in any pending or subsequent judicial proceeding commenced by the Government of Iran, any political subdivision of Iran, or any agency, instrumentality or entity owned or controlled by tne Government of Iran or any political subdivision thereof.

(iii) Nothing in this paragraph (b)(3) shall preclude the commencement of an action for the purpose of tolling the period of limitations for commencement of such action.

(iv) Nothing in this paragraph (b)(3) shall require dismissal of any action for want of prosecution.

(c) For purposes of this section, contested and contingent liabilities and property interests of the Government of Iran, its agencies, instrumentalities, or controlled entities, including debts, shall be deemed to be subject to § 535.215.

(d) A judicial proceeding is not authorized by this section if it is based on transactions which violated the prohibitions of this part.

(e) Judicial proceedings to obtain attachments on standby letters of credit, performance bonds or similar obligations and on substitute blocked accounts established under § 535.568 relating to standby letters of credit, performance bonds and similar obligations are not authorized or licensed.

(Secs. 201-207, 91 Stat. 1626, 50 U.S.C. 1701-1706; E.O. 12170, 44 FR 65729; E.O. 12205, 45 FR 24099; E.O. 12211, 45 FR 26685; E.O. 12276, 46 FR 7913; E.O. 12279, 46 FR 7919;

E.O. 12280, 46 FR 7921; E.O. 12281, 46 FR 7923; E.O. 12282, 46 FR 7925; E.O. 12283, 46 FR 7927, and E.O. 12294, 46 FR 14111)

[46 FR 14336, Feb. 26, 1981, as amended at 46 FR 26477, May 13, 1981; 47 FR 29529, July 7, 1982; 47 FR 55482, Dec. 10, 1982; 48 FR 57129, Dec. 28, 1983]

§ 535.508 Payments to blocked accounts in domestic banks.

(a) Any payment or transfer of credit, including any payment or transfer by any U.S.-owned or controlled foreign firm or branch to a blocked account in a domestic bank in the name of Iran or any Iranian entity is hereby authorized: *Provided,* Such payment or transfer shall not be made from any blocked account if such payment or transfer represents, directly or indirectly, a transfer of the interest of Iran or an Iranian entity to any other country or person.

(b) This section does not authorize:

(1) Any payment or transfer to any blocked account held in a name other than that of Iran or the Iranian entity who is the ultimate beneficiary of such payment or transfer; or

(2) Any foreign exchange transaction including, but not by way of limitation, any transfer of credit, or payment of an obligation, expressed in terms of the currency of any foreign country.

(c) This section does not authorize any payment or transfer of credit comprising an integral part of a transaction which cannot be effected without the subsequent issuance of a further license.

(d) This section does not authorize the crediting of the proceeds of the sale of securities held in a blocked account or a sub-account thereof, or the income derived from such securities to a blocked account or sub-account under any name or designation which differs from the name or designation of the specific blocked account or sub-account in which such securities were held.

(e) This section does not authorize any payment or transfer from a blocked account in a domestic bank to a blocked account held under any name or designation which differs from the name or designation of the specified blocked account or sub-account from which the payment or transfer is made.

(f) The authorization in paragraph (a) of this section is subject to the condition that a notification from the domestic bank receiving an authorized payment or transfer is furnished by the transferor to the Office of Foreign Assets Control confirming that the payment or transfer has been deposited in a blocked account under the regulations in this part and providing the name and address of Iran or the Iranian entity in whose name the account is held.

[44 FR 66590, Nov. 20, 1979]

§535.528 Certain transactions with respect to Iranian patents, trademarks and copyrights authorized.

(a) The following transactions by any person subject to the jurisdiction of the United States are authorized:

(1) The filing and prosecution of any application for an Iranian patent, trademark or copyright, or for the renewal thereof;

(2) The receipt of any Iranian patent, trademark or copyright;

(3) The filing and prosecution of opposition or infringement proceedings with respect to any Iranian patent, trademark, or copyright, and the prosecution of a defense to any such proceedings;

(4) The payment of fees currently due to the government of Iran, either directly or through an attorney or representative, in connection with any of the transactions authorized by paragraphs (a)(1), (2), and (3) of this section or for the maintenance of any Iranian patent, trademark or copyright; and

(5) The payment of reasonable and customary fees currently due to attorneys or representatives in Iran incurred in connection with any of the transactions authorized by paragraphs (a)(1), (2), (3) or (4) of this section.

(b) Payments effected pursuant to the terms of paragraphs (a)(4) and (5) of this section may not be made from any blocked account.

(c) As used in this section the term "Iranian patent, trademark, or copyright" shall mean any patent, petty patent, design patent, trademark or copyright issued by Iran.

[45 FR 29288, May 2, 1980]

§535.531 Payment of certain checks and drafts.

(a) A bank subject to the jurisdiction of the United States is hereby authorized to make payments from blocked accounts with such banking institution of checks and drafts drawn or issued prior to the effective date, *Provided,* That:

(1) The amount involved in any one payment, acceptance, or debit does not exceed $3000; or

(2) The check or draft was within the United States in process of collection by a domestic bank on or prior to the effective date and does not exceed $50,000.

(3) The authorization contained in this paragraph shall expire at the close of business on January 14, 1980.

(b) A bank subject to the jurisdiction of the United States as its own obligation may make payment to a person subject to the jurisdiction of the United States who is the beneficiary of any letter of credit issued or confirmed by it, or on a draft accepted by it, prior to the effective date, where the letter of credit was issued or confirmed on behalf of Iran or an Iranian entity, *Provided,* That:

(1) Notwithstanding the provisions of §535.902, no blocked account may at any time be debited in connection with such a payment.

(2) Such a payment shall give the bank making payment no special priority or other right to blocked accounts it holds in the event that such blocked accounts are vested or otherwise lawfully used in connection with a settlement of claims.

(3) Nothing in this paragraph prevents payment being made to the beneficiary of any draft or letter of credit or to any banking institution pursuant to §535.904.

(c) The office will consider on a case-by-case basis, without any commitment on its part to authorize any transaction or class of transactions, applications for specific licenses to make payments from blocked accounts of documentary drafts drawn under irrevocable letters of credit issued or confirmed by a domestic bank prior to the effective date, in favor of any person subject to the jurisdiction of the United States. Any bank or payee submitting such an application should include data on all such letters of credit in which it is involved. Applications should be submitted not later than January 10, 1980.

(d) Paragraphs (a) and (b) of this section do not authorize any payment to Iran or an Iranian entity except payments into a blocked account in a domestic bank unless Iran or the Iranian entity is otherwise licensed to receive such payment.

[44 FR 75352, Dec. 19, 1979]

§ 535.532 Completion of certain securities transactions.

(a) Banking institutions within the United States are hereby authorized to complete, on or before November 21, 1979, purchases and sales made prior to the effective date of securities purchased or sold for the account of Iran or an Iranian entity provided the following terms and conditions are complied with, respectively.

(1) The proceeds of such sale are credited to a blocked account in a banking institution in the name of the person for whose account the sale was made; and

(2) The securities so purchased are held in a blocked account in a banking institution in the name of the person for whose account the purchase was made.

(b) This section does not authorize the crediting of the proceeds of the sale of securities held in a blocked account or a sub-account thereof, to a blocked account or sub-account under any name or designation which differs from the name or designation of the specific blocked account or sub-account in which such securities were held.

§ 535.540 Disposition of certain tangible property.

(a) Specific licenses may be issued in appropriate cases at the discretion of the Secretary of the Treasury for the public sale and transfer of certain tangible property that is encumbered or contested within the meaning of § 535.333 (b) and (c) and that, because it is blocked by § 535.201, may not be sold or transferred without a specific

license, provided that each of the following conditions is met:

(1) The holder or supplier of the property has made a good faith effort over a reasonable period of time to obtain payment of any amounts owed by Iran or the Iranian entity, or adequate assurance of such payment;

(2) Neither payment nor adequate assurance of payment has been received;

(3) The license applicant has, under provisions of law applicable prior to November 14, 1979, a right to sell, or reclaim and sell, such property by methods not requiring judicial proceedings, and would be able to exercise such right under applicable law, but for the prohibitions in this part, and

(4) The license applicant shall enter into an indemnification agreement acceptable to the United States providing for the applicant to indemnify the United States, in an amount up to 150 percent of the proceeds of sale, for any monetary loss which may accrue to the United States from a decision by the Iran-U.S. Claims Tribunal that the United States is liable to Iran for damages that are in any way attributable to the issuance of such license. In the event the applicant and those acting for or on its behalf are the only bidders on the property, the United States shall have the right to establish a reasonable indemnification amount.

(b) An applicant for a license under this section shall provide the Office of Foreign Assets Control with documentation on the points enumerated in paragraph (a) of this section. The applicant normally will be required to submit an opinion of legal counsel regarding the legal right claimed under paragraph (a)(3) of this section.

(c) Any sale of property licensed under this section shall be at public auction and shall be made in good faith in a commercially reasonable manner. Notwithstanding any provision of State law, the license applicant shall give detailed notice to the appropriate Iranian entity of the proposed sale or transfer at least 30 days prior to the sale or other transfer. In addition, if the license applicant has filed a claim with the Iran-U.S. Claims Tribunal, the license applicant shall give at least 30 days' advance notice of the sale to the Tribunal.

(d) The disposition of the proceeds of any sale licensed under this section, minus such reasonable costs of sale as are authorized by applicable law (which will be licensed to be deducted), shall be in accordance with either of the following methods:

(1) Deposit into a separate blocked, interest-bearing account at a domestic bank in the name of the licensed applicant; or

(2) Any reasonable disposition in accordance with provisions of law applicable prior to November 14, 1979, which may include unrestricted use of all or a portion of the proceeds, provided that the applicant shall post a bond or establish a standby letter of credit, subject to the prior approval of the Secretary of the Treasury, in favor of the United States in the amount of the proceeds of sale, prior to any such disposition.

(e) For purposes of this section, the term "proceeds" means any gross amount of money or other value realized from the sale. The proceeds shall include any amount equal to any debt owed by Iran which may have constituted all or part of a successful bid at the licensed sale.

(f) The proceeds of any such sale shall be deemed to be property governed by § 535.215 of this part. Any part of the proceeds that constitutes Iranian property which under § 535.215 is to be transferred to Iran shall be so transferred in accordance with that section.

(g) Any license pursuant to this section may be granted subject to conditions deemed appropriate by the Secretary of the Treasury.

(h) Any person licensed pursuant to this section is required to submit a report to the Chief of Licensing, Office of Foreign Assets Control, within ten business days of the licensed sale or other transfer, providing a full accounting of the transaction, including the costs, any payment to lienholders or others, including payments to Iran or Iranian entities, and documentation concerning any blocked account established or payments made.

(Sec. 201-207, 91 Stat. 1626, 50 U.S.C. 1701-1706; E.O. 12170, 44 FR 65729; E.O. 12205, 45 FR 24099; E.O. 12211, 45 FR 26605; E.O. 12276, 46 FR 7913; E.O. 12279, 46 FR 7919; E.O. 12280, 46 FR 7921; E.O. 12281, 46 FR 7923; E.O. 12282, 46 FR 7925; and E.O. 12294, 46 FR 14111)

[47 FR 31683, July 22, 1982]

§ 535.566 **Unblocking of foreign currency deposits held by U.S.-owned or controlled foreign firms.**

Deposits held abroad in currencies other than U.S. dollars by branches and subsidiaries of persons subject to the jurisdiction of the United States are unblocked, provided however that conversions of blocked dollar deposits into foreign currencies are not authorized.

[44 FR 66833, Nov. 21, 1979]

§ 535.567 **Payment under advised letters of credit.**

(a) Specific licenses may be issued for presentation, acceptance, or payment of documentary drafts under a letter of credit opened by an Iranian entity and advised by a domestic bank or an Iranian bank subject to the jurisdiction of the United States, *provided,* That:

(1) The letter of credit was advised prior to the effective date;

(2) The property which is the subject of the payment under the letter of credit was not in the possession or control of the exporter on or after the effective date;

(3) The Beneficiary is a person subject to the jurisdiction of the United States.

(b) As a general matter, licenses will not be issued if the amount to be paid to a single payee exceeds $500,000, or if hardship cannot be shown.

[44 FR 75354, Dec. 19, 1979]

§ 535.568 **Certain standby letters of credit and performance bonds.**

(a) Notwithstanding any other provision of law, payment into a blocked account in a domestic bank by an issuing or confirming bank under a standby letter of credit in favor of an Iranian entity is prohibited by § 535.201 and not authorized, notwithstanding the provisions of § 535.508, if either:

(1) A specific license has been issued pursuant to the provisions of paragraph (b) of this section, or

(2) Eight business days have not expired after notice to the account party pursuant to paragraph (b) of this section.

(b) Whenever an issuing or confirming bank shall receive such demand for payment under a standby letter of credit, it shall promptly notify the person for whose account the credit was opened. Such person may then apply within five business days for a specific license authorizing the account party to establish a blocked account on its books in the name of the Iranian entity in the amount payable under the credit, in lieu of payment by the issuing or confirming bank into a blocked account and reimbursement therefor by the account party.

(c) Where there is outstanding a demand for payment under a standby letter of credit, and the issuing or confirming bank has been enjoined from making payment, upon removal of the injunction, the person for whose account the credit was opened may apply for a specific license for the same purpose and in the same manner as that set forth in paragraph (b) of this section. The issuing or confirming bank shall not make payment under the standby letter of credit unless:

(1) Eight business days have expired since the bank has received notice of the removal of the injunction and;

(2) A specific license issued to the account party pursuant to the provisions of this paragraph has not been presented to the bank.

(d) If necessary to assure the availability of the funds blocked, the Secretary may at any time require the payment of the amounts due under any letter of credit described in paragraph (a) of this section into a blocked account in a domestic bank or the supplying of any form of security deemed necessary.

(e) Nothing in this section precludes any person for whose account a standby letter of credit was opened or any other person from at any time contesting the legality of the demand from the Iranian entity or from raising any other legal defense to payment under the standby letter of credit.

(f) This section does not affect the obligation of the various parties of the instruments covered by this section if the instruments and payment thereunder are subsequently unblocked.

(g) For the purposes of this section, the term "standby letter of credit" shall mean a letter of credit securing performance of, or repayment of, any advance payments of deposits, under a contract with Iran or an Iranian entity, or any similar obligation in the nature of a performance bond.

(h) The regulations do not authorize any person subject to the jurisdiction of the United States to reimburse a non-U.S. bank for payment to Iran or an Iranian entity under a standby letter of credit, except by payment into a blocked account in accordance with § 535.508 or paragraph (b) or (c) of this section.

(i) A person receiving a specific license under paragraph (b) or (c) of this section shall certify to the Office of Foreign Assets Control within five business days after receipt of that license that it has established the blocked account on its books as provided for in those paragraphs. However, in appropriate cases, this time may be extended upon application to the Office of Foreign Assets Control when the account party has filed a petition with an appropriate court seeking a judicial order barring payment by the issuing or confirming bank.

(j) The extension or renewal of a standby letter of credit is authorized.

[47 FR 12339, Mar. 23, 1982]

§ 535.569 Licensed letter of credit transactions; forwarding of documents.

When payment of a letter of credit issued, advised, or confirmed by a bank subject to the jurisdiction of the United States is authorized by either general or specific license, the forwarding of the letter of credit documents to the account party is authorized.

[45 FR 1877, Jan. 9, 1980]

§ 535.576 Payment of non-dollar letters of credit to Iran.

Notwithstanding the prohibitions of §§ 535.201 and 535.206(a)(4), payment of existing non-dollar letters of credit in favor of Iranian entities or any person in Iran by any foreign branch or subsidiary of a U.S. firm is authorized, provided that the credit was opened prior to the respective effective date.

[45 FR 29288, May 2, 1980]

§ 535.579 Authorization of new transactions concerning certain Iranian property.

(a) Transactions involving property in which Iran or an Iranian entity has an interest are authorized where:

(1) The property comes within the jurisdiction of the United States or into the control or possession of any person subject to the jurisdiction of the United States after January 19, 1981, or

(2) The interest in the property of Iran or an Iranian entity (e.g. exports consigned to Iran or an Iranian entity) arises after January 19, 1981.

(b) Transactions involving standby letters of credit, performance or payment bonds and similar obligations, entered into prior to January 20, 1981, described in § 535.568 remain subject to the prohibitions and procedures contained in §§ 535.201 and 535.568.

(c) Property not blocked under § 535.201 as of January 19, 1981, in which the Government of Iran or an Iranian entity has an interest, which after that date is or becomes subject to the jurisdiction of the United States or comes within the control or possession of a person subject to the jurisdiction of the United States for the express purpose of settling claims against Iran or Iranian entities, is excluded from any authorization in this part for any attachment, injunction or other order of similar or analogous effect and any such attachment, injunction or order is prohibited by §§ 535.201 and 535.203.

(Secs. 201-207, 91 Stat. 1626, 50 U.S.C. 1701-1706; E.O. 12170, 44 FR 65729; E.O. 12205, 45 FR 24099; E.O. 12211, 45 FR 26685; E.O. 12276, 46 FR 7913; E.O. 12279, 46 FR 7919; E.O. 12280, 46 FR 7921; E.O. 12281, 46 FR 7923; E.O. 12282, 46 FR 7925; E.O. 12283, 46 FR 7927, and E.O. 12294, 46 FR 14111)

[46 FR 14336, Feb. 26, 1981]

§ 535.580 Necessary living expenses of relatives of the former Shah of Iran.

The transfer, payment or withdrawal of property described in § 535.217 is authorized to the extent necessary to pay living expenses of any individual listed in that section. Living expenses for this purpose shall include food, housing, transportation, security and other personal expenses.

(Secs. 201-207, 91 Stat. 1626, 50 U.S.C. 1701-1706; E.O. 12170, 44 FR 65729; E.O. 12211, 45 FR 26685; E.O. 12284, 46 FR 7929)

[46 FR 14330, Feb. 26, 1981]

Subpart F—Reports

§ 535.601 Records.

Every person engaging in any transaction subject to the provisions of this part shall keep a full and accurate record of each such transaction engaged in by him, regardless of whether such transaction is effected pursuant to license or otherwise, and such record shall be available for examination for at least two years after the date of such transaction.

[44 FR 75354, Dec. 19, 1979]

§ 535.602 Reports to be furnished on demand.

Every person is required to furnish under oath, in the form of reports or otherwise, from time to time and at any time as may be required by the Secretary of the Treasury or any person acting under his direction or authorization complete information relative to any transaction subject to the provisions of this part or relative to any property in which any foreign country or any national thereof has any interest of any nature whatsoever, direct or indirect. The Secretary of the Treasury or any person acting under his direction may require that such reports include the production of any books of account, contracts, letters or other papers, connected with any such transaction or property, in the custody or control of the persons required to make such reports. Reports with respect to transactions may be required either before or after such transactions are completed. The Secretary of the Treasury may, through any person

§ 535.615

or agency, investigate any such transaction or property or any violation of the provisions of this part regardless of whether any report has been required or filed in connection therewith.

[44 FR 75354, Dec. 19, 1979]

§ 535.615 Reports on Form TFR-615.

(a) *Requirement for report.* Reports on Form TFR-615 are hereby required to be filed on or before May 15, 1980, in the manner prescribed herein, with respect to all property subject to the jurisdiction of the United States or in the possession or control of any person subject to the jurisdiction of the United States at any time between the effective date and March 31, 1980, in which Iran or an Iranian entity has or has had any interest.

(1) *Who must report.* Reports on Form TFR-615 must be filed by each of the following:

(i) Any person subject to the jurisdiction of the United States or his successor, who on the effective date or any subsequent date up to and including March 31, 1980, had in his custody, possession or control, directly or indirectly, in trust or otherwise, property in which there was any direct or indirect interest of Iran or any Iranian entity, whether or not the property continued to be held by that person on March 31, 1980; and

(ii) Any business or non-business entity in the United States in which Iran or an Iranian entity held any financial interest on the effective date or on any subsequent date.

(2) *Property not required to be reported.* A report on Form TFR-615 is not required with respect to:

(i) Property of a private Iranian national; and

(ii) Patents, copyrights, trademarks and inventions; *Provided, however,* That a report is required with respect to any royalties due and unpaid in connection with such property.

(b) *Filing Form TFR-615.* Reports on Form TFR-615 shall be prepared in triplicate. On or before May 15, 1980, two copies shall be sent in a set to Unit 615, Office of Foreign Assets Control, Department of the Treasury, Washington, DC 20220. The third copy

must be retained with the reporter's records.

(c) *Certification.* Every report on Form TFR-615 shall contain the certification required in Part F of the Form. Failure to complete the certification shall render the report ineffective, and the submission of such a report shall not constitute compliance with this section.

(d) *Confidentiality of reports.* Reports on Form TFR-615 are regarded as privileged and confidential.

[45 FR 24408, Apr. 9, 1980]

§ 535.616 Reports on Form TFR-616.

(a) *Requirement for reports.* Reports on Form TFR-616 are hereby required to be filed on or before May 15, 1980, in the manner prescribed herein, with respect to claims for losses due to expropriation, nationalization, or other taking of property or businesses in Iran, including any special measures such as Iranian exchange controls directed against such property or businesses; claims for debt defaults, for damages for breach of contract or similar damages; and personal claims for salaries or for injury to person or property.

(b) *Who must report.* Reports on Form TFR-616 must be filed by every person subject to the jurisdiction of the United States which had a claim against Iran or an Iranian entity which arose before April 15, 1980. No report is to be submitted by a U.S. branch of a foreign firm not owned or controlled by a person subject to the jurisdiction of the United States or by a nonresident alien.

(c) *Filing Form TFR-616.* Reports on Form TFR-616 shall be prepared in triplicate. On or before May 15, 1980, two copies shall be sent in a set to Unit 616, Office of Foreign Assets Control, Department of the Treasury, Washington, DC 20220. The third copy must be retained with the reporter's record.

(d) *Certification.* Every report on Form TFR-616 shall contain the certification required on Part E of the Form. Failure to complete the certification shall render the report ineffective, and the submission of such a

report shall not constitute compliance with this section.

(e) *Confidentiality of reports.* Reports on Form TFR-616 are regarded as privileged and confidential.

[45 FR 24408, Apr. 9, 1980]

§ 535.618   **Report of contested property.**

(a) *Requirement for reports.* Reports are required to be filed within 15 days of receipt of a direction from Iran to transfer any interests in property claimed or believed to be an interest of Iran which was blocked by the Iranian Assets Control Regulations if the party receiving the direction to transfer has not transferred such claimed interest in property.

(b) *Who must report.* Reports must be filed by every person subject to the jurisdiction of the United States who does not transfer any interest or claimed interest in property described in paragraph (a) of this section within 15 days of a direction from Iran to transfer it.

(c) *Contents of report.* Each report shall contain the following information.

(1) Name and address of entity making the report.

(2) Name of person and entity directing the transfer.

(3) Date of the direction and date of its receipt.

(4) Description of the interest or claimed interest in property directed to be transferred.

(5) Statement or estimate of value of the interest or claimed interest in property.

(6) Explanation why property was not transferred as directed.

(7) Statement of any planned actions with respect to the interest or claimed interest in the property described.

(d) *Filing.* Reports shall be prepared in triplicate. Two copies shall be sent in a set to Unit 617, Office of Foreign Assets Control, Department of the Treasury, Washington, DC 20220. The third copy must be retained with the reporter's records.

(e) *Confidentiality of reports.* Reports under this section are regarded as privileged and confidential.

(Secs. 201-207, 91 Stat. 1626, 50 U.S.C. 1701-1706; E.O. 12170, 44 FR 65729; E.O. 12205, 45 FR 24099; E.O. 12211, 45 FR 26685; E.O. 12276, 46 FR 7913; E.O. 12279, 46 FR 7919; E.O. 12280, 46 FR 7921; E.O. 12281, 46 FR 7923; E.O. 12282, 46 FR 7925; E.O. 12283, 46 FR 7927, and E.O. 12294, 46 FR 14111)

[46 FR 14337, Feb. 26, 1981]

§ 535.619   **Reports on Form TFR-619.**

(a) *Reporting requirements.* Within 30 days after publication in the FEDERAL REGISTER of the name of any person or estate in § 535.217(b), the following persons who are subject to the jurisdiction of the United States shall file reports on Form TFR-619 with respect to their knowledge of the property of such person or estate at any time between November 3, 1979 and the date designated after the name of any person in § 535.217(b):

(1) Any person whose name is published for inclusion in § 535.217(b);

(2) Any person who has or had, from November 3, 1979 to the date of designation of the relevant person in § 535.217(b), actual or constructive possession or control, directly or indirectly, in trust or otherwise, of property in which there was any direct or indirect interest of any person listed in § 535.217(b) of the Regulations;

(3) Any business or non-business entity in the United States in which any person listed in § 535.217(b) of the Regulations held any financial interest at any time between November 3, 1979 and the date of designation of the relevant person in § 535.217(b);

(4) Any person having knowledge of property or assets of a person listed in § 535.217(b) of the Regulations, by reason of a business relationship with such property;

(5) Any person having actual knowledge of property of a person named in § 535.217(b) because of a personal relationship with the named person; and

(6) Any agency of the United States Government which has in any of its official financial books and records any information which serves to identify any property or assets of a person listed in § 535.217(b) of the Regulations.

(b) *What must be reported.* Form TFR-619 reports shall include the information specified in the form with respect to any interest of any nature whatsoever that a person named in § 535.217(b) had in any property subject to the jurisdiction of the United States between November 3, 1979, and the date of any designation of the relevant person in § 535.217(b). The term "property" is defined in § 535.311 of this part.

(c) *Filing Form TFR-619.* Reports on Forms TFR-619 shall be prepared in triplicate, two copies of which shall be sent in a set to Unit 619, Office of Foreign Assets Control, Department of the Treasury, Washington, DC 20220. The third copy is to be retained for the reporter's records.

(d) *Certification.* Every reporter is required to complete the certification portion of Form TFR-619. Failure to complete the certification shall render the report ineffective and the submission shall not constitute compliance with this section.

(Secs. 201-207, 91 Stat. 1626, 50 U.S.C. 1701-1706; E.O. 12170, 44 FR 65729; E.O. 12211, 45 FR 26685; E.O. 12284, 46 FR 7929)

[46 FR 26478, May 13, 1981]

§ 535.620 **Report on transfer of domestic bank assets and financial assets held by nonbanking institutions.**

(a) *Requirement for reports.* A report shall be filed by June 26, 1981 on Form TFR-620 by any bank or nonbanking institution regarding any transfer to the Federal Reserve Bank of New York that is required by § 535.213 or § 535.214. Any reporter that transfers property to the Federal Reserve Bank of New York by June 19, pursuant to § 535.213 or § 535.214, shall describe the property so transferred. Property (including interest through July 8, 1981, not transferred but required by § 535.213 or § 535.214 to be transferred shall be separately described.

(b) *Contents of report.* Each report shall contain the following information:

(1) Name and address of the transferor (indicate whether bank or nonbanking institution).

(2) Name and telephone number of person to be contacted about the transfer.

(3) Description of the property transferred or required to be trans-

ferred with a list of accounts, including branch, account party, account number, and account amount, with breakdown between principal and interest (as of date transferred or as of July 8 if not yet transferred).

(4) Total value (market value in the case of securities) of each transfer.

(5) Date and time of transfer (if applicable).

(6) A statement as to how interest was calculated, including rate(s) of interst and period(s) for which the rate(s) was applied.

(c) *Filing.* Reports shall be prepared in triplicate. Two copies shall be sent in a set to Unit 620, Office of Foreign Assets Control, Department of the Treasury, Washington, DC 20220. The third copy shall be retained for the reporter's records.

(d) *Confidentiality of reports.* Reports under this section are regarded as privileged and confidential but may be disclosed to Iran.

(e) *Updating of reports.* The Form TFR-620 report shall be updated within five business days of the transfer date to be determined by the Treasury Department by any reporter that does not transfer to the Federal Reserve Bank of New York, on or before that date, the property described in the reporter's TFR-620 report. The required updating shall include a full explanation as to why the property actually transferred was not the same as the property described in the reporter's TFR-620 report.

(Secs. 201-207, 91 Stat. 1626, 50 U.S.C. 1701-1706; E.O. 12170, 44 FR 65729; E.O. 12205, 45 FR 24099; E.O. 12211, 45 FR 26685; E.O. 12276, 46 FR 7913; E.O. 12279, 46 FR 7919; E.O. 12280, 46 FR 7921; E.O. 12281, 46 FR 7923; E.O. 12282, 46 FR 7925; E.O. 12283, 46 FR 7927, and E.O. 12294, 46 FR 14111)

[46 FR 31630, June 16, 1981]

§ 535.621 **Registration of bank claims against the escrow account at the Bank of England.**

(a) *Registration requirements.* Any U.S. banking institution that has, and intends to assert, a claim against the account established by the deposit of $1.418 billion in escrow ("the Escrow Account," also known as "Dollar Account No. 2") at the Bank of England pursuant to Paragraph 2(B) of the Undertakings of the Government of the United States of America and the Government of the Islamic Republic of Iran with Respect to the Declaration of the Government of the Democratic and Popular Republic of Algeria, is required to register with the Office of Foreign Assets Control, in writing, on or before December 16, 1981.

(b) *Contents of registration notice.* The required registration shall refer to this section of the Regulations and contain the following:

(1) Name and address of the banking institution; and

(2) Name, title, and telephone number of person who may be contacted about this registration.

(c) *Filing.* One copy of this registration notice, which shall be in the form of a letter or a telex (Telex No. 710-822-9201), should be sent to Unit 621, Office of Foreign Assets Control, Department of the Treasury, Washington, DC 20220. Telexed notices should also include the telephone number (376-0968) of the Census Unit. A copy of the notice should be retained for the submitter's records.

(d) *Failure to register.* Any banking institution which does not submit a registration notice pursuant to this section shall be precluded from asserting any claim against the Escrow Account.

(Secs. 201-207, 91 Stat. 1626, 50 U.S.C. 1701-1706; E.O. 12170, 44 FR 65729; E.O. 12205, 45 FR 24099; E.O. 12211, 45 FR 26685; E.O. 12276, 46 FR 7913; E.O. 12279, 46 FR 7919; E.O. 12280, 46 FR 7921; E.O. 12281, 46 FR 7923; E.O. 12282, 46 FR 7925; and E.O. 12294, 46 FR 14111)

[46 FR 59939, Dec. 7, 1981]

§ 535.622 Registration of bank claims against the No. 1 Account, and the escrow account at the Bank of England (Dollar Account No. 2); registration of January Interest claims.

(a) *Bank claims against the No. 1 Account—* (1) *Registration requirements.* Any U.S. banking institution that is a member of a syndicate of banking institutions and has, or any member of the syndicate has, and intends to assert, a claim against the balance remaining (the "No. 1 Account") of the $3.667 billion transferred to the Federal Reserve Bank of New York (the "Fed") pursuant to Paragraph 2(A) of the January 19, 1981 Undertakings of the Government of the United States of America and the Government of the Islamic Republic of Iran With Respect to the Declaration of the Government of the Democratic and Popular Republic of Algeria (the "Undertakings") is required to register with the Office of Foreign Assets Control, in writing, on or before November 17, 1986, unless at least one other U.S. banking institution that is a member of the syndicate has properly filed a registration pursuant to this subsection relating to such claim. Each registration shall relate only to one syndicate.

(2) *Contents of registration.* The required registration shall refer to this subsection and contain the following:

(i) Name and address of the registrant banking institution;

(ii) Name, title, and telephone number of person who may be contacted about the registration;

(iii) Identification of the syndicate;

(iv) The basis for each kind of claim together with the name of each syndicate member (including the registrant, if applicable) on whose behalf the registrant is asserting that kind of claim and the dollar amount of that kind of claim for each such syndicate member;

(v) If there is more than one kind of claim, for each kind of claim the total dollar amount claimed for all syndicate members (including the registrant if applicable) on whose behalf the registrant is asserting that kind of claim;

(vi) The aggregate total dollar amount claimed for all syndicate members (including the registrant, if applicable) on whose behalf the registrant is asserting claims; and

(vii) The interest rate(s) at which interest would accrue after September 30, 1986, and, if different rates apply to different portions of the aggregate total dollar amount claimed, the dollar amount to which each rate applies.

All dollar amounts are to be stated as of September 30, 1986. Dollar amounts and other information relating to a claim for interest (including interest thereon) related to the period after December 31, 1980, on the syndicated loans and credits referred to in Paragraph 2(A) of the Undertakings ("January Interest") shall not be included in registrations pursuant to this subsection. If the interest rate(s) referred to in clause (a)(2)(vii) may only be stated with reference to an index, that index and the applicable margin shall be provided. For all interest rates referred to in clause (a)(2)(vii), the calculation period (*e.g.,* semiannual), the starting date of the first interest calculation period beginning after September 30, 1986, and the calculation basis (*e.g.,* 365/365, 365/360) shall be provided.

(3) *Filing.* One copy of the registration, which shall be in the form of a letter or a telex (Telex No. 710–822–9201), shall be sent to Unit 622(a), Office of Foreign Assets Control, Department of the Treasury, Washington, DC 20220. Telexed registrations should also include the telephone number of the Census Unit (376–0968). A copy of the registration should be retained for the registrant banking institution's records.

(4) *Failure to register.* All members of a syndicate are precluded from asserting any claim against the No. 1 Account arising out of the syndicate, or participation in the syndicate, unless at least one U.S. banking institution that is a member of the syndicate has registered a claim against the No. 1 Account pursuant to this subsection and the claim asserted is consistent with information provided in such registration and with the purpose of Paragraph 2(A) of the Undertakings.

(b) *Bank claims against the escrow account (Dollar Account No. 2) at the Bank of England*—(1) *Registration requirements.* Any U.S. banking institution that has, and intends to assert, any remaining claim against the account established by the deposit of $1.418 billion in escrow (the "Escrow Account," also known as Dollar Account No. 2") at the Bank of England pursuant to paragraph 2(B) of the Undertakings is required to register with the Office of Foreign Assets Control, in writing, on or before November 17, 1986.

(2) *Contents of registration.* The required registration shall refer to this subsection and contain the following:

(i) Name and address of the registrant banking institution;

(ii) Name, title, and telephone number of person who may be contacted about the registration;

(iii) The basis for each kind of claim together with the dollar amount of that kind of claim;

(iv) The total dollar amount claimed; and

(v) The interest rate(s) at which interest would accrue after September 30, 1986, and, if different rates apply to different portions of the total dollar amount claimed, the dollar amount to which each rate applies.

All dollar amounts are to be stated as of September 30, 1986. Dollar amounts and other information relating to a January Interest claim shall not be included in registrations pursuant to this subsection. If the interest rate(s) referred to in clause (b)(2)(v) may only be stated with reference to an index, that index and the applicable margin shall be provided. For all interest rates referred to in clause (b)(2)(v), the calculation period (*e.g.,* semiannual), the starting date of the first interest calculation period beginning after September 30, 1986, and the calculation basis (*e.g.,* 365/365, 365/360) shall be provided.

(3) *Filing.* One copy of the registration, which shall be in the form of a letter or a telex (Telex No. 710–822–9201), shall be sent to Unit 622(b), Office of Foreign Assets Control, Department of the Treasury, Washington, DC 20220. Telexed registrations should also include the telephone number (376–0968) of the Census Unit. A copy of the registration should be retained for the registrant banking institution's records.

(4) *Failure to register.* Except for a January Interest claim, U.S. banking institutions are precluded from asserting any claim against the Escrow Account unless the U.S. banking institution has registered a claim against the Escrow Account pursuant to this subsection and has previously registered pursuant to § 535.621 and the claim asserted is consistent with information provided in the registration pursuant to this subsection and with the purpose of Paragraph 2(A) of the Undertakings.

(c) *January Interest registration*—(1) *Registration requirements.* Any U.S. banking institution that is a member of a syndicate of banking institutions and has, or any member of the syndicate has, and intends to assert, a claim for January Interest against the Escrow Account is required to register with the Office of Foreign Assets Control, in writing, on or before November 17, 1986, unless at least one other U.S. banking institution that is a member of the syndicate has properly filed a registration pursuant to this subsection relating to such claim.

(2) *Contents of registration.* The required registration shall refer to this subsection and contain the following:

(i) Name and address of the registrant banking institution;

(ii) Name, title, and telephone number of person who may be contacted about the registration;

(iii) Identification of syndicate(s);

(iv) For each syndicate the name of each syndicate member (including the registrant, if applicable) on whose behalf the registrant is asserting a claim and the dollar amount of the claim for such syndicate member;

(v) If there is more than one syndicate, for each syndicate the total dollar amount claimed for all syndicate members (including the registrant if applicable) on whose behalf the registrant is asserting a claim;

(vi) The aggregate total dollar amount claimed for all syndicate members (including the registrant, if applicable) on whose behalf the registrant is asserting claims; and

(vii) The interest rate(s) at which interest would accrue after September 30, 1986, and, if different rates apply to different portions of the aggregate total dollar amount claimed, the dollar amount to which each rate applies.

All dollar amounts are to be stated as of September 30, 1986. If the interest rate(s) referred to in clause (c)(2)(vii) may only be stated with reference to an index, that index and the applicable margin shall be provided. For all interest rates referred to in clause (c)(2)(vii), the calculation period (*e.g.,* semiannual), the starting date of the first interest calculation period beginning after September 30, 1986, and the calculation basis (*e.g.,* 365/365, 365/360) shall be provided.

(3) *Filing.* One copy of the registration, which shall be in the form of a letter or a telex (Telex No. 710–822–9201), shall be sent to Unit 622(c), Office of Foreign Assets Control, Department of the Treasury, Washington, DC 20220. Telexed registrations should also include the telephone number of the Census Unit (376–0968). A copy of the registration should be retained for the registrant banking institution's records.

(4) *Failure to register.* All members of a syndicate are precluded from asserting any January Interest claim against the Escrow Account arising out of the syndicate, or participation in the syndicate, unless at least one U.S. banking institution that is a member of the syndicate has registered a claim against the Escrow Account pursuant to this subsection and the claim asserted is consistent with information provided in such registration and with the purpose of Paragraph 2(B) of the Undertakings.

[51 FR 37569, Oct. 23, 1986]

§ 535.625 **Reports on Form TFR–625.**

(a) *Requirement for report.* Reports on Form TFR–625 are hereby required to be filed on or before July 1, 1982, in the manner prescribed herein, with respect to all tangible property subject to the jurisdiction of the United States or in the possession or control of any person subject to the jurisdiction of the United States at any time between November 14, 1979, and January 19, 1981, in which Iran or an Iranian entity has or has had any interest or asserted interest.

(b) *Who must report.* Reports on Form TFR–625 must be filed by any person, or the successor to such person, subject to the jurisdiction of the United States who has an interest in, or who, between November 14, 1979, and January 19, 1981, had in his custody, control, or possession, directly or indirectly, in trust or otherwise, tangible property in which there was or is any direct or indirect interest or an asserted interest of Iran or an Iranian entity. This includes, but is not limited to, all persons who reported holding tangible property as of March 31, 1980 on Treasury Department Form TFR-615, "Census of Blocked Iranian Assets."

(c) *Filing Form TFR-625.* Reports on Form TFR-625 shall be prepared in triplicate. On or before July 1, 1982, two copies shall be sent in a set to Unit 625, Office of Foreign Assets Control, Department of the Treasury, Washington, DC 20220. The third copy must be retained with the reporter's records.

(d) *Certification.* Every report on Form TFR-625 shall contain the certification required in Part D of the Form. Failure to complete the certification shall render the report ineffective, and the submission of such a report shall not constitute compliance with this section.

(e) *Confidentiality of reports.* Reports on Form TFR-625 are regarded as privileged and confidential.

(Approved by the Office of Management and Budget under control number 1505-0056)

(Secs. 201-207, 91 Stat. 1626, 50 U.S.C. 1701-1706; E.O. 12170, 44 FR 65729; E.O. 12205, 45 FR 24099; E.O. 12211, 45 FR 26685; E.O. 12276, 46 FR 7913; E.O. 12279, 46 FR 7919; E.O. 12280, 46 FR 7921; E.O. 12281, 46 FR 7923; E.O. 12282, 46 FR 7925; and E.O. 12294, 46 FR 14111)

[47 FR 22361, May 24, 1982]

EDITORIAL NOTE: For a notice document affecting § 535.625 Form TFR-625, see 47 FR 25003, June 9, 1982.

Subpart G—Penalties

§ 535.701 Penalties.

(a) Attention is directed to section 206 of the International Emergency Economic Powers Act which provides in part:

(a) A civil penalty of not to exceed $10,000 may be imposed on any person who violates any license, order, or regulation issued under this title.

(b) Whoever willfully violates any license, order, or regulation issued under this title shall, upon conviction be fined not more than $50,000, or, if a natural person, may be imprisoned for not more than ten years, or both; and any officer, director, or agent of any corporation who knowingly participates in such violation may be punished by a like fine, imprisonment or both.

This section of the International Emergency Economic Powers Act is applicable to violations of any provision of this part and to violations of the provisions of any license, ruling, regulation, order, direction or instruction issued by or pursuant to the direction or authorization of the Secretary of the Treasury pursuant to this part or otherwise under the International Emergency Economic Powers Act.

(b) Attention is also directed to 18 U.S.C. 1001 which provides:

Whoever, in any matter within the jurisdiction of any department or agency of the United States knowingly and willfully falsifies, conceals or covers up by any trick, scheme, or device a material fact, or makes any false, fictitious or fraudulent statements or representation or makes or uses any false writing or document knowing the same to contain any false, fictitious or fraudulent statement or entry, shall be fined not more than $10,000 or imprisoned not *more than five years, or both.*

§ 535.702 Prepenalty notice.

(a) *When required.* If the Director of the Office of Foreign Assets Control (hereinafter "Director") has reasonable cause to believe that there has occurred a violation of any provision of this part or a violation of the provisions of any license, ruling, regulation, order, direction or instruction issued by or pursuant to the direction or authorization of the Secretary of the Treasury pursuant to this part or otherwise under the International Emergency Economic Powers Act, and the Director determines that further proceedings are warranted, he shall issue to the person concerned a notice of his intent to impose a monetary penalty. The prepenalty notice shall be issued whether or not another agency has taken any action with respect to this matter.

(b) *Contents*—(1) *Facts of violation.* The prepenalty notice shall: (i) Describe the violation.

(ii) Specify the laws and regulations allegedly violated.

(iii) State the amount of the proposed monetary penalty.

(2) *Right to make presentations.* The prepenalty notice also shall inform the person of his right to make a written presentation within thirty (30)

days of mailing of the notice as to why a monetary penalty should not be imposed, or, if imposed, why it should be in a lesser amount than proposed.

[53 FR 7356, Mar. 8, 1988]

§ 535.703 Presentation responding to prepenalty notice.

(a) *Time within which to respond.* The named person shall have 30 days from the date of mailing of the prepenalty notice to make a written presentation to the Director.

(b) *Form and contents of written presentation.* The written presentation need not be in any particular form, but shall contain information sufficient to indicate that it is in response to the prepenalty notice. It should contain responses to the allegations in the prepenalty notice and set forth the reasons why the person believes the penalty should not be imposed or, if imposed, why it should be in a lesser amount than proposed.

[53 FR 7356, Mar. 8, 1988]

§ 535.704 Penalty notice.

(a) *No violation.* If, after considering any presentations made in response to the prepenalty notice, the Director determines that there was no violation by the person named in the prepenalty notice, he promptly shall notify the person in writing of that determination and that no monetary penalty will be imposed.

(b) *Violation.* If, after considering any presentations made in response to the prepenalty notice, the Director determines that there was a violation by the person named in the prepenalty notice, he promptly shall issue a written notice of the imposition of the monetary penalty to that person.

[53 FR 7356, Mar. 8, 1988]

§ 535.705 Referral to United States Department of Justice.

In the event that the person named does not pay the penalty imposed pursuant to this subpart or make payment arrangements acceptable to the Director within thirty days of the mailing of the written notice of the imposition of the penalty, the matter shall be referred to the United States Department of Justice for appropriate

action to recover the penalty in a civil suit in a Federal district court.

[53 FR 7356, Mar. 8, 1988]

Subpart H—Procedures

Source: 44 FR 66833, Nov. 21, 1979, unless otherwise noted.

§ 535.801 Licensing.

(a) *General licenses.* General licenses have been issued authorizing under appropriate terms and conditions many types of transactions which are subject to the prohibitions contained in Subpart B of this part. All such licenses are set forth in Subpart E of this part. It is the policy of the Office of Foreign Assets Control not to grant applications for specific licenses authorizing transactions to which the provisions of an outstanding general license are applicable. Persons availing themselves of certain general licenses are required to file reports and statements in accordance with the instructions specified in the licenses.

(b) *Specific licenses*—(1) *General course of procedure.* Transactions subject to the prohibitions contained in Subpart B of this part which are not authorized by general license may be effected only under specific license. The specific licensing activities of the Office of Foreign Assets Control are performed by its Washington Office and by the Federal Reserve Bank of New York. When an unusual problem is presented, the proposed action is cleared with the Director of the Office of Foreign Assets Control or such person as he may designate.

(2) *Applications for specific licenses.* Applications for specific licenses to engage in any transaction prohibited by or pursuant to this part are to be filed in duplicate on Form TFAC-27 with the Federal Reserve Bank of New York. Any person having an interest in a transaction or proposed transaction may file an application for a license authorizing the effecting of such transaction, and there is no requirement that any other person having an interest in such transaction shall or should join in making or filing such application.

(3) *Information to be supplied.* Applicant must supply all information specified by the respective forms and instructions. Such documents as may be relevant shall be attached to each application as a part of such application except that documents previously filed with the Office of Foreign Assets Control may, where appropriate, be incorporated by reference. Applicants may be required to furnish such further information as is deemed necessary to a proper determination by the Office of Foreign Assets Control. If an applicant or other party in interest desires to present additional information or discuss or argue the application, he may do so at any time before or after decision. Arrangements for oral presentation should be made with the Office of Foreign Assets Control.

(4) *Effect of denial.* The denial of a license does not preclude the reopening of an application or the filing of a further application. The applicant or any other party in interest may at any time request explanation of the reasons for a denial by correspondence or personal interview.

(5) *Reports under specific licenses.* As a condition upon the issuance of any license, the licensee may be required to file reports with respect to the transaction covered by the license, in such form and at such times and places as may be prescribed in the license or otherwise.

(6) *Issuance of license.* Licenses will be issued by the Office of Foreign Assets Control acting on behalf of the Secretary of the Treasury or by the Federal Reserve Bank of New York, acting in accordance with such regulations, rulings and instructions as the Secretary of the Treasury or the Office of Foreign Assets Control may from time to time prescribe, in such cases or classes of cases as the Secretary of the Treasury or the Office of Foreign Assets Control may determine, or licenses may be issued by the Secretary of the Treasury acting directly or through any person, agency, or instrumentality designated by him.

§ 535.802 Unblocking.

Any interested person desiring the unblocking of accounts or other property on the ground that neither Iran nor any Iranian entity has an interest in the property may file such an application. Such application shall be filed in the manner provided in § 535.801(b) and shall contain full information in support of the administrative action requested.

The applicant is entitled to be heard on the application. If the applicant desires a hearing, arrangements should be made with the Office of Foreign Assets Control.

§ 535.803 Decision.

The Office of Foreign Assets Control or the Federal Reserve Bank of New York will advise each applicant of the decision respecting applications filed by him. The decision of the Office of Foreign Assets Control acting on behalf of the Secretary of the Treasury with respect to an application shall constitute final agency action.

§ 535.804 Records and reporting.

Records are required to be kept by every person engaging in any transaction subject to the provisions of this part.

Reports may be required from any person with respect to any transaction subject to the provisions of this chapter or relative to any property in which any foreign country or any national thereof has any interest.

§ 535.805 Amendment, modification, or revocation.

The provisions of this part and any rulings, licenses, authorizations, instructions, orders, or forms issued thereunder may be amended, modified, or revoked at any time.

§ 535.806 Rule making.

(a) In general, rule making by the Office of Foreign Assets Control involves foreign affairs functions of the United States to which the provisions of the Administrative Procedure Act, 5 U.S.C. 553, requiring notice of proposed rule making, the opportunity for public participation and a delay in effective date are inapplicable. However, the Office of Foreign Assets Control may consult with interested groups or persons in connection with the issuance of rules or the establishment of licensing policies.

(b) Any interested person may recommend in writing to the Director of the Office of Foreign Assets Control the issuance, amendment or the repeal of any rule.

[44 FR 75353, Dec. 19, 1979]

Subpart I—Miscellaneous Provisions

§ 535.901 Dollar accounts at banks abroad.

Any domestic bank is hereby authorized to effect withdrawals or other transfers from any account held in the name of a non-Iranian bank located in a foreign country, provided such non-Iranian foreign bank is not a person subject to the jurisdiction of the United States.

§ 535.902 Set-offs by U.S. owned or controlled firms abroad.

(a) Branches and subsidiaries in foreign countries of persons subject to the jurisdiction of the United States are licensed to set-off their claims against Iran or Iranian entities by debit to blocked accounts held by them for Iran or Iranian entities.

(b) The general license in paragraph (a) of this section is revoked as of January 19, 1981.

(c) For purposes of this section, set-offs include combinations of accounts and any similar actions.

(Secs. 201-207, 91 Stat. 1626, 50 U.S.C. 1701-1706; E.O. 12170, 44 FR 65729; E.O. 12205, 45 FR 24099; E.O. 12211, 45 FR 26685; E.O. 12276, 46 FR 7913; E.O. 12279, 46 FR 7919; E.O. 12280, 46 FR 7921; E.O. 12281, 46 FR 7923; E.O. 12282, 46 FR 7925; E.O. 12283, 46 FR 7927, and E.O. 12294, 46 FR 14111)

[46 FR 14337, Feb. 26, 1981]

§ 535.904 Payment by Iranian entities of obligations to persons within the United States.

The transfer of funds after the effective date by, through or to any U.S. banking institution or other person within the United States solely for purposes of payment of obligations by Iranian entities owed to persons within the United States is authorized: *Provided,* That there is no debit to a blocked account. Property is not blocked by virtue of being transferred or received pursuant to this section.

[44 FR 66591, Nov. 20, 1979]

§ 535.905 Paperwork Reduction Act notice.

The information collection requirements in §§ 535.568 and 535.801 have been approved by the Office of Management and Budget and assigned control number 1505-0075.

[50 FR 27438, July 3, 1985]

PART 540—NICARAGUAN TRADE CONTROL REGULATIONS

hereunder may be amended, modified, or revoked at any time.

§ 555.804 Rulemaking.

(a) All rules and other public documents are issued by the Secretary of the Treasury upon recommendation of the Director of the Office of Foreign Assets Control. Except to the extent that there is involved any military, naval, or foreign affairs function of the United States or any matter relating to agency management or personnel or to public property, loans, grants, benefits, or contracts, and except when interpretive rules, general statements of policy, or rules of agency organization, practice, or procedure are involved, or when notice and public procedure are impracticable, unnecessary, or contrary to the public interest, interested persons will be afforded an opportunity to participate in rulemaking through the submission of written data, views, or arguments, with oral presentation in the discretion of the Director. In general, rulemaking by the Office of Foreign Assets Control involves foreign affairs functions of the United States. Wherever possible, however, it is the practice to hold informal consultations with interested groups or persons before the issuance of any rule or other public document.

(b) Any interested person may petition the Director of the Office of Foreign Assets Control in writing for the issuance, amendment or revocation of any rule.

§ 555.805 Delegation by the Secretary of the Treasury.

Any action that the Secretary of the Treasury is authorized to take with respect to the subject matter of this part may be taken by the Director of the Office of Foreign Assets Control, or by any other person to whom the Secretary of the Treasury has delegated authority so to act.

§ 555.806 Rules governing availability of information.

(a) The records of the Office of Foreign Assets Control that are required by 5 U.S.C. 552 to be made available to the public shall be made available in accordance with the definitions, proce-

dures, payment of fees, and other provisions of the regulations on the disclosure of records of the Office of the Secretary and of other bureaus and offices of the Department issued under 5 U.S.C. 552 and published as Part 1 of this Title 31 of the Code of Federal Regulations.

(b) Any form issued for use in connection with this part may be obtained in person from or by writing to the Office of Foreign Assets Control, Treasury Department, Washington, D.C. 20220, or the Foreign Assets Control Division, Federal Reserve Bank of New York, 33 Liberty Street, New York, NY 10045.

PART 560—IRANIAN TRANSACTIONS REGULATIONS

AUTHORITY: 22 U.S.C. 2349aa-9; E.O. 12613, 52 FR 41940, Oct. 30, 1987.

SOURCE: 52 FR 44076, Nov. 17, 1987, unless otherwise noted.

Subpart A—Relation of This Part to Other Laws and Regulations

§ 560.101 Relation of this part to other laws and regulations.

(a) This part is separate from, and independent of, the other parts of this chapter, including Part 535, "Iranian Assets Control Regulations." No license or authorization contained in or issued pursuant to those other parts authorizes any transaction prohibited by this part. No license or authorization contained in or issued pursuant to any other provision of law or regulations authorizes any transaction prohibited by this part.

(b) No license or authorization contained in or issued pursuant to this part relieves the involved parties from complying with any other applicable laws or regulations.

Subpart B—Prohibitions

§ 560.201 Prohibited importation of goods and services from Iran.

Except as authorized by regulations, rulings, instructions, licenses, or otherwise, no goods or services of Iranian origin may be imported into the United States, with the following exceptions:

(a) Iranian-origin publications and materials imported for news publications or news broadcast dissemination;

(b) Petroleum products refined from Iranian crude oil in a third country; and

(c) Articles imported directly from Iran prior to the effective date.

§ 560.202 Prohibited related transactions.

No person may order, buy, act as broker or facilitator for, receive, conceal, store, use, sell, loan, dispose of, transfer, transport, finance, forward, or otherwise service, in whole or in part, any goods or services subject to the prohibitions of this part, with knowledge or reason to know that a violation of this part, or any regulation, order, or license issued pursuant hereto or to section 505 of the Act, has occurred, is about to occur, or is intended to occur with respect to such goods or services.

§ 560.203 Evasions.

Any transaction for the purpose of, or which has the effect of, evading or avoiding any of the prohibitions set forth in this subpart is hereby prohibited.

Subpart C—General Definitions

§ 560.301 Effective date.

The term "effective date" means 12:01 p.m., Eastern Standard Time, October 29, 1987.

§ 560.302 The Act.

For purposes of this part, the term "Act" means the International Security and Development Cooperation Act of 1985 (Pub. L. 99–83).

§ 560.303 Iran; Iranian.

The term "Iran" means the country of Iran and any Iranian territory, dependency, colony, protectorate, mandate, dominion, possession or place subject to the jurisdiction thereof, or any territory which, at the time of the relevant transaction, is controlled or occupied by the military, naval or police forces or other authorities of Iran. The term "Iranian" means pertaining to Iran as defined in this section.

§ 560.304 Government of Iran.

(a) The "Government of Iran" includes:

(1) The state and the Government of Iran, as well as any political subdivision, agency, or instrumentality thereof;

(2) Any partnership, association, corporation, or other organization substantially owned or controlled by the foregoing;

(3) Any person to the extent that such person is, or has been, or to the extent that there is reasonable cause to believe that such person is, or has been, since the effective date acting or purporting to act directly or indirectly on behalf of any of the foregoing.

§ 560.305 Person.

The term "person" means an individual, partnership, association, corporation or other organization.

§ 560.306 Iranian origin goods and services.

The term "goods or services of Iranian origin" includes:

(a) Goods grown, produced, manufactured, extracted, or processed in Iran;

(b) Goods which have entered into Iranian commerce; and

(c) Services performed in Iran or by the Government of Iran, as defined in § 560.304, where the benefit of such services will be received in the United States. Services of Iranian origin are not imported into the United States when such services are provided in the United States by an Iranian national resident in the United States. The term "services of Iranian origin" does not include:

(1) Diplomatic and consular services performed by or on behalf of the Government of Iran, or

(2) Diplomatic and consular services performed by or on behalf of the Government of the United States.

§ 560.307 United States.

The term "United States" means the United States, including its territories and possessions.

§ 560.308 Importation.

The term "importation" means the bringing of any goods into the United States, except that in the case of goods transported by vessel, "importation" shall mean the bringing of any goods into the United States with the intent to unlade it.

§ 560.309 Publications.

The term "publications" includes, but is not limited to, books, newspapers, magazines, films, phonograph records, tape recordings, photographs, microfilm, microfiche, videotapes, and posters, as well as items described in the following:

(a) 15 CFR 399.1, Commodity Control List, Group 5, CCL No. 7599I: microfilm that reproduces the content of certain publications, and similar materials.

(b) 15 CFR 399.1, Commodity Control List, Group 9, CCL No. 7999I: certain publications and related materials.

§ 560.310 License.

Except as otherwise specified, the term "license" means any license or authorization contained in or issued pursuant to this part.

§ 560.311 General license.

The term "general license" means any license or authorization the terms of which are set forth in this part.

§ 560.312 Specific license.

The term "specific license" means any license or authorization not set forth in this part but issued pursuant to this part in response to a written application.

Subpart D—Interpretations

§ 560.401 Reference to amended sections.

Reference to any section of this part or to any regulation, ruling, order, instruction, direction, or license issued pursuant to this part shall be deemed to refer to the same as currently amended unless otherwise so specified.

§ 560.402 Effect of amendment of sections of this part or of other orders, etc.

Any amendment, modification, or revocation of any section of this part or of any order, regulation, ruling, instruction, or license issued by or under the direction of the Secretary of the Treasury pursuant to section 505 of the Act shall not, unless otherwise specifically provided, be deemed to affect any act done or omitted to be done, or any suit or proceeding had or commenced in any civil or criminal case prior to such amendment, modification, or revocation. All penalties, forfeitures, and liabilities under any such order, regulation, ruling, instruction, or license shall continue and may be enforced as if such amendment, modification, or revocation had not been made.

§ 560.403 Exports from Iran prior to the effective date.

Goods may be imported pursuant to exception (c) in § 560.201 if, prior to the effective date, the goods were loaded on board a vessel or aircraft in Iran or a third country ready for export to the United States, or were in transit from Iran or a third country for direct importation into the United States.

§ 560.404 Certain offshore transactions and other transactions related thereto.

The prohibitions contained in § 560.201 do not apply to the importation into locations outside the United States of goods or services of Iranian origin. The prohibitions also do not extend to payments or other transactions, wherever concluded, by any person relating to such transactions outside the United States, such as U.S. financial, service, or brokerage transactions involving offshore transactions with Iran. Payments relating to such non-prohibited transactions, and payments relating to the exceptions designated in § 560.201, are not prohibited.

§ 560.405 Goods; technical data.

The term "goods" shall include merchandise; articles; and technical data in tangible form including, but not limited to, a model, prototype, blueprint, drawing, operating manual, computer software, tape recording, microfiche, or other material in machine readable form. The term "goods" does not apply to oral transmission of technical data in the course of performance of services, telephone communications, lectures, seminars, or plant visits.

§ 560.406 Transshipment through United States prohibited.

The prohibitions in § 560.201 apply to the importation into the United States, for transshipment or transit, of goods of Iranian origin which are intended or destined for third countries.

§ 560.407 Importation from third countries; transshipment.

(a) Importation into the United States from third countries of goods containing raw materials or components of Iranian origin is not prohibited if those raw materials or components have been incorporated into manufactured products or substantially transformed in a third country.

(b) Importation into the United States of goods of Iranian origin that have been transshipped through a third country without being incorporated into manufactured products or substantially transformed in a third country is prohibited.

§ 560.408 Importation into and release from a bonded warehouse or foreign trade zone.

The prohibitions in § 560.201 apply to importation into a bonded warehouse or a foreign trade zone of the United States. However, § 560.201 does not prohibit the release from a bonded warehouse or a foreign trade zone of goods of Iranian origin imported into a bonded warehouse or a foreign trade zone prior to the effective date.

Subpart E—Licenses, Authorizations, and Statements of Licensing Policy

§ 560.501 Effect of license or authorization.

(a) No license or other authorization contained in this part, or otherwise issued by or under the direction of the Secretary of the Treasury pursuant to section 505 of the Act, shall be deemed to authorize or validate any transaction effected prior to the issuance of the license, unless specifically provided in such license or other authorization.

(b) No regulation, ruling, instruction, or license authorizes a transaction prohibited under this part unless the regulation, ruling, instruction, or license is issued by the Treasury Department and specifically refers to this part. No regulation, ruling, instruction, or license referring to this part shall be deemed to authorize any transactions prohibited by any provision of this chapter unless the regulation, ruling, instruction or license specifically refers to such provision.

(c) Any regulation, ruling, instruction or license authorizing a transaction otherwise prohibited under this part has the effect of removing a prohibition or prohibitions in Subpart B from the transaction, but only to the extent specifically stated by its terms. Unless the regulation, ruling, instruction or license otherwise specifies, such an authorization does not create any right, duty, obligation, claim, or interest in, or with respect to, any property which would not otherwise exist under ordinary principles of law.

§ 560.502 Exclusion from licenses and authorizations.

The Secretary of the Treasury reserves the right to exclude any person from the operation of any license, or from the privileges therein conferred, or to restrict the applicability thereof with respect to particular persons, transactions or property or classes thereof. Such action shall be binding upon all persons receiving actual or constructive notice thereof.

§ 560.503 Importation pursuant to prior contractual agreements.

Specific licenses may be issued, on a case-by-case basis, authorizing the importation of goods of Iranian origin into the United States after the effective date and before January 1, 1988, if the importer furnishes the Office with a certification supported by written evidence establishing that—

(a) Payment for the goods was made, or payment was irrevocably committed to be made, prior to the effective date, *or*

(b) A written agreement to purchase the goods was entered into prior to the effective date; *and*

(c) Prior to the effective date, the goods were intended for importation into the United States.

§ 560.504 Iranian goods in third countries prior to effective date.

(a) Specific licenses may be issued authorizing the importation of non-fungible goods of Iranian origin, such as carpets and artwork, provided the applicant submits satisfactory documentary proof that the goods are located outside Iran prior to the effective date and that no payment or other benefit has accrued or will accrue to Iran after the effective date. For purposes of this section, a payment or other benefit to Iran includes a payment or other economic benefit accruing to the Government of Iran or to a person or persons residing or located in Iran.

(b) Fungible goods of Iranian origin, such as oil and agricultural products, may qualify for importation after the effective date only under the provisions of §§ 560.201 and 560.503.

(c) The type of documentation that would constitute satisfactory proof of the location of non-fungible goods outside Iran as of the effective date may vary depending upon the facts of a particular case. However, independent corroborating documentary evidence issued and certified by a disinterested party will be required. This might include contracts, insurance documents, shipping documents, warehouse receipts, and appropriate customs documents, accompanied by a certification of an insurance agent, warehouse agent, or other appropriate person, identifying with particularity the goods sought to be imported and attesting that the goods concerned were located outside Iran at a time prior to the effective date. In general, affidavits, statements, and other documents prepared by the applicant or another interested party will not, by themselves, constitute satisfactory proof.

EXAMPLE: A Persian carpet stored in a warehouse in Europe since January 1986, and purchased by a U.S. resident in November 1987, may be licensed for importation into the United States if the importer provides, for example, (1) a warehouse receipt dated prior to the effective date, and a certification from the warehouse that the carpet sought to be imported is the same carpet that was in storage, identifying such characteristics as predominant colors and design by description or photograph; and (2) insurance documents dated prior to the effective date and containing sufficient information to identify the specific carpet insured in a location outside Iran.

§ 560.505 Certain services relating to participation in various events authorized.

The importation of services of Iranian origin into the United States is authorized where an Iranian national enters the United States on a visa issued by the State Department for the purpose of participating in a public conference, performance, exhibition or similar event.

§ 560.506 Importation of certain gifts authorized.

The importation into the United States is authorized for goods of Iranian origin sent as gifts to persons in the United States where the value of the gift is not more than $100.

§ 560.507 Importation of accompanied baggage authorized.

Persons entering the United States directly or indirectly from Iran are authorized to import into the United States Iranian-origin accompanied baggage normally incident to travel. This authorization does not extend to Iranian-origin goods the value of which exceeds the personal exemption from Customs duty, currently at $400 per individual, or for Iranian-origin goods brought to the United States from third countries as accompanied baggage.

EXAMPLE: Under this section, a U.S. resident returning from Iran may import personal effects acquired in Iran such as clothing and small purchases, provided their value is below the personal exemption amount, currently $400. A U.S. tourist returning from a vacation in Canada with a Persian carpet purchased there is not eligible for the general license in this section, as the individual would not be entering the United States directly or indirectly from Iran. In the latter case, the carpet could be imported only under a specific license issued pursuant to another section, such as §§ 560.503 or 560.504.

§ 560.508 Telecommunications and mail transactions authorized.

All transactions of common carriers incident to the receipt or transmission of telecommunications and mail between the United States and Iran are authorized. For purposes of this section, the term "mail" shall include parcels only to the extent the parcels contain goods excepted from these Regulations or otherwise eligible for importation from Iran under a general or specific license.

§ 560.509 Certain services performed in Iran with respect to patents, trademarks and copyrights.

(a) All transactions incident to the following services rendered by a resident of Iran to or on behalf of a U.S. person are hereby authorized:

(1) The filing and prosecution of any application in Iran to obtain a patent, trademark, copyright or other form of intellectual property protection.

(2) The receipt of an Iranian patent, trademark, copyright or other form of intellectual property protection.

(3) The renewal of maintenance of a patent, trademark, copyright or other form of intellectual property protection in Iran.

(4) The filing and prosecution of opposition or infringement proceedings in Iran with respect to a patent, trademark, copyright or other form of intellectual property protection; or the entrance of a defense to any such proceedings.

(b) Nothing in this section affects obligations under any other provision of law.

§ 560.510 Certain goods and services relating to legal proceedings.

All transactions are authorized pertaining to the importation of goods and services necessary for the conduct of legal proceedings, including administrative, judicial, and arbitral proceedings.

§ 560.511 Importation of goods awarded by the Hague Tribunal.

(a) Specific licenses will be issued on a case-by-case basis to permit the importation of goods of Iranian origin in connection with awards, decisons, or orders of the Iran-United States Claims Tribunal in the Hague, established pursuant to the Algiers Accords of January 19, 1981.

(b) Specific licenses may be issued on a case-by-case basis to permit the importation of Iranian origin goods in connection with agreements settling claims brought before the Iran-United States Claims Tribunal.

§ 560.512 Certain imports for diplomatic or official personnel authorized.

All transactions ordinarily incident to the importation of any goods or services into the United States from Iran are authorized if such imports are destined for official or personal use by personnel employed by Iranian missions to international organizations located in the United States, and such imports are not for resale.

Subpart F—Reports

§ 560.601 Required records.

Every person engaging in any transaction subject to the provisons of this part shall keep a full and accurate record of each transaction in which he engages, regardless of whether such transaction is effected pursuant to license or otherwise, and such record shall be available for examination for at least two years after the date of such transaction.

§ 560.602 Reports to be furnished on demand.

Every person is required to furnish under oath, in the form of reports or otherwise, from time to time and at any time as may be required, complete information relative to any transaction, regardless of whether such transaction is effected pursuant to license or otherwise, subject to the provisions of this part. Such reports may be required to include the production of any books of account, contracts, letters or other papers, connected with any such transaction or property, in the custody of control of the persons required to make such reports. Reports with respect to transactions may be required either before or after such transactions are completed. The Secretary of the Treasury may, through any person or agency, conduct investigations, hold hearings, administers oaths, examine witnesses, receive evidence, take depositions, and require by subpoena the attendance and testimony of witnesses and the production of all books, papers, and documents relating to any matter under investigation, regardless of whether any report has been required or filed in connection therewith.

Subpart G—Penalties

§ 560.701 Penalties.

(a) Attention is directed to 18 U.S.C. 545, which provides:

Whoever knowingly and willfully, with intent to defraud the United States, smuggles, or clandestinely introduces into the United States any merchandise which should have been invoiced, or makes out or passes, or attempts to pass, through the customhouse any false, forged, or fraudulent invoice, or other document or paper; or

Whoever fraudulently or knowingly imports or brings into the United States, any merchandise contrary to law, or receives, conceals, buys, sells, or in any manner facilitates the transportation, concealment, or sale of such merchandise after importation, knowing the same to have been imported or brought into the United States contrary to law—

Shall be fined not more that $10,000 or imprisoned not more than five years, or both.

Proof of defendant's possession of such goods, unless explained to the satisfaction of the jury, shall be deemed evidence sufficient to authorize conviction for violation of this section.

Merchandise introduced into the United States in violation of this section, or the value thereof, to be recovered from any person described in the first or second paragraph of this section, shall be forfeited to the United States.

(b) Attention is directed to 18 U.S.C. 1001, which provides:

Whoever, in any matter within the jurisdiction of any department or agency of the United States knowingly and willfully falsifies, conceals or covers up by any trick, scheme, or device a material fact, or makes any false, fictitious or fraudulent statements or representation or makes or uses any false writing or document knowing the same to contain any false, fictitious or fraudulent statement or entry, shall be fined not more than $10,000 or imprisoned not more than five years, or both.

(c) Attention is directed to 19 U.S.C. 1592, which provides, in part:

(a) Prohibition.—
(1) General rule.—Without regard to whether the United States is or may be deprived of all or a portion of any lawful duty thereby, no person, by fraud, gross negligence, or negligence—
(A) may enter, introduce, or attempt to enter or introduce any merchandise into the commerce of the United States by means of—
(i) any document, written or oral statement, or act which is material and false, or
(ii) any omission which is material, or
(B) may aid or abet any other person to violate subparagraph (A) * * *.
(c) Maximum penalties.—
(1) Fraud.—A fraudulent violation of subsection (a) of this section is punishable by a civil penalty in an amount not to exceed the domestic value of the merchandise.
(2) Gross negligence.—A grossly negligent violation of subsection (a) of this section is

punishable by a civil penalty in an amount not to exceed—
(A) the lesser of—
(i) the domestic value of the merchandise, or
(ii) four times the lawful duties of which the United States is or may be deprived, or
(B) if the violation did not affect the assessment of duties, 40 percent of the dutiable value of the merchandise.
(3) Negligence.—A negligent violation of subsection (a) of this section is punishable by a civil penalty in an amount not to exceed—
(A) the lesser of—
(i) the domestic value of the merchandise, or
(ii) two times the lawful duties of which the United States is or may be deprived, or
(B) if the violation did not affect the assessment of duties, 20 percent of the dutiable value of the merchandise.

(d) Attention is also directed to 19 U.S.C. 1595a, which provides:

(a) * * * [E]very vessel, vehicle, animal, aircraft, or other thing used in, to aid in, or to facilitate, by obtaining information or in any other way, the importation, bringing in, unloading, landing, removal, concealing, harboring, or subsequent transportation of any article which is being or has been introduced, or attempted to be introduced, into the United States contrary to law, whether upon such vessel, vehicle, animal, aircraft or other thing or otherwise, may be seized and forfeited together with its tackle, apparel, furniture, harness, or equipment.
(b) Every person who directs, assists financially or otherwise, or is in any way concerned in any unlawful activity mentioned in the preceding subsection shall be liable to a penalty equal to the value of the article or articles introduced or attempted to be introduced.
(c) Any merchandise that is introduced or attempted to be introduced into the United States contrary to law (other than in violation of section 1592 of this title) may be seized and forfeited.

§ 560.702 Detention of shipments.

Import shipments into the United States of goods of Iranian origin in violation of § 560.201 shall be detained. No such import shall be permitted to proceed, except as specifically authorized by the Secretary of the Treasury. Such shipments shall be subject to licensing, penalties, or seizure and forfeiture action, under the Customs laws or other applicable provisions of law, depending on the circumstances.

Subpart H—Procedures

§560.801 Licensing.

(a) *General licenses.* General licenses have been issued authorizing under appropriate terms and conditions certain types of transactions which are subject to the prohibitions contained in Subpart B of this part. All such licenses are set forth in Subpart E of this part. It is the policy of the Office of Foreign Assets Control not to grant applications for specific licenses authorizing transactions to which the provisions of an outstanding general license are applicable. Persons availing themselves of certain general licenses may be required to file reports and statements in accordance with the instructions specified in those licenses.

(b) *Specific licenses*—(1) *General course of procedure.* Transactions subject to the prohibitions contained in Subpart B of this part which are not authorized by general license may be effected only under specific licenses. The specific licensing activities of the Office of Foreign Assets Control are performed by its Washington Office and by the Foreign Assets Control Division of the Federal Reserve Bank of New York.

(2) *Applications for specific licenses.* Applications for specific licenses to engage in any transactions prohibited by or pursuant to this part may be filed in duplicate by letter or on an application form with the Office of Foreign Assets Control or the Federal Reserve Bank of New York. Any person having an interest in a transaction or proposed transaction may file an application for a license authorizing such transaction, and there is no requirement that any other person having an interest in such transaction shall or should join in making or filing such application.

(3) *Information to be supplied.* The applicant must supply all information specified by relevant instructions and/or forms. Such documents as may be relevant shall be attached to each application as a part of such application except that documents previously filed with the Office of Foreign Assets Control may, where appropriate, be incorporated by reference. Applicants may be required to furnish such further information as is deemed necessary to a proper determination by the Office of Foreign Assets Control. If an applicant or other party in interest desires to present additional information or discuss or argue the application, he may do so at any time before or after decision. Arrangements for oral presentation should be made with the Office of Foreign Assets Control.

(4) *Effect of denial.* The denial of a license does not preclude the reopening of an application or the filing of a further application. The applicant or any other party in interest may at any time request explanation of the reasons for a denial by correspondence or personal interview.

(5) *Reports under specific licenses.* As a condition upon the issuance of any license, the licensee may be required to file reports with respect to the transaction covered by the license, in such form and at such times and places as may be prescribed in the license or otherwise.

(6) *Issuance of license.* Licenses will be issued by the Office of Foreign Assets Control acting on behalf of the Secretary of the Treasury, or by the Federal Reserve Bank of New York acting in accordance with such regulations, rulings and instructions as the Secretary of the Treasury or the Office of Foreign Assets Control may from time to time prescribe, or licenses may be issued by the Secretary of the Treasury acting directly or through any specifically designated person, agency, or instrumentality.

§560.802 Decisions.

The Office of Foreign Assets Control or the Federal Reserve Bank of New York will advise each applicant of the decision respecting filed applications. The decision of the Office of Foreign Assets Control acting on behalf of the Secretary of the Treasury with respect to an application shall constitute final agency action.

§560.803 Amendment, modification, or revocation.

The provisions of this part and any rulings; licenses, whether general or specific; authorizations; instructions; orders; or forms issued hereunder may be amended, modified, or revoked at any time.

§ 560.804 Rulemaking.

(a) All rules and other public documents are issued by the Secretary of the Treasury upon recommendation of the Director of the Office of Foreign Assets Control. In general, rulemaking by the Office of Foreign Assets Control involves foreign affairs functions of the United States, and for that reason is exempt from the requirements under the Administrative Procedure Act (5 U.S.C. 553) for notice of proposed rulemaking, opportunity for public comment, and delay in effective date. Wherever possible, however, it is the practice of the Office of Foreign Assets Control to receive written submissions or hold informal consultations with interested parties before the issuance of any rule or other public document.

(b) Any interested person may petition the Director of the Office of Foreign Assets Control in writing for the issuance, amendment, or repeal of any rule.

§ 560.805 Delegation by the Secretary of the Treasury.

Any action which the Secretary of the Treasury is authorized to take pursuant to Executive Order No. 12613 or section 505 of the Act may be taken by the Director, Office of Foreign Assets Control, or by any other person to whom the Secretary of the Treasury has delegated authority so to act.

§ 560.806 Customs procedures: Goods specified in § 560.201.

(a) With respect to goods specified in § 560.201, and not otherwise licensed or excepted from the scope of that section, appropriate Customs officers shall not accept or allow any:

(1) Entry for consumption or warehouse (including any appraisement entry, any entry of goods imported in the mails, regardless of value, and any informal entries);

(2) Entry for immediate exportation;

(3) Entry for transportation and exportation;

(4) Withdrawal from warehouse;

(5) Admission, entry, transfer or withdrawal to or from a foreign trade zone; or

(6) Manipulation or manufacture in a warehouse or in a foreign trade zone.

(b) Customs officers shall accept or allow the importation of Iranian-origin goods under the procedures listed in subsection (a) if:

(1) The merchandise was imported prior to 12:01 p.m., October 29, 1987,

(2) A specific license pursuant to this part is presented, or

(3) Instructions authorizing the transaction are received from the Office of Foreign Assets Control, either directly or through the Federal Reserve Bank of New York.

(c) Whenever a specific license is presented to an appropriate Customs officer in accordance with this section, one additional legible copy of the entry, withdrawal or other appropriate document with respect to the merchandise involved shall be filed with the appropriate Customs officers at the port where the transaction is to take place. Each copy of any such entry, withdrawal or other appropriate document, including the additional copy, shall bear plainly on its face the number of the license pursuant to which it is filed. The orignial copy of the specific license shall be presented to the appropriate Customs officers in respect of each such transaction and shall bear a notation in ink by the licensee or person presenting the license showing the description, quantity and value of the merchandise to be entered, withdrawn or otherwise dealt with. This notation shall be so placed and so written that there will exist no possibility of confusing it with anything placed on the license at the time of its issuance. If the license in fact authorizes the entry, withdrawal, or other transaction with regard to the merchandise, the appropriate Customs officer, or other authorized Customs employee, shall verify the notation by signing or initialing it after first assuring himself that it accurately describes the merchandise it purports to represent. The license shall thereafter be returned to the person presenting it and the additional copy of the entry, withdrawal or other appropriate document shall be forwarded by the appropriate Customs officer to the Office of Foreign Assets Control.

(d) If it is unclear whether an entry, withdrawal or other action affected by this section requires a specific Foreign Assets Control license, the appropriate Customs officer shall withhold any action thereon and shall advise such person to communicate directly with the Federal Reserve Bank of New York, Foreign Assets Control Division, 33 Liberty Street, New York, New York 10045, to request that instructions be sent to the Customs officer to authorize him to take action with regard thereto.

§ 560.807 Rules governing availability of information.

(a) The records of the Office of Foreign Assets Control which are required by 5 U.S.C. 552 to be made available to the public shall be made available in accordance with the definitions, procedures, payment of fees, and other provisions of the regulations on the Disclosure of Records of the Office of the Secretary and of other bureaus and offices of the Department isssued under 5 U.S.C. 552 and published as Part 1 of this Title 31 of the Code of Federal Regulations.

(b) Any form issued for use in connection with the Iranian Transactions Regulations may be obtained in person or by writing to the Office of Foreign Assets Control, Treasury Department, Washington, DC 20220, or the Foreign Assets Control Division, Federal Reserve Bank of New York, 33 Liberty Street, New York, NY 10045.

Subpart I—Paperwork Reduction Act

§ 560.901 Paperwork Reduction Act Notice.

The information collection requirements in §§ 560.601, 560.602, and 560.801 have been approved by the Office of Management and Budget and assigned control number 1505-0106.

[53 FR 37556, Sept. 27, 1988]

PART 565—PANAMANIAN TRANSACTIONS REGULATIONS

Supplementary Material: US

DEPARTMENT OF THE TREASURY
WASHINGTON

OFFICE OF FOREIGN ASSETS CONTROL
KUWAITI ASSETS CONTROL REGULATIONS
IRAQI SANCTIONS REGULATIONS

GENERAL LICENSE NO. 12

<u>Donations of Food to Relieve Human Suffering</u>

(a) Specific licenses may be issued on a case-by-case basis to permit exportation to Iraq or Kuwait of donated food, intended to relieve human suffering, where the shipment of foodstuffs has been authorized by the Security Council of the United Nations or a duly authorized body subordinate thereto acting pursuant to, and in accordance with, the provisions of United Nations Security Council resolution 666 (1990), a copy of which is attached hereto. Authorization will be sought from the United Nations Security Council or duly authorized subordinate body by the United States following application to this Office meeting the requirements of subsection (c) of this license.

(b) In general, and subject to paragraph (a), specific licenses will only be granted for donations of food to be provided through the United Nations in cooperation with the International Committee of the Red Cross or other appropriate humanitarian agencies and distributed by them or under their supervision, or in such other manner as may be approved under United Nations Security Council resolution 666 (1990), in order to ensure that such donations reach the intended beneficiaries.

(c) Applications for specific licenses pursuant to paragraph (a) shall be made in advance of the proposed exportation, and provide notice and evidence of:

(1) the nature, quantity, value, and intended use of the donated food; and

(2) compliance with such terms and conditions of distribution as may have been adopted by the United Nations Security Council or duly authorized subordinate body to govern the shipment of foodstuffs under applicable United Nations Security Council resolutions, including resolutions 661 (1990) and 666 (1990).

Issued: September 26, 1990

R/ Richard Newcomb
Director
Office of Foreign Assets Control

DEPARTMENT OF THE TREASURY
WASHINGTON

OFFICE OF FOREIGN ASSETS CONTROL
IRAQI SANCTIONS REGULATIONS
GENERAL LICENSE NO. 13

Certain standby letters of credit and performance bonds.

(a) Notwithstanding any other provision of law, payment
into a blocked account in a U.S. financial institution by an
issuing or confirming bank under a standby letter of credit in
favor of an Iraqi entity is prohibited if either (1) a
specific license has been issued pursuant to the provisions of
paragraph (b) of this license or (2) ten business days have
not expired after notice to the account party pursuant to
paragraph (b) of this license.

(b) Whenever an issuing or confirming bank shall receive
such demand for payment under such a standby letter of credit,
it shall promptly notify the account party. The account party
may then apply within five business days for a specific
license authorizing the account party to establish a blocked
account on its books in the name of the Iraqi beneficiary in
the amount payable under the credit, in lieu of payment by the
issuing or confirming bank into a blocked account and
reimbursement therefor by the account party. Nothing in this
license relieves any such bank or such account party from
giving any notice of defense against payment or reimbursement
that is required by applicable law.

(c) Where there is outstanding a demand for payment
under a standby letter of credit, and the issuing or

confirming bank has been enjoined from making payment, upon removal of the injunction, the account party may apply for a specific license for the same purpose and in the same manner as that set forth in paragraph (b) of this license. The issuing or confirming bank shall not make payment under the standby letter of credit unless (1) ten business days have expired since the bank has received notice of the removal of the injunction and (2) a specific license issued to the account party pursuant to the provisions of this paragraph has not been presented to the bank.

(d) If necessary to assure the availability of the funds blocked, the Secretary of the Treasury may at any time require the payment of the amounts due under any letter of credit described in paragraph (a) of this license into a blocked account in a U.S. financial institution or the supplying of any form of security deemed necessary.

(e) Nothing in this license precludes the account party on any standby letter of credit or any other person from at any time contesting the legality of the demand from the Iraqi beneficiary or from raising any other legal defense to payment under the standby letter of credit.

(f) This license does not affect the obligation of the various parties to the instruments covered by this license if the instruments and payments thereunder are subsequently unblocked.

(g) This license does not authorize any U.S. person to reimburse a non-U.S. bank for payment to an Iraqi beneficiary under a standby letter of credit, except by payments into a blocked account in accordance with paragraph (b) or (c) of this license.

(h) A person receiving a specific license under paragraph (b) or (c) of this license shall certify to the Office of Foreign Assets Control within five business days after receipt of the specific license that it has established the blocked account on its books as provided in those paragraphs. However, in appropriate cases, this time period may be extended upon application to the Office of Foreign Assets Control when the account party has filed a petition with an appropriate court seeking a judicial order barring payment by the issuing or confirming bank.

(i) The extension or renewal of a standby letter of credit is authorized.

(j) Terms used in this license are defined as follows:

(1) The term "standby letter of credit" shall mean a letter of credit securing performance of, or repayment of any advance payments or deposits under, a contract, or any similar obligation in the nature of a performance bond.

(2) The term "account party" shall mean the person for whose account the standby letter of credit is opened.

(3) The term "U.S. financial institution" shall mean any U.S. person (including foreign branches) that is engaged in the business of accepting deposits or making,

granting, transferring, holding, or brokering loans or credits, or of purchasing or selling foreign exchange, commodity futures or options, or procuring purchasers and sellers thereof, as principal or agent, including, but not limited to, banks, savings banks, trust companies, securities brokers and dealers, commodity futures and options brokers and dealers, forward contract and foreign exchange merchants, securities and commodities exchanges, clearing corporations, investment companies, employee benefit plans, and U.S. holding companies, U.S. affiliates, or U.S. subsidiaries of any of the foregoing.

(4) The term "blocked account" shall mean an account with respect to which payments, transfers or withdrawals, or other dealings may not be made or effected except pursuant to an authorization or license from the Office of Foreign Assets Control authorizing such action.

Issued: October 3, 1990

R. Richard Newcomb
Director
Office of Foreign Assets Control

TREASURY NEWS

Department of the Treasury • Washington, D.C. • Telephone 566-20⸰

FOR IMMEDIATE RELEASE   Contact: Desiree Tucker-Sorini (202)566-8773
October 4, 1990   Cheryl Crispen   (202)566-5252

THE DEPARTMENT OF THE TREASURY RELEASES LIST CLARIFYING STATUS OF
94 KUWAITI BANKS AND COMPANIES.

Washington, D.C. -- The Treasury Department today released a list
clarifying the status of 94 Kuwaiti banks and companies under the
Executive Orders issued by the President when he froze assets
belonging to the Governments of Kuwait and Iraq on August 2, 1990.

The list divides the Kuwaiti entities into three categories:

"Controlled/Blocked," which means they are controlled by the
Government of Kuwait and/or the Government of Iraq and their
assets are frozen;

"Controlled/Licensed to Operate," which means they are
controlled by the legitimate Government of Kuwait and have
been licensed by the Treasury Department to operate;

"Not Controlled/No Restrictions," which means they are not
regarded by the Treasury Department as controlled by the
Government of Kuwait or the Government of Iraq. This category
was included solely for the purpose of clarification because
the Treasury Department has received many requests concerning
the status of those particular entities.

The Treasury Department will update the list when new or
significant information becomes available. Additions or revisions
affecting all three categories are anticipated.

oOo

DEPARTMENT OF THE TREASURY
WASHINGTON

OFFICE OF FOREIGN ASSETS CONTROL
KUWAITI ASSETS CONTROL REGULATIONS
General Notice No. 1

NOTIFICATION OF STATUS OF KUWAITI ENTITIES
(10/04/90)

The Treasury Department has been asked about the status of various entities in which Kuwait or Kuwaiti nationals may have an interest for purposes of Executive Order Nos. 12722-12725. Based on information currently available to the Office of Foreign Assets Control, the following lists have been compiled.

The entities listed as "Controlled/Blocked" have been determined to be controlled by the Government of Kuwait and/or the Government of Iraq and should be regarded as blocked entities. This means U.S. persons are prohibited from engaging in transactions with these entities and all assets under U.S. jurisdiction owned or controlled by those entities are blocked. U.S. persons are not prohibited, however, from paying funds owed to these entities into blocked accounts held in U.S. financial institutions.

The entities listed as "Controlled/Licensed to Operate" should also be regarded as controlled by the Government of Kuwait, but as licensed to operate. This means the Office of Foreign Assets Control has determined that the entities are under the effective control of the legitimate Government of Kuwait and U.S. persons are authorized to engage in transactions with them. These authorized transactions include entering into contracts, making and receiving payments, and conducting other commercial or financial transactions. If questions arise, U.S. financial and commercial institutions should request, from the entities concerned, to see copies of the operating licenses.

The entities listed as "Not Controlled/No Restrictions" are not regarded by the Office of Foreign Assets Control as controlled by the Government of Kuwait or the Government of Iraq. The names of these entities appear on the list solely for the purpose of clarification because requests regarding their status have been received. Some of the entities on this list may be subject to special Treasury Department licensing/reporting requirements.

Warning: These lists are subject to revision should new information become available and are not inclusive. Additions to the lists are anticipated. The absence of a particular entity on any of the lists should not be regarded as indicative of whether the entity is owned or controlled by the Government of Kuwait or the Government of Iraq.

For further information concerning this notice contact the Office of Foreign Assets Control at (202) 566-2701.

Issued: October 4, 1990

R. Richard Newcomb
Director
Office of Foreign Assets Control

OFFICE OF FOREIGN ASSETS CONTROL

Status of Kuwaiti Entities
10/04/90

Controlled/Blocked

AlAhli Bank of Kuwait
AlAhlia Insurance Company
Arab Fund for Economic and Social Development
Arab Trust Company
Bahrain Arab International Bank
Bank of Kuwait & Middle East
Burgan Bank
Central Bank of Kuwait
Commercial Bank of Kuwait
Commercial Facilities Company
Gulf Insurance Company
Industrial Bank of Kuwait
International Financial Advisor
Kuwait Finance House
KREIC Singapore
Kuwait Cement Company
Kuwait Clearing Company
Kuwait Hotels Company
Kuwait Metal Pipe Industries Company
Kuwait Real Estate Bank
Kuwait Real Estate Investment Consortium (KREIC)
Kuwait Reinsurance Company
Kuwait Supply Company
Kuwait United Poultry Company
Mobile Telephone Systems
Mubarakiah Poultry and Feed Company
National Industries Company K.S.C.
National Real Estate Company
Public Warehousing Company
Rawdatain Water Bottling Company
Refrigeration Industries Company
Savings and Credit Bank
Securities Group Company
Securities House Company
The Gulf Bank
United Fisheries of Kuwait
United Realty Company
Univest Invest Company
Warba Insurance Company

OFFICE OF FOREIGN ASSETS CONTROL

Status of Kuwaiti Entities
10/04/90

Controlled/Licensed to Operate

Credit des Bergues
Georgetown Industries, Inc. (including
    subsidiaries)
KFIC, Inc. (including subsidiaries)
Kuwait Airways Corporation
Kuwait Asia Bank
Kuwait Investment Office (including controlled
    entities)
Kuwait Investment Authority
Kuwait Maritime Transport Company
Kuwait & Middle East Financial Investment Company
Kuwait Oil Tanker Company
Kuwait Petroleum Corporation (London) (including
    licensed affiliates)
Kuwait Petroleum - North Sea Holdings Ltd.
    (including subsidiaries)
Santa Fe International Corporation (including
    subsidiaries and affiliates)
Wafra Intervest Corporation (Cayman) (including
    subsidiaries and affiliates)

Not Controlled/No Restrictions *

Alexandria Kuwait International Bank
Arab African International Bank
Arab Banking Corporation
Arab Financial Services Company
Arab Hellenic Bank
Arab Insurance Group
Arab Maritime Petroleum Transport
Arab Mining Company
Arab Petroleum Investments Corporation
Arab Turkish Bank
Bahrain Islamic Bank

* Some of these entities may be subject to special Treasury
Department licensing/reporting requirements.

OFFICE OF FOREIGN ASSETS CONTROL

Status of Kuwaiti Entities
10/04/90

Not Controlled/No Restrictions *
(continued from previous page)

Bahrain Islamic Investment Company
Bahrain Middle East Bank
Banco Arabe Espanol
Banco Atlantico
Bank of Bahrain and Kuwait
Bank of Oman, Bahrain & Kuwait
CHENI
Dao Heng Bank
FRAB Bank International
Gulf International Bank
Gulf Investment Corporation
Independent Petroleum Group
International Contracting Group
Jordan Fertilizer Industry Company
Jordan Kuwait Bank
Korea Kuwait Banking Corporation
Kuwait French Bank
Kuwait Investment Projects Company
Kuwait Lebanon Bank
Kuwait National Cinema Company
National Bank of Kuwait
National Investment Company
Oman Housing Bank
Pearl Holding Company
Swiss Kuwaiti Bank
The Arab Investment Company
UBAF Arab American Bank
United Arab Shipping Company
United Bank of Kuwait
United Gulf Bank
Yemen Kuwait Bank

* Some of these entities may be subject to special Treasury
Department licensing/reporting requirements.

STOP PRESS October 19, 1990

General License No. 4 has been revoked and License Nos. 3 and 7 have been amended. The revised texts follow on pages 184b to 184j.

SHEARMAN & STERLING

CITICORP CENTER
153 EAST 53rd STREET
NEW YORK, N.Y. 10022
212 848-4000

FAX: 212-848-5255
212-848-5252
TELEX: 668789 WUI

SAN FRANCISCO
LOS ANGELES
WASHINGTON, D.C.
TORONTO
LONDON
PARIS
TOKYO
ABU DHABI

WRITER'S DIRECT DIAL NUMBER:

October 19, 1990

Memorandum to: Interested Clients

The Office of Foreign Assets Control has revoked General License No. 4 ("Transactions by U.S. Entities Owned or Controlled by the Government of Kuwait"). This license allowed U.S. financial institutions to engage in transactions involving blocked accounts held in the name of companies located in the U.S. and controlled by the Government of Kuwait or its agencies, provided the company had registered with OFAC. OFAC does not expect to replace General License No. 4 with another general license. Instead, OFAC will henceforth require such companies to obtain special licenses.

OFAC has issued many such special licenses to Kuwaiti-controlled companies since August 2, including, for example, Sante Fe International Corp. Before engaging in transactions involving payments into or out of blocked accounts, U.S. financial institutions should require evidence of a special license from the account holder.

We are continuing to monitor this situation and will advise you of further developments. If we can be of any assistance, please contact your usual contacts at Shearman & Sterling, or in their absence, one of the following:

John E. Hoffman, Jr.	(212) 848-4181
Danforth Newcomb	4184
Henry Weisburg	4193
Michael Gruson	8060
Jonathan M. Weld	8075
Edward B. Schwartz	4596
Philip Urofsky	5136

SHEARMAN & STERLING

DEPARTMENT OF THE TREASURY
WASHINGTON

OFFICE OF FOREIGN ASSETS CONTROL
KUWAIT ASSETS CONTROL REGULATIONS
GENERAL LICENSE NO. 3   (AMENDED)

This license is being amended to expand its application to include funds held in blocked accounts in the name of the Government of Iraq.

Investment of Government of Kuwait or Government of Iraq Funds Held in Blocked Accounts.

(a)   U.S. financial institutions are hereby authorized to invest and reinvest funds held in blocked accounts in the name of the Government of Kuwait, subject to the following conditions:

(1) The proceeds of such investments and reinvestments are credited to a blocked account or sub-account which is in the name of the Government of Kuwait and which is subject to the jurisdiction of the United States;

(2) The proceeds of such investments and reinvestments are not credited to a blocked account or sub-account under any name or designation which differs from the name or designation of the specific blocked account or sub-account in which such funds or securities were held; and

(3) no financial or economic benefit accrues to the Government of Iraq as a result of the transaction.

(b)   U.S. financial institutions are hereby authorized to invest and reinvest funds held in blocked accounts in the name of the Government of Iraq, subject to the following conditions:

(1) The proceeds of such investments and reinvestments are credited to a blocked account or

sub-account which is in the name of the Government of Iraq and which is subject to the jurisdiction of the United States;

(2) The proceeds of such investments and reinvestments are not credited to a blocked account or sub-account under any name or designation which differs from the name or designation of the specific blocked account or sub-account in which such funds or securities were held.

(c) (1) U.S. persons seeking to avail themselves of this authorization must register with the Office of Foreign Assets Control, Blocked Assets Section.

(2) Transactions conducted pursuant to this section must be reported to the Office of Foreign Assets Control, Blocked Assets Section, within ten (10) days of completion of the transaction.

(d) Terms used in this license are defined as follows:

(1) The term "Government of Iraq" includes:

(A) The state and the Government of Iraq, as well as any political subdivision, agency, or instrumentality thereof, including the Central Bank of Iraq;

(B) Any partnership, association, corporation, or other organization substantially owned or controlled by the foregoing;

(C) Any person to the extent that such person is, or has been, or to the extent that there is reasonable cause to believe such person is, or has been, since the effective date, acting or purporting to act, directly or indirectly on behalf of any of the foregoing;

(D) Any other person or organization determined by the Secretary of the Treasury to be included within section (d)(1).

(2) The term "Government of Kuwait" shall mean

(A) The state and the Government of Kuwait or any entity purporting to be the Government of Kuwait, as well as any political subdivision, agency, or instrumentality thereof, including the Central Bank of Kuwait;

(B) Any partnership, association, corporation, or other organization substantially owned or controlled by the foregoing;

(C) Any person to the extent that such person is, or has been, or to the extent that there is reasonable cause to believe such person is, or has been, since the effective date, acting or purporting to act, directly or indirectly on behalf of any of the foregoing; and

(D) Any other person or organization determined by the Secretary of the Treasury to be included within section (d)(2).

(3) The term "blocked account" shall mean an account with respect to which account payments, transfers or withdrawals or other dealings may not be made or effected except pursuant to an authorization or license from the Office of Foreign Assets Control authorizing such action.

(4)   The term "U.S. financial institution" shall
mean any U.S. person (including foreign branches) that is
engaged in the business of accepting deposits or making,
granting, transferring, holding, or brokering loans or
credits, or of purchasing or selling foreign exchange,
commodity futures or options, or procuring purchasers and
sellers thereof, as principal or agent, including, but not
limited to, banks, savings banks, trust companies,
securities brokers and dealers, commodity futures and
options brokers and dealers, forward contract and foreign
exchange merchants, securities and commodities exchanges,
clearing corporations, investment companies, employee
benefit plans, and U.S. holding companies, U.S. affiliates,
or U.S. subsidiaries of any of the foregoing.

Issued: October 15, 1990

R. Richard Newcomb
Director
Office of Foreign Assets Control

DEPARTMENT OF THE TREASURY
WASHINGTON

OFFICE OF FOREIGN ASSETS CONTROL
KUWAIT ASSETS CONTROL REGULATIONS
IRAQI SANCTIONS REGULATIONS
GENERAL LICENSE NO. 7, AMENDED

Payment For Goods or Services Exported Prior to Effective Date
to Iraq or Kuwait or to the Government of Iraq or Government of
Kuwait.

(a) Specific licenses may be issued on a case-by-case
basis to permit payment involving an irrevocable letter of
credit issued or confirmed by a U.S. bank, or a letter of
credit reimbursement confirmed by a U.S. bank, from a blocked
account or otherwise, of amounts owed to or for the benefit of
a person with respect to goods or services exported prior to
the effective date directly or indirectly to Iraq or Kuwait, or
to third countries for an entity operated from Iraq or Kuwait
or for the benefit of the Government of Iraq or the Government
of Kuwait, where the license application presents evidence
satisfactory to the Office of Foreign Assets Control that:

(1) the exportation occurred prior to the effective
date (such evidence may include, e.g., bill of lading, air
waybill, the purchaser's written confirmation of completed
services, customs documents, insurance documents), and

(2) if delivery or performance occurred after the
effective date, due diligence was exercised to divert delivery
of the goods from Iraq or Kuwait and to effect final delivery
of the goods to a non-prohibited destination, or to prevent
performance of the services.

(b) This general license does not authorize exportations
or the performance of services after the effective date

pursuant to a contract entered into or partially performed prior to the effective date.

(c) Transactions conducted under specific licenses granted pursuant to this general license must be reported in writing to the Office of Foreign Assets Control, Blocked Assets Section, within ten (10) days of the date of payment.

(d) Separate criteria may be applied to the issuance of specific licenses authorizing payment from an account held in a blocked U.S. bank.

(e) Terms used in this general license are defined as follows:

(1) The term "effective date" shall mean (A) 5:00 a.m. Eastern Daylight Time, August 2, 1990, in the case of exportations to Iraq or for the benefit of the Government of Iraq or the Government of Kuwait; or (B) 8:55 p.m. Eastern Daylight Time, August 9, 1990, in the case of exportations to Kuwait, or to an entity operated from Iraq or Kuwait but not controlled by the Government of Iraq or the Government of Kuwait.

(2) The term "Government of Iraq" shall mean

(A) The state and the Government of Iraq, as well as any political subdivision, agency, or instrumentality thereof, including the Central Bank of Iraq;

(B) Any partnership, association, corporation, or other organization owned or controlled by the foregoing;

(C) Any person to the extent that such person is, or has been, or to the extent that there is reasonable cause to believe such person is, or has been, since the effective date, acting or purporting to act, directly or indirectly on behalf of any of the foregoing, and

(D) Any other person or organization determined by the Secretary of the Treasury to be included within section (e)(2).

(3) The term "Government of Kuwait" shall mean

(A) The state and the Government of Kuwait or any entity purporting to be the Government of Kuwait, as well as any political subdivision, agency, or instrumentality thereof, including the Central Bank of Kuwait;

(B) Any partnership, association, corporation, or other organization owned or controlled by the foregoing;

(C) Any person to the extent that such person is, or has been, or to the extent that there is reasonable cause to believe such person is, or has been, since the effective date, acting or purporting to act, directly or indirectly on behalf of any of the foregoing, and

(D) Any other person or organization determined by the Secretary of the Treasury to be included within section (e)(3).

(4) The term "blocked account" shall mean an account in a U.S. bank with respect to which account payments,

transfers or withdrawals or other dealings may not be made or effected except pursuant to an authorization or license from the Office of Foreign Assets Control authorizing such action.

(5) The term "exportation" shall mean (A) the actual departure of goods from the territorial jurisdiction of the country from which exported, or (B) the performance of services that are intended to result in a benefit to the Government of Iraq, the Government of Kuwait, a person in Iraq or Kuwait, or an entity operated from Iraq or Kuwait.

Issued: October 18, 1990

R. Richard Newcomb
Director
Office of Foreign Assets Control

Canada

Source of government materials and this section and the accompanying Supplementary section: Privy Council Office and External Affairs and International Trade Canada.

These materials are reproduced by permission of the Minister of Supply and Services Canada 1990.

TORY TORY DesLAURIERS & BINNINGTON

CANADA'S UNITED NATIONS IRAQ REGULATIONS: AN ANALYSIS AND COMMENT

I   Introduction

Reaction by the Government of Canada to Iraq's invasion of Kuwait was swift and unprecedented. Anxious to condemn Iraq and protect Kuwaiti assets, but lacking statutory authority to impose sanctions in the absence of a resolution of the United Nations, the Canadian Government took a controversial step. On August 3, 1990, the Superintendent of Financial Institutions issued a Direction to all banks in Canada pursuant to subsection 313.1 (1) of the Bank Act which empowers the Superintendent to direct a bank to cease and refrain from an unsafe or unsound practice. This Direction, unprecedented, narrow in scope and controversial, ordered each of the banks "to refrain from acting on instructions from or on behalf of, or purporting to be from or on behalf of, a Kuwait government agency ..." other than instructions approved in writing by the Superintendent of Financial Institutions or instructions received as to matters necessary to effect contractually binding obligations of Kuwait government agencies entered into prior to July 31, 1990[1].

On August 7, 1990, following adoption by the United Nations Security Council of Security Council Resolution 661 (1990) (the "Security Council Resolution") the Governor General-in-Council issued the United Nations Iraq Regulations (the "Regulations") pursuant to Canada's United Nations Act. The United Nations Act empowers the Governor-in-Council to issue orders to give effect in Canada to decisions of the Security Council of the United Nations. The Regulations are unique in that their validity rests on the existence of the Security Council Resolution.

---

[1]   In view of the enactment of the United Nations Iraq Regulations, the Superintendent of Financial Institutions rescinded the Direction under Subsection 313.1 of the Bank Act on August 8, 1990.

The Regulations implement the Security Council Resolution in Canada[2] and effect a complete freeze on all trade (imports, exports and trans-shipments) and financial dealings with or directed by the Government of Iraq or Kuwait, any agencies of or bodies controlled by Iraq or Kuwait and any person in Iraq or Kuwait or on the direction or order of any such person. The enactment of the Regulations had an immediate impact on all trade relations and financial transactions with Iraq and Kuwait.

II   Scope of the Regulations

With respect to trade, the Regulations prohibit, inter alia, the import into Canada by a **"person in Canada"** of Iraqi or Kuwaiti goods, the export of goods to Iraq or Kuwait by a **"person in Canada"**, and participation by **"a person in Canada or a Canadian outside Canada"**, in the sale or supply of any goods that are outside Iraq or Kuwait to any person in Iraq or Kuwait. With respect to financial matters and financial assets, the Regulations prohibit inter alia, all financial dealings and transactions between a **"person"** in Canada or a **"Canadian outside Canada"** and **"any person in Iraq or Kuwait"** or on account of, on behalf of, or in the name of **"the Government of Iraq or Kuwait or any agencies of or bodies controlled by Iraq or Kuwait"**. Additionally, the Regulations prohibit making financial resources available to any persons outside Iraq or Kuwait **"on the direction or order of any person in Iraq or Kuwait"**.

A **"person in Canada"** has its plain meaning and includes individuals in Canada as well as bodies corporate. Thus individuals and all incorporated entities in Canada are subject to the Regulations.

---

[2] The Regulations implementing the Security Council Resolution impose prohibitions more restrictive than those called for by the United Nations. For instance, Canada has explicitly forbidden the remitting of funds at the direction of someone in Iraq or Kuwait to someone outside of those countries. Under the Security Council Resolution there is no such prohibition. The Security Council Resolution requires that financial resources not be made available to the Government of Iraq or to any commercial, industrial or public undertaking in Iraq or Kuwait. The Regulations go further essentially prohibiting any transaction involving the Governments of Iraq or Kuwait whether or not such dealings would result in financial resources becoming available to those countries. The Security Council Resolution does not extend to the "Government of Kuwait", the Regulations, however, apply the same sanctions to the Governments of Iraq and Kuwait.

"**Canadian**" is defined in the Regulations, as "a person who is a citizen within the meaning of the Citizenship Act or a body corporate incorporated by or under the laws of Canada or a province". Thus, the Regulations apply not only to citizens working outside of Canada but also to branches of Canadian companies operating in foreign jurisdictions. The Regulations do not extend to foreign incorporated subsidiaries of Canadian companies which are bound by foreign local law in this matter. Canadian citizens working abroad, however, would be subject to the Regulations and could find themselves in a conflict situation to the extent that the prohibitions in the Regulations conflict with local law.

The Regulations prohibit financial dealings and transactions on behalf of, on account of, or in the name of "**agencies of or bodies controlled by Iraq or Kuwait**". The Regulations contain no further amplifying language to assist in the determination of whether an entity is an agency of or body controlled by Iraq or Kuwait. However, the Government has issued a "Statement of Guidance regarding entities controlled by the Government of Iraq or by persons in Iraq or Kuwait". The purpose of this document is to assist in the interpretation of the Regulations. The Statement of Guidance contains three lists. List (I) contains names of entities which have been determined to be controlled by the Government of Iraq or by persons within Iraq or Kuwait and as such are considered "bodies controlled by Iraq or Kuwait" within the meaning of the Regulations. List (II) contains names of entities not controlled by the Government of Iraq or the Government of Kuwait or by persons within Iraq or Kuwait. As such, these entities are not considered "bodies controlled by Iraq or Kuwait". List (III) contains names of entities, the status of which is still being considered and for which no determination has been made. While interaction with the entities on List II is not per se prohibited by the Regulations, transactions involving such entities may be prohibited as a result of the nature of the transaction. "UK branches of the United Bank of Kuwait, incorporated under the laws of the United Kingdom"[3] have been separately certified as not being intended to be covered by the Security Council Resolution and thus exempt from the application of the Regulations.

The Regulations are not intended nor drafted in such a way as to prohibit Iraqi or Kuwaiti citizens who find themselves temporarily in Canada or Canadian residents of Iraqi or Kuwaiti origin or citizenship from dealing with their own assets. With respect to individuals, the intent of the Regulations is to prohibit financial dealings and transactions with "any person in Iraq or Kuwait".

---

[3] Certificate signed by Donald Campbell on August 10, 1990.

The Regulations provide that where an offence has been committed under the Regulations by a corporation, every officer, director or agent of the corporation who directed, authorized, assented to, acquiesced in or participated in commission of the offence is a party to and guilty of the offence and liable on conviction to the penalties set out in the Regulations.

III   <u>Extraterritorial Application of the Regulations</u>

As explained above, the Regulations are applicable to "all persons in Canada" and to a "Canadian" outside Canada which would include individuals and foreign branches of a Canadian corporate entity[4]. The application of the Regulations extraterritorially is unique as Canada has consistently opposed the extraterritorial reach of foreign (most notably U.S.) laws. The extraterritorial scope of the Regulations is consistent, however, with the Security Council Resolution which calls on members to ensure that sanctions are observed within their territories and by their nationals. As such, the Regulations do not constitute a unilateral extension of Canadian jurisdictional authority, but are an assertion of jurisdiction fully consistent with Canada's obligations as a member of the United Nations and thus consistent with international law.

IV   <u>Certificates Modifying the Scope of the Regulations</u>

Unlike the United Kingdom and the United States, Canada has had little experience with the freezing of foreign assets in Canada. This may explain why the enactment of the Regulations was not followed immediately by the issuance of general licences, general certificates or explanatory regulations.

In drafting the Regulations, the Government was cognizant of the need for a mechanism to permit exemption from the prohibitions in the Regulations. Accordingly, the Regulations provide that it is not an offence to proceed with an action if prior to doing so the Secretary of State for External Affairs has certified

---

[4]   Subsections 6(4) and 6(5) of the Regulations, as drafted, prohibit a "person" from engaging in specified actions. There is no reference to the "person" being in Canada or, if outside Canada, being a Canadian citizen or a branch of a Canadian person. While it could be argued that this wording extends the reach of these subsections to actions engaged in anywhere by anyone, we do not believe that this was the intention of the Government. These subsections should be read to prohibit actions by persons in Canada and Canadians outside Canada.

that the action is not intended to be prohibited by the Security Council Resolution or the action is for the purpose of assisting the legitimate Government of Kuwait.

General Certificates

The Canadian Government has now issued a number of "General Certificates" which have the effect of exempting a range of generic activities, engaged in by "financial institutions" (defined in the Certificates to include, banks, trust companies, life insurance companies, investment dealers and other firms in the financial area) from the application of the Regulations.

Briefly, General Certificate No. 1 permits financial institutions in Canada to: change the mix of investments in a blocked account, accept deposits for blocked accounts, make investments and reinvestments of assets in such accounts and effect the transfer of blocked assets within Canada. Specifically, financial transactions are permitted which involve the release or delivery of financial assets and the receipt of other financial assets in exchange therefor so long as fair market value is received by the blocked account. Transactions consummated in conventional markets would meet this test. However, non-arm's length transactions or transactions of an unusual nature would most likely not meet the test. General Certificate No. 1 also permits financial institutions to receive financial assets for deposit to a blocked account and allows funds in blocked accounts to be invested or reinvested or debited to pay amounts owing to financial institutions (e.g fees or reimbursement of amounts paid pursuant to a contractual commitment). Finally, General Certificate No. 1 permits the transfer of financial assets from one blocked account to another blocked account in Canada of the same party. Financial institutions intending to rely on the permissions in Certificate No. 1 must so indicate to the Department of External Affairs (see "Reporting and Record Keeping" below).

General Certificate No. 2 permits the completion by financial institutions of transactions of a financial nature (but not including term deposits) entered into, prior to 5:00 a.m., eastern daylight time, August 2, 1990. A financial institution taking actions to perform obligations with respect to such a transaction must not have reasonable cause to believe that completion of the transaction would result in payments giving rise to a benefit to the Government of Iraq, any agencies of or bodies controlled by the Government of Iraq, or to any person in Iraq or Kuwait. The permission to complete the transactions contemplated in General Certificate No. 2 requires a pre-existing customer relationship (i.e. a bank could not complete a transaction for a blocked account opened after August 2, 1990). General Certificate No. 2 contains a reporting requirement (see: "Reporting and Record Keeping" below).

General Certificate No. 3 tempers substantially the extraterritorial reach of the Regulations. This General Certificate recognizes the measures taken in the United Kingdom and the United States to enforce the Security Council Resolution. General Certificate No. 3 specifies that acts or things done by a Canadian within the "territory" of the United Kingdom or of the United States to effect transactions within the jurisdictional scope of the rules adopted in those jurisdictions to implement the Security Council Resolution are not prohibited. Certificate No. 3 defines "territory of the United Kingdom" as including the Channel Islands and Isle of Man. "Territory of the United States" includes the fifty states and the District of Columbia. Thus, while rules adopted in the U.K. may permit activities in e.g. Gibraltar, Certificate No. 3 could not be relied upon to authorize a transaction in Gibraltar as it is not in the "territory of the United Kingdom" for the purposes of the Certificate. In order to rely on the permission in Certificate No. 3, the Canadian involved must not have reasonable cause to believe the transaction will assist the Government of Iraq, agencies of or bodies controlled by that government or any person in Iraq or Kuwait.

Reporting and Record Keeping

Financial institutions intending to rely on General Certificate Nos. 1 or 2 must so indicate to the Department of External Affairs, Export Control Division. The notification need only be given once, but a separate notice would be required where a financial institution subsidiary intended to rely on the Certificate. Certificate Nos. 1 and 2 also impose on financial institutions the obligation to keep records of actions taken in reliance on those Certificates. The notice requirement will enable External Affairs and regulators of financial institutions (e.g. the Office of the Superintendent of Financial Institutions) to know which institutions are relying on Certificates in order to be in a position to examine particular transactions if necessary. A nice question arises as to the confidentiality of such records in order to safeguard e.g. a bank-customer relationship.

Specific Certificates

A number of certificates exempting certain entities and specific transactions of a financial nature have been issued. Some of these certificates are potentially significant but confidential. The practice has been for the Secretary of State for External Affairs or the Deputy Minister for International Trade and Associate Under Secretary of State for External Affairs[5] to issue the exempting certificate in regard to a particular matter. While exemption from the application of the Regulations is within the sole and exclusive authority of the Secretary of State for External Affairs, there is in practice extensive involvement by the Department of Finance and the Office of the Superintendent of Financial Institutions.

V	**The Spirit of the Regulations**

Readers should bear in mind that Canadian authorities have had little experience with the freezing of foreign assets in Canada. It should also be noted that while Canadian officials have demonstrated flexibility and reasonableness in response to requests for specific exemptions to mitigate hardships which might result from strict adherence to the terms of the Regulations, the Government of Canada is fully committed to upholding its responsibilities in this matter as a Member of the United Nations. Further, while the Regulations extend to both Iraq and Kuwait in similar fashion, the Government of Canada may well exhibit more flexibility with respect to transactions involving Kuwaiti individuals or Kuwaiti entities acting outside of Kuwait than they would to Iraqi citizens or Iraqi entities operating outside of Iraq or Kuwait.

The object of the sanctions imposed by the United Nations and implemented by the Regulations is to ensure that the benefit of economic activity does not accrue to Iraq. In the end, though there is no specific provision in the

---

[5] Pursuant to a certificate signed by the Secretary of State for External Affairs (undated) Donald W. Campbell, Deputy Minister for International Trade and Associate Under Secretary of State for External Affairs was authorized to exercise and perform the powers, duties and functions of the Secretary of State pursuant to section 9 of the United Nations Iraq Regulations.

Regulations to this effect, this is the ultimate test which the Government of Canada will apply in assessing the appropriateness of any activity.

Barry R. Campbell
September 17, 1990

CANADA

PRIVY COUNCIL • CONSEIL PRIVÉ

P.C. 1990-1676
7 August, 1990

HIS EXCELLENCY THE GOVERNOR GENERAL IN COUNCIL, on the recommendation of the Secretary of State for External Affairs, pursuant to section 2 of the United Nations Act, is pleased hereby to make the annexed Regulations giving effect to a resolution of the Security Council of the United Nations concerning Iraq.

CERTIFIED TO BE A TRUE COPY - COPIE CERTIFIÉE CONFORME

CLERK OF THE PRIVY COUNCIL - LE GREFFIER DU CONSEIL PRIV

90-725-01
(SOR/DORS)

REGULATIONS GIVING EFFECT
TO A RESOLUTION OF THE
SECURITY COUNCIL OF THE UNITED NATIONS
CONCERNING IRAQ

Short Title

1. These Regulations may be cited as the United Nations Iraq Regulations.

Interpretation

2. In these Regulations,

"Canadian" means a person who is a citizen within the meaning of the Citizenship Act or a body corporate incorporated by or under the laws of Canada or a province; (Canadien)

"Canadian ship" has the same meaning as in the Canada Shipping Act; (navire canadien)

"credit" includes loans, overdrafts, letters of credit, guarantees, bankers' acceptances, credit insurance, and performance or payment bonds; (crédit)

"goods" includes commodities, articles or products of any kind but does not include medical supplies or food intended solely for humanitarian purposes; (biens)

"property" means any real or personal property; (propriété)

"security" means any share of a body corporate or any bond, debenture, note or other evidence of indebtedness. (titre)

Her Majesty

3. These Regulations are binding on Her Majesty in right of Canada or a province.

Prohibitions

4. (1) No person in Canada shall knowingly import into Canada any goods originating in Iraq or Kuwait that are exported therefrom after August 6, 1990.

(2) No person in Canada and no Canadian outside Canada shall knowingly sell, supply, tranship or otherwise deal in, or attempt to sell, supply, tranship or otherwise deal in, any goods originating in Iraq or Kuwait that are exported therefrom after August 6, 1990.

(3) No person in Canada and no Canadian outside Canada shall knowingly do anything that causes, assists or promotes, or is intended to cause, assist or promote, any act or thing prohibited by subsections (1) and (2).

5. (1) No person in Canada shall knowingly export any goods to any person in Iraq or Kuwait.

(2) No person in Canada and no Canadian outside Canada shall knowingly sell or supply or attempt to sell or supply any goods that are outside Iraq or Kuwait to any person in Iraq or Kuwait.

(3) No person in Canada and no Canadian outside Canada shall knowingly do anything that causes, assists or promotes, or is intended to cause, assist or promote, any act or thing prohibited by subsections (1) and (2).

6. (1) No person in Canada and no Canadian outside Canada shall knowingly send, pay, transfer or remit, directly or indirectly, any money, cheques, bank deposits or other financial resources, or cause any money, cheques, bank deposits or other financial resources to be sent, paid, transferred or remitted, directly or indirectly, to any person in Iraq or Kuwait or to any other person on the direction or order of any person in Iraq or Kuwait.

(2) No person in Canada and no Canadian outside Canada shall knowingly send, transfer, remit or assign any money, cheques, bank deposits or other financial resources held by, on behalf of or on account of the Government of Iraq or Kuwait or any agencies of or bodies controlled by Iraq or Kuwait.

(3) No person in Canada and no Canadian outside Canada shall knowingly make available to or permit the use by the Government of Iraq or any commercial, industrial or public utility undertaking in Iraq or Kuwait of any funds, monetary resources, credit, extension of credit or deposit facilities.

(4) No person shall knowingly transfer, sell, assign, dispose of, export, endorse or guarantee the signature on any security held by, on behalf of or in the name of the Government of Iraq or Kuwait or any agencies of or bodies controlled by Iraq or Kuwait.

(5) No person shall knowingly transfer, pay for, export, dispose of or otherwise deal with any property or any interest in property held by the Government of Iraq or Kuwait or any agencies of or bodies controlled by Iraq or Kuwait.

7. No owner or master of a Canadian ship shall knowingly carry, or cause or permit to be carried, any goods

(a) originating in Iraq or Kuwait and exported therefrom after August 6, 1990; or

(b) destined for Iraq or Kuwait.

Offences

8. (1) Every person who contravenes any provision of these Regulations is guilty of an offence and liable

(a) on summary conviction, to a fine not exceeding two hundred dollars or to imprisonment for a term not exceeding three months, or to both; or

(b) on conviction on indictment, to a fine not exceeding five thousand dollars or to imprisonment for a term not exceeding five years, or to both.

(2) Where an offence has been committed under these Regulations by a corporation, every officer, director or agent of the corporation who directed, authorized, assented to, acquiesced in or participated in the commission of the offence is a party to and guilty of the offence and is liable on conviction to the punishment provided for the offence, whether or not the corporation has been prosecuted or convicted.

9. Notwithstanding sections 4 to 7, no person commits an offence under these Regulations by doing any act or thing prohibited by these Regulations if, before that person does that act or thing, the Secretary of State for External Affairs certifies in writing that, in the opinion of the Secretary of State for External Affairs,

(a) United Nations Security Council Resolution 661 (1990) of August 6, 1990 does not intend that such acts or things be prohibited; or

(b) such acts or things are for the purpose of assisting the legitimate Government of Kuwait.

CHAPTER U-2

An Act respecting Article 41 of the Charter of the United Nations

SHORT TITLE

Short title **1.** This Act may be cited as the *United Nations Act*. R.S., c. U-3, s. 1.

ORDERS AND REGULATIONS OF THE GOVERNOR IN COUNCIL

Application of Security Council decisions **2.** When, in pursuance of Article 41 of the Charter of the United Nations, set out in the schedule, the Security Council of the United Nations decides on a measure to be employed to give effect to any of its decisions and calls on Canada to apply the measure, the Governor in Council may make such orders and regulations as appear to him to be necessary or expedient for enabling the measure to be effectively applied. R.S., c. U-3, s. 2.

Offence and punishment **3.** (1) The Governor in Council may prescribe a fine not exceeding five thousand dollars or a term of imprisonment not exceeding five years, or both, as punishment for contravention of any order or regulation made under this Act and may also prescribe whether the punishment shall be imposed on summary conviction or on conviction on indictment or on either summary conviction or conviction on indictment, but in the case of summary conviction the fine prescribed shall not exceed two hundred dollars and the term of imprisonment prescribed shall not exceed three months.

Forfeiture (2) Any goods, wares or merchandise dealt with contrary to any order or regulation made under this Act may be seized and detained and are liable to forfeiture at the instance of the Minister of Justice, on proceedings in the Federal Court, or in any superior court, and any such court may make rules governing the

CHAPITRE U-2

Loi concernant l'Article 41 de la Charte des Nations Unies

TITRE ABRÉGÉ

1. *Loi sur les Nations Unies.* S.R., ch. U-3, Titre abrégé art. 1.

DÉCRETS ET RÈGLEMENTS DU GOUVERNEUR EN CONSEIL

2. Le gouverneur en conseil peut prendre les Décisions du Conseil de décrets et règlements qui lui semblent utiles Sécurité des pour l'application d'une mesure que le Conseil Nations Unies de Sécurité des Nations Unies, en conformité avec l'Article 41 de la Charte des Nations Unies — reproduit à l'annexe —, invite le Canada à mettre en œuvre pour donner effet à l'une de ses décisions. S.R., ch. U-3, art. 2.

3. (1) Le gouverneur en conseil peut insti- Infractions et peines tuer, pour sanctionner la violation d'un décret ou d'un règlement pris en application de la présente loi, une amende maximale de cinq mille dollars et un emprisonnement maximal de cinq ans, ou l'une de ces peines; il peut aussi décider du mode de poursuite de l'infraction : par mise en accusation ou par procédure sommaire, ou encore au choix. En cas de déclaration de culpabilité par procédure sommaire, toutefois, le maximum de la peine encourue est de deux cents dollars et de trois mois d'emprisonnement.

(2) Les marchandises ou autres articles Confiscation ayant servi ou donné lieu à une infraction aux décrets ou règlements pris en application de la présente loi peuvent être saisis et retenus et faire l'objet d'une confiscation sur instance introduite par le ministre de la Justice devant la Cour fédérale — ou toute autre juridiction

procedure on any proceedings taken before the court or a judge thereof under this section. R.S., c. U-3, s. 3; R.S., c. 10(2nd Supp.), s. 64.

Tabling in
Parliament

4. (1) Every order and regulation made under this Act shall be laid before Parliament forthwith after it has been made or, if Parliament is not then sitting, forthwith after the commencement of the next ensuing session.

Resolution

(2) If both the Senate and House of Commons within the period of forty days, beginning with the day on which an order or regulation is laid before Parliament pursuant to subsection (1) and excluding any time during which Parliament is dissolved or prorogued or during which both the Senate and House of Commons are adjourned for more than four days, resolve that it be annulled, it ceases to have effect, but without prejudice to its previous operation or anything duly done or suffered thereunder or any offence committed or any punishment incurred. R.S., c. U-3, s. 4.

supérieure —, laquelle peut établir les règles de procédure applicables à l'instance exercée devant elle ou l'un de ses juges. S.R., ch. U-3, art. 3; S.R., ch. 10(2ᵉ suppl.), art. 64.

4. (1) Les décrets ou règlements pris en application de la présente loi sont immédiatement déposés devant le Parlement ou, si celui-ci ne siège pas, dès l'ouverture de la session suivante.

Présentation au
Parlement

(2) Si le Sénat et la Chambre des communes, dans un délai de quarante jours à compter de la date de dépôt, déduction faite des périodes de dissolution ou de prorogation du Parlement ou d'ajournement simultané de plus de quatre jours des deux chambres, en décident l'annulation, le décret ou le règlement cesse d'avoir effet, sans préjudice toutefois de son application antérieure, l'annulation restant inopérante en ce qui concerne tout acte régulier en découlant, notamment en matière d'infractions et de peines. S.R., ch. U-3, art. 4; 1976-77, ch. 28, art. 49.

Résolution de
rejet

SCHEDULE

(*Section 2*)

ARTICLE 41—The Security Council may decide what measures not involving the use of armed force are to be employed to give effect to its decisions, and it may call upon the Members of the United Nations to apply such measures. These may include complete or partial interruption of economic relations and of rail, sea, air, postal, telegraphic, radio, and other means of communication, and the severance of diplomatic relations.
R.S., c. U-3, Sch.

ANNEXE

(*article 2*)

ARTICLE 41 — Le Conseil de Sécurité peut décider quelles mesures n'impliquant pas l'emploi de la force armée doivent être prises pour donner effet à ses décisions et peut inviter les Membres des Nations Unies à appliquer ces mesures. Celles-ci peuvent comprendre l'interruption complète ou partielle des relations économiques et des communications ferroviaires, maritimes, aériennes, postales, télégraphiques, radio-électriques et des autres moyens de communication, ainsi que la rupture des relations diplomatiques.
S.R., ch. U-3, ann.

Canada

August 3, 1990

TO: All Banks named in Schedules I and II to the Bank Act (the "Banks")

DIRECTION

WHEREAS the Bank may hold deposits and assets (the "Kuwait property") belonging to the Government of Kuwait and/or its agencies, instrumentalities and controlled entities, including the Kuwait Investment Office, the Central Bank of Kuwait, the Bank of Kuwait, and other emanations of the Government of Kuwait (the "Kuwait government agencies");

AND WHEREAS in view of the invasion of Kuwait by armed forces of the Government of Iraq there is uncertainty as to whether instructions received or which may be received by a Bank from or on behalf of a Kuwait government agency are duly authorized by the Government of Kuwait;

AND WHEREAS the action by a Bank in accepting instructions from or on behalf of a Kuwait government agency at this time or completing a transaction as so instructed or delivering to a third party Kuwaiti property or the proceeds of sale might give rise to a liability of the Bank and would therefore in my opinion be an unsafe or unsound business practice in conducting the business of the Bank;

AND WHEREAS under the provisions of subsection 313.1(1) of the Bank Act, the Superintendent may direct a Bank to cease or refrain from doing any act that may be an unsafe or unsound practice in conducting the business of the Bank, and to perform such acts as are in his opinion necessary to remedy the situation.

AND WHEREAS to allow time for representations before giving this Direction could, in my opinion, be prejudicial to the public interest.

NOW THEREFORE, the Superintendent of Financial Institutions does hereby direct each of the Banks to refrain from acting on instructions from or on behalf of, or purporting to be from or on behalf of, a Kuwait government agency during the period this Direction remains in effect other than:

(a)   instructions the action to be taken by the Bank in respect of which is first approved by me in writing, or

(b)   instructions received or as to matters necessary to effect contractually binding obligations of the Kuwait government agencies that were entered into prior to July 31, 1990.

This action is effective immediately and shall remain in force unless it is revoked or set aside under the provisions of the Bank Act.

Pursuant to subsection 313.1(4) of the Bank Act, you have the right to make representations to me in respect of this matter. Should you wish to make representations, please do so in writing delivered prior to the expiry of the 15th day after the date hereof, at either of our Toronto or Ottawa offices. The addresses are as follows:

Office of the Superintendent
of Financial Institutions
1 Front Street West
2nd Floor
Toronto, Ontario
M5W 1A3

Office of the Superintendent
of Financial Institutions
255 Albert Street
Ottawa, Ontario
K1A 0H2

DATED AT TORONTO at 5 p.m. Eastern Daylight Time this 3rd day of August, 1990.

Michael Mackenzie
Superintendent

DEPARTMENT OF EXTERNAL AFFAIRS

UNITED NATIONS IRAQ REGULATIONS

General Certificate No. 1, dated August 24, 1990

Pursuant to section 9 of the United Nations Iraq Regulations. I hereby certify that the following transactions are not intended to be prohibited by Security Council resolution 661 (1990), of August 6, 1990:

(1) financial transactions involving the release or delivery of financial assets and the receipt of other financial assets in exchange therefor, that are effected by a financial institution in Canada for an account with a financial institution in Canada maintained by the Government of Kuwait, any agencies of or bodies controlled by the Government of Kuwait, or by a person in Kuwait, unless the financial institution has reasonable cause to believe that fair market value is not being received by the particular account;

(2) the receipt by a financial institution in Canada of financial assets for an account of the Government of Kuwait, of any agencies of or bodies controlled by the Government of Kuwait, or of any person in Kuwait and the application of financial assets within that account by way of investment or re-investment or the payment of amounts owing to the financial institution; or

(3) the transfer of financial assets from one account of the Government of Kuwait, any of the agencies of or bodies controlled by the Government of Kuwait, or any person in Kuwait, with a financial institution in Canada, to another such account of the same party with a financial institution in Canada.

It is a condition of this certificate that financial institutions in Canada intending to rely on the present general certificate shall notify the Export Controls Division of the Department of External Affairs in writing and shall keep available for inspection records of the actions taken by them in reliance on it.

For purposes of this certificate, the term "financial institution" means

(*a*) a bank to which the Bank Act applies;

(*b*) a trust company to which the Trust Companies Act applies;

(*c*) a loan company to which the Loan Companies Act applies;

(*d*) a cooperative credit society to which the Cooperative Credit Associations Act applies;

(*e*) an insurance company to which Parts I to VII of the Canadian and British Insurance Companies Act apply;

MINISTÈRE DES AFFAIRES EXTÉRIEURES

RÈGLEMENT DES NATIONS UNIES SUR L'IRAQ

Attestation générale n° 1 établie en date du 24 août 1990

Conformément à l'article 9 du Règlement des Nations Unies sur l'Iraq, j'atteste par la présente que la Résolution 661 (1990) du Conseil de sécurité des Nations Unies, en date du 6 août 1990, ne vise pas à interdire les transactions suivantes :

(1) les transactions financières concernant la libération ou la remise d'avoirs financiers de même que la réception d'autres avoirs financiers en échange, qui sont effectuées par une institution financière au Canada sur un compte que détient auprès d'une institution financière au Canada le Gouvernement du Koweit ou tout agence ou organisme contrôlé par lui ou par une personne au Koweit, sauf si l'institution financière a raisonnablement lieu de penser que ladite transaction ne correspond pas à la juste valeur marchande;

(2) la réception, par une institution financière au Canada, d'avoirs financiers destinés à un compte du Gouvernement du Koweit, d'agences ou d'organismes contrôlés par lui ou par une personne au Koweit, et l'investissement ou le réinvestissement d'avoirs financiers existant dans ledit compte, ou le versement de sommes dues à l'institution financière; ou

(3) le transfert d'avoirs financiers d'un compte que détient auprès d'une institution financière au Canada le Gouvernement du Koweit, une agence ou un organisme contrôlé par lui, ou une personne au Koweit, dans un compte que le Gouvernement du Koweit, une agence ou un organisme contrôlé par lui, ou une personne au Koweit, pourrait avoir auprès d'une autre institution financière au Canada.

Les institutions financières au Canada qui ont l'intention d'invoquer la présente sont tenues d'en aviser par écrit la Direction du contrôle des exportations des Affaires extérieures et Commerce extérieur et de tenir aux fins d'inspection une liste des mesures qu'elles auront prises conformément à la présente.

Aux fins de la présente attestation, l'expression «institution financière» s'entend de :

a) toute banque visée par la *Loi sur les banques*;

b) toute compagnie fiduciaire visée par la *Loi sur les compagnies fiduciaires*;

c) toute compagnie de prêt visée par la *Loi sur les compagnies de prêt*;

d) toute société coopérative de crédit visée par la *Loi sur les associations coopératives de crédit*;

e) toute compagnie d'assurances visée par les Parties numérotées de I à VII de la *Loi sur les compagnies d'assurances canadiennes et britanniques*;

(*f*) a trust, loan or insurance corporation incorporated by or under an Act of the legislature of a province;

(*g*) a cooperative credit society incorporated and regulated by or under an Act of the legislature of a province;

(*h*) an entity that is incorporated or formed by or under an Act of Parliament or of the legislature of a province, the activities of which are limited to dealing in securities, including portfolio management and investment counselling; or

(*i*) an investment company to which the Investment Companies Act applies.

General Certificate No. 2, dated August 24, 1990

Pursuant to section 9 of the United Nations Iraq Regulations, I hereby certify that actions taken by persons which are financial institutions in Canada and branches of such institutions outside Canada to perform obligations with respect to transactions of a financial nature, but not including term deposits, if:

(*a*) such transactions were entered into; and

(*b*) actions are taken in accordance with customer relationships in place

prior to 5:00 a.m. Eastern Daylight Time of August 2, 1990, are not intended to be prohibited by Security Council resolution 661 (1990), of August 6, 1990, provided that the financial institution does not have reasonable cause to believe that the completion of the transactions would result in payments giving rise to a benefit to the Government of Iraq, to any agencies of or bodies controlled by the Government of Iraq, or to any person in Iraq or Kuwait.

It is a condition of this certificate that financial institutions in Canada intending to rely on the present general certificate shall notify the Export Controls Division of the Department of External Affairs in writing and shall keep available for inspection records of the actions taken by them in reliance on it.

For purposes of this certificate, the term "financial institution" means

(*a*) a bank to which the Bank Act applies;

(*b*) a trust company to which the Trust Companies Act applies;

(*c*) a loan company to which the Loan Companies Act applies;

(*d*) a cooperative credit society to which the Cooperative Credit Associations Act applies;

(*e*) an insurance company to which Parts I to VII of the Canadian and British Insurance Companies Act apply;

(*f*) a trust, loan or insurance corporation incorporated by or under an Act of the legislature of a province;

(*g*) a cooperative credit society incorporated and regulated by or under an Act of the legislature of a province;

(*h*) an entity that is incorporated or formed by or under an Act of Parliament or of the legislature of a province, the activities of which are limited to dealing in securities,

f) toute corporation de fiducie, société de prêt ou corporation d'assurances incorporée par ou en vertu d'une loi provinciale;

g) toute société coopérative de crédit incorporée et régie par ou en vertu d'une loi provinciale;

h) toute entité qui est incorporée ou formée par ou en vertu d'une loi du Parlement ou d'une loi provinciale, dont les activités sont limitées à la négociation de titres, y compris la gestion de portefeuilles et les conseils en matière d'investissement; ou

i) toute société d'investissement visée par la *Loi sur les sociétés d'investissement*.

Attestation générale nᵒ 2 établie en date du 24 août 1990

Conformément à l'article 9 du Règlement des Nations Unies sur l'Iraq, j'atteste par la présente que les mesures prises par des personnes qui sont des institutions financières au Canada et par les succursales de ces institutions à l'étranger dans le but de s'acquitter des obligations concernant les transactions de nature financière, à l'exception des dépôts à terme, sous réserve que :

a) ces transactions aient été engagées; et

b) les mesures en question aient été prises conformément aux rapports existants avec le client

avant 5 heures, heure avancée de l'Est, le 2 août 1990, ne sont pas visées par la Résolution 661 (1990) du Conseil de sécurité des Nations Unies, en date du 6 août 1990, à condition que l'institution financière en question n'ait pas raisonnablement lieu de penser que la réalisation desdites transactions donnera lieu à des paiements au bénéfice du Gouvernement de l'Iraq, des agences ou organismes contrôlés par lui, ou de toute personne en Iraq ou au Koweit.

Les institutions financières au Canada qui ont l'intention d'invoquer la présente sont tenues d'en aviser par écrit la Direction du contrôle des exportations des Affaires extérieures et Commerce extérieur et de tenir aux fins d'inspection une liste des mesures qu'elles auront prises conformément à la présente.

Aux fins de la présente attestation, l'expression «institution financière» s'entend de :

a) toute banque visée par la *Loi sur les banques*;

b) toute compagnie fiduciaire visée par la *Loi sur les compagnies fiduciaires*;

c) toute compagnie de prêt visée par la *Loi sur les compagnies de prêt*;

d) toute société coopérative de crédit visée par la *Loi sur les associations coopératives de crédit*;

e) toute compagnie d'assurances visée par les Parties numérotées de I à VII de la *Loi sur les compagnies d'assurances canadiennes et britanniques*;

f) toute corporation de fiducie, société de prêt ou corporation d'assurances incorporée par ou en vertu d'une loi provinciale;

g) toute société coopérative de crédit incorporée et régie par ou en vertu d'une loi provinciale;

h) toute entité qui est incorporée ou formée par ou en vertu d'une loi du Parlement ou d'une loi provinciale, dont les activités sont limitées à la négociation de titres, y compris la

including portfolio management and investment counselling: or

(*i*) an investment company to which the Investment Companies Act applies.

General Certificate No. 3, dated August 24, 1990

Pursuant to section 9 of the United Nations Iraq Regulations and having taken note of the measures taken by the Government of the United Kingdom and the Government of the United States to implement and enforce Security Council resolution 661 (1990) of August 6, 1990, I hereby certify that Security Council resolution 661 (1990) does not intend to prohibit acts or things done by a Canadian within the territory of the United Kingdom or of the United States of America to effect a transaction that meets the following conditions:

(*a*) the transaction is within the jurisdictional scope of the rules adopted by the Government of the United Kingdom or the Government of the United States of America relating to the implementation of Security Council resolution 661 (1990), but is not prohibited under those rules; and

(*b*) the Canadian does not have reasonable cause to believe that the transaction concerned is intended to assist the Government of Iraq, agencies of or bodies controlled by the Government of Iraq or any person in Iraq or Kuwait.

For purposes of this certificate the term "territory of the United Kingdom" includes the Channel Islands and the Isle of Man but does not include any other territories or dependencies; and the term "territory of the United States" means the fifty States of the United States and the District of Columbia.

JOE CLARK
Secretary of State for External Affairs
[37-1-o]

Attestation générale nº 3 établie en date du 24 août 1990

Conformément à l'article 9 du Règlement des Nations Unies sur l'Iraq, et ayant pris note des mesures prises par le Gouvernement du Royaume-Uni et le Gouvernement des États-Unis afin d'appliquer et de faire respecter la Résolution 661 (1990) du Conseil de sécurité des Nations Unies, en date du 6 août 1990, j'atteste par la présente que ne sont pas interdits par ladite Résolution les actes ou faits d'un Canadien résidant sur le territoire du Royaume-Uni ou sur le territoire des États-Unis afin d'effectuer une transaction satisfaisant aux conditions ci-après :

a) la transaction en question se situe dans les limites juridictionnelles des règlements adoptés par le Gouvernement du Royaume-Uni ou le Gouvernement des États-Unis concernant l'application de la Résolution 661 (1990) du Conseil de sécurité, mais n'est pas interdite en vertu de ces règlements; et

b) que ledit Canadien n'ait pas raisonnablement lieu de penser que la transaction en question a pour but d'aider le Gouvernement de l'Iraq, les agences ou organismes contrôlés par lui, ou une personne en Iraq ou au Koweit.

Aux fins de la présente attestation, l'expression «territoire du Royaume-Uni» inclut les îles Anglo-Normandes et l'île de Man, mais n'inclut pas les autres territoires ou dépendances, et l'expression «territoire des États-Unis» s'entend des cinquante États des États-Unis et du District de Columbia.

Le secrétaire d'État aux Affaires extérieures
JOE CLARK
[37-1-o]

I✦I External Affairs and   Affaires extérieures et
International Trade Canada   Commerce extérieur Canada

Deputy Minister   Sous-ministre
International Trade   du Commerce extérieur

Statement of Guidance regarding entities controlled by the Government of Iraq or by persons in Iraq or Kuwait, dated September 6, 1990

The purpose of this Statement is to provide guidance in the interpretation of the United Nations Iraq Regulations. The Annex to this Statement contains three lists of entities:

- List I contains names of entities that are controlled by the Government of Iraq or by persons within Iraq or Kuwait, and as such are considered "bodies controlled by Iraq or Kuwait" within the meaning of the Regulations;

- List II contains names of entities not controlled by the Government of Iraq or the Government of Kuwait or by persons within Iraq or Kuwait, and as such are not considered "bodies controlled by Iraq or Kuwait" within the meaning of the Regulations;

- List III contains names of entities, the status of which is currently being considered but for which it has not yet been possible to make a determination that they should be added to either List I or List II.

Donald W. Campbell

ANNEX

(subject to amendment)

List I: Entities controlled by the Government of Iraq or by persons in Iraq or Kuwait

Al Fao State Establishment
Central Bank of Iraq
The Ministry of Transport and Communication
Rafidian Bank
Rasheed Bank
State Engineering Co. for Industrial Design & Construction
Alahli Bank of Kuwait
Bank of Kuwait & Middle East
Burgan Bank
Commercial Bank of Kuwait
The Gulf Bank
Industrial Bank of Kuwait
Kuwait Foreign Trading Contracting and Investment Co.
Kuwait Institute for Scientific Research
Kuwait Investment Company
Kuwait Real Estate Bank

List II: Entities not controlled by the Government of Iraq or by the Government of Kuwait or by persons in Iraq or Kuwait

Arab Banking Corp.
Arab Banking Corp. - Daus & Co. GMBH
Arab Hellenic Bank
Banco Atlantico
Dao Heng Bank
Gulf International Bank BSC
Gulf Investment Corporation
International Bank of Asia
UBAF Arab American Bank
United Bank of Kuwait PLC

List III: Entities the status of which is currently under examination

Bahrain Middle East Bank
Breadstreet Moorgate
Central Bank of Kuwait
Financial Group of Kuwait
Kuwait and Bahrain Bank
Kuwait Financial Centre
Kuwait French Bank
Kuwait International Investment Company
National Bank of Kuwait
NBK Financa S.A. - Geneva
National Bank of Kuwait - France
National Bank of Kuwait New York Branch
Sante Fe International Corp. & Subs.
United Trading Group

<u>List III: Entities the status of which is currently under examination</u>

Kuwait French Bank
National Bank of Kuwait (all branches)
National Bank of Kuwait - France
United Trading Group

*   see Statement of Guidance

External Affairs and
International Trade Canada

Affaires extérieures et
Commerce extérieur Canada

Deputy Minister
International Trade

Sous-ministre
du Commerce extérieur

September 17, 1990

Amendment to the Statement of Guidance regarding entities controlled by the Government of Iraq or by persons in Iraq or Kuwait, dated September 17, 1990

The Annex to the Statement of Guidance issued by me on September 6, 1990 is hereby amended so as to add the following entities to List I (entities controlled by the Government of Iraq or by the Government of Kuwait or by persons in Iraq or Kuwait) or List II (entities not controlled by the Government of Iraq or by the Government of Kuwait or by persons in Iraq or Kuwait) and to make consequential changes to List III (entities the status of which is currently under examination). A copy of the amended list is attached replacing the list issued on September 6.

Added to List I

Central Bank of Kuwait
Kuwait Asia Bank
Kuwait International Investment Company
Financial Group of Kuwait
Kuwait Financial Centre

Added to List II

Bahrain Middle East Bank
Bank of Bahrain and Kuwait
Sante Fe International Corp. and Subs
NBK Finance S.A. - Geneva
NBK Investment Management Ltd.

In addition, the Secretary of State for External Affairs has issued certificates permitting three entities controlled by the Government of Kuwait to carry out transactions within the terms of the certificate. These entities, Kuwait Airways Corp, Kuwait Investment Authority and Kuwait Investment Office, are indicated by an asterisk in the attached Annex.

Donald W. Campbell

Supplementary Material: Canada

█◆█ External Affairs and   Affaires extérieures et
International Trade Canada   Commerce extérieur Canada

Deputy Minister   Sous-ministre
International Trade   du Commerce extérieur

September 27, 1990

<u>First Amendment to General Certificate No. 3,
dated August 24, 1990</u>

Pursuant to section 9 of the <u>United Nations Iraq
Regulations</u> and the authority provided to me by the Secretary of
State for External Affairs, I certify that, for purposes of
General Certificate No. 3, dated August 24, 1990, the term
"territory of the United States" means the fifty States of the
United States, the District of Columbia, Puerto Rico and the
United States Virgin Islands.

Donald W. Campbell
Deputy Minister for
International Trade and
Associate Under-Secretary of
State for External Affairs

CANADA

PRIVY COUNCIL • CONSEIL PRIVÉ

P.C. 1990-2158
1 October, 1990

HIS EXCELLENCY THE GOVERNOR GENERAL IN COUNCIL, on the recommendation of the Secretary of State for External Affairs, pursuant to section 2 of the United Nations Act, is pleased hereby to amend the United Nations Iraq Regulations, made by Order in Council P.C. 1990-1676 of August 7, 1990, in accordance with the schedule hereto.

CERTIFIED TO BE A TRUE COPY - COPIE CERTIFIÉE CONFORME

CLERK OF THE PRIVY COUNCIL - LE GREFFIER DU CONSEIL PRIVÉ

SCHEDULE

1. The long title of the United Nations Iraq Regulations is revoked and the following substituted therefor:

"REGULATIONS GIVING EFFECT TO CERTAIN RESOLUTIONS OF THE SECURITY COUNCIL OF THE UNITED NATIONS CONCERNING IRAQ"

2. (1) The definition "goods" in section 2 of the said Regulations is revoked.

(2) Section 2 of the said Regulations is further amended by adding thereto, in alphabetical order, the following definition:

""Security Council Resolutions" means United Nations Security Council Resolution 661 (1990) of August 6, 1990 and Resolution 670 (1990) of September 25, 1990. (résolutions du Conseil de Sécurité)"

3. The said Regulations are further amended by adding thereto, immediately after section 7 thereof, the following sections:

"7.1 No operator of an aircraft registered in Canada shall knowingly carry, or cause or permit to be carried, any goods originating in or destined for Iraq or Kuwait.

7.2 No person in Canada shall operate an aircraft that the person knows is intended to carry goods to or from Iraq or Kuwait.

7.3 No person shall operate over the territory of Canada an aircraft that the person knows is destined to land in Iraq or Kuwait unless

(a) an inspection of the aircraft at an airfield has verified that no goods are being carried on board the aircraft in contravention of any measures taken by Members of the United Nations to implement the Security Council Resolutions; or

(b) a certificate in respect of the overflight has been issued under section 9.

7.4 (1) No person shall cause a ship that is registered in Iraq and that the person knows is or has been used in contravention of any measures taken by Members of the United Nations to implement the Security Council Resolutions to enter a port in Canada, except where the entry is necessary in order to safeguard human life.

(2) Every ship registered in Iraq that enters a port in Canada in contravention of subsection (1) shall be detained."

4. Section 9 of the said Regulations is revoked and the following substituted therefor:

"9. Notwithstanding sections 4 to 7.4, no person commits an offence under these Regulations by doing any act or thing prohibited by these Regulations if, before that person does that act or thing, the Secretary of State for External Affairs issues a certificate stating that, in the opinion of the Secretary of State for External Affairs,

(a) the Security Council Resolutions do not intend that such acts or things be prohibited;

(b) such acts or things are for the purpose of assisting the legitimate Government of Kuwait; or

(c) such acts or things have been approved by the United Nations Security Council or the Committee of the Security Council established by United Nations Security Council Resolution 661 (1990) of August 6, 1990."

▌✦▌ External Affairs and
International Trade Canada

Affaires extérieures et
Commerce extérieur Canada

Deputy Minister
International Trade

Sous-ministre
du Commerce extérieur

September 19, 1990

Second Amendment to the Statement of Guidance regarding entities controlled by the Government of Iraq or by persons in Iraq or Kuwait, dated September 6, 1990

The Annex to the Statement of Guidance issued by me on September 6, 1990 is hereby further amended so as to delete the following entity from List I (Entities controlled by the Government of Iraq or by the Government of Kuwait or by persons in Iraq or Kuwait) and to add the following entity to List II (entities not controlled by the Government of Iraq or by the Government of Kuwait or by persons in Iraq or Kuwait) and to make consequential changes to List III (entities the status of which is currently under examination). A copy of the amended list is attached replacing the list issued on September 14.

Added to List II

National Bank of Kuwait

Added to List III from List I

Kuwait French Bank

In addition, the Secretary of State for External Affairs has issued certificates permitting three entities controlled by the Government of Kuwait to carry out transactions within the terms of the certificate. These entities, Kuwait Airways Corp, Kuwait Investment Authority and Kuwait Investment Office, are indicated by an asterisk in the attached Annex.

Donald W. Campbell

ANNEX

List I: Entities controlled by the Government of Iraq or by the government of Kuwait or by persons in Iraq or Kuwait

Al Fao State Establishment
Alahli Bank of Kuwait
Bank of Kuwait & Middle East
Burgan Bank
Central Bank of Iraq
Central Bank of Kuwait
Commercial Bank of Kuwait
Financial Group of Kuwait
The Gulf Bank
Industrial Bank of Kuwait
Kuwait Asia Bank
Kuwait Financial Centre
Kuwait Foreign Trading Contracting and Investment Co.
* Kuwait Airways Corp. (KAC)
* Kuwait Investment Authority (KIA)
* Kuwait Investment Office (KIO)
Kuwait International Investment Company
Kuwait Investment Company
Kuwait Real Estate Bank
Rafidian Bank
Rasheed Bank
State Engineering Co. for Industrial Design & Construction

List II: Entities not controlled by the Government of Iraq or by the Government of Kuwait or by persons in Iraq or Kuwait

Arab Banking Corp.
Arab Banking Corp. - Daus & Co. GMBH
Arab Hellenic Bank
Bahrain Middle East Bank
Banco Atlantico
Dao Heng Bank
Gulf International Bank BSC
Gulf Investment Corporation
International Bank of Asia
Bank of Bahrain and Kuwait
National Bank of Kuwait
NBK Finance S.A. - Geneva
NBK Investment Management Ltd.
Sante Fe International Corp. & Subs.
UBAF Arab American Bank
United Bank of Kuwait PLC

List III: Entities the status of which is currently under examination

Kuwait French Bank
National Bank of Kuwait - France
United Trading Group

* see Statement of Guidance

European Community

<u>Complete text of the declaration of the 12 members of the EEC
concerning the Iraqi invasion of Kuwait - ROME, August 4</u>

"The European Economic Community and its Member states affirm
their unreserved condemnation of the brutal Iraqi invasion of
Kuwait and demand an immediate unconditional retreat of the
Iraqi armed forces from the Kuwaiti territory, as already
expressed in their declaration of August 2.

Iraq's motives justifying its military invasion of Kuwait are
deemed unjustified and inacceptable by the members of the
economic community which will refrain from any action which
could be considered as an implicit recognition of the
government imposed by the invaders in Kuwait.

To protect the interests of the legitimate government in
Kuwait, the members decided to take steps in order to protect
all assets belonging directly or indirectly to Kuwait.

The European Economic Community and its Member states confirm
their backing of resolution 660 of the United Nations Security
Council and request that Iraq respect the provisions of this
resolution. If the Iraqi authorities do not respect these
provisions, the European Economic Community and its Member
states shall apply a resolution of the Security Council
introducing obligatory global sanctions.

The following decisions were reached with immediate effect:

- an embargo on petrol imports from Iraq and Kuwait.

- appropriate measures in order to freeze Iraqi assets in
Member states of the European Economic Community.

- an embargo on the sale of arms and other military equipment
to Iraq.

- the suspension of all military cooperation with Iraq.

- the suspension of technical and scientific cooperation with
Iraq.

- the suspension and application of the general preference
system in Iraq.

The European Economic Community and its Member states reiterate
their firm conviction that any dispute between countries should
be resolved pacifically and that they are prepared to
participate wholeheartedly in assisting to reduce the tension
in the region.

They are in close contact with the governments of several Arab
countries and follow attentively all discussions within the
Arab League and the Cooperation Council of the Gulf. They hope
that Arab initiatives will contribute to the reestablishment of
international order and of the legitimate Kuwaiti government.
The European Economic Community and its Member states are
prepared to strongly back these initiatives as well as all
efforts to resolve the problem by negotiating the disputes
between the concerned countries.

The European Economic Community and its Member states are
attentively following the situation of their fellow countrymen
resident in Iraq and in Kuwait. They are closely coordinating
in order to assure their security."

I

(Acts whose publication is obligatory)

COUNCIL REGULATION (EEC) No 2340/90

of 8 August 1990

preventing trade by the Community as regards Iraq and Kuwait

THE COUNCIL OF THE EUROPEAN COMMUNITIES,

Whereas the serious situation resulting from the invasion of Kuwait by Iraq, which was the subject of United Nations Security Council Resolution 660 (1990) of 2 August 1990, has led to a declaration by the Community and its Member States, adopted on 4 August 1990 in the framework of political cooperation, condemning outright the invasion of Kuwait by Iraq and demanding an immediate and unconditional withdrawal of Iraqi forces from the territory of Kuwait, as well as to the Decision that economic measures will be taken against Iraq;

Whereas, faced with Iraq's refusal to conform to Resolution 660, the Security Council adopted Resolution 661 (1990) of 6 August 1990 establishing an embargo on trade with Iraq and Kuwait;

Whereas, in these conditions, the Community's trade as regards Iraq and Kuwait must be prevented;

Whereas the Community and its Member States have agreed to have recourse to a Community instrument in order to ensure uniform implementation, throughout the Community, of the measures concerning trade with Iraq and Kuwait decided upon by the United Nations Security Council;

Whereas it is appropriate to avoid a situation in which this Regulation affects exports from these countries conducted before 7 August 1990 as well as the supply of products intended strictly for medical purposes, and, where humanitarian reasons so warrant, of foodstuffs;

Having regard to the Treaty establishing the European Economic Community, and in particular Article 113 thereof,

Having regard to the proposal from the Commission,

HAS ADOPTED THIS REGULATION:

Article 1

As from 7 August 1990, the following shall be prohibited:

1. the introduction into the territory of the Community of all commodities or products originating in, or coming from, Iraq or Kuwait;

2. the export to the said countries of all commodities or products originating in, or coming from, the Community.

Article 2

As from the date referred to in Article 1, the following shall be prohibited in the territory of the Community or by means of aircraft and vessels flying the flag of a Member State, and when carried out by any Council national:

1. all activities or commercial transactions, including all operations connected with transactions which have already been concluded or partially carried out, the object or effect of which is to promote the export of any commodity or product originating in, or coming from, Iraq or Kuwait;

2. the sale or supply of any commodity or product, wherever it originates or comes from:

— to any natural or legal person in Iraq or Kuwait,

— to any other natural or legal person for the purposes of any commercial activity carried out in or from the territory of Iraq or Kuwait;

3. any activity the object or effect of which is to promote such sales or supplies.

Article 3

1. Article 1 (2) and Article 2 (2) shall not apply to the products listed in the Annex.

2. Article 1 (1) and Article 2 (1) shall not prevent the introduction into the territory of the Community of the commodities or products referred to in Article 1 (1) which originate in, or come from, Iraq or Kuwait and are exported before 7 August 1990.

Article 4

This Regulation shall enter intor force on the day of its publication in the *Official Journal of the European Communities.*

This Regulation shall be binding in its entirety and directly applicable in all Member States.

Done at Brussels, 8 August 1990.

For the Council
The President
G. DE MICHELIS

———

ANNEX

LIST OF PRODUCTS REFERRED TO IN ARTICLE 3 (1)

A. Medical products

ex chapter 29

All the products which are international nonproprietary names (INN) or modified international nonproprietary names (INNM) of the World Health Organization

2937 Hormones, natural or reproduced by synthesis ; derivatives thereof, used primarily as hormones ; other steroids used primarily as hormones

2941 Antibiotics

3001 Glands and other organs for organotherapeutic uses, dried, whether or not powdered ; extracts of glands or other organs or of their secretions for organotherapeutic uses ; heparin and its salts ; other human or animal substances prepared for therapeutic or prophylactic uses, not elsewhere specified or included

3002 Human blood ; animal blood prepared for therapeutic, prophylactic or diagnostic uses ; antisera and other blood fractions ; vaccines, toxins, cultures of micro-organisms (excluding yeasts) and similar products

3003 Medicaments (excluding goods of heading Nos 3002, 3005 or 3006) consisting of two or more constituents which have been mixed together for therapeutic or prophylactic uses, not put up in measured doses or in forms or packings for retail sale

3004 Medicaments (excluding goods of heading Nos 3002, 3005 or 3006) consisting of mixed or unmixed products for therapeutic or prophylactic uses, put up in measured doses or in forms or packings for retail sale

3005 Wadding gauze, bandages and similar articles (for example, dressings, adhesive plasters, poultices), impregnated or coated with pharmaceutical substances or put up in forms or packings for retail sale for medical, surgical, dental or veterinary purposes

3006 Pharmaceutical goods specified in note 3 to this chapter

B. Foodstuffs

Any foodstuff intended for humanitarian purposes as part of emergency aid operations.

Corrigendum to Council Regulation (EEC) No 2340/90 of 8 August 1990 prevending trade by the Community as regards Iraq and Kuwait

(Official Journal of the European Communities No L 213 of 9 August 1990)

On page 1 in Article 2, introductory part:

for: '... Member State, and when carried out by any Community national :',

read: '... Member State, or when carried out by any Community national :'.

European Coal and Steel Community

II

(Acts whose publication is not obligatory)

COUNCIL

DECISION OF THE REPRESENTATIVES OF THE GOVERNMENTS OF THE MEMBER STATES OF THE EUROPEAN COAL AND STEEL COMMUNITY, MEETING WITHIN THE COUNCIL

of 8 August 1990

preventing trade as regards Iraq and Kuwait

(90/414/ECSC)

THE REPRESENTATIVES OF THE GOVERNMENTS OF THE MEMBER STATES OF THE EUROPEAN COAL AND STEEL COMMUNITY, MEETING WITHIN THE COUNCIL,

Whereas the serious situation resulting from the invasion of Kuwait by Iraq, which was the subject of United Nations Security Council Resolution 660 (1990) of 2 August 1990, has led to a declaration by the Community and its Member States, adopted on 4 August 1990 in the framework of political cooperation, condemning outright the invasion of Kuwait by Iraq and demanding an immediate and unconditional withdrawal of Iraqi forces from the territory of Kuwait, as well as to the decision that economic measures will be taken against Iraq;

Whereas, faced with Iraq's refusal to conform to Resolution 660, the Security Council adopted Resolution 661 (1990) of 6 August 1990 establishing an embargo on trade with Iraq and Kuwait;

Whereas, in these conditions, trade in commodities and products covered by the ECSC Treaty must be prevented as regards Iraq and Kuwait;

Whereas the Community and its Member States have agreed to ensure uniform implementation, throughout the Community, of measures concerning trade with Iraq and Kuwait decided upon by the United Nations Security Council; whereas, as a result, Council Regulation (EEC) No 2340/90 of 8 August 1990 preventing trade by the Community as regards Iraq and Kuwait (¹) was adopted in order to cover commodities and products other than those covered by the ECSC Treaty; whereas it is necessary to adopt a Decision concerning these last mentioned products;

Whereas it is appropriate to avoid a situation in which this Decision affects exports from these countries conducted before 7 August 1990,

In agreement with the Commission,

HAVE DECIDED AS FOLLOWS:

Article 1

As from 7 August 1990, the following shall be prohibited:

1. the introduction into the territory of the Community of all commodities or products covered by the ECSC Treaty and originating in, or coming from, Iraq or Kuwait;

2. the export to the said countries of all commodities or products covered by the said Treaty and originating in, or coming from, the Community.

Article 2

As from the date referred to in Article 1, the following shall be prohibited in the territory of the Community or by means of aircraft and vessels flying the flag of a Member State, and when carried out by any Community national:

1. all activities or commercial transactions, including all operations connected with transactions which have already been concluded or partially carried out, the object or effect of which is to promote the export of any commodity or product covered by the ECSC Treaty and originating in, or coming from, Iraq or Kuwait;

(¹) See page 1 of this Official Journal.

2. the sale or supply of any commodity or product covered by the said Treaty wherever it originates or comes from :

— to any natural or legal person in Iraq or Kuwait,

— to any other natural or legal person for the purposes of any commercial activity carried out in or from the territory of Iraq or Kuwait ;

3. any activity the object or effect of which is to promote such sales or supplies.

Article 3

Article 1 (1) and Article 2 (1) shall not prevent the introduction into the territory of the Community of the commodities or products referred to in Article 1 (1) which originate in, or come from, Iraq or Kuwait and are exported before 7 August 1990.

Article 4

This Decision shall enter into force on the day of its publication in the *Official Journal of the European Communities.*

Done at Brussels, 8 August 1990.

The President

G. DE MICHELIS

Corrigendum to Decision 90/414/ECSC of the Representatives of the Governements of the Member States of the European Coal and Steel Community, meeting within the Council, of 8 August 1990, preventing trade as regards Iraq and Kuwait

(Official Journal of the European Communities No L 213 of 9 August 1990)

On page 3 in Article 2, introductory part:

for: '... Member State, and when carried out by any Community national :',

read: '... Member State, or when carried out by any Community national :'.

France

DECRET N° 90-681 DU 2 AOUT 1990
REGLEMENTANT LES RELATIONS FINANCIERES
AVEC CERTAINS PAYS

Article 1er

Sont soumis à autorisation préalable du ministre chargé de l'économie les opérations de change, les mouvements de capitaux et les règlements de toute nature entre la France et l'étranger effectués pour le compte de personnes physiques ou morales résidentes au Koweit et en Irak ou de nationalité koweitienne ou irakienne. Sont également soumises à autorisation préalable du ministre chargé de l'économie la constitution et la liquidation d'investissements d'origine koweitienne et irakienne en France.

Article 2

Le ministre chargé de l'économie peut par arrêté dispenser certaines catégories d'opérations de l'autorisation prévue à l'article 1er ci-dessus.

Article 3

Le ministre d'Etat, ministre de l'économie, des finances et du budget, et le ministre des départements et territoires d'outre-mer, porte-parole du Gouvernement, sont chargés, chacun en ce qui le concerne, de l'exécution du présent décret, qui sera publié au Journal Officiel de la République française et qui, vu l'urgence, entrera immédiatement en vigueur.

Fait à Paris, le 2 août 1990

DECREE N° 90-681 OF AUGUST 2 1990
REGULATING FINANCIAL RELATIONSHIPS
WITH CERTAIN COUNTRIES

Article 1

Foreign exchange transactions, transfer of funds and settlement of any kind between France and other countries made on behalf of individuals or companies resident in Kuwait and in Iraq, or of Kuwaiti or Iraqi nationality, are subject to the prior authorization of the Minister of Economy. The constitution and liquidation in France of investments originating in Kuwait or Iraq are also subject to the prior authorization of the Minister of Economy.

Article 2

The Minister of Economy may exempt certain transactions from the authorization outlined in Article 1 above.

Article 3

The Minister of State, Minister of Economy, Finances and Budget, the Minister of Overseas Territories, representing the Government, must, respectively, enforce this decree, which will be published in the Official Journal of the French Republic (Journal Officiel) and which, given the urgency, will be effective immediately.

Paris, August 2, 1990

MINISTÈRE DE L'ÉCONOMIE, DES FINANCES ET DU BUDGET

**Arrêté du 4 août 1990 relatif
aux relations financières avec certains pays**

NOR : *ECOX9010897A*

Le ministre d'Etat, ministre de l'économie, des finances et du budget,

Vu la loi n° 66-1008 du 28 décembre 1966 relative aux relations financières avec l'étranger ;

Vu la loi n° 84-46 du 24 janvier 1984 relative à l'activité et au contrôle des établissements de crédit ;

Vu le décret du 5 novembre 1870 relatif à la promulgation des lois et décrets, et notamment son article 2 (deuxième alinéa) ;

Vu le décret n° 89-938 du 29 décembre 1989 réglementant les relations financières avec l'étranger, modifié par le décret n° 90-58 du 13 janvier 1990 ;

Vu le décret n° 90-681 du 2 août 1990 réglementant les relations financières avec certains pays,

Arrête :

Art. 1er. - Pour l'application du décret du 2 août 1990 susvisé et du présent arrêté, il faut entendre par :

1. *Investissements*

Les avoirs de toute nature, y compris notamment les dépôts dans les établissements de crédit ou autres, les titres, les investissements directs, les actifs immobiliers, ainsi que les droits y afférents.

2. *Investissements d'origine irakienne ou koweïtienne*

Les investissements réalisés par des personnes physiques de nationalité ou de résidence koweïtienne ou irakienne, et les investissements des personnes morales ayant leur siège au Koweït ou en Irak ou dont des personnes de nationalité ou de résidence koweïtienne ou irakienne ou une collectivité publique située au Koweït ou en Irak ou un de ces Etats lui-même contrôlent directement ou indirectement 50 p. 100 ou plus du capital ou des droits de vote, ou exercent sur elles par tout autre moyen une influence déterminante.

3. *Etablissements de crédit ou autres*

Les établissements relevant des articles 1er et 99 de la loi du 24 janvier 1984 susvisée relative à l'activité et au contrôle des établissements de crédit, les institutions et services énumérés à l'article 8 de ladite loi, et les sociétés de bourse.

Art. 2. - Sont dispensées de l'autorisation préalable prévue à l'article 1er du décret du 2 août 1990 susvisé les opérations suivantes :

- les opérations de change manuel ;
- les versements effectués par tout moyen au crédit des comptes ouverts dans les établissements de crédit ou autres, au nom des personnes visées à l'article 1er du décret du 2 août 1990 susvisé ;
- les opérations de débit de toute nature effectuées, dans la limite d'un montant cumulé d'un million de francs par compte, sur les comptes visés à l'alinéa précédent.

Art. 3. - Les règlements relatifs aux dépenses courantes des personnes physiques visées à l'article 1er du décret du 2 août 1990 susvisé et aux opérations courantes des personnes morales visées à l'article 1er du décret précité dont l'activité revêt un caractère industriel ou commercial sont autorisés, sous réserve de la présentation à l'établissement chargé du mouvement des fonds conformément à l'article 2 du décret du 29 décembre 1989 susvisé des justificatifs permettant à celui-ci de vérifier la réalité de la transaction.

Art. 4. - Sont également autorisées, sous réserve, le cas échéant, de l'application des dispositions aux investissements directs étrangers en France, les opérations d'achats ou de ventes de titres émis ou cotés en France, d'actifs immobiliers situés en France ou de droits y afférents dès lors que le règlement de ces opérations est assuré respectivement par débit ou crédit d'un compte ouvert dans un établissement de crédit ou autre situé en France, au nom de la personne pour le compte de laquelle ces opérations sont réalisées et à condition qu'aient été produits à l'établissement concerné les justificatifs permettant à celui-ci de s'assurer de la réalité de la transaction.

Art. 5. - Les règlements qui ont fait l'objet d'ordres adressés à l'établissement chargé du mouvement des fonds avant le 3 août 1990, ou qui sont relatifs à des transactions sur titres ou instruments financiers conclues avant le 3 août 1990 ou à des ordres exécutés avant cette même date, sont autorisés sous réserve de présentation à l'établissement concerné des justificatifs appropriés.

Art. 6. - Les demandes d'autorisation préalable doivent être adressées par les établissements concernés au ministre d'Etat, ministre de l'économie, des finances et du budget, direction du Trésor, bureau D 3.

Art. 7. - Le présent arrêté sera publié au *Journal officiel* de la République française et qui, vu l'urgence, entrera immédiatement en vigueur.

Fait à Paris, le 4 août 1990.

PIERRE BÉRÉGOVOY

S & S TRANSLATION

MINISTRY OF THE ECONOMY, FINANCE AND BUDGET

Decree dated August 4, 1990 relating
to financial relationships with certain countries
NOR: ECOX9010897A

The Minister of State, Minister of the Economy, Finance
and Budget,
Whereas the Law no. 66-1008 dated December 28, 1966
relating to financial relationships abroad;
Whereas the Law no. 84-46 dated January 24, 1984 relating
to the activity and to the control of credit institutions;
Whereas the Decree dated November 5, 1870 relating to the
promulgation of laws and decrees and, in particular, its
Article 2 (second paragraph);
Whereas the Decree no. 89-938 dated December 29, 1989
regulating the financial relationships abroad, amended by the
Decree no. 90-58 dated January 15, 1990;
Whereas the Decree no. 90-681 dated August 2, 1990
regulating the financial relationships with certain countries,

Decrees:

Art. 1. - For the application of the Decree dated August
2, 1990 referred to above and of the present decree, the
following are defined:

1.   Investments

Assets of any type, including, in particular, deposit
accounts in credit or other institutions, securities, direct
investments, fixed assets, as well as the rights pertaining
to these.

2.   Investments with origin in Iraq or Kuwait

Investments realized by natural persons of Kuwaiti or
Iraqi nationality or residence and investments of legal
entities with registered offices in Kuwait or in Iraq or
those of persons of Kuwaiti or Iraqi nationality or residence
or a public organization located in Kuwait or in Iraq or one
of these States itself controlling directly or indirectly
50% or more of the capital or the voting rights or exercising
a determining influence over it by any other means.

S & S TRANSLATION

3. Credit or Other Institutions

The pertinent institutions of Articles 1 and 99 of the Law dated January 24, 1984 referred to above relating to the activity and control of the credit institutions, institutions and services listed in Article 8 of said law and stock brokers.

Art. 2. - The following transactions are exempt from prior authorization stipulated in Article 1 of Decree dated August 2, 1990 referred to above:

- transactions of exchange by hand;
- payments effected by any means to the credit of accounts opened in credit or other institutions in the name of persons referred to in Article 1 of the Decree dated August 2, 1990 referred to above;
- debit transactions of any nature effected within the limit of a cumulative amount of one million French Francs per account, on accounts referred to in the preceding paragraph.

Art. 3 - The regulations relating to current expenses of natural persons referred to in Article 1 of Decree dated August 2, 1990 referred to above and to current transactions of legal entities referred to in Article 1 of the aforementioned decree, the activity of which bears an industrial or commercial character, are authorized, subject to the presentation to the institution in charge of the movement of funds in conformance with Article 2 of the Decree dated December 29, 1989 referred to above of vouchers permitting them to verifiy the actuality of the transaction.

Art. 4 - Likewise authorized, subject, if need be, to the application of stipulations for direct foreign investments in France, are transactions for the purchase or sale of securities issued or listed in France, for fixed assets located in France or for rights pertaining thereto since the regulation of these transactions is assured, respectively, by debit or credit of an account opened in a credit or other type of institution located in France, in the name of the person for the account of which these transactions are realized and on condition that there had been issued at the institution involved the vouchers permitting them to make sure of the actuality of the transaction.

Art. 5. - The regulations which are the subject of orders sent to the institution in charge of the movement of funds before August 3, 1990, or which are related to transactions on securities or financial instruments entered into before August 3, 1990 or to orders executed before this same date,

S & S TRANSLATION

are authorized subject to the presentation of the appropriate vouchers to the institution concerned.

Art. 6 - Requests for previous authorization must be sent by the institutions concerned to the Minister of State, Minister of the Economy, Finance and Budget, Treasury Department, Office D 3.

Art. 7 - The present decree will be published in the Journal Officiel [Official Journal] of the French Republic and which, given the urgency, will enter into force immediately.

Issued in Paris on August 4, 1990.

PIERRE BEREGOVOY

Germany

SHEARMAN & STERLING

August 6, 1990

Memorandum to: Emmanuel Gaillard

<u>Iraq/Kuwait: West Germany</u>

The deputy speaker of the German Federal Government, Dieter Vogel, makes the following announcement:

<u>Original German text</u>:

"Der Stellvertretende Sprecher der Bundesregierung, Dieter Vogel, teilt mit:

Die Bundesregierung hat bereits gestern die brutale Invasion Kuwaits durch den Irak mit aller Entschiedenheit verurteilt. Sie stellt mit Befriedigung fest, dass in dieser Frage ein weitgespannter Konsens besteht. Die Partnerschaft und Kooperation zwischen den Vereinigten Staaten von Amerika und der Sowjetunion ist dabei besonders hervozuheben; das weltweite Echo auf die Agression gegen Kuwait sollte auch bei der irakischen Regierung seinen Eindruck hinterlassen.

Die Bundesregierung belässt es nicht bei Appellen. Die Ressorts haben die folgenden Massnahmen vorbereitet, die nun dem Kabinett zur Beschlussfassung vorgelegt werden:

1. Alle Konten und Depots im staatlichen Eigentum Kuwaits, die sich in der Bundesrepublik Deutschland befinden, werden eingefroren. Damit soll und kann verhindert werden, dass sich der Irak über von ihm kontrollierte Stellen Kuwaits kuwaitische Vermögenswerte aneignet.

2. Ausfuhrgewährleistungen, z.b. Hermes-Bürgschaften, sind ausgesetzt.

3. Die Bundesregierung stellt sicher, dass der Wirtschaftsverkehr vom Irak nicht zu militärischen Zwecken missbraucht werden kann. Deshalb wird die Durchfuhr von Waffen und Nuklearwaren über das Territorium der Bundesrepublik Deutschland in den Irak der aussenwirtschaftlichen Kontrolle unterworfen und damit genehmigungspflichtig.

Ueber die schon bestehenden Exportbeschränkungen hinaus
wird der Export zusätzlicher Waren, die sowohl
militärischen wie zivilen Zwecken dienen können, aus der
Bundesrepublik in den Irak genehmigungspflichtig gemacht.
Beispiele dafür sind Hubschrauber und Hubschrauberteile,
schwere Schmieden und Pressen, einige Maschinentypen und
-teile, die möglicherweise nicht nur für friedliche Zwecke
verwendet werden können.

Das Bundesamt für Wirtschaft in Eschborn ist angewiesen
worden, für alle Waren, die sowohl zivil wie militärisch
verwendet werden können, bis auf weiteres keine
Exportgenehmigungen mehr in den Irak zu erteilen. Der Zoll
wird Lieferungen in den Irak besonders sorgfältig
kontrollieren."

Unofficial draft translation

"Yesterday, the Federal Government strongly condemned the
brutal invasion of Kuwait by Irak. It has noted with
satisfaction that there is a widespread consent on this
question. The partnership and cooperation between the United
States of America and the Soviet Union is to be noted,
especially in this case. The worldwide reaction to the
aggression against Kuwait should leave its traces even with the
Iraqi government.

The Federal Government, however, does not restrict itself to
appeals. The departments have prepared the following measures,
which will now be submitted to the cabinet to be resolved upon:

1. All accounts and deposits belonging to the State of Kuwait
    in Germany will be frozen. This should and can prevent
    Iraq from appropriating Kuwaiti assets now under its
    control.

2. Export guarantees as, for example, Hermes-Guarantees have
    been suspended.

3. The Federal Government undertakes to guarantee that the
    economic transactions cannot be misused for military
    purposes by Iraq. For this reason, the trading of arms and
    nuclear weapon products on the territory of the Federal
    Republic of Germany will be subject to foreign trade
    control and hence subject to approbation.

    In addition to the already existing export restrictions,
    the export of supplementary products which could serve for
    military as well as for civil purposes from the Federal
    Republic to Iraq is subject to approbation. Examples for
    this would be helicopters and helicopter parts, heavy
    forging ovens and presses, some types of machines and
    machine parts which could be used for other than peaceful
    purposes.

The Federal Office for Economy in Eschborn has been
instructed not to issue any additional export licences to
Iraq for all products destined for civil as well as for
military purposes. Customs authorities will effect
particularly careful controls on deliveries to Iraq.

Marianne Nitsch

248

Amtlicher Teil

Verkündungen

Der Bundesminister für Wirtschaft

Neunte Verordnung
zur Änderung der Außenwirtschaftsverordnung
Vom 7. August 1990

Auf Grund des § 27 Abs. 1 Satz 1 und 2 in Verbindung mit § 2 Abs. 1 und § 7 Abs. 1 des Außenwirtschaftsgesetzes in der im Bundesgesetzblatt Teil III, Gliederungs-Nr. 7400-1, veröffentlichten bereinigten Fassung, von denen § 27 Abs. 1 Satz 1 und 2 durch das Gesetz vom 6. Oktober 1980 (BGBl. I S. 1905) neu gefaßt worden ist, verordnet die Bundesregierung:

Artikel 1

Die Außenwirtschaftsverordnung vom 18. Dezember 1986 (BGBl. I S. 2671), zuletzt geändert durch die Verordnung vom 21. Juni 1990 (BGBl. I S. 1121), wird wie folgt geändert:

1. § 5 Abs. 2 Satz 2 wird wie folgt gefaßt:

„Satz 1 gilt nicht für Waren der Nummern 1075a, 1087, 1213, 1366, 1461, 1462, 1471, 1517e und 1710 der Ausfuhrliste sowie für Datenverarbeitungsprogramme (Software)."

§ 33 wird wie folgt geändert:

a) Nach Absatz 2 wird folgender Absatz 3 eingefügt:

„(3) Die Durchfuhr der in Teil I Abschnitte A und B der Ausfuhrliste (Anlage AL) genannten Waren oder Unterlagen zur Fertigung von Waren bedarf der Genehmigung, wenn Empfangsland der Irak oder Kuwait ist."

b) Die bisherigen Absätze 3 bis 5 werden die Absätze 4 bis 6.

3. Nach § 51 wird folgender § 52 eingefügt:

§ 52
Beschränkung nach § 7 Abs. 1 Nr. 2 und Nr. 3 AWG

Gebietsansässige Kreditinstitute bedürfen der Genehmigung für die Ausführung von Verfügungen über Konten, Depots oder sonstige in Verwahrung oder Verwaltung befindliche Vermögenswerte Iraks oder Kuwaits, amtlicher Stellen in Irak oder Kuwait oder deren Beauftragter. Der Genehmigung bedürfen auch Verfügungen Iraks oder Kuwaits, amtlicher Stellen in Irak oder Kuwait oder deren Beauftragter über Vermögenswerte, die nicht bei gebietsansässigen Kreditinstituten gehalten werden."

4. § 70 wird wie folgt geändert:

a) Absatz 1 Nr. 7 wird wie folgt gefaßt:

„7. entgegen § 33 Abs. 1 bis 4 Waren oder Unterlagen durchführt",

b) Nach Absatz 1 Nr. 7 wird folgende Nummer 8 eingefügt:

„8. entgegen § 52 ohne Genehmigung Verfügungen vornimmt"

c) Absatz 3 Nr. 2 wird wie folgt gefaßt:

„2. entgegen § 33 Abs. 3 ohne Genehmigung die dort bezeichneten Waren durchführt oder".

Artikel 2

Diese Verordnung gilt nach § 14 des Dritten Überleitungsgesetzes in Verbindung mit § 51 Abs. 4 des Außenwirtschaftsgesetzes auch im Land Berlin, soweit sie sich nicht auf Rechtsgeschäf-

te und Handlungen bezieht, die nach dem Gesetz Nr. 43 des Kontrollrates vom 20. Dezember 1946 oder nach sonstigem in Berlin geltendem Recht verboten sind oder der Genehmigung bedürfen.

Artikel 3

Diese Verordnung tritt am Tage nach der Verkündung in Kraft.

Bonn, den 7. August 1990

Der Bundeskanzler
Dr. Helmut Kohl

Der Bundesminister für Wirtschaft
H. Haussmann

★

Neunundsechzigste Verordnung
zur Änderung der Ausfuhrliste
— Anlage AL zur Außenwirtschaftsverordnung —
Vom 7. August 1990

Auf Grund des § 27 Abs. 1 Satz 1 und 2 in Verbindung mit § 2 Abs. 1 und § 7 des Außenwirtschaftsgesetzes in der im Bundesgesetzblatt Teil III, Gliederungs-Nr. 7400-1, veröffentlichten bereinigten Fassung, von denen § 27 Abs. 1 Satz 1 und 2 durch das Gesetz vom 6. Oktober 1980 (BGBl. I S. 1905) neu gefaßt worden ist, verordnet die Bundesregierung:

Artikel 1

Die Ausfuhrliste — Anlage AL zur Außenwirtschaftsverordnung — in der Fassung der Verordnung vom 20. Februar 1990 (BAnz. Nr. 54a vom 17. März 1990), geändert durch Verordnung vom 21. Juni 1990 (BAnz. S. 3269) wird wie folgt geändert:

1. In Teil I Abschnitt C wird Nr. 1075 wie folgt gefaßt:

„1075a
Drück- und Fließdrückmaschinen mit numerischer Steuerung oder Teach-in-Steuerung und besonders konstruierte Werkzeuge für die Herstellung von Teilen für kerntechnische Anlagen, Flugkörper und Raketen und andere militärische Güter

Amtlicher Teil Bundesanzeiger Nr. 147 vom 9.8.90

Verkündungen

Der Bundesminister für Wirtschaft

**Berichtigung
der Neunten Verordnung zur Änderung
der Außenwirtschaftsverordnung
und
der Neunundsechzigsten Verordnung zur
Änderung der Ausfuhrliste — Anlage AL
zur Außenwirtschaftsverordnung —**

Die Neunte Verordnung zur Änderung der Außenwirtschaftsverordnung vom 7. August 1990 (BAnz. S. 4013) und die Neunundsechzigste Verordnung zur Änderung der Ausfuhrliste — Anlage AL zur Außenwirtschaftsverordnung — vom 7. August 1990 (BAnz. S. 4013) sind wie folgt zu berichtigen:

Artikel 3 lautet jeweils wie folgt:

Artikel 3

Diese Verordnung tritt am Tage der Verkündung in Kraft."

S & S TRANSLATION

Official Part   [handwritten: Bundesanzeiger
                                                August 8, 1990]

Announcements   Page 4013; Number 146
The Federal Minister for the Economy

Ninth Decree
in Modification of the Foreign Trade Regulations

Dated August 7, 1990

On the basis of § 27 Para. 1 Sentences 1 and 2 in
connection with § 2 Para. 1 and § 7 Para. 1 of the Foreign
Trade Law in the revised version published in the
Bundesgesetzblatt [Federal Law Gazette] Part III, Category
7400-1, of which § 27 Para. 1 Sentences 1 and 2 were revised
by Law dated October 6, 1980 (BGB1. [FLG] I p. 1905), the
Federal Government decrees:

Article 1

The Foreign Trade Regulations dated December 18, 1986
(BGB1.I p. 2671) last modified through the Decree dated June
21, 1990 (BGB1.I p. 1121), is modified as follows:

1. § 5 Para. 2 Sentence 2 is drafted as follows:

    "Sentence 1 is not valid for goods of Numbers 1075a,
    1087, 1313, 1366, 1461, 1462, 1471, 1517a and 1710 of the
    export list or for data-processing programs (Software)."

2. § 38 is amended as follows:

    a) Following Paragraph 2, the following Paragraph 3 is
    inserted:

        "(3) The transit of goods named in Part I Sections A
            and B of the export list (Appendix AL) or of
            documents for the preparation of goods requires
            authorization if the country of receipt is Iraq
            or Kuwait."

    b) The previous Paragraphs 3 to 5 become Paragraphs 4 to
    6.

S & S TRANSLATION

3.   After § 51, the following § 52 is inserted:

"§ 52

Restriction according to § 7 Para. 1 No. 2 and No. 3 AWG

Resident credit institutions require authorization for the execution of instructions regarding accounts, deposit accounts or other assets of Iraq or Kuwait, of official agencies in Iraq or Kuwait or of their agents which are in custody or under management. Authorization is also required for instructions of Iraq or Kuwait, of official agencies in Iraq or Kuwait or of their agents regarding assets which are not held in resident credit institutions."

4.   § 70 is modified as follows:

a)   Paragraph 1 No. 7 is drafted as follows:

"7.   contrary to § 38 Paras. 1 to 4 transports goods or documents",

b)   After Paragraph 1 No.7, the following Number 8 is inserted:

"8.   contrary to § 52 undertakes instructions without authorization."

c)   Paragraph 3 No. 2 is drafted as follows:

"2.   contrary to § 38 Para. 5 transports the goods designated there without authorization or".

Article 2

According to § 14 of the Dritten Ueberleitungsgesetz [Third Transitory Law] in connection with § 51 Para. 4 of the Aussenwirtschaftsgesetzes [Foreign Trade Law], this decree is also valid in the Berlin Land, as long as it does not pertain to legal transactions and acts which are prohibited according to Law No. 43 of the Kontrollrat [Control Board] dated December 20, 1945 or according to other law valid in Berlin or which require authorization.

S & S TRANSLATION

Article 3

This decree enters into force on the day following its promulgation.

Bonn, on August 7, 1990

Chancellor of the Federation
Dr. Helmut Kohl

Federal Minister of the Economy
H. Haussmann

*

Sixty-ninth Decree
in Modification of the Export List
-Appendix AL to the Foreign Trade Decree-

Dated August 7, 1990

On the basis of § 27 Para. 1 Sentences 1 and 2 in connection with § 2 Para. 1 and § 7 of the Foreign Trade Law in the revised version published in the Bundesgesetzblatt [Federal Law Gazette] Part III, Category 7400-1, of which § 27 Para. 1 Sentences 1 and 2 were revised by Law dated October 6, 1980 (BGBl. [FLG] I p. 1905), the Federal Government decrees:

Article 1

The Export List--Appendix AL to the Foreign Trade Decree--in the wording of Decree dated February 20, 1990 (BAnz. No. 54a dated March 17, 1990), modified through Decree dated Jun 21, 1990 (BAnz. p. 3269), is modified as follows:

1. In Part I Section C, No. 1075 is drafted as follows:

"1075a
Hydraulic and other printing presses (?) with numerical control or Teach-in control and in particular tools constructed for the production of parts for nuclear plants, flying hulls and rockets and other military goods [...]

CENTRAL LEGAL AND TAX DIVISION
LEGAL DEPARTMENT

S & S TRANSLATION

Official Part

Bundesanzeiger No. 147
dated 8/9/90 p. 4025

Announcements
The Federal Minister for the Economy

Correction
of the Ninth Decree in Modification
of the Foreign Trade Reguations

and

of the Sixty-ninth Decree
in Modification of the Export List
-Appendix AL to the Foreign Trade Decree-

The Ninth Decree in Modification of the Foreign Trade
Regulations dated August 7, 1990 (BAnz. p. 4013) and the
Sixty-ninth Decree in Modification of the Export
List--Appendix AL to the Foreign Trade Decree--dated August
7, 1990 (BAnz. p. 4013) are to be corrected as follows:

Article 3 reads, in each case, as follows:

"Article 3

This decree enters into force on the day of its
promulgation."

Fernkopierer-Station	
Filiale	**Abteilung:** _____
Bd.-Nr.:	Absender:
Seitenzahl **4**	Commerzbank Frankfurt ZRSt - Dr. Rethorn
Datum: ·27.8.90	Empfänger:
Uhrzeit: 09.45 h	Herr Michael Gruson, Shearman & Sterling
Handzeichen d. Bedienent:	New York

Lieber Herr Gruson,

wie immer recht herzlichen - Dank für Ihre Information
zu Kuwait/Irak.
Das Beigefügte ist vielleicht für Sie von Interesse.

Mit freundlichen Grüßen

Zehnte Verordnung
zur Änderung der Außenwirtschaftsverordnung

Vom 9. August 1990

Auf Grund des § 27 Abs. 1 Satz 1 und 2 in Verbindung mit § 2 Abs. 1, § 5 und § 7 Abs. 1 und Abs. 3 des Außenwirtschaftsgesetzes in der im Bundesgesetzblatt Teil III, Gliederungsnummer 7400-1, veröffentlichten bereinigten Fassung, von denen § 27 Abs. 1 Satz 1 und 2 durch das Gesetz vom 6. Oktober 1980 (BGBl. I S. 1905) neugefaßt und § 7 Abs. 3 durch das Gesetz vom 20. Juli 1990 (BGBl. I S. 1457) eingefügt worden ist, verordnet die Bundesregierung:

Artikel 1

Die Außenwirtschaftsverordnung vom 18. Dezember 1986 (BGBl. I S. 2671), zuletzt geändert durch die Verordnung vom 7. August 1990 (BAnz. S. 4013, 4025), wird wie folgt geändert:

1. Nach Kapitel VII wird folgendes Kapitel VII a eingefügt:

Kapitel VII a
Besondere Beschränkungen gegen Irak und Kuwait

§ 69 a
Beschränkungen der Europäischen Gemeinschaften

Zur Gewährleistung der Straf- und Bußgeldbewehrung entsprechender Verbote der Europäischen Gemeinschaften sind verboten:

(1)

1. Die Einfuhr aller Erzeugnisse mit Ursprung in oder Herkunft aus Irak oder Kuwait.

2. die Ausfuhr in diese Länder aller Erzeugnisse mit Ursprung in oder Herkunft aus der Gemeinschaft.

(2) Die folgenden Tätigkeiten im Geltungsbereich dieser Verordnung oder durch ein Schiff oder Luftfahrzeug, das berechtigt ist, die Bundesflagge oder das Staatszugehörigkeitszeichen der Bundesrepublik Deutschland zu führen, sowie jedem Deutschen im Sinne des § 69 d:

1. jegliche Handelstätigkeit oder jegliches Handelsgeschäft, einschließlich jeglicher Tätigkeit im Zusammenhang mit bereits geschlossenen oder teilweise erfüllten Geschäften, die das Ziel oder die Wirkung haben, die Ausfuhr jeglichen Erzeugnisses mit Ursprung in oder Herkunft aus Irak oder Kuwait zu fördern.

2. der Verkauf oder die Lieferung jeglichen Erzeugnisses gleich welchen Ursprungs und welcher Herkunft

a) an jegliche natürliche oder juristische Person in Irak oder in Kuwait,

b) an jegliche sonstige natürliche oder juristische Person zum Zwecke jeglicher Handelstätigkeit auf oder ausgehend von dem Gebiet Iraks oder Kuwaits,

3. jegliche Tätigkeit, die das Ziel oder die Wirkung haben, diese Verkäufe oder diese Lieferungen zu fördern.

(3) Absatz 1 Nr. 1 und Absatz 2 Nr. 1 steht der Verbringung in den Geltungsbereich dieser Verordnung der in Absatz 1 Nr. 1 genannten Erzeugnisse mit Ursprung in oder Herkunft aus Irak oder Kuwait, die vor dem 7. August 1990 ausgeführt wurden, nicht entgegen.

(4) Absatz 1 Nr. 2 und Absatz 2 Nr. 2 gelten nicht für die folgenden Erzeugnisse:

a) Medizinische Erzeugnisse

aus Kapitel 29 des Harmonisierten Systems zur Bezeichnung und Codierung der Waren.

Alle Erzeugnisse, die gemeinsame internationale Bezeichnungen (International Nonproprietary Names — INN) oder geänderte gemeinsame internationale Bezeichnungen (Modified International Nonproprietary Names — MINN) der Weltgesundheitsorganisation tragen:

2937 Natürliche, auch synthetisch hergestellte Hormone, ihre hauptsächlich als Hormone gebrauchten Derivate, andere hauptsächlich als Hormone gebrauchte Steroide,

2941 Antibiotika.

3001 Drüsen und andere Organe zu organotherapeutischen Zwecken, getrocknet, auch als Pulver; Auszüge aus Drüsen oder anderen Organen oder ihren Absonderungen zu organotherapeutischen Zwecken; Heparin und seine Salze; andere menschliche oder tierische Stoffe zu therapeutischen oder prophylaktischen Zwecken, zubereitet, anderweit weder genannt noch inbegriffen,

3002 menschliches Blut; tierisches Blut zu therapeutischen, prophylaktischen oder diagnostischen Zwecken zubereitet; Antisera und andere Blutfraktionen; Vaccine, Toxine, Kulturen von Mikroorganismen (ausgenommen Hefe) und ähnliche Erzeugnisse,

3003 Arzneiwaren (ausgenommen Erzeugnisse der Position 3002, 3005 oder 3006), die aus zwei oder mehr zu therapeutischen oder prophylaktischen Zwecken gemischten Bestandteilen bestehen, weder dosiert noch in Aufmachungen für den Einzelverkauf,

3004 Arzneiwaren (ausgenommen Erzeugnisse der Position 3002, 3005 oder 3006), die aus gemischten oder ungemischten Erzeugnissen zu therapeutischen oder prophylaktischen Zwecken bestehen, dosiert oder in Aufmachungen für den Einzelverkauf,

3005 Watte, Gaze, Binden und dergleichen (z. B. Verbandzeug, Pflaster zum Heilgebrauch, Senfpflaster) mit medikamentösen Stoffen getränkt oder überzogen oder in Aufmachungen für den Einzelverkauf zu medizinischen, chirurgischen, zahnärztlichen oder tierärztlichen Zwecken,

3006 pharmazeutische Zubereitungen und Waren im Sinne der Anmerkung 3 zu Kapitel 30 des Harmonisierten Systems zur Bezeichnung und Codierung der Waren.

b) Nahrungsmittel

Alle für humanitäre Zwecke bestimmten Nahrungsmittel im Rahmen von Soforthilfelieferungen.

§ 69 b
Beschränkung nach § 7 Abs. 1 AWG

Die Durchfuhr aller Waren durch das Wirtschaftsgebiet ist verboten, wenn Empfangsland, Verkäufer- oder Ursprungsland der Irak oder Kuwait ist.

§ 69 c
Beschränkung nach § 7 Abs. 1 AWG

Die Weitergabe der in § 45 Abs. 2 genannten Kenntnisse an Gebietsfremde, die im Irak oder Kuwait ansässig sind, ist verboten.

§ 69 c
Beschränkung nach § 7 Abs. 1 AWG und Abs. 3 AWG

Dienstleistungen Deutscher in Irak oder Kuwait sind verboten, wenn sich die Dienstleistungen auf Waren und sonstige Gegenstände nach § 7 Abs. 2 Nr. 1 AWG einschließlich ihrer Entwicklung und Herstellung beziehen und wenn der Deutsche

1. Inhaber eines Personaldokumentes der Bundesrepublik Deutschland ist oder

2. verpflichtet wäre, einen Personalausweis zu besitzen, falls er eine Wohnung im Geltungsbereich dieses Gesetzes hätte.

§ 69 e
Beschränkung nach § 7 Abs. 1 AWG

(1) Die Leistung von Zahlungen oder die Übertragung von Vermögenswerten durch Gebietsansässige im Zusammenhang mit nach § 69 a verbotenen Handelsgeschäften an Gebietsfremde, die in Irak oder Kuwait ansässig sind, ist verboten.

(2) Sonstige Zahlungen oder die Übertragung sonstiger Vermögenswerte durch Gebietsansässige

   a) an Irak oder Kuwait,

   b) an amtliche Stellen in Irak oder Kuwait oder deren Beauftragte,

   c) an Gebietsfremde in Irak oder Kuwait,

   d) an Gebietsfremde, wenn die Zahlungen oder Übertragungen für Irak oder Kuwait, amtliche Stellen in Irak oder Kuwait oder deren Beauftragte oder für Unternehmen mit Sitz in Irak oder Kuwait bestimmt sind, auch wenn die Zahlungen oder Übertragungen nicht in Irak oder Kuwait selbst erfolgen,

bedürfen der Genehmigung."

2. § 70 Abs. 1 wird wie folgt geändert:

   a) In Nummer 8 wird der Punkt durch das Wort „oder" ersetzt.

   b) Nach Nummer 8 wird folgende Nummer 9 eingefügt:

   „9. einer Vorschrift der §§ 69 a, 69 b, 69 c, 69 d oder 69 e über Beschränkungen gegen Irak und Kuwait zuwiderhandelt."

Artikel 2

Diese Verordnung gilt nach § 14 des Dritten Überleitungsgesetzes in Verbindung mit § 51 Abs. 4 des Außenwirtschaftsgesetzes auch im Land Berlin, soweit sie sich nicht auf Rechtsgeschäfte und Handlungen bezieht, die nach dem Gesetz Nr. 43 des Kontrollrates vom 20. Dezember 1946 oder nach sonstigem in Berlin geltendem Recht verboten sind oder der Genehmigung bedürfen.

Artikel 3

Diese Verordnung tritt am Tage der Verkündung in Kraft.

Bonn, den 9. August 1990

Der Bundeskanzler
Dr. Helmut Kohl

Der Bundesminister für Wirtschaft
H. Haussmann

S & S TRANSLATION DOC ID 18211

No. 149 dated 8/11/1990
(p. 4065)

Tenth Decree
in Modification of the Foreign Trade Regulations

Dated August 9, 1990

On the basis of § 27 Para. 1 Sentences 1 and 2 in connection with § 2 Para.2, § 5 and § 7 Para. 1 and Para. 3 of the Foreign Trade Law in the revised version published in the Bundesgesetzblatt [Federal Law Gazette] Part III, Category 7400-1, of which § 27 Para. 1 Sentences 1 and 2 were revised by Law dated October 6, 1980 (BGBl. [FLG] I p. 1905) and § 7 Para. 3 was inserted by Law dated July 20, 1990 (BGBl.I p. 1457), the Federal Government decrees:

Article 1

The Foreign Trade Regulations dated December 18, 1986 (BGBl.1 p. 2671) last modified through the Decree dated August 7, 1990 (BAnz. p. 4013, 4025), is modified as follows:

1. After Chapter VII, the following Chapter VII a is inserted:

"Chapter VII a

Special Restrictions against Iraq and Kuwait

§ 69 a

Restrictions of the European Community

To guarantee the enforcement of the sanctions and penalties corresponding to the prohibitions of the European Community, prohibited are:

(1)

1. The importation of all products with origin in or derivation from Iraq or Kuwait,

2. the exportation into these countries of all products with origin in or derivation from the Community.

S & S TRANSLATION DOC ID 18211

(2) The following activities within the purview of this decree or through a vessel or airplane which is authorized to carry the federal flag or marks of citizenship of the Federal German Republic, as well as for all Germans in the wording of § 69 d:

1. all commercial activities and all commercial transactions, including any activity in connection with transactions which are partially fulfilled or already concluded which have the goal or effect of.promoting the exportation of any products with origin in or derivation from Iraq or Kuwait,

2. the sale or delivery of any products regardless of origin and derivation

   a) to any natural person or legal entity in Iraq or in Kuwait,

   b) to any other natural person or legal entity for the purpose of any commercial activity to or out of the regions of Iraq and Kuwait,

3. all activities which have the goal or effect of promoting these sales or deliveries.

(3) Paragraph 1 No. 1 and Paragraph 2 No. 1 do not prevent the incorporation of the products with origin in or derivation from Iraq or Kuwait which have been exported before August 7, 1990 into the range of application of this decree.

(4) Paragraph 1 No. 2 and Paragraph 2 No. 2 are not valid for the following products:

   a)   Medical products

   from Chapter 29 of the Harmonized System for the Designation and Coding of Goods.

   All products which bear common international designations (International Nonproprietary Names --INN) or modified common international designations (Modified International Nonproprietary Names--MINN) of the World Health Organization:

2937 natural, as well as synthetically produced hormones, their derivatives used principally as hormones, other steroids used principally as hormones,

2941 antibiotics,

3001 glands and other organs for organ-therapeutic purposes, dried or as powder, extracts from glands or other organs or their secretions for organ-therapeutic purposes, Heparin and its salts, other human or animal substances prepared for therapeutic or prophylactic purposes, not otherwise named or included,

3002 human blood, animal blood prepared for therapeutic, preventive or diagnostic purposes, antiserums and other blood components, vaccines, toxins, cultures of micro-organisms (except for yeast) and similar products,

3003 medical supplies (except for products of items 3002, 3005 or 3006), which are made up of two or more mixed components for therapeutic or prophylactic purposes, neither measured out nor in packages for individual sale,

3005 cotton, gauze, bandages and similar items (for example, dressing, healing plasters, mustard plasters) saturated or coated with medicinal materials or in packages for individual sale for medicinal, surgical, dental or purposes of such a nature,

3006 pharmaceutical preparations and goods in the wording of Note 3 to Chapter 30 of the Harmonized System for the Designation and Coding of Goods.

b) Foodstuffs

All foodstuffs determined for humanitarian purposes within the scope of emergency relief aid supplies.

§ 69 b

Restriction according to § 7 Para. 1 AWG

The transit of all goods through the trade region is prohibited if the country of receipt, sale or origination is Iraq or Kuwait.

S & S TRANSLATION DOC ID 18211

§ 69 c

Restriction according to § 7 Para. 1 AWG

The transmission of knowledge indicated in § 45 Para. 2 to non-residents who are residents in Iraq or Kuwait is prohibited.

§ 69 d

Restriction according to § 7 Para. ? AWG and Para. 3 AWG.

The German performance of services is prohibited in Iraq or Kuwait if the services are related to goods or other objects according to § 7 Para. 2 No. 2 AWG including their development and production and if the German individual

1. is the holder of a personal identification document of the Federal Republic of Germany or

2. would be required to possess an identification card if he/she had a residence within the scope of application of this Law.

[At the bottom of original page 1]: <u>Distribution</u>

RD   Hantke
ORR'in   Wülker-Mirbach
N.N.
N.N.
ZI'in z.A. Thole
VA   Emig

S & S TRANSLATION DOC ID 18211

§ 69 e

Restriction according to § 7 Para. 1 AWG

(1) The execution of payments or the transfer of assets through residents in the region in connection with commercial transactions prohibited according to § 69 a to non-residents who are residents in Iraq or Kuwait is prohibited.

(2) Other payments or the tranfer of other assets through residents in the region

a)   to Iraq or Kuwait,

b)   to government offices in Iraq or Kuwait or their agents,

c)   to non-residents in Iraq or Kuwait,

d)   to non-residents if the payments or transfers are designated for Iraq or Kuwait, government offices in Iraq or Kuwait or their agents or for enterprises with domicile in Iraq or Kuwait, even if the payments or transfers are not effected in Iraq or Kuwait proper,

require authorization."

2.   § 70 Para. 1 is modified as follows:

a)   In Number 8 the period is replaced with the word "or".

b)   After Number 8 the following Number 9 is inserted:

"9. violates a provision of the § § 69 a, 69 b, 69 c, 69 d or 69 e about restrictions against Iraq and Kuwait."

Article 2

According to § 14 of the Dritten Ueberleitungsgesetz [Third Transitory Law] in connection with § 51 Para. 4 of the Aussenwirtschaftsgesetzes [Foreign Trade Law], this decree is also valid in the Berlin Land, as long as it does not pertain to legal transactions and acts which are prohibited according to Law No. 43 of the Kontrollrat [Control Board] dated December 20, 1945 or according to other law valid in Berlin or which require authorization.

S & S TRANSLATION DOC ID 18211

Article 3

This decree enters into force on the day of its promulgation.

Bonn, on August 9, 1990

Chancellor of the Federation
Dr. Helmut Kohl

Federal Minister of the Economy
H. Haussmann

Italy

SHEARMAN & STERLING

August 8, 1990

Memorandum to: Emmanuel Gaillard

IRAQ/KUWAIT : ITALY

Original Italian text

DECRETO-LEGGE 6 agosto 1990, n. 220
Misure urgenti relative ai beni della Repubblica dell'Iraq

IL PRESIDENTE DELLA REPUBBLICA

"Visti gli articoli 77 e 87 della Costituzione:
Vista la dichiarazione sulla invasione del Kuwait da parte dell'Iraq, resa il 4 agosto 1990 dalla Comunità economica europea o dai suoi Stati membri;
Viste le misure concordate e previste nella suddetta dichiarazione, tra le quali figura l'adozione di adeguati provvedimenti intesi a congelare i beni iracheni nel territorio degli Stati membri;
Visto il perdurare della occupazione del Kuwait da parte dell'Iraq;
Ritenuta la straordinaria necessità ed urgenza di dare esecuzione da parte italiana alla decisione della Comunità;
Vista la deliberazione del Consiglio dei Ministri, adottata nella riunione del 5 agosto 1990;
Sulla proposta del Presidente del Consiglio dei Ministri e del Ministro degli affari esteri, di concerto con i Ministri di grazia e giustizia, del tesoro, delle partecipazione statali e del commercio con l'estero;

EMANA

il seguente decreto-legge:

Art. 1

1. Sono vietati gli atti di disposizione e le transazioni, a qualsiasi titolo effettuati, concernenti beni mobili anche immateriali, beni immobili, aziende o altre universalità di beni, valori o titoli di natura finanziaria o valutaria comunque denominali, allorché detti beni, valori o titoli appartengano, anche tramite intermediari, alla Repubblica dell'Iraq o a qualsiasi soggetto, agenzia, ente od organismo partecipato, controllato o diretto dalla Repubblica dell'Iraq medesima.

Art. 2

1. Gli atti compiuti in violazione del divieto di cui all'articolo I sono nulli.

Art. 3

1. I soggetti che, anche indirettamente, prendono parte agli atti per i quali sussiste il divieto di cui all'articolo I sono civilmente rsponsabili dei danni derivanti dal compimento degli atti nulli. Si applica altresi nei loro confronti la sanzione amministrativa consistente nel pagamento di una somma di danaro non inferiore alla metà del valore dell'operazione e non superiore al valore medesimo.

2. Per l'accertamento delle violazioni del divieto di cui all'articolo I e per l'irrogazione delle relative sanzioni si applicano le disposizioni del titolo II, Capi I et II, dal testo unico delle norme di legge in materia valutaria, approvato con decreto del Presidente della Repubblica 31 marzo 1988, n. 148;

Art. 4

1. Deroghe al divieto di cui all'articolo I possono essere disposte con decreto del Presidente del Consiglio dei Ministri, su proposta del Ministro degli affari esteri, sentiti i Ministri del tesoro e del commercio con l'estero.

Art. 5

Il presente decreto, munito del sigillo dello Stato, sarà inserito nella Raccolta ufficiale degli atti normativi della Repubblica italiana. E fatto obbligo a chiunque spetti di osservarlo e di farlo osservare.

Dato a Roma, addi 6 agosto 1990."

Claire Brice

SHEARMAN & STERLING

August 8, 1990

Memorandum to: Mr. Gaillard

Iraq/Kuwait : Italian Decree-Law
of August 6, 1990, n° 220

Urgent measures concerning the assets of the Republic of Iraq

The President of the Republic,

Considering Articles 77 and 87 of the Constitution;

Considering the declaration made on August 4, 1990 by the European Community and by its member states on the invasion of Kuwait by Iraq;

Considering the unanimous measures provided for by said declaration, among which lists the adoption of adequate measures aimed at freezing Iraqi assets in the respective territories of each of the member states;

Considering the continuation of the occupation of Kuwait by Iraq, the extraordinary necessity and urgence for Italy to execute the Community's decision;

Considering the Council of Ministers' resolution adopted in the meeting of August 5, 1990;

By proposal of the President of the Council of Ministers and the Foreign Secretary, together with the Minister "di grazia e giustizia" (Minister of Grace and Justice), the Minister of Finance, Nationalized Industry and Foreign Trade;

Issues the following decree-law

Art. 1

1.   Are forbidden, all dispositions and transactions, regardless of their denomination, concerning personal and real property, companies or other entities,

values or rights of financial nature or other values regardless of their denomination, to the extent that such assets, values or rights belong to, even through intermediaries, the Republic of Iraq or to whatever person, agency, entity or organization in which the Republic of Iraq holds shares or which is controlled or managed by the Republic of Iraq itself.

Art. 2

1.   Any action in violation of the prohibition set out in Article 1 will be void.

Art. 3

1.   Any person, taking part in whatever action by which he persists in violating the provisions of Article 1 will be held personally liable for all damages arising from the performance of such void acts. Such person will also be subject to an administrative sanction requiring the payment of an amount not less than half of, and not exceeding the entire value of the action.

2.   The provisions of the Title II, Chapter I and II of the single text of the law concerning shares, approved by decree N° 148 of the President of the Republic on March 31, 1988, will be applied to such violations of the prohibitions of Article 1 and the related sanctions.

Art. 4

The prohibitions of Article 1 can be amended by decree of the President of the Council of Ministers on proposal of the foreign secretary with the Minister of Finance's and Minister of Foreign Trade's consent.

Art. 5

The present decree will enter into force on the day of its publication in the "Gazzetta Ufficiale" of the Italian Republic and will be presented to the Cabinet in order to be passed law.

The present decree executed by the Italian state seal will be registered in the official collection of legal acts of the Italian Republic.

This decree is binding to everyone concerned and enforceable by anyone.

Done in Rome on August 6, 1990.

Signed by Androtti, President of the Council of Ministers, De Michaelis, Foreign Secretary, Vassalli, Minister of "Grace and Justice", Carli, Minister of Finance, Piga, Minister of Nationalized Industries, Ruggero, Minister of Foreign Trade.

Marianna Nitsch

Japan

Sanctions against Iraq Taken by the Japanese Government

1. Importation
    (promulgated and enforced on August 9)

    Importing goods of Iraqi or Kuwaiti origin, or goods shipped from Iraq or Kuwait, is forbidden, excluding exporting goods already in transit.

2. Exportation
    (promulgated on August 15 and enforced on August 22)

    (1)   All export activity with Iraq and Kuwait is forbidden, excluding exporting goods which are meant for medical and humanitarian purposes.

    (2)   Exporting goods for Iraq or Kuwait shipped on or after August 7 is requested to be canceled voluntarily.

3. Services and Transit Trades
    (promulgated on August 15 and enforced on August 22)

    (1)   All service transactions, excluding those meant for medical and humanitarian purposes, with natural persons and corporations in Iraq and Kuwait is forbidden.

    (2)   Contracts made with natural persons and corporations in Iraq and Kuwait on or after August 10 are requested to be canceled.

    (3)   Transit trades of goods of Iraqi or Kuwaiti origin, or goods shipped from or heading for Iraq or Kuwait, excluding goods meant for medical and humanitarian purposes, are prohibited.

4. Financial Transactions
    (promulgated on August 15 and enforced on August 22)

    All financial transactions with Iraq or Kuwait are suspended.

5. Payments
    (promulgated and enforced on August 15)

    All payments for imported goods and services must be reported. They will not be allowed with few exceptions.

6. Remittance
    (promulgated and enforced on August 15)

All other remittances related with transactions with Iraq and Kuwait are forbidden.

MOF Ordinance No. 134

Dated August 10, 1990

Amendment of Foreign Exchange and Foreign Trade Control Law:

Effective August 10, 1990, under the Foreign Exchange Control Law Chapt. 6 prior licence should be obtained from MOF for the payment or receipt of funds by resident or non-resident of Japan, i.e., individuals, corporations, or organizations whose address is either in Iraq or Kuwait. (Including overseas offices of said corporations or organizations)

The corporation means those corporations, more than 50% of which share/capital is owned by residents of Iraq or Kuwait or majority of directors of the corporations are residents of Iraq or Kuwait.

Switzerland

DECREE INSTITUTING ECONOMIC MEASURES

TOWARDS THE REPUBLIC OF IRAK AND THE STATE OF KUWAIT

OF AUGUST 7, 1990

The Swiss Federal Council, considering article 102 (8) and article 102 (9) of the Constitution,

Decides :

Article 1
PROHIBITION TO TRADE

1. All trading activity with the Republic of Irak and the State of Kuwait is forbidden.

2. Among other activities, the following are forbidden :

    a) Importing and receiving in transit any goods of Iraqi or Kuwait origin;

    b) Exporting any goods towards the Republic of Irak or the State of Kuwait;

    c) Purchasing, selling or furnishing goods of Kuwaiti or Iraqi origin, as well as any brokerage activity related thereto.

    d) Transporting any goods of Iraqi or Kuwaiti origin and making any freight facilities available for that prpose by entities operating road, sea or air transport facilities.

Article 2
FINANCIAL TRANSACTIONS, CREDITS

1. Payments or loans to Iraqi or Kuwaiti persons or legal entities, whether private or public, in relation with any transactions contemplated by article 1 are forbidden.

2. Any other financial transactions related to the Iraqi government or to commercial or industrial entities or public services located in Irak or Kuwait are also forbidden.

3. The protection of assets held in Switzerland by the legitimate Government of Kuwait shall be the object of a separate decree.

Article 3
DUTY TO DISCLOSE

1. All operations and negotiations conducted between persons or legal entities in Switzerland and Iraqi or Kuwaiti persons or legal entities, whether public or private, which, at the time of this decree coming into force, were not brought to an end through their execution by both parties, shall be disclosed.

2. Disclosure shall be made to the Federal Department of Public Economy.

Article 4
EXCEPTIONS

1. The following shall constitute exceptions to this decree :

    a) Exporting or receiving in transit goods which are meant for medical or humanitarian purposes;

    b) Exporting or receiving in transit food products in exceptional situations, related to humanitarian assistance;

    c) Transferring luggage for people travelling to or from the Repubic of Irak or the State of Kuwait;

    d) Exporting or receiving in transit goods or carrying out financial transactions related to the normal use or to the maintenance of Swiss representatives in the Republic of Irak and the State of Kuwait, as well as the International Committee of the Red Cross and Swiss companies established there;

    e) Importing goods and carrying out financial transactions in favour of the Iraqi Embassy in Switzerland as well as the Mission of the State of Kuwait at the United Nations in Geneva, to the extent provided by International public law;

    f) Hardship cases.

2. The Federal Department of Public Economy may grant exceptional authorizations, in coordination with other Departments. The decision may be brought to the Federal Council.

Article 5
SANCTIONS

1. Shall be punishable any person who :

   a) Carries out transactions within the meaning of articles 1 and 2 with persons or legal entities, whether public or private, of the republic of Irak or the State of Kuwait;

   b) Carries out such transactions with third parties whilst knowing or having a duty to presume that the real beneficiaries are persons or legal entities, whether public or private, of the republic of Irak or the State of Kuwait;

   c) Violates the duty to disclose set forth at article 3.

2. The sanctions shall be the following :

   a) Violations of the prohibition to trade, or to carry out payments or credits, shall be punished by a fine of up to ten times the internal value of the goods concerned. The internal value shall be calculated according to market prices applicable at the time the violation is discovered. For financial transactions, the penalty shall be a fine of up to ten times the amount involved.

   b) The violation of the duty to disclose shall be fined up to SF 2,000.--.

3) The Federal statute on penal administrative law shall be applicable. The Federal Department of Public Economy shall have jurisdiction to prosecute and decide on any violations.

Article 6
IMPLEMENTING REGULATIONS

The Federal Department of Public Economy shall be entitled to decide and adopt those regulations which may be necessary to implement this decree, in agreement with the Federal Department of Foreign Affairs and the Federal Department of Finances.

Article 7
APPLICATION TO EXISTING TRANSACTIONS AND VALIDITY

1. This decree shall apply to all operations which, at the time of its coming into force, had not yet been finalised through their execution by both parties.

2. This decree shall be in force as from August 7, 1990 at 11a.m.

IMPLEMENTING REGULATION ADOPTED BY THE FEDERAL DEPARTMENT OF

PUBLIC ECONOMY WITH REGARD TO THE DECREE INSTITUTING

ECONOMIC MEASURES TOWARDS THE REPUBLIC OF IRAK

AND THE STATE OF KUWAIT

OF AUGUST 8, 1990

The Department of Public Economy

Pursuant to Article 6 of the August 7, 1990 decree instituting economic measures towards the Repubic of Irak and the State of Kuwait (hereafter the decree),

Decides :

Article 1
TRADING ACTIVITY

1. A "trading activity" within the meaning of Article 1 (1) of the decree, shall also mean any brokerage activity in transactions concerning goods coming from or destined to the Republic of Irak and the State of Kuwait.

2. The aforesaid term shall also include any new technical measures with regard to transportation, taken whilst goods of a third origin are in transit through Switzerland.

Article 2
EXCEPTIONAL AUTHORIZATIONS

1. Whoever wishes to obtain an exceptional authorization pursuant to Article 4 of the decree shall submit a request with motivation to the Federal Department of Public Economy, Federal Office of External Economic Affairs.

2. The request shall among other include indications with regard to the type of the goods, the exact purpose of their use, their value, their shipper, their addressee and the carrier of the goods, or, for financial transactions, the corresponding indications.

3.   For the goods and financial transactions under Article 4 (1) (d) of the decree, the Swiss diplomatic offices in the Republic of Irak and in the State of Kuwait, as well as the International Committee of the Red Cross, are granted a general authorization. This also applies to the Embassy and the Mission of the Republic of Irak in Switzerland and the Mission of the State of Kuwait at the United Nations in Geneva (Article 4 (1) (e) of the decree).

4.   Similarly, a general authorization is hereby granted for the personal objects pursuant to Article 4 (1) (c) of the decree.

Article 3
DUTY TO DISCLOSE

Disclosure of the transactions falling under Article 3 of the decree shall be made in writing before September 14, 1990. The disclosure shall include indication on the type, the purpose and the scope of the transaction as well as on the parties involved.

Article 4
ASSISTANCE BY CUSTOMS AUTHORITIES

The goods within the purpose of Article 1 of the decree shall be withheld by the customs authorities. They shall advise the Federal Department of Public Economy which shall decide the matter.

Article 5
VALIDITY

This implementing regulation shall be deemed to have been in force as of August 7, 1990 at 11:00a.m.

DECREE ON THE PROTECTION OF ASSETS OF THE STATE OF KUWAIT

IN SWITZERLAND OF AUGUST 10, 1990

The Swiss Federal Council, considering article 102 (8) and article 102 (9) of the Constitution

Decides :

Article 1
PURPOSE

The purpose of this decree shall be to ensure the protection of assets of the State of Kuwait in Switzerland as long as the Federal Council considers that the issue of the right to dispose of such assets has not been resolved.

Article 2
FREEZE OF THE RIGHT TO DISPOSE

1. Assets in Switzerland or being managed from Switzerland and belonging to the State of Kuwait or to enterprises, foundations or similar institutions belonging to or controlled by the State of Kuwait (beneficial owner), may not be transferred either to other legal entities or inside the Republic of Irak or the State of Kuwait.

2. Disposing of assets shall be permitted when they remain entirely under the control of the same beneficial owners and when there is no reason to think that the republic of Irak or a Kuwaiti regime controlled by Irak may dispose of such assets.

Article 3
FROZEN ASSETS

Shall be frozen among others, fiduciery deposits in Swiss or foreign currencies, commercial papers and similar rights (1), bank notes, precious metals, valuable objects, property rights, shares and real estate, managed on behalf or in favour of the beneficial owners mentioned at article 2 or registered under their names.

(1) Translator's note : under "Commercial papers and similar rights", one should understand, stocks, bonds, options, etc.

Article 4
EXCEPTIONS

1. Upon request, the Federal Department of Finances may authorize the transfer of assets to other legal entities on a case by case basis or to certain beneficial owners generally, when there is no reason to think that the Republic of Irak or a Kuwaiti regime controlled by Irak may dispose of such assets or that assets belonging to the State of Kuwait would thus be illicitly transferred to private owners.

2. The decisions of the Federal Department of finances may be appealed to the Federal Council.

3. Procedural matters shall be governed by the Federal Statute on Administrative Procedure.

Article 5
SANCTIONS

1. Whoever intentionally and without authorization transfers assets or causes assets to be illicitly transferred to other legal entities shall be punished by a jail term of maximum three months or by a fine of up to SF 500,000.--.

2. If the offence was committed by negligence, the maximum penalty shall be a fine of up to SF 200,000.--.

3. The Federal Statute on Penal Administrative Law shall be applicable. The Federal Department of Finances shall have jurisdiction to prosecute and decide on any violations.

Article 6
VALIDITY

This decree shall be in force as from August 10, 1990 at 12 a.m.

United Kingdom

FREEZING OF KUWAITI AND IRAQI ASSETS

SANCTIONS AGAINST IRAQ

Simmons & Simmons
14 Dominion Street
London EC2M 2RJ

CONTENTS

FREEZING OF KUWAITI AND IRAQI ASSETS
SANCTIONS AGAINST IRAQ

There follows a summary of the various freezing and sanctions measures in force as at 13th September 1990.

UK FREEZING OF ASSETS

A.   **The Control of Gold, Securities, Payments and Credits (Kuwait) Directions 1990**

Key points

-    no order given by a Kuwaiti resident to anyone in the UK concerning payments, gold or securities to be carried out.

-    accounts of Kuwaiti residents to be identified and designated.

-    no restriction on payments <u>to</u> Kuwaiti accounts, except in relation to payments under contract bonds.

-    no payments <u>from</u> Kuwaiti accounts or otherwise to Kuwaiti residents except in accordance with general or specific permissions.

1.   These Directions were made on 2nd August 1990, under the Emergency Laws (Re-enactments and Repeals) Act 1964, and prohibit (except with Treasury permission) any recipient in the United Kingdom, the Channel Islands or the Isle of Man of an order from the government of, or any person resident in, Kuwait from carrying out that order insofar as the order (a) requires the recipient to make any payment or to part with any gold or securities or (b) requires any change to be made in the persons to whose credit any sum is to stand or to whose order any gold or securities is to be held.

      By Statutory Instruments made on 6th August 1990, similar prohibitions were made in respect of orders addressed to persons in Anguilla, British Virgin Islands, Cayman Islands, Monserrat and Turks & Caicos Islands, and in Hong Kong.

2.   On 3rd August 1990, the Bank of England announced that bargains entered into in the money, foreign exchange and securities (including share purchases and taking up of rights issues) markets, or payments instructions received for immediate execution, involving Kuwaiti counterparties, prior to 3.00 p.m. BST (2.00 p.m GMT) on Thursday 2nd August 1990, may be completed without infringing the Directions.

3.   On 3rd August 1990, the Bank of England announced that authorised institutions (banks) and building societies may permit private Kuwaiti individuals to draw on their personal accounts in the UK without infringing the Directions.

4.   On 7th August 1990, the Bank of England issued a Notice amplifying the effect of the Directions, and giving certain permissions

thereunder. The Directions (and the Iraqi Directions (see B below)) were themselves the subject of discussions between the Bank of England and the British Bankers' Association, and the BBA on 15th August 1990 issued further guidance to it́s members, endorsed by the Bank of England:

4.1 Residents of Kuwait

A. A resident of Kuwait is a person (including a company) "normally resident" there on 2nd August 1990, or thereafter. There is no definition of "normally resident", but it is a question of fact, and a Kuwaiti resident may be a UK expatriate, although on 3rd September 1990 the Bank of England issued Supplement No. 2 to the Notice, setting out the circumstances in which banks may cease to treat as Kuwaiti (or Iraqi) accounts the accounts of UK nationals who had been caught by the Directions because resident in Kuwait (or Iraq) at the relevant time, but who have since returned to the UK.

Under the old Exchange Control Notices and Regulations a person was treated as "resident" if he had been so for a period of three years.

B. A branch in Kuwait of any business is treated as resident there.

C. Orders given by overseas branches of companies resident or head-quartered in Kuwait are treated as given by Kuwaiti residents.

D. UK companies managed and controlled from the UK are treated as resident in the UK unless a controlling interest is held by the government of Kuwait.

E. Specific adjudications:

Resident in Kuwait: Kuwait Investment Office (although permission may be given to KIO to conduct its business on a transaction by transaction basis); Kuwait Petroleum Corporation; UK branches of National Bank of Kuwait (it is understood that special arrangements are to be made to enable KPC and NBK to carry on their UK business).

Resident in UK: UK branches of United Bank of Kuwait.

4.2 Overseas branches of UK companies and business

Overseas branches of companies and businesses incorporated or headquartered in the UK are not affected by the Directions, except that instructions received by persons who are subject to the Directions should not be re-directed off-shore for execution. Counsel has confirmed that the Directions do apply to securities held outside the UK but managed by a UK fund manager for Kuwaiti residents. No transaction should be carried out in respect of such securities.

4.3 Kuwaiti accounts

A. Sterling, foreign currency and gold bullion accounts of Kuwaiti residents ("Kuwaiti accounts") with UK banks or building societies should be specially designated and funds held by solicitors, accountants, stockbrokers etc. on behalf of Kuwaiti residents should be transferred to separate accounts (Banks need not enquire as to the beneficial ownership of funds held by eg solicitors for others).

Joint accounts, where one holder only is a Kuwaiti resident, are subject to the restrictions, but banks should give the non-Kuwaiti person the opportunity to open a separate non-restricted account.

B. The general embargo under the Directions on payments on the directions of Kuwaiti residents is waived in respect of payments, credits, loans and overdrafts to Kuwaiti accounts.

However, on 25th August 1990, the Bank of England issued Supplement No.1 to the Notice, stating that permission would not be given for payments to Kuwaiti (or Iraqi) accounts in compliance with calls on contract bonds.

On 12th September 1990, the Bank of England announced that in future payments due under insurance contracts to Kuwaiti or Iraqi residents, whether insurers, re-insurers or insureds, could only be made with DTI permission.

C. There may be no change without permission in the ownership of Kuwaiti accounts.

D. Certain payments are permitted from Kuwaiti accounts:

(a) living, medical, educational and similar expenses of residents of Kuwait in the UK, including under existing reasonable overdraft commitments;

(b) payments in respect of goods (including oil) which have been shipped or otherwise despatched to the UK against evidence of shipment or despatch and production of any necessary import licence;

(c) payments to reimburse UK banks who have made payments in respect of Kuwaiti trade under irrevocable letters of credit:

(d) payments to other Kuwaiti accounts in the UK;

(e) payments of interest, or repayment of capital, on borrowings from UK residents by residents of Kuwait:

(f) payments to UK residents in connection with the operations of vessels and aircraft owned by, or on charter to, residents of Kuwait;

(g) payment to UK residents of insurance premiums under existing (but not new) contracts;

(h) payment of charges to banks in the UK;

(i) payment of sums due to the Inland Revenue and HM Customs and Excise;

(j) distributions and payments to residents of the UK under wills and intestacies and under trusts set up before 2 August 1990;

(k) payments against cheques within cheque card limits.

E. The Bank of England will consider applications to debit Kuwaiti accounts for the following purposes:-

(a) payments to meet travel expenditure by residents of Kuwait leaving the UK;

(b) payments for charitable purposes:

(c) payments of the types described in paragraphs D (e), (f), (g) and (j), above, to residents outside the UK.

F. Credit and debit card companies are not under any duty to identify card holders who are Kuwaiti (or Iraqi) residents, but if they have specific notice (eg an address in Kuwait (or Iraq) for correspondence) they should decline to honour transactions above floor limits, and should request the return of the card.

4.4 Provision of cash to residents of Kuwait in the UK

Banks and other persons in the UK may provide cash in reasonable amounts (judged primarily by reference to past usage) in sterling in the UK to residents of Kuwait:

(a) in exchange for foreign currency of equivalent value;

(b) against cheques, travellers' cheques, travellers' letters of credit, credit and debit cards and other payment instruments;

(c) through automated teller machines.

4.5 Payments by UK branches of companies resident in Kuwait

UK branches of companies or businesses resident in Kuwait may make salary and pension payments to persons living in the UK.

The Bank of England will consider applications from such branches to make other payments.

4.6 Pensions etc due to residents of Kuwait

Pensions due to residents of Kuwait and of widows' and widowers' annuities associated with deceased husbands' and wives' employments may be paid, even outside the UK.

4.7 Syndicated credits

Any necessary permission will be given on application for banks which are agents for syndicated loans and credits to the government or residents of Kuwait to distribute capital repayments and interested payments to participants in the syndicates, provided that the necessary funds are received from outside the UK.

4.8 Maturing bills of exchange

Maturing bills of exchange drawn by residents of Kuwait and accepted by persons subject to the Directions to be paid by the acceptor on maturity and for Kuwaiti accounts to be debited in reimbursement.

4.9 Definitions

A.   Gold

Gold includes gold coin or gold bullion wherever located.

B.   Securities

The Emergency Laws (Re-enactments and Repeals) Act 1964 as amended defines securities as including:-

(a)   shares, stocks, bonds, notes (other than promissory notes), debentures, debentures, certificates of deposit and Treasury and other government bills;

(b)   a deposit receipt in respect of the deposit of securities;

(c)   a unit or a sub-unit of a unit trust:

(d)   an annuity granted under the Government Annuities Act 1929, or to which either Part I or Part II of that Act applies, and a life assurance policy or other contract entered into with an assurance company for securing the payment in the future of any capital sum or sums, or of an annuity;

(e)   a warrant conferring an option to acquire a security;

(f)   a share in an oil royalty;

but excludes bills of exchange.

For the purposes of the permissions covered in the Notice "securities" includes those instruments defined as "investments" in Schedule 1 of the Financial Services Act 1986.

4.10 Portfolio management

As noted at 4.2 above, Counsel has confirmed that the Directions apply to securities managed for Kuwaiti residents by a person in the UK, even if the securities are held outside the UK. However, the Bank of England will consider applications from persons engaged in the discretionary management of portfolios of securities on behalf of residents of Kuwait to continue to manage the portfolios in question. Permission will not normally be given to allow the release of portfolios from UK control.

4.11 Payments in respect of securities

Where securities are registered in the name of a person resident in Kuwait, no order requiring payments of capital monies, dividends or interest to any person outside the UK may be complied with without permission, provided payment is to a Kuwaiti account. Such permission is also given where persons subject to the directions hold bearer securities for account of persons resident in Kuwait. All other cases should be referred to the Bank of England.

4.12 Transactions in Kuwaiti securities

No permissions are necessary for transfers of securities issued by residents of Kuwait except when a person subject to the Directions is required, by order given by or on behalf of a resident of Kuwait, to part with any such security or to make any change in the persons to whose order any such security is to be held.

Application should be made to the Bank of England for any permission needed by paying agents in the United Kingdom from Kuwaiti securities to make interest, dividend or redemption payments on, or to buy in, such securities.

4.13 Applications and enquiries

Application should be made to the Bank of England in respect of any transaction which is not covered by the permissions given in the Notice.

Applications for permissions should be addressed to the Bank of England, Threadneedle Street, London, EC2R 8AH, and marked for the attention of the Iraq and Kuwait Emergency Unit (IKEU). Applications may also be made by facsimile transmission (071-601-4309).

Telephone enquiries may be made to 071-601-3250/3309/3764/3848/4768/5463

B. **The Control of Gold, Securities, Payments and Credits (Republic of Iraq) Directions 1990**

<u>Key points</u>

–   no order given by an Iraqi resident to anyone in the UK concerning payments, gold or securities to be carried out.

–   accounts of Iraqi residents to be identified and designated.

–   no restriction on payments <u>to</u> Iraqi accounts, except in relation to calls on contract bonds.

–   no payments <u>from</u> Iraqi accounts except in very limited circumstances.

1.   The Directions were made on 4th August 1990, and prohibit (except with Treasury permission) any recipient in the United Kingdom, the Channel Islands or the Isle of Man of an order from the government of or any person resident in the Republic of Iraq from carrying out that order insofar as the order (a) requires the recipient to make any payment or to part with any gold or securities or (b) requires any change to be made in the person to whose credit any sum is to stand or to whose order any gold or securities is to be held.

The Directions are therefore similar to those made in respect of Kuwait, except that the effective time is 4.30 BST (3.30 GMT) on Saturday 4th August 1990.

2.   On 7th August 1990, as in the case of Kuwait, the Bank of England issued a Notice amplifying the effect of the Directions, but confirming that they will be operated much more restrictively than those in respect of Kuwait.

The provisions of the Iraq Notice are similar to those in the Kuwait Notice (including a similar ban on payments <u>to</u> Iraqi accounts in connection with calls on contract bonds), except that:

2.1   **Iraqi accounts**

A.   Transfers between Iraqi accounts will not normally be permitted

B.   These are no general permissions for transfers from Iraqi accounts, except for:

   (a)   charges to banks in the United Kingdom, and payments on cheques within cheque card limits;

   (b)   sums due to the Inland Revenue and HM Customs and Excise, provided no overdraft is thereby created on an Iraqi account;

   (c)   distributions and payments to residents of the UK under wills and intestacies and under trusts set up before 4 August 1990; and

(d) payments for oil, provided the necessary import licence and evidence of shipment are exhibited.

C. The Bank of England will consider applications to debit Iraqi Accounts for the following purposes:-

(a) living, medical, educational and similar expenses of residents of Iraq in the UK. Payments to meet travel expenditure by residents of Iraq leaving the UK will also be considered. For all of these purposes, reasonable amounts will normally be permitted;

(b) payments in respect of goods which have been shipped or otherwise despatched to the UK. Production of any necessary import licence and evidence of shipment or despatch will be required;

(c) payments to reimburse UK banks who have made payments in respect of Iraqi trade under irrevocable letters of credit;

(d) payments for charitable purposes.

D. For the time being, permission will not normally be given for Iraqi accounts to be debited for the following purposes:-

(a) payments to other Iraqi accounts:

(b) payment of interest, or repayment of capital, on borrowings by residents of Iraq;

(c) payments in connection with the operations of vessels and aircraft owned by, or on charter to, residents of Iraq;

(d) payment of insurance premiums.

E. Capital payments by UK branches of Iraq-incorporated or head-quartered companies will not normally be permitted.

F. Cash may not be provided to Iraqi residents in the UK in exchange for Iraqi or Kuwaiti dinars.

G. Whre an Iraqi resident has transferred the entire interest in trust property ("fully divested himself of his powers") in favour of a discretionary trustee in the UK, the trust is deemed to fall outside the restrictions.

2.2 Credits, loans and overdrafts

For the time being, permissions will not normally be given to enable existing or intending lenders subject to the Directions to comply with any order given by or on behalf of a person resident of Iraq to make any payment - without such permission no further drawings may be made under existing facilities. No new arrangements should be entered into, no bills of exchange drawn by a resident of Iraq should be issued, confirmed or advised for account of, or in favour of, or on behalf of, a resident of Iraq.

Irrevocable credits opened before 4 August 1990 in respect of transactions with Iraq may be honoured. Iraqi accounts may not be debited in reimbursement except where otherwise permitted in the Notice.

2.3 Maturing bills of exchange

Maturing bills of exchange drawn by residents of Iraq and accepted before 4 August 1990 by persons subject to the Directions may be paid by the acceptor on maturity. Iraqi accounts may not be debited in reimbursement without permission.

2.4 Roll-overs

Persons subject to the Directions who have made loans to residents of Iraq before 4 August 1990 and who wish to roll-over such loans in accordance with the terms of the loan agreement should refer to the Bank of England. Attention should be drawn to the reasons for any reduction in the interest rate or change in currency composition. Permission will not normally be given to enable the drawn down amount of the loan or credit to be increased on roll-over.

[C.   **Ban on Oil and Oil Products from Iraq and Kuwait**

Following agreement at the emergency meeting of the Political Committee of the European Communities in Rome on 4 August, the UK has imposed restrictions on the import of crude oil and petroleum products originating in Iraq or Kuwait. The restrictions were brought into force at midnight on Sunday 5 August 1990.

By an amendment to the Open General Import Licence of 4 December 1987 under the Import of Goods (Control) Order, 1954, such goods originating in Iraq or Kuwait are prohibited to be imported into the UK except under the authority of an individual import licence issued by the Department of Trade and Industry.

It will not be the normal policy to issue licences for these goods. However applications for licences will be considered where a firm contract existed before the restrictions entered into force. Licenses will normally be issued for goods in transit before 6 August 1990.] [See now D below.]

D   **The Export of Goods (Control) (Iraq and Kuwait Sanctions) Order 1990 SI 1640**
The Iraq and Kuwait (United Nations Sanctions) Order 1990 SI 1651

On 8th August 1990, the UK took steps to implement UN Security Council resolution 661 imposing sanctions on Iraq and Kuwait. The new restrictions came into force at 00.01 BST, 9 August 1990.

The restrictions will apply to Iraq and to Kuwait to avoid trade diversion by Iraq.

Exports

Exports are prohibited under the Export of Goods (Control) (Iraq and Kuwait Sanctions) Order 1990, made under the Import, Export and Customs Powers (Defence) Act 1939.

This Order prohibits the export from the UK or the Isle of Man, without a licence under the Order, of all goods to Iraq or Kuwait or to any destination in any other country for delivery to a person for the purposes of any business on in or operated from Iraq or Kuwait.

Imports

All products originating in Iraq or Kuwait are prohibited to be imported by an amendment to the Open General Import Licence of 4th December 1987 under the Import of Goods (Control) Order 1954 except under the authority of an individual import licence issued by the Department of Trade and Industry. It will not be the normal policy to issue licences for such goods. However licences will normally be issued for goods in transit.

These restrictions supersede those already imposed by the UK on 5th August 1990 (see C, above) against imports of crude oil and petroleum products originating in Iraq or Kuwait.

Other Restrictions

The Iraq and Kuwait (United Nations Sanctions) Order 1990 also came into effect at 00.01 BST, 9th August 1990.

In summary, in accordance with the requirements of UN resolution 661 it prohibits, except when licensed, activities in connection with the export of goods from Iraq or Kuwait including acts calculated to promote such exports, dealing in goods exported from Iraq and Kuwait after 6th August, and activities in connection with the supply or delivery of goods to Iraq and Kuwait. These prohibitions apply to British citizens worldwide. Provisions are also made to prohibit the use of ships, aircraft and land transport vehicles for these purposes. These provisions will operate in parallel with the restrictions noted above on imports and exports under the Import, Export and Customs Powers (Defence) Act 1939.

The Order was amended on 29th August 1990 by the Iraq and Kuwait (United Nations Sanctions) Order 1990 SI 1768, which, with effect from 30th August 1990, prohibited payments under contract bonds in respect of contracts illegal under the principal order, extended enforcement powers to land vehicles and made certain other minor amendments.

Dependent territories

Statutory instruments made on 8th August 1990 and on 29th August 1990 have made similar provisions in relation to UK Dependent Territories, being Anguilla, Bermuda, British Antarctic Territory,

British Indian Ocean Territory, Cayman Islands, Falkland Islands, South Georgia and South Sandwich Islands, Gibraltar, Hong Kong, Monserrat, Pitcairn, St. Helena, Turks and Caicos Islands, Virgin Islands, and in relation to the Channel Islands.

INTERNATIONAL MEASURES

A.   European Community

On 4th August 1990, the European Political Cooperation Council announced that the EC and its Member States had decided to adopt:

- an embargo on oil imports from Iraq and Kuwait;

- appropriate measures aimed at freezing Iraqi assets in the territory of Member States;

- an embargo on sales of arms and other military equipment to Iraq;

- the suspension of any cooperation in the military sphere with Iraq;

- the suspension of technical and scientific cooperation with Iraq;

- the suspension of the application to Iraq of the system of generalised preferences.

The EC's commitment to the implementation of the UN Security Council Resolutions concerning Iraq and Kuwait was emphasized by a Declaration on 10th August 1990 following an Extraordinary Ministerial Meeting of the EPC.

On 8th August 1990, the EC adopted Regulation No 2340/90, pursuant to UN Resolution 660 and 661. The EC Resolution provides

"Article 1

As from 7 August 1990, the following shall be prohibited:

1   the introduction into the territory of the Community of all commodities or products originating in, or coming from, Iraq or Kuwait;

2   the export to the said countries of all commodities or products originating in, or coming from, the Community.

Article 2

As from the date referred to in Article 1, the following shall be prohibited in the territory of the Community or by means of aircraft and vessels flying the flag of a Member State, or when carried out by any Council national:

1   all activities or commercial transactions, including all operations connected with transactions which have already been concluded or partially carried out, the object or effect of which is to promote the export of any commodity or product originating in, or coming from, Iraq or Kuwait;

2   the sale or supply of any commodity or product, wherever it originates or comes from:

—   to any natural or legal persons in Iraq or Kuwait,

—   to any other natural or legal person for the purposes of any commercial activity carried out in or from the territory of Iraq or Kuwait;

3   any activity the object or effect of which is to promote such sales or supplies.

Article 3

1   Article 1(2) and Article 2(2) shall not apply to the products listed in the Annex [medical products].

2   Article 1(1) and Article 2(1) shall not prevent the introduction into the territory of the Community of the commodities or products referred to in Article 1(1) which originate in, or come from, Iraq or Kuwait and are exported before 7 August 1990.

Article 4

This Regulation shall enter into force on the day of its publication in the Official Journal of the European Communities [9th August 1990]".

On 8th August 1990, the EC Coal and Steel Community adopted a restriction in similar terms, banning the import to the EC of coal and steel originating in Iraq or Kuwait.

B.   **USA**

1.   On 2nd August 1990, the following measures were introduced:

Under Executive Order 12722, all property and interests in property of the Government of Iraq and any of its agencies or entities in the United States or under the control of United States persons are blocked. In addition, virtually all commercial and financial transactions involving Iraq are prohibited although exceptions may be contained in rules and regulations to be issued by the Secretary of the Treasury to implement the Executive Order.

Under Executive Order 12723, all property and interests in property of the Government of Kuwait and any of its agencies or entities in the United States or under the control of the United States persons are blocked.

The Department of State announced in Public Notice 1238 the immediate revocation of all licences and approvals to export or transfer defence articles and services to Iraq. Similarly, all such licences and approvals with respect to Kuwait are suspended.

2. **General Licence No.1, 3rd August 1990**

    US financial institutions are permitted to complete, on or before 16th August 1990, securities and forex transactions entered into for the account of the Government of Kuwait, provided that the proceeds of sale in the securities are held in a blocked account in the US.

3   **General Licence No.2, 8th August 1990**

    The import of Iraqi and Kuwaiti oil is permitted under contracts made prior to 2nd August 1990, provided payment is made to a blocked account in the US.

4   **General Licence No.3, 8th August 1990**

    Portfolio managers may continue to manage and reinvest assets held for the Government of Kuwait, provided the assets are held in blocked accounts.

5   **General Licence No.4, 8th August 1990**

    US entities controlled by the Government of Kuwait are enabled to operate bank accounts, provided no benefit accrues to Iraq.

6   **General Licence No.6, Telecommunications Payments**

7   **General Licence No.7, Payments for pre-zero exports to Kuwait and Iraq**

8   The Treasury Department issued on 5th August 1990 a list of banks it regards, in a preliminary determination, as being de jure or de facto owned by the Government of Kuwait, and of others which were required by 18th August 1990 to produce further evidence of their ownership.

9. On 10th August 1990, two further Executive Orders were made, pursuant to UN Security Council Resolution 661, and the earlier Executive Orders referred to at 1 above. The Orders, with effect from 8.55 p.m. EDT, 9th August 1990:

    -   prohibit exports and imports of good and services between the United States and Iraq or Kuwait, and any activity that promotes or is intended to promote such exportation or importation;

    -   prohibit any dealing by a U.S. person in connection with property of Iraqi or Kuwaiti origin exported from Iraq or Kuwait after August 6, 1990, or intended for exportation to or from Iraq or Kuwait to any country, and related activities;

- prohibit transactions related to travel to or from Iraq or Kuwait or to activities by any U.S. person with Iraq or Kuwait, except for transactions necessary for prompt departure from Iraq or Kuwait, the conduct of official business of the United States Government or of the United Nations, or journalistic travel;

- prohibit transactions related to transportation to or from Iraq or Kuwait, or the use of vessels or aircraft registered in Iraq or Kuwait by U.S. persons;

- prohibit the performance by any U.S. person of any contract in support of certain categories of projects in Iraq or Kuwait;

- prohibit the commitment or transfer of funds or other financial or economic resources by any U.S. person to the Government of Iraq or the Government of Kuwait, or any other person in Iraq or Kuwait;

- block all property of the Government of Iraq or the Government of Kuwait now or hereafter located in the United States or in the possession or control of U.S. persons, including their foreign branches; and

- clarify that the definition of U.S. persons includes vessels of U.S. registry.

United Nations

On 6th August 1990, the Security Council unanimously (except for abstentions by Cuba and Yemen) passed mandatory sanctions Resolution 661 (affirming Resolution 660, which had called upon Iraq to withdraw, and to commence negotiations) including the following terms:

"3. Decides that all States shall prevent:

(a) The import into their territories of all commodities and products originating in Iraq or Kuwait exported therefrom after the date of these Resolutions;

(b) Any activities by their nationals or in their territories which could promote or are calculated to promote the export or transshipment of any commodities or products from Iraq or Kuwait; and any dealings by their nationals or their flag vessels or in their territories in any commodities or products originating in Iraq or Kuwait and exported therefrom after the date of this resolution, including, in particular, any transfer of funds to Iraq or Kuwait for the purposes of such activities or dealings;

(c) The sale or supply by their nationals or from their territories or using their flag vessels of any commodities or products, including weapons or any other military equipment, whether or not originating in their territories but not including supplies, intended strictly for medical purposes, and, in Kuwait or to any person or body for the purposes of any business carried on in their territories which promote or are calculated to promote such sale or supply of such commodities or products;

"4. Decides that all States shall not make available to the Government of Iraq or to any commercial, industrial or public utility undertaking in Iraq or Kuwait, any funds or any other financial or economic resources and shall prevent their nationals and any persons within their territories from removing from their territories or otherwise making available to the Government or to any such undertaking any such funds or resources and from remitting any other funds to persons or bodies within Iraq or Kuwait, except payments exclusively for strictly medical to humanitarian purposes and, in special humanitarian circumstances, foodstuffs."

On 9th August 1990, Security Council Resolution 662 again demanded Iraqi withdrawal from Kuwait, and described the annexation as "null and void".

On 18th August 1990, Security Council Resolution 664 reaffirmed Resolutions 660, 661 and 662, demanded that Iraq respect the rights of foreign nationals and permit them to leave Kuwait and Iraq, and that Iraq should rescind its closure of diplomatic missions in Kuwait and withdrawal of diplomatic status.

On 25th August 1990, Security Council Resolution 665 reaffirmed previous resolutions and called upon those Member States deploying maritime forces to the Gulf to use such measures commensurate to the specific circumstances as may be necessary under the authority of the Security Council to halt all inward and outward maritime shipping in order to inspect and verify their cargoes and destinations and to ensure strict implementation of the provisions related to such shipping laid down in Resolution 661. The Security Council thereby approved the naval blockade of Iraq and Kuwait.

General

On 16th August 1990, the Association of International Bond Dealers issued a Notice advising its members to seek local legal advice on issues arising from transactions with Kuwaiti counterparties, in particular in relation to Rules 430, 459 and 487 of its Rules. The AIBD however expressed the view that its Rules 420, 450 and 480 provide "an appropriate means of closing out Kuwaiti related transactions under the given circumstances."

Simmons & Simmons
14 Dominion Street
London EC2M 2RJ

13th September 1990

STATUTORY INSTRUMENTS

1990 No. 1591

EMERGENCY POWERS

The Control of Gold, Securities, Payments and Credits (Kuwait) Directions 1990

Made - - -	*2nd August 1990*
Coming into force -	*2nd August 1990*
Laid before Parliament	*3rd August 1990*

Whereas the Treasury are satisfied that action to the detriment of the economic position of the United Kingdom is being or is likely to be taken by the government of or persons resident in Kuwait.

Now, therefore, the Treasury, in exercise of the powers conferred upon them by section 2 of the Emergency Laws (Re-enactments and Repeals) Act 1964(a) hereby give the following directions:–

1. These directions may be cited as the Control of Gold, Securities, Payments and Credits (Kuwait) Directions 1990 and shall come into force on 2nd August 1990.

2. Except with permission granted by or on behalf of the Treasury, no order given by or on behalf of the government of or any person resident in Kuwait at the time of the coming into force of these directions or at any later time while these directions are in force, shall be carried out, insofar as the order–

    (i) requires the person to whom the order is given to make any payment or to part with any gold or securities; or

    (ii) requires any change to be made in the persons to whose credit any sum is to stand or to whose order any gold or securities is to be held.

Thomas Sackville
John Major
Two of the Lords Commissioners
2nd August 1990   of Her Majesty's Treasury

(a) 1964 c.60; section 2 was amended by the Finance Act 1968 (c.44), section 61(10) and Schedule 20, Part V.

EXPLANATORY NOTE

(This note is not part of the Order)

These Directions prohibit (except with Treasury permission) any recipient in the United Kingdom, the Channel Islands or the Isle of Man of an order from the government of or any person resident in Kuwait from carrying out that order insofar as the order (a) requires the recipient to make any payment or to part with any gold or securities or (b) requires any change to be made in the persons to whose credit any sum is to stand or to whose order any gold or securities is to be held.

Bank of England

Press Notice

Press Office
Threadneedle Street
London EC2R 8AH
Telephone 01-601 4411

THE CONTROL OF GOLD, SECURITIES, PAYMENTS AND CREDITS (KUWAIT) DIRECTIONS 1990

The Bank of England, on behalf of HM Treasury, announce that bargains entered into in the money, foreign exchange and securities markets, or payments instructions received for immediate execution, involving Kuwaiti counterparties, prior to 3.00pm BST (2.00pm GMT) on Thursday 2 August, may be completed without infringing the above Directions.

Questions regarding the above, or in relation to other pre-existing commitments, should be referred to the Bank of England, telephone numbers:

            071-601 3764
            071-601 5463
            071-601 4768
            071-601 3309
            071-601 3250
            071-601 3848

3 August 1990

STATUTORY INSTRUMENTS

1990 No. 1616

EMERGENCY POWERS

The Control of Gold, Securities, Payments and Credits (Republic of Iraq) Directions 1990

Made - - - -	*4th August 1990*
Coming into force	*4th August 1990*
Laid before Parliament	*6th August 1990*

Whereas the Treasury are satisfied that action to the detriment of the economic position of the United Kingdom is being or is likely to be taken by the government of or persons resident in the Republic of Iraq;

Now, therefore, the Treasury, in exercise of the powers conferred upon them by section 2 of the Emergency Laws (Re-enactments and Repeals) Act 1964(**a**) hereby give the following directions:

1. These directions may be cited as the Control of Gold, Securities, Payments and Credits (Republic of Iraq) Directions 1990 and shall come into force on 4th August 1990.

2. Except with permission granted by or on behalf of the Treasury, no order given by or on behalf of the government of or any person resident in the Republic of Iraq at the time of the coming into force of these directions or at any later time while these directions are in force, shall be carried out, insofar as the order–

(i) requires the person to whom the order is given to make any payment or to part with any gold or securities; or

(ii) requires any change to be made in the persons to whose credit any sum is to stand or to whose order any gold or securities is to be held.

Thomas Sackville
John Major
Two of the Lords Commissioners
of Her Majesty's Treasury

4th August 1990

(**a**) 1964 c.60; section 2 was amended by the Finance Act 1968 (c.44), section 61(10) and Schedule 20, Part V.

EXPLANATORY NOTE

(This note is not part of the Order)

These Directions prohibit (except with Treasury permission) any recipient in the United Kingdom, the Channel Islands or the Isle of Man of an order from the government of or any person resident in the Republic of Iraq from carrying out that order insofar as the order (a) requires the recipient to make any payment or to part with any gold or securities or (b) requires any change to be made in the persons to whose credit any sum is to stand or to whose order any gold or securities is to be held.

Bank of England Notice

EMERGENCY LAWS (RE-ENACTMENTS AND REPEALS) ACT 1964

KUWAIT

7 August 1990

This Notice draws attention in convenient form to the effect of the law contained in the Act and to the Treasury directions given thereunder. The purpose of these directions is to prevent the misappropriation of Kuwaiti assets in the United Kingdom. By virtue of powers delegated by HM Treasury, this Notice gives certain permissions which are subject to the condition that they shall not apply in any case where it is so directed by or on behalf of HM Treasury.

References in this Notice to the United Kingdom should be read to include the Channel Islands and the Isle of Man.

This Notice supersedes the guidance set out in the Bank of England's Press Notices issued on 3 August 1990.

INTRODUCTION

1 On 2 August 1990 HM Treasury issued directions under the Emergency Laws (Re-enactments and Repeals) Act 1964 which have the effect of freezing certain Kuwaiti assets.

2 The directions are contained in Statutory Instrument 1990 No 1591 which may be cited as The Control of Gold, Securities, Payments and Credits (Kuwait) Directions 1990. Copies may be obtained from HM Stationery Office.

3 Article 2 of the Statutory Instrument reads as follows:- ''Except with permission granted by or on behalf of the Treasury, no order given by or on behalf of the government of or any person resident in Kuwait at the time of the coming into force of these directions or at any later time while these directions are in force, shall be carried out, insofar as the order:-

 (i) requires the person to whom the order is given to make any payment or to part with any gold or securities; or

 (ii) requires any change to be made in the persons to whose credit any sum is to stand or to whose order any gold or securities is to be held.''

4 These directions apply to all persons (including bodies corporate) in the United Kingdom, including the Channel Islands and the Isle of Man, and to all other persons, wherever they may be, who are ordinarily resident in the United Kingdom and who are citizens of the United Kingdom and Colonies* or British protected persons.

Residents of Kuwait

5 For the purposes of the directions, a resident of Kuwait is any person, including any body corporate, normally resident in that country on 2 August 1990 or at any later time. A branch in Kuwait of any business is treated as if the branch were a body corporate resident in Kuwait. Orders given by branches outside Kuwait of any body corporate resident in Kuwait or by branches of any business whose head office is in Kuwait are given on behalf of persons resident in Kuwait, irrespective of the location of such branches. Persons resident or becoming resident in Kuwait should not subsequently be treated as resident elsewhere without prior reference to the Bank of England.

6 Bodies incorporated in the United Kingdom whose day-to-day control and management are established in the United Kingdom are to be treated for the purposes of this Notice as resident in the United Kingdom unless a controlling interest is held by the government of Kuwait.

7 Residential status should be determined by reference to the facts. Among bodies to be regarded as residents of Kuwait are Kuwait Investment Office, Kuwait Petroleum Corporation and branches in the United Kingdom of the National Bank of Kuwait. Branches in the United Kingdom of the United Bank of Kuwait are to be regarded as residents of the United Kingdom. Cases of doubt should be referred to the Bank of England.

*In this paragraph "citizens of the United Kingdom and Colonies" means a British citizen, a British Dependent Territories citizen or a British Overseas citizen or a person who under the Hong Kong (British Nationality) Order 1986 is a British National (Overseas). See the British Nationality Act 1981 Section 51 (3) (a) (ii).

Overseas Branches of United Kingdom companies and businesses

8 Branches outside the United Kingdom of companies incorporated in the United Kingdom and of businesses whose head offices are in the United Kingdom may continue to comply with orders from persons who are resident in Kuwait but permissions will not normally be given to enable orders received by persons subject to the directions from persons resident in Kuwait to be transferred to and executed by branches outside the United Kingdom.

Kuwaiti Accounts

9 The sterling, foreign currency and gold bullion accounts of persons resident in Kuwait held in the United Kingdom with institutions authorised under the Banking Act 1987 or the Building Societies Act 1986 ("banks") should be designated and are referred to below as "Kuwaiti Accounts". Funds held by solicitors, accountants, stockbrokers etc. on behalf of Kuwaiti residents should be placed in a separate account.

Payments ordered by or on behalf of residents of Kuwait

10 Any payment required by an order given by or on behalf of the government of Kuwait or a resident of Kuwait to a person subject to the directions (see paragraph 4) is prohibited except with permission. Permission is hereby given for any such payment whether in sterling or in foreign currency to be made to a "Kuwaiti Account". Permission will not normally be given for any such payment to any account held outside the United Kingdom.

Balances on "Kuwaiti Accounts"

11 Permission will not normally be given for any change to be made in the persons to whose credit any sum held on a "Kuwaiti Account" is to stand.

Payments from "Kuwaiti Accounts"

12 Permission is hereby given to debit the accounts of residents of Kuwait (see paragraph 5) for the following purposes:-

(a) living, medical, educational and similar expenses of residents of Kuwait in the United Kingdom;

(b) payments in respect of goods which have been shipped or otherwise despatched to the United Kingdom against evidence of shipment or despatch and production of any necessary import licence;

(c) payments to reimburse United Kingdom banks who have made payments in respect of Kuwaiti trade under irrevocable letters of credit;

(d) payments to other "Kuwaiti Accounts" in the United Kingdom;

(e) payment of interest, or repayment of capital, on borrowings from United Kingdom residents by residents of Kuwait;

(f) payments to United Kingdom residents in connection with the operations of vessels and aircraft owned by, or on charter to, residents of Kuwait;

(g) payment to United Kingdom residents of insurance premiums;

(h) payment of charges to banks in the United Kingdom;

(i) payment of sums due to the Inland Revenue and HM Customs and Excise;

(j)   distributions and payments to residents of the United Kingdom under wills and intestacies and under trusts set up before 2 August 1990.

13 The Bank of England will consider applications to debit ''Kuwaiti Accounts'' for the following purposes:-

(a)   payments to meet travel expenditure by residents of Kuwait leaving the United Kingdom;

(b)   payments for charitable purposes;

(c)   payments of the types described in paragraphs 12 (e), (f), (g) and (j) to residents outside the United Kingdom.

Provision of cash to residents of Kuwait in the United Kingdom

14 Banks and other persons in the United Kingdom may provide cash in reasonable amounts in sterling in the United Kingdom to residents of Kuwait -

(a)   in exchange for foreign currency of equivalent value;

(b)   against cheques, travellers' cheques, travellers' letters of credit, credit and debit cards and other payment instruments;

(c)   through automated teller machines.

Payments by branches in the United Kingdom of companies resident in Kuwait

15 Permission is hereby given for branches in the United Kingdom of companies or businesses resident in Kuwait to make salary and pension payments to persons living in the United Kingdom.

16 The Bank of England will consider applications from branches in the United Kingdom of companies or businesses resident in Kuwait to make other payments.

Pensions etc due to residents of Kuwait

17 Any necessary permission is hereby given for the payment outside the United Kingdom of pensions due to residents of Kuwait and of widows' and widowers' annuities associated with deceased husbands' and wives' employments.

Credits, loans and overdrafts

18 Any necessary permissions are hereby given for credits or loans to, and overdrafts on, ''Kuwaiti Accounts''. Except where covered by the terms of paragraph 12 (e) above, permission will be required for payments by debit of a ''Kuwaiti Account'' to service such loans.

19 Any necessary permission will be given on application for banks which are agents for syndicated loans and credits to the government or residents of Kuwait to distribute capital repayments and interest payments to participants in the syndicates, provided that the necessary funds are received from outside the United Kingdom.

Maturing bills of exchange

20 All necessary permissions are hereby given for maturing bills of exchange drawn by residents of Kuwait and accepted by persons subject to the directions to be paid by the acceptor on maturity and for ''Kuwaiti Accounts'' to be debited in reimbursement.

Gold

21 Permission is required for persons subject to the directions to do anything which involves parting with any gold coin or gold bullion wherever located or making any change in the persons to whose order any gold coin or gold bullion is to be held in compliance with an order given by or on behalf of the government or residents of Kuwait.

Securities

22 The Emergency Laws (Re-enactments and Repeals) Act 1964 as amended defines securities as including :-

(a)   shares, stocks, bonds, notes (other than promissory notes), debentures, debenture stock, certificates of deposit and Treasury and other government bills;

(b)   a deposit receipt in respect of the deposit of securities;

(c)   a unit or a sub-unit of a unit trust;

(d)   an annuity granted under the Government Annuities Act 1929, or to which either Part I or Part II of that Act applies, and a life assurance policy or other contract entered into with an assurance company for securing the payment in the future of any capital sum or sums, or of an annuity;

(e)   a warrant conferring an option to acquire a security;

(f)   a share in an oil royalty;

but excludes bills of exchange.

For the purposes of the permissions covered in this Notice "securities" includes those instruments defined as "investments" in Schedule 1 of the Financial Services Act 1986.

23 Permission is required for persons subject to the directions to do anything which involves parting with any securities or making any change in the persons to whose order any securities are to be held in compliance with an order given by or on behalf of residents of Kuwait.

24 The Bank of England will consider applications from persons engaged in the discretionary management of portfolios of securities on behalf of residents of Kuwait to continue to manage the portfolios in question. Permission will not normally be given to allow the release of portfolios from United Kingdom control.

25 Where securities are registered in the name of a person resident in Kuwait, no order requiring payments of capital monies, dividends or interest to any person outside the United Kingdom may be complied with without permission, which is hereby given provided payment is to a "Kuwaiti Account". Such permission is also given where persons subject to the directions hold bearer securities for account of persons resident in Kuwait. All other cases should be referred to the Bank of England.

Kuwaiti securities

26 No permissions are necessary for transfers of securities issued by residents of Kuwait except when a person subject to the directions is required, by order given by or on behalf of a resident of Kuwait, to part with any such security or to make any change in the persons to whose order any such security is to be held.

27 Application should be made to the Bank of England for any permission needed by paying agents in the United Kingdom for Kuwaiti securities to make interest, dividend or redemption payments on, or to buy in, such securities.

Pre-zero transactions

28 Any necessary permissions are hereby given for any bargains entered into in the money, foreign exchange, commodities (other than physical oil) and securities markets, including derivatives, or any payment instructions received for immediate execution, involving Kuwaiti counterparties, prior to 3.00pm BST (2.00pm GMT) on 2 August 1990, to be completed.

Oil

29 Permission is hereby given for payments to be made by debit of a "Kuwaiti Account" for shipments of oil, provided the necessary import licence and evidence of shipment are exhibited.

Applications and Enquiries

30 Application should be made to the Bank of England in respect of any transaction which is not covered by the permissions given in this Notice.

31 Applications for permissions should be addressed to the Bank of England, Threadneedle Street, London, EC2R 8AH, and marked for the attention of the Iraq and Kuwait Emergency Unit (IKEU). Applications may also be made by facsimile transmission (071-601 4309).

32 Telephone enquiries may be made to 071-601 3250/3309/3764/3848/4768/5463

Bank of England
7 August 1990

Bank of England Notice

EMERGENCY LAWS (RE-ENACTMENTS AND REPEALS) ACT 1964

IRAQ

7 August 1990

This Notice draws attention in convenient form to the effect of the law contained in the Act and to the Treasury Directions given thereunder. By virtue of powers delegated by HM Treasury, this Notice gives certain permissions which are subject to the condition that they shall not apply in any case where it is so directed by or on behalf of HM Treasury.

References in this Notice to the United Kingdom should be read to include the Channel Islands and the Isle of Man.

This Notice supersedes the guidance set out in the Bank of England's Press Notice issued on 4 August 1990.

INTRODUCTION

1 On 4 August 1990 HM Treasury issued directions under the Emergency Laws (Re-enactments and Repeals) Act 1964 which have the effect of freezing certain Iraqi assets held in the United Kingdom.

2 The directions are contained in Statutory Instrument 1990 No 1616 which may be cited as The Control of Gold, Securities, Payments and Credits (Republic of Iraq) Directions 1990. Copies may be obtained from HM Stationery Office.

3 Article 2 of the Statutory Instrument reads as follows:- ''Except with permission granted by or on behalf of the Treasury, no order given by or on behalf of the government of or any person resident in the Republic of Iraq at the time of the coming into force of these directions or at any later time while these directions are in force, shall be carried out, insofar as the order :-

(i) requires the person to whom the order is given to make any payment or to part with any gold or securities; or

(ii) requires any change to be made in the persons to whose credit any sum is to stand or to whose order any gold or securities is to be held.''

4 These directions apply to all persons (including bodies corporate) in the United Kingdom, including the Channel Islands and the Isle of Man, and to all other persons, wherever they may be, who are ordinarily resident in the United Kingdom and who are citizens of the United Kingdom and Colonies* or British protected persons.

Residents of Iraq

5 For the purposes of the directions, a resident of Iraq is any person, including any body corporate, normally resident in that country on 4 August 1990 or at any later time. A branch in Iraq of any business is treated as if the branch were a body corporate resident in Iraq. Orders given by branches outside Iraq of any body corporate resident in Iraq or by branches of any business whose head office is in Iraq are given on behalf of persons resident in Iraq, irrespective of the location of such branches. Persons resident or becoming resident in Iraq should not subsequently be treated as resident elsewhere without prior reference to the Bank of England.

6 Residential status should be determined by reference to the facts. Cases of doubt should be referred to the Bank of England.

Overseas Branches of United Kingdom companies and businesses

7 Branches outside the United Kingdom of companies incorporated in the United Kingdom and of businesses whose head offices are in the United Kingdom may continue to comply with orders from persons who are resident in Iraq but permissions will not normally be given to enable orders received by persons subject to the directions from persons resident in Iraq to be transferred to and executed by branches outside the United Kingdom.

Iraqi Accounts

8 The sterling, foreign currency and gold bullion accounts of persons resident in Iraq held in the United Kingdom with institutions authorised under the Banking Act 1987 or the Building Societies Act 1986 ("banks") should be designated and are referred to below as "Iraqi Accounts". Funds held by stockbrokers, solicitors, accountants, etc, on behalf of Iraqi residents, should be placed in a separate account.

*In this paragraph "citizens of the United Kingdom and Colonies" means a British citizen, a British Dependant Territories citizen or a British Overseas citizen or a person who under the Hong Kong (British Nationality) Order 1986 is a British National (Overseas). See the British Nationality Act 1981 Section 51 (3) (a) (ii).

Payments ordered by or on behalf of residents of Iraq

9 Any payment required by an order given by or on behalf of the government of Iraq or a resident of Iraq to a person subject to the directions (see paragraph 4) is prohibited except with permission. Permission will not normally be given for any such payment to any account held outside the United Kingdom. Permission is hereby given for any such payment whether in sterling or in foreign currency to be made to an "Iraqi Account". No payment or transfer may be made from one "Iraqi Account" to another "Iraqi Account" without permission, which will not normally be given.

Balances on "Iraqi Accounts"

10 Permission will not normally be given for any change to be made in the persons to whose credit any sum held on an "Iraqi Account" is to stand.

Payments from "Iraqi Accounts"

11 The Bank of England will consider applications to debit "Iraqi Accounts" for the following purposes:-

  (a) living, medical, educational and similar expenses of residents of Iraq in the United Kingdom. Payments to meet travel expenditure by residents of Iraq leaving the United Kingdom will also be considered. For all of these purposes, reasonable amounts will normally be permitted;

  (b) payments in respect of goods which have been shipped or otherwise despatched to the United Kingdom. Production of any necessary import licence and evidence of shipment or despatch will be required;

  (c) payments to reimburse United Kingdom banks who have made payments in respect of Iraqi trade under irrevocable letters of credit;

  (d) payments for charitable purposes.

12 For the time being, permission will not normally be given for "Iraqi Accounts" to be debited for the following purposes:-

  (a) payments to other "Iraqi Accounts";

  (b) payment of interest, or repayment of capital, on borrowings by residents of Iraq;

  (c) payments in connection with the operations of vessels and aircraft owned by, or on charter to, residents of Iraq;

  (d) payment of insurance premiums.

13 Permission is hereby given for the payment from "Iraqi Accounts" of -

  (a) charges to banks in the United Kingdom;

  (b) sums due to the Inland Revenue and HM Customs and Excise, provided no overdraft is thereby created on an "Iraqi Account";

  (c) distributions and payments to residents of the United Kingdom under wills and intestacies and under trusts set up before 4 August 1990.

Provision of cash to residents of Iraq in the United Kingdom

14 Banks and other persons in the United Kingdom may provide cash in reasonable amounts in sterling in the United Kingdom to residents of Iraq -

(a) in exchange for foreign currency (other than Iraqi or Kuwaiti dinars) of equivalent value;

(b) against cheques, travellers' cheques, travellers' letters of credit, credit and debit cards and other payment instruments except for those payable in Iraqi dinars;

(c) through automated teller machines.

Payments by branches in the United Kingdom of companies resident in Iraq

15 Permission is hereby given for branches in the United Kingdom of Iraqi companies or businesses resident in Iraq to make salary and pension payments to persons living in the United Kingdom.

16 The Bank of England will consider applications from branches in the United Kingdom of companies or businesses resident in Iraq to make other payments of a current nature. Payments of a capital nature will not normally be permitted.

Pensions, etc, due to residents of Iraq

17 Any necessary permission is hereby given for the payment outside the United Kingdom of pensions due to residents of Iraq and of widows' and widowers' annuities associated with deceased husbands' and wives' employments.

Credits, loans and overdrafts

18 For the time being, permissions will not normally be given to enable existing or intending lenders subject to the directions (see paragraph 4 above) to comply with any order given by or on behalf of a person resident of Iraq to make any payment - without such permission no further drawings may be made under existing facilities. No new arrangements should be entered into, no bills of exchange drawn by a resident of Iraq should be accepted, and no credits, discount or acceptance facilities of any sort should be issued, confirmed or advised for account of, or in favour of, or on behalf of, a resident of Iraq.

19 Any necessary permission is, however, hereby given for irrevocable credits opened before 4 August 1990 in respect of transactions with Iraq to be honoured. "Iraqi Accounts" may not be debited in reimbursement except where otherwise permitted in this Notice.

Maturing bills of exchange

20 All necessary permissions are hereby given for maturing bills of exchange drawn by residents of Iraq and accepted before 4 August 1990 by persons subject to the directions to be paid by the acceptor on maturity. "Iraqi Accounts" may not be debited in reimbursement without permission.

Servicing of syndicated loans

21 Any necessary permission will be given for banks which are agents for syndicated loans and credits to the government or residents of Iraq to distribute capital repayments and interest payments to participants in the syndicates, provided that the necessary funds are received from outside the United Kingdom. Applications for such permission should be made to the Bank of England. Permission will not normally be given to use balances on "Iraqi Accounts".

Roll-overs

22 Persons subject to the directions who have made loans to residents of Iraq before 4 August 1990 and who wish to roll-over such loans in accordance with the terms of the loan agreement should refer to the Bank of England. Attention should be drawn to the reasons for any reduction in the interest rate or change in currency composition. Permission will not normally be given to enable the drawn down amount of the loan or credit to be increased on roll-over.

Gold

23 Permission is required for persons subject to the directions to do anything which involves parting with any gold coin or gold bullion wherever located or making any change in the persons to whose order any gold coin or gold bullion is to be held in compliance with an order given by or on behalf of the government or residents of Iraq. Such permission will not normally be given.

Securities

24 The Emergency Laws (Re-enactments and Repeals) Act 1964 as amended defines securities as including -

(a)   shares, stocks, bonds, notes (other than promissory notes), debentures, debenture stock, certificates of deposit and Treasury and other government bills;

(b)   a deposit receipt in respect of the deposit of securities;

(c)   a unit or a sub-unit of a unit trust;

(d)   an annuity granted under the Government Annuities Act 1929 or to which either Part I or Part II of that Act applies, and a life assurance policy or other contract entered into with an assurance company for securing the payment in the future of any capital sum or sums or of an annuity;

(e)   a warrant conferring an option to acquire a security;

(f)   a share in an oil royalty;

but excludes bills of exchange.

For the purposes of the permissions covered in this Notice "securities" includes those instruments defined as "investments" in Schedule 1 of the Financial Services Act 1986.

25 Permission is required for persons subject to the directions to do anything which involves parting with any securities or making any change in the persons to whose order any securities are to be held in compliance with an order given by or on behalf of residents of Iraq.

26 The Bank of England will consider applications from persons engaged in the discretionary management of portfolios of securities on behalf of residents of Iraq to continue to manage the portfolios in question. Permission will not normally be given to allow the release of portfolios from United Kingdom control.

27 Where securities are registered in the name of a person resident in Iraq, no order requiring payments of capital monies, dividends or interest to any person outside the United Kingdom may be complied with. Permission is hereby given for such payments to be made to "Iraqi Accounts". Such permission is also given where persons subject to the directions hold bearer securities for account of persons resident in Iraq.

Iraqi securities

28 No permissions are necessary for transfers of securities issued by residents of Iraq except when a person subject to the directions is required, by order given by or on behalf of a resident of Iraq, to part with any such security or to make any change in the persons to whose order any such security is to be held.

29 Applications should be made to the Bank of England for any permission needed by paying agents in the United Kingdom for Iraqi securities to make interest, dividend or redemption payments on, or to buy in, such securities.

Pre-zero transactions

30 Any necessary permissions are hereby given for any bargains entered into in the money, foreign exchange, commodities (other than physical oil) and securities markets, including derivatives, or any payment instructions received for immediate execution, involving Iraqi counterparties, prior to 4.30 p.m. BST (3.30 p.m. GMT) on 4 August 1990, to be completed.

Oil

31 Permission is hereby given for payments to be made by debit of an "Iraqi Account" for shipments of oil, provided the necessary import licence and evidence of shipment are exhibited.

Application and enquiries

32 Application should be made to the Bank of England in respect of any transaction which is not covered by the permissions given in this Notice.

33 Applications for permissions should be addressed to the Bank of England, Threadneedle Street, London, EC2R 8AH, and marked for the attention of the Iraq and Kuwait Emergency Unit (IKEU). Applications may also be made by facsimile transmission (071-601 4309).

34 Telephone enquiries may be made to 071-601 3250/3309/3764/3848/4768/5463.

Bank of England
7 August 1990

S T A T U T O R Y   I N S T R U M E N T S

1990 No. 1640

CUSTOMS AND EXCISE

The Export of Goods (Control) (Iraq and Kuwait Sanctions) Order 1990

Made - - - -	*8th August 1990*
Coming into force	*9th August 1990*

The Secretary of State, in exercise of powers conferred by section 1 of the Import, Export and Customs Powers (Defence) Act 1939**(a)** and now vested in him **(b)**, and of all other powers enabling him in that behalf, hereby makes the following Order:–

Citation, commencement and interpretation

1.—(1) This Order may be cited as the Export of Goods (Control) (Iraq and Kuwait Sanctions) Order 1990 and shall come into force on 9th August 1990.

(2) Unless the context otherwise requires, any expression used in this Order shall have the meaning it bears in the Export of Goods (Control) Order 1989**(c)**.

Prohibition on exportation to Iraq and Kuwait

2.—(1) Subject to article 3 of this Order, all goods are prohibited to be exported from the United Kingdom to any destination in Iraq or Kuwait, or to any destination in any other country for delivery, directly or indirectly, to a person for the purposes of any business carried on in or operated from Iraq or Kuwait.

(2) Any licence granted by the Secretary of State under any other Order relating to the control of exports made by virtue of the powers conferred by section 1 of the Import, Export and Customs Powers (Defence) Act 1939, and any licence granted under any other enactment prohibiting or restricting the exportation of goods, shall be subject to paragraph (1) of this article.

Exceptions

3. Nothing in article 2 of this Order shall prohibit the exportation of any goods under the authority of a licence granted by the Secretary of State under this Order, provided that all conditions attaching to the said licence are complied with.

(a) 1939 c.69.
(b) *See* S.I. 1970/1537.
(c) S.I. 1989/2376, amended by S.I. 1990/128, 735, 893 and 1588.

Enforcement

4. Articles 5, 6 and 7 of the Export of Goods (Control) Order 1989 (customs powers for demanding evidence of destination, offences in connection with applications for licences and conditions attaching to licences, and declarations as to goods and powers of search) shall apply for the enforcement of the provisions of this Order as they apply for the enforcement of the said Order of 1989.

Modification and revocation of licences

5. Any licence granted by the Secretary of State in pursuance of article 3 of this Order may be modified or revoked by him at any time.

R. J. Meadway
An Under Secretary,
Department of Trade and Industry

8th August 1990

EXPLANATORY NOTE

(This note is not part of the Order)

This Order prohibits the export, without a licence under the Order from the Secretary of State, of all goods to Iraq and Kuwait, or to any other destination where the goods are to be delivered to a person for the purposes of a business carried on in or operated from Iraq or Kuwait.

STATUTORY INSTRUMENTS

1990 No. 1651

UNITED NATIONS

The Iraq and Kuwait (United Nations Sanctions) Order 1990

Made - - - -	*8th August 1990*
Laid before Parliament	*8th August 1990*
Coming into force	*9th August 1990*

At the Court at HM Yacht Britannia the 8th day of August 1990

Present,

The Queen's Most Excellent Majesty in Council

Whereas under Article 41 of the Charter of the United Nations the Security Council of the United Nations have, by a resolution adopted on 6th August 1990, called upon Her Majesty's Government in the United Kingdom and all other States to apply certain measures to give effect to a decision of that Council in relation to the situation between Iraq and Kuwait.

Now therefore Her Majesty, in exercise of the powers conferred on Her by section 1 of the United Nations Act 1946 (**a**), is pleased, by and with the advice of Her Privy Council, to order, and it is hereby ordered, as follows:

Citation and commencement, extent and interpretation

1.—(1) This Order may be cited as the Iraq and Kuwait (United Nations Sanctions) Order 1990.

(2) This Order shall come into force on the 9th August 1990.

(3) This Order shall extend to the United Kingdom and the Isle of Man.

(4) In this Order the following expressions have the meanings hereby respectively assigned to them, that is to say–

"commander", in relation to an aircraft, means the person designated as commander of the aircraft by the operator thereof, and includes any person who is for the time being in charge of command of the aircraft;

"land transport vehicle" includes a barge;

"master", in relation to a ship, includes any person (other than a pilot) for the time being in charge of the ship;

"operator", in relation to an aircraft or to a land transport vehicle, means the person for the time being having the management of the aircraft or the vehicle;

"owner", where the owner of a ship is not the operator, means the operator and any person to whom it is chartered; and

"person in Iraq or Kuwait" includes any body constituted or incorporated under the law of Iraq or Kuwait and any body carrying on business (whether within Iraq or

---

(**a**) 1946 c.45.

N

Kuwait or not) which is controlled by persons or bodies resident in Iraq or Kuwait or constituted or incorporated as aforesaid.

Exportation of Goods from Iraq or Kuwait

2.—(1) Except under the authority of a licence granted by the Secretary of State under this Order or the Import of Goods (Control) Order 1954(**a**), the Control of Gold, Securities, Payments and Credits (Republic of Iraq) Directions 1990(**b**), the Control of Gold, Securities, Payments and Credits (Kuwait) Directions 1990(**c**), the Hong Kong (Control of Gold, Securities, Payments and Credits: Kuwait and Republic of Iraq) Order 1990 or the Caribbean Territories (Control of Gold, Securities, Payments and Credits: Kuwait and Republic of Iraq) Order 1990(**d**) no person shall–

    (a) make or carry out any contract for the exportation of any goods from either Iraq or Kuwait;

    (b) make or carry out any contract for the sale of any goods which he intends or has reason to believe that another person intends to export from either Iraq or Kuwait; or

    (c) do any act calculated to promote the exportation of any goods from either Iraq or Kuwait.

(2) No person shall deal in any goods that have been exported from Iraq or Kuwait after the 6th August 1990, that is to say, shall, by way of trade or otherwise for gain, acquire or dispose of such goods or of any property or interest in them or any right to or charge upon them or process them or do any act calculated to promote any such acquisition, disposal or processing by himself or any other person. Provided that the aforesaid prohibition shall not apply, if a licence has been granted under paragraph (1) of this Article, to any dealing authorised by the said licence.

Supply of goods to Iraq and Kuwait

3. Except under the authority of a licence granted by the Secretary of State under this Order or under the Export of Goods (Control) (Iraq and Kuwait Sanctions) Order 1990 (**e**) no person shall–

    (a) supply or deliver or agree to supply or deliver to or to the order of any person in either Iraq or Kuwait any goods that are not in either country;

    (b) supply or deliver or agree to supply or deliver any such goods to any person, knowing or having reasonable cause to believe that they will be supplied or delivered to or to the order of a person in either Iraq or Kuwait or that they will be used for the purposes of any business carried on in or operated from Iraq or Kuwait; or

    (c) do any act calculated to promote the supply or delivery of any goods to any person in Iraq or Kuwait or for the purpose of any business carried on in Iraq or Kuwait in contravention of the foregoing provisions of this paragraph.

Application of Articles 2 and 3

4.—(1) The provisions of Articles 2 and 3 shall apply to any person within the United Kingdom or any place to which this Order extends and to any person elsewhere who–

    (a) is a British citizen, a British Dependent Territories citizen, a British Overseas citizen, a British Subject or a British protected person; or

    (b) is a body incorporated or constituted under the law of the United Kingdom or the law of any other place to which this Order extends.

(2) Any person specified in paragraph 1 of this Article who contravenes the provisions of Article 2(1) or (2) or Article 3 shall be guilty of an offence.

Carriage of certain goods exported from or destined for Iraq or Kuwait

5.—(1) Without prejudice to the generality of Article 2 of this Order, no ship or aircraft to which this Article applies and no land transport vehicle within the United Kingdom shall be used for the carriage of any goods if those goods are being or have been

---

(**a**) S.I. 1954/23, amended by S.I. 1954/627, 1975/2117 and 1978/806.   (**b**) S.I. 1990/1616.
(**c**) S.I. 1990/1591.   (**d**) S.I. 1990/1625.   (**e**) S.I. 1990/1640.

exported from Iraq or Kuwait in contravention of Article 2(1) öf this Order.

(2) Without prejudice to the generality of Article 3 of this Order, no ship or aircraft to which this Article applies and no land transport vehicle within the United Kingdom shall be used for the carriage of any goods if the carriage is, or forms part of, carriage from any place outside Iraq or Kuwait to any destination therein or to any person for the purposes of any business carried on in or operated from Iraq or Kuwait.

(3) This Article applies to British ships registered in the United Kingdom or in any other country or place to which this Order extends, to aircraft so registered and to any other ship or aircraft that is for the time being chartered to any person who is–

(a) a British citizen, a British Dependent Territories citizen, a British Overseas citizen or a British protected person; or

(b) a body incorporated or constituted under the law of the United Kingdom or the law of any other place to which this Order extends.

(4) If any ship, aircraft or land transport vehicle is used in contravention of paragraph (1) of this Article, then each of the following persons–

(a) in the case of a British ship registered in the United Kingdom or in any other place to which this Order extends or any aircraft so registered, the owner and master of the ship or, as the case may be, the operator and the commander of the aircraft; or

(b) in the case of any other ship or aircraft, the person to whom the ship or aircraft is for the time being chartered and, if he is such a person as is referred to in sub-paragraph (a) or sub-paragraph (b) of paragraph (3) of this Article, the master of the ship or, as the case may be, the operator and the commander of the aircraft; or

(c) in the case of a land transport vehicle, the operator of the vehicle;

shall be guilty of an offence against the Order unless he proves that he did not know and had no reason to suppose that the goods were being or had been exported from Iraq or Kuwait in contravention of Article 2(1) of this Order.

(5) If any ship, aircraft or land transport vehicle is used in contravention of paragraph (2) of this Article, then–

(a) in the case of a British ship registered in the United Kingdom or in any other country or place to which this Order extends or any aircraft so registered, the owner and the master of the ship or, as the case may be, the operator and the commander of the aircraft; or

(b) in the case of any other ship or aircraft, the person to whom the ship or aircraft is for the time being chartered and, if he is such a person as is referred to in sub-paragraph (a) or sub-paragraph (b) of paragraph (3) of this Article, the master of the ship or, as the case may be, the operator and the commander of the aircraft; or

(c) in the case of a land transport vehicle, the operator of the vehicle,

shall be guilty of an offence against this Order unless he proves that he did not know and had no reason to suppose that the carriage of the goods in question was, or formed part of, carriage from any place outside Iraq or Kuwait to any destination therein or to any person for the purposes of any business carried on in or operated from Iraq or Kuwait.

(6) Nothing in this Article applies to goods in respect of which a licence granted by the Secretary of State is in force under–

(a) Article 2(1) of this Order; or

(b) Article 3 of this Order.

(7) Nothing in this Article shall be construed so as to prejudice any other provision of law prohibiting or restricting the use of ships, aircraft or land transport vehicles.

Investigation, etc. of suspected British ships and aircraft

6.—(1) Where any authorised officer, that is to say, any such officer as is referred to in section 692(1) of the Merchant Shipping Act 1894(**a**), has reason to suspect that any British ship registered in the United Kingdom or in any other country or place to which this Order extends has been or is being or is about to be used in contravention of

(**a**) S.I. 1894 c.60.

paragraph (1) or paragraph (2) of Article 5 of the Order, he may (either alone or accompanied and assisted by persons under his authority) board the ship and search her and, for that purpose, may use or authorise the use of reasonable force, and he may request the master of the ship to furnish such information relating to the ship and her cargo and produce for his inspection such documents so relating and such cargo as he may specify; and an authorised officer (either there and then or upon consideration of any information furnished or document or cargo produced in pursuance of such a request) may, in the case of a ship that is reasonably suspected of being or of being about to be used in contravention of Article 5(2) of this Order, exercise the following further powers with a view to the prevention of the commission (or the continued commission) of any such contravention or in order that enquiries into the matter may be pursued, that is to say, he may either direct the master to refrain, except with the consent of an authorised officer, from landing at any port specified by the officer any part of the ship's cargo that is so specified or request the master to take any one or more of the following steps–

(a) to cause the ship not to proceed with the voyage on which she is then engaged or about to engage until the master is notified by any authorised officer that the ship may so proceed;

(b) if the ship is then in a port in the United Kingdom or in any other country or place to which this Order extends, to cause her to remain there until the master is notified by any authorised officer that the ship may depart;

(c) if the ship is then in any other place, to take her to any such port specified by the officer and to cause her to remain there until the master is notified as mentioned in sub-paragraph (b) of this paragraph; and

(d) to take her to any other destination that may be specified by the officer in agreement with the master;

and the master shall comply with any such request or direction.

(2) Without prejudice to the provisions of paragraph (8) of this Article, where a master refuses or fails to comply with a request made under this Article that his ship shall or shall not proceed to or from any place or where an authorised officer otherwise has reason to suspect that such a request that has been so made may not be complied with, any such officer may take such steps as appear to him to be necessary to secure compliance with that request and, without prejudice to the generality of the foregoing, may for that purpose enter upon, or authorise entry upon, that ship and use, or authorise the use of, reasonable force.

(3) Where any officer of customs and excise or any person authorised by the Secretary of State for that purpose either generally or in a particular case has reason to suspect that any aircraft registered in the United Kingdom or in any other country or place to which this Order extends or any aircraft for the time being chartered to any person specified in paragraph 3 of Article 5 of this Order has been or is being or is about to be used in contravention of paragraph (1) or paragraph (2) of Article 5 of this Order, that authorised person or that officer may request the charterer, the operator and the commander of the aircraft or any of them to furnish such information relating to the aircraft and its cargo and produce for their or his inspection such documents so relating and such cargo as they or he may specify, and that authorised person or that officer may (either alone or accompanied and assisted by persons under his authority) board the aircraft and search it and, for that purpose, may use or authorise the use of reasonable force; and, if the aircraft is then in the United Kingdom any such authorised person or any such officer (either there and then or upon consideration of any information furnished or document or cargo produced in pursuance of such a request) may further request the charterer, operator and the commander or any of them to cause the aircraft to remain in the United Kingdom until notified that the aircraft may depart; and the charterer, the operator and the commander shall comply with any such request.

(4) Without prejudice to the provisions of paragraph (8) of this Article, where any person authorised as aforesaid or any such officer as aforesaid has reason to suspect that any request that an aircraft should remain in the United Kingdom that has been made under paragraph (3) of this Article may not be complied with, that authorised person or that officer may take such steps as appear to him to be necessary to secure compliance with that request and, without prejudice to the generality of the foregoing, may for that purpose–

(a) enter, or authorise entry, upon any land and upon that aircraft;

(b) detain, or authorise the detention of, that aircraft; and

(c) use, or authorise the use of, reasonable force.

(5) A person authorised by the Secretary of State to exercise any power for the purposes of paragraph (3) or paragraph (4) of this Article shall, if requested to do so, produce evidence of his authority before exercising that power.

(6) No information furnished or document produced by any person in pursuance of a request made under this Article shall be disclosed except–

(a) with the consent of the person by whom the information was furnished or the document was produced–

Provided that a person who has obtained information or is in possession of a document only in his capacity as servant or agent of another person may not give consent for the purposes of this sub-paragraph but such consent may instead be given by any person who is entitled to that information or to the possession of that document in his own right; or

(b) to any person who would have been empowered under this Article to request that it be furnished or produced or to any person holding or acting in any office under or in the service of the Crown in respect of the Government of the United Kingdom or under or in the service of the Government of any other place to which this Order extends; or

(c) on the authority of the Secretary of State, to any organ of the United Nations or to any person in the service of the United Nations or of the Government of any other country for the purpose of assisting the United Nations or that Government in securing compliance with or detecting evasion of measures in relation to Iraq or Kuwait decided upon by the Security Council of the United Nations; or

(d) with a view to the institution of, or otherwise for the purposes of, any proceedings for an offence against this Order or, with respect to any of the matters regulated by this Order, for an offence against any enactment relating to customs or for an offence against any provision of law with respect to similar matters that is for the time being in force in any place to which this Order extends.

(7) Any power conferred by this Article to request the furnishing of information or the production of a document or of cargo for inspection shall include a power to specify whether the information should be furnished orally or in writing and in what form and to specify the time by which and the place in which the information should be furnished or the document or cargo produced for inspection.

(8) Each of the following persons shall be guilty of an offence against this Order, that is to say–

(a) A master of a ship who disobeys any direction given under paragraph (1) of this Article with respect to the landing of any cargo;

(b) A master of a ship or a charterer or an operator or a commander of the aircraft who, without reasonable excuse, refuses or fails within a reasonable time to comply with any request made under this Article by any person empowered to make it or who wilfully furnishes false information or produces false documents to such a person in response to such a request;

(c) A master or a member of a crew of a ship or a charterer or an operator or a commander or a member of a crew of an aircraft who wilfully obstructs any such person (or any person acting under the authority of any such person) in the exercise of his powers under this Article.

(9) Nothing in this Article shall be construed so as to prejudice any other provision of law conferring powers or imposing restrictions or enabling restrictions to be imposed with respect to ships or aircraft.

Obtaining of evidence and information

7. The provisions of the Schedule to this Order shall have effect in order to facilitate the obtaining, by or on behalf of the Secretary of State or the Commissioners of Customs

and Excise, of evidence and information for the purpose of securing compliance with or detecting evasion of this Order and in order to facilitate the obtaining, by or on behalf of the Secretary of State or the Commissioners of Customs and Excise, of evidence of the commission of an offence against this Order or with respect to any of the matters regulated by this Order, of an offence relating to customs.

Penalties and proceedings

8.—(1) Any person guilty of an offence against his Order shall be liable–

    (a) on conviction on indictment to imprisonment for a term not exceeding two years or to a fine or to both; or

    (b) on summary conviction to imprisonment for a term not exceeding six months or to a fine not exceeding the statutory maximum or to both.

(2) Where any body corporate is guilty of an offence against this order, and that offence is proved to have been committed with the consent or connivance of, or to be attributable to any neglect on the part of, any director, manager, secretary or other similar officer of the body corporate of any person who was purporting to act in any such capacity, he, as well as the body corporate, shall be guilty of that offence and shall be liable to be proceeded against and punished accordingly.

(3) Summary proceedings for an offence against this Order, being an offence alleged to have been committed outside the United Kingdom, may be commenced at any time not later than twelve months from the date on which the person charged first enters the United Kingdom after committing the offence.

(4) Proceedings against any person for an offence against this Order may be taken before the appropriate court in the United Kingdom, or in any place to which this Order extends, having jurisdiction in the place where that person is for the time being.

(5) No proceedings for an offence against this Order shall be instituted in England, Wales, Northern Ireland or in the Isle of Man except by the Secretary of State or with the consent of the Attorney General or, as the case may be, the Attorney General for Northern Ireland or the Isle of Man.

Provided that this paragraph shall not prevent the arrest, or the issue or execution of a warrant for the arrest, of any person in respect of such an offence, or the remand in custody or on bail of any person charged with such an offence, notwithstanding that the necessary consent to the institution of proceedings for the offence has not been obtained.

Exercise of powers of the Secretary of State

9.—(1) The Secretary of State may to such extent and subject to such restrictions and conditions as he may think proper, delegate or authorise the delegation of any of his powers under this Order (other than the power to give authority under Schedule 1 to this Order to apply for a search warrant) to any person, or class or description of persons, approved by him, and references in this Order to the Secretary of State shall be construed accordingly.

(2) Any licences granted under this Order may be either general or special, may be subject to or without conditions, may be limited so as to expire on a specified date unless renewed and may be varied or revoked by the authority that granted them.

Miscellaneous

10.—(1) This Order applies to or in relation to any ship or aircraft or any body corporate that purports to be registered in any particular place or, as the case may be, that purports to be incorporated or constituted under the law of that place as it applies to or in relation to any ship or aircraft that is so registered or any body corporate that is so incorporated or constituted.

(2) Any provision of this Order which prohibits the doing of a thing except under the authority of a licence granted by the Secretary of State shall not have effect in relation to any such thing done in a place other than the United Kingdom to which this Order extends or done elsewhere outside the United Kingdom by a person who is ordinarily resident in, or by a body incorporated or constituted under the law of, that place, provided that it is so done under the authority of a licence or with permission granted, in

accordance with any law in force in that place (being a law substantially corresponding to the relevant provision of this Order), by the authority competent in that behalf under that law.

G. I. de Deney
Clerk of the Privy Council

SCHEDULE   Article 7

EVIDENCE AND INFORMATION

1.—(1) Without prejudice to any other provision of this Order, or any provision of any other law, the Secretary of State (or any person authorised by him for that purpose either generally or in a particular case) or the Commissioners of Customs and Excise may request any person in or resident in the United Kingdom to furnish to him or them (or to that authorised person) any information in his possession or control, or to produce to him or them (or to that authorised person) any document in his possession or control, which he or they (or that authorised person) may require for the purpose of securing compliance with or detecting evasion of this Order; and any person to whom such a request is made shall comply with it within such time and in such manner as may be specified in the request.

(2) Nothing in the foregoing sub-paragraph shall be taken to require any person who has acted as counsel or solicitor for any person to disclose any privileged communication made to him in that capacity.

(3) Where a person is convicted on indictment for failing to furnish information or produce a document when requested so to do under this paragraph, the court may make an order requiring him, within such period as may be specified in the order, to furnish the information or produce the document.

(4) The power conferred by this paragraph to request any person to produce documents shall include power to take copies of or extracts from any document so produced and to request that person, or, where that person is a body corporate, any other person who is a present or past officer of, or is employed by, the body corporate, to provide an explanation of any of them.

2.—(1) If any justice of the peace is satisfied by information on oath given by a person authorised by the Secretary of State or the Commissioners of Customs and Excise to act for the purposes of this paragraph either generally or in a particular case–

(a) that there is reasonable ground for suspecting that an offence against this Order or, with respect to any of the matters regulated by this Order, an offence against any enactment relating to customs has been or is being committed and that evidence of the commission of the offence is to be found on any premises specified in the information, or in any vehicle, vessel or aircraft so specified; or

(b) that any documents which ought to have been produced under paragraph 1 of this Schedule and have not been produced are to be found on any such premises or in any such vehicle, vessel or aircraft,

he may grant a search warrant authorising any constable, together with any other persons named in the warrant and any other constables, to enter the premises specified in the information or, as the case may be, any premises upon which the vehicle, vessel or aircraft so specified may be, at any time within one month from the date of the warrant and to search the premises, or, as the case may be, the vehicle, vessel or aircraft.

(2) A person authorised by any such warrant as aforesaid to search any premises or any vehicle, vessel or aircraft may search every person who is found in, or whom he has reasonable ground to believe to have recently left or to be about to enter, those premises or that vehicle, vessel or aircraft and may seize any document or article found on the premises or in the vehicle, vessel or aircraft or on such person which he has reasonable ground to believe to be evidence of the commission of any such offence as aforesaid or any documents which he has reasonable ground to believe ought to have been produced under paragraph 1 of this Schedule or to take in relation to any such article or document any other steps which may appear necessary for preserving it and preventing interference with it–

Provided that no female shall, in pursuance of any warrant issued under this paragraph, be searched except by a female.

(3) Where, by virtue of this paragraph, a person is empowered to enter any premises, vehicle, vessel or aircraft he may use such force as is reasonably necessary for that purpose.

(4) Any documents or articles of which possession is taken under this paragraph may be retained for a period of three months or, if within that period there are commenced any proceedings for such an offence as aforesaid to which they are relevant, until the conclusion of those proceedings.

(5) In the application of this paragraph to Scotland any reference to a justice of the peace includes a reference to the sheriff.

3. A person authorised by the Secretary of State to exercise any power for the purposes of this Schedule shall, if requested to do so, produce evidence of his authority before exercising that power.

4. No information furnished or document produced (including any copy of extract made of any document produced) by any person in pursuance of a request made under this Schedule and no document seized under paragraph 2(2) of this Schedule shall be disclosed except–

(a) with the consent of the person by whom the information was furnished or the document was produced or the person from whom the document was seized:

Provided that a person who has obtained information or is in possession of a document only in his capacity as servant or agent of another person may not give consent for the purposes of this sub-paragraph but such consent may instead be given by any person who is entitled to that information or to the possession of that document in his own right; or

(b) to any person who would have been empowered under this Schedule to request that it be furnished or produced or to any person holding or acting in any office under or in the service of the Crown; or

(c) on the authority of the Secretary of State, to any organ of the United Nations or to the Government of any other country for the purpose of assisting the United Nations or that Government in securing compliance with or detecting evasion of measures in relation to this Order decided upon by the Security Council of the United Nations; or

(d) with a view to the institution of, or otherwise for the purposes of, any proceedings for an offence against this Order or, with respect to any of the matters regulated by this Order, for an offence against any enactment relating to customs or for an offence against any provision of law with respect to similar matters that is for the time being in force in any country or place to which this Order extends.

5. Any person who–

(a) without reasonable excuse, refuses or fails within the time and in the manner specified (or, if no time has been specified, within a reasonable time) to comply with any request made under this Schedule by any person who is empowered to make it; or

(b) wilfully furnishes false information or a false explanation or otherwise wilfully obstructs any person in the exercise of his powers under this Schedule; or

(c) with intent to evade the provisions of this Schedule, destroys, mutilates, defaces, secretes or removes any document,

shall be guilty of an offence against this Order.

EXPLANATORY NOTE

(This note is not part of the Order)

This Order imposes restrictions pursuant to a decision of the Security Council of the United Nations in Resolution No. 661 of 6th August 1990, on the exportation of goods from Iraq and Kuwait and on supply of goods to Iraq and Kuwait as well as certain related activities and dealings, including the carriage of such goods in British ships or aircraft. The Order also makes provision for the investigation of ships and aircraft that are suspected of contravening the Order.

Bank of England

Press Notice

Press Office
Threadneedle Street
London EC2R 8AH
Telephone 01-601 4411

KUWAIT AND IRAQ - EMERGENCY LAWS (RE-ENACTMENTS AND REPEALS) ACT 1964

CONTRACT BONDS (INCLUDING PERFORMANCE BONDS)

In accordance with the powers delegated by HM Treasury, the Bank of England is withdrawing, with effect from 25 August, the permission contained in their Notices of 7 August under which payments may be made to Kuwaiti Accounts or Iraqi Accounts in compliance with calls on contract bonds.   Such permission will not in future be given.

24 August 1990

Notes for Editors

In the present emergency, a significant number of UK export contracts to Iraq and Kuwait have been halted. As a result, many UK exporters face the possibility that they would have to pay if an Iraqi or Kuwaiti importer made a call on a contract or performance bond given by the exporter's UK bank on frustrated contracts. Although payment would go to an Iraqi or Kuwaiti account and be blocked at that point, the exporter would still be out of funds.

The Bank and the Government are urgently considering possible long-term solutions to this issue. In the meantime they are withdrawing the delegated authority for payments.

On 7 August the Bank of England published its detailed guidance on the operation of the freezes on certain Kuwaiti and Iraqi assets held in the United Kingdom. Questions arising should be addressed to the Iraq and Kuwait Emergency Unit, telephone numbers 071-601 3764/5463/4768/3309/3250/3848. Press enquiries should as usual be directed to the Bank's Press Office 071 601 4411.

EMERGENCY LAWS (RE—ENACTMENTS AND REPEALS) ACT 1964

Bank of England Notice dated 7 August 1990:   **IRAQ**

Supplement No. 1
25 August 1990

CONTRACT BONDS (INCLUDING PERFORMANCE BONDS)

1   The purpose of this Supplement, which is issued in accordance with the powers delegated by HM Treasury, is to withdraw the authority whereby calls under all types of contract bond may be met by payments to "Iraqi Accounts" in the United Kingdom. With effect from the date of this Supplement, no such permission will be given.

2   Accordingly, delete paragraph 9 and substitute the following:

"Payments ordered by or on behalf of residents of Iraq

9   Any payment required by an order given by or on behalf of the government of Iraq or a resident of Iraq to a person subject to the directions (see paragraph 4) is prohibited except with permission. Permission will not be given for payments to meet calls under contract bonds. Nor will permission normally be given for any payment to any account held outside the United Kingdom. Permission is hereby given for any other payment whether in sterling or in foreign currency to be made to an "Iraqi Account" in the United Kingdom. No payment or transfer may be made from one "Iraqi Account" to another "Iraqi Account" without permission, which will not normally be given."

BANK OF ENGLAND
25 August 1990

EMERGENCY LAWS (RE—ENACTMENTS AND REPEALS) ACT 1964

Bank of England Notice dated 7 August 1990: **KUWAIT**

Supplement No. 1
25 August 1990

CONTRACT BONDS (INCLUDING PERFORMANCE BONDS)

1 The purpose of this Supplement, which is issued in accordance with the powers delegated by HM Treasury, is to withdraw the authority whereby calls under all types of contract bond may be met by payments to "Kuwaiti Accounts" in the United Kingdom. With effect from the date of this Supplement, no such permission will be given.

2 Accordingly, delete paragraph 10 and substitute the following:

"Payments ordered by or on behalf of residents of Kuwait

10 Any payment required by an order given by or on behalf of the government of Kuwait or a resident of Kuwait to a person subject to the directions (see paragraph 4) is prohibited except with permission. Permission will not be given for payments to meet calls under contract bonds. Nor will permission normally be given for any payment to any account held outside the United Kingdom. Permission is hereby given for any other payment whether in sterling or in foreign currency to be made to a "Kuwaiti Account" in the United Kingdom."

BANK OF ENGLAND
25 August 1990

EMERGENCY LAWS (RE—ENACTMENTS AND REPEALS) ACT 1964

Bank of England Notice dated 7 August 1990:   **IRAQ**

Supplement No. 2
3 SEPTEMBER 1990

RETURNING UK NATIONALS

1   The purpose of this Supplement, which is issued in accordance with the powers delegated by HM Treasury, is to permit banks (as defined in paragraph 8 of the Notice) to remove restrictions on the accounts of UK Nationals who were resident in Iraq on 4 August and who have since returned to the United Kingdom.

2   Accordingly, notwithstanding the terms of the last sentence of paragraph 5 of the Notice, banks may, without reference to the Bank of England, redesignate as UK resident the "Iraqi Accounts" of personal customers provided that:-

(a)   the person concerned is a UK passport holder;

(b)   he/she was in Iraq on 4 August 1990; **and**

(c)   has since returned to the United Kingdom;

(d)   in the case of joint accounts both accountholders are now in the United Kingdom.

3   If conditions (a) - (c) above are met but if condition (d) is not fulfilled, banks may make available reasonable amounts to such persons by debit to "Iraqi Accounts" to meet living, medical, educational and similar expenses.

BANK OF ENGLAND
3 SEPTEMBER 1990

EMERGENCY LAWS (RE—ENACTMENTS AND REPEALS) ACT 1964

Bank of England Notice dated 7 August 1990:   **KUWAIT**

Supplement No. 2
3 SEPTEMBER 1990

RETURNING UK NATIONALS

1   The purpose of this Supplement, which is issued in accordance with the powers delegated by HM Treasury, is to permit banks (as defined in paragraph 9 of the Notice) to remove restrictions on the accounts of UK Nationals who were resident in Kuwait on 2 August and who have since returned to the United Kingdom.

2   Accordingly, notwithstanding the terms of the last sentence of paragraph 5 of the Notice, banks may, without reference to the Bank of England, redesignate as UK resident the "Kuwaiti Accounts" of personal customers provided that:-

(a)   the person concerned is a UK passport holder;

(b)   he/she was in Kuwait on 2 August 1990; **and**

(c)   has since returned to the United Kingdom;

(d)   in the case of joint accounts both accountholders are now in the United Kingdom.

3   If condition (d) is not fulfilled, Banks are reminded that paragraphs 12 and 14 of the Notice give permission for funds to be released from Kuwaiti Accounts to meet living, medical, educational and similar expenses within the United Kingdom.

BANK OF ENGLAND
3 SEPTEMBER 1990

STATUTORY INSTRUMENTS

1990 No. 1768

UNITED NATIONS

The Iraq and Kuwait (United Nations Sanctions) (Amendment) Order 1990

Made - - - -	*29th August 1990*
Laid before Parliament	*29th August 1990*
Coming into force	*30th August 1990*

At the Court at Balmoral, the 29th day of August 1990

Present,

The Queen's Most Excellent Majesty in Council

Whereas under Article 41 of the Charter of the United Nations the Security Council of the United Nations have, by a resolution adopted on 6th August 1990, called upon Her Majesty's Government in the United Kingdom and all other States to apply certain measures to give effect to a decision of that Council in relation to the situation between Iraq and Kuwait;

Now therefore Her Majesty, in exercise of the powers conferred on Her by section 1 of the United Nations Act 1946(**a**), is pleased, by and with the advice of Her Privy Council, to order, and it is hereby ordered, as follows:

Citation and commencement

1.—(1) This Order may be cited as the Iraq and Kuwait (United Nations Sanctions) (Amendment) Order 1990 and shall come into force on 30th August 1990.

(2) This Order and the Iraq and Kuwait (United Nations Sanctions) Order 1990(**b**) (hereinafter referred to as "the principal Order") may be cited together as the Iraq and Kuwait (United Nations Sanctions) Orders 1990.

(3) This Order shall be construed as one with the principal Order.

Amendment of Article 2 of the principal Order

2. Article 2 of the principal Order shall be replaced by the following article–

"Exportation of goods from Iraq or Kuwait and dealing and processing

2.—(1) Except under the authority of a licence granted by the Secretary of State under this Order or the Import of Goods (Control) Order 1954(**c**), or a permission granted under the Control of Gold, Securities, Payments and Credits (Republic of Iraq) Directions 1990(**d**), the Control of Gold, Securities, Payments and Credits (Kuwait) Directions 1990(**e**), the Hong Kong (Control of Gold, Securities, Payments and Credits: Kuwait and Republic of Iraq) Order 1990, the Caribbean Territories (Control of Gold, Securities, Payments and Credits: Kuwait and

---

(**a**) 1946 c.54.   (**b**) S.I. 1990/1651.   (**c**) S.I. 1954/23, amended by S.I. 1954/627, 1975/2117 and 1978/806.
(**d**) S.I. 1990/1616.   (**e**) S.I. 1990/1591.

Republic of Iraq) Order 1990(**a**) or the Iraq and Kuwait (United Nations Sanctions) (Bermuda) Order 1990(**b**) no person shall–

(a) make or carry out any contract for the exportation of any goods from either Iraq or Kuwait;

(b) make or carry out any contract for the sale of any goods which he intends or has reason to believe that another person intends to export from either Iraq or Kuwait; or

(c) do any act calculated to promote the exportation of any goods from either Iraq or Kuwait.

(2) Except under the authority of a licence granted by the Secretary of State under this Order, no person shall deal in any goods that have been exported from Iraq or Kuwait after 6th August 1990, that is to say, shall, by way of trade or otherwise for gain, acquire or dispose of such goods or of any property or interest in them or any right to or charge upon them or process them or do any act calculated to promote any such acquisition, disposal or processing by himself or any other person.

(3) Nothing in paragraph 1(b) or (c) or (2) of this article shall apply where the exportation of the goods from Iraq or Kuwait is authorised by a licence granted by the Secretary of State under this Order, or the importation of the goods into the United Kingdom or any place to which this Order extends is authorised by a licence granted by the Secretary of State under the Import of Goods (Control) Order 1954."

Amendment of Article 3 of the principal Order

3. Article 3 of the principal Order shall be replaced by the following Article–

"Supply of Goods to Persons in Iraq or Kuwait

3.—(1) Except under the authority of a licence granted by the Secretary of State under this Order or under the Export of Goods (Control) (Iraq and Kuwait Sanctions) Order 1990(**c**) no person shall–

(a) supply or deliver or agree to supply or deliver to or to the order of any person in either Iraq or Kuwait any goods that are not in either country;

(b) supply or deliver or agree to supply or deliver any such goods to any person, knowing or having reasonable cause to believe that they will be supplied or delivered to or to the order of any person in either Iraq or Kuwait or to any person for the purposes of any business carried on in or operated from Iraq or Kuwait; or

(c) do any act calculated to promote the supply or delivery of any such goods to any person in Iraq or Kuwait or to any person for the purposes of any business carried on in or operated from Iraq or Kuwait.

(2) Nothing in paragraph (1)(b) or (c) of this article shall apply where the supply or delivery of the goods to or to the order of the person concerned is authorised by a licence granted by the Secretary of State under this Order or under the Export of Goods (Control) (Iraq and Kuwait Sanctions) Order 1990."

Addition of New Article 4A to principal Order

4. The following article shall be inserted in the principal Order immediately after article 4–

"Payments under bonds

4A.—(1) Except under the authority of permission granted by or on behalf of

(a) the Treasury under this Order or under the Control of Gold, Securities, Payments and Credits (Republic of Iraq) Directions 1990(**d**) or the Control of Gold, Securities, Payments and Credits (Kuwait) Directions 1990(**e**)

(b) the Financial Secretary under the Hong Kong (Control of Gold, Securities, Payments and Credits: Kuwait and Republic of Iraq) Order 1990, or

(c) the Governor under the Caribbean Territories (Control of Gold, Securities, Payments and Credits: Kuwait and Republic of Iraq) Order 1990(**f**) or the

---

(**a**) S.I. 1990/1625.
(**d**) S.I. 1990/1616.

(**b**) S.I. 1990/1769.
(**e**) S.I. 1990/1591.

(**c**) S.I. 1990/1640.
(**f**) S.I. 1990/1625.

Iraq and Kuwait (United Nations Sanctions) (Bermuda) Order 1990(**a**), no person shall make any payment to or to the order of any person in Iraq or Kuwait under or in respect of a bond to which this article applies.

(2) Except under the Authority of a permission granted by or on behalf of the Treasury under this Order no person shall do any act to the purpose of obtaining payment, or make any payment, in respect of any right to indemnity in respect of any bond to which this article applies, where payment under the bond is, or would if payment were to be made by a person referred to in paragraph (6) below be, unlawful by virtue of paragraph (1) above.

(3) A bond to which this article applies is a bond given in respect of a contract the performance of which is unlawful wholly or in part by virtue of this Order, or the Export of Goods (Control) (Iraq and Kuwait Sanctions) Order 1990.

(4) In this article–
  (a) "bond" means an agreement under which a person ("the obligor") agrees that, if called upon to do so, or if a third party fails to fulfil contractual obligations owed to another, the obligor will make payment to or to the order of the other party to the agreement; and
  (b) "make payment" means make payment by any method, including but not restricted to, the grant or any agreement to the exercise of, any right of set off, accord and satisfaction and adjustment of any account.

(5) Any person who does any act for the purpose of obtaining payment, or who makes payment, in contravention of paragraph (1) or (2) of this article shall be guilty of an offence against this Order.

(6) Paragraphs (1) and (2) of this article shall apply to any person within the United Kingdom or any place to which this Order extends, and to any person elsewhere who
  (a) is a British Citizen, a British Dependent Territory citizen, a British overseas citizen or a British protected person; or
  (b) is a body incorporated or constituted under the law of any part of the United Kingdom or the law of any other place to which this Order extends.

(7) Any permission granted under this Article may be either general or special, may be subject to or without conditions, may be limited so as to expire on a specified date unless renewed and may be varied or revoked by the authority that granted it."

Amendment of Article 5 of the principal Order

5.—(1) The following paragraphs shall be substituted for paragraphs (1) and (2) of article 5 of the principal Order–

"**5.**—(1) Without prejudice to the generality of article 2 of this Order and except under the authority of a licence granted by the Secretary of State under this Order, no ship or aircraft to which this article applies and no land transport vehicle within the United Kingdom or any place to which this Order extends shall be used for the carriage of any goods if those goods are being or have been exported from Iraq or Kuwait after 6th August 1990.

(2) Without prejudice to the generality of article 3 of this Order and except under the authority of a licence granted by the Secretary of State under this Order, no ship or aircraft to which this article applies and no land transport vehicle within the United Kingdom or any place to which this Order extends shall be used for the carriage of any goods if the carriage is, or forms part of, carriage from any place outside Iraq or Kuwait to any destination therein, or to any person for the purposes of any business carried on in or operated from Iraq or Kuwait".

(2) In paragraph (4) of article 5 for the words "in contravention of article 2(1) of this Order" which appear at the end of that paragraph there shall be substituted the words "after 6th August 1990".

(**a**) S.I. 1990/1769.

(3) Paragraph (6) of article 5 shall be replaced by the following paragraph–

"(6) Nothing in paragraph (1) of this article shall apply where the exportation of the goods concerned from Iraq or Kuwait was authorised by a licence granted by the Secretary of State under this Order, or the importation of the goods concerned into the United Kingdom or any place to which this Order extends was authorised by a licence granted by the Secretary of State under the Import of Goods (Control) Order 1954."

(4) The following paragraph shall be inserted after paragraph (6) of Article 5–

"(6A) Nothing in paragraph (2) of this article shall apply where the supply or delivery or exportation from the United Kingdom of the goods concerned to that destination was authorised by a licence granted by the Secretary of State under this Order or the Export of Goods (Control) (Iraq and Kuwait Sanctions) Order 1990(a)"

Amendment of Article 6 of the principal Order

6.—(1) Paragraph (3) of article 6 of the principal Order shall be amended by the insertion, after the words "United Kingdom" where they appear for the second and third time in that paragraph, of the words "or in any other place to which this Order extends".

(2) Paragraph (4) of article 6 of the principal Order shall be amended by the insertion after the words "United Kingdom" of the words "or in any other place to which this Order extends".

(3) The following paragraphs shall be inserted in article 6 of the principal Order immediately after paragraph (4)–

"(4A) Where any officer of customs and excise or any person authorised by the Secretary of State for that purpose either generally or in a particular case has reason to suspect that any land transport vehicle in the United Kingdom or in any place to which this Order extends has been or is being or is about to be used in contravention of paragraph (1) or paragraph (2) of article 5 of this Order, that authorised person or that officer may request the operator and driver of the vehicle or either of them to furnish such information relating to the vehicle and any goods contained in it and produce for their or his inspection such documents so relating and such goods as they or he may specify, and that authorised person or that officer may (either alone or accompanied and assisted by persons under his authority) board the vehicle and, for that purpose, may use or authorise the use of reasonable force; any such authorised person or such officer (either there and then or upon consideration of any information furnished or document or goods produced in pursuance of such a request) may further require the operator or driver to cause the vehicle to remain in the United Kingdom or any other place to which this Order extends until notified that the vehicle may depart; and the operator and the driver shall comply with any such request.

(4B) Without prejudice to the provisions of paragraph (8) of this article where any person authorised as aforesaid has reason to suspect that a request that a land transport vehicle should remain in the United Kingdom or in any other place to which this Order extends that has been made under paragraph (4A) of this article may not be complied with, that authorised person or that officer may take such steps as appear to him to be necessary to secure compliance with that request and, without prejudice to the generality of the foregoing, may for that purpose–

(a) enter, or authorise entry, upon any land and upon that vehicle;

(b) detain, or authorise the detention of, that vehicle; and

(c) use, or authorise the use of reasonable force."

(4) Paragraph (8) of article 6 of the principal Order shall be amended by insertion after the word "aircraft" in sub-paragraphs (b) and (c) of the words "or an operator or a driver of the land transport vehicle".

(a) S.I. 1990/1640.

Amendment of Article 10 of the principal Order

7.   Paragraph (2) of article 10 of the principal Order shall be amended by the deletion of the words "granted by the Secretary of State" in line 2, and by the insertion in the same line immediately after the words "of a licence", of the words "or permission".

R. P. Bulling
Clerk of the Privy Council

EXPLANATORY NOTE

(This note is not part of the Order)

This Order is made under the United Nations Act 1946 and amends the Iraq and Kuwait (United Nations Sanctions) Order 1990 ("the principal Order"). It inserts a new Article 4A which prohibits payments under any bond in respect of a contract the performance of which is unlawful by virtue of the principal Order or the Export of Goods (Control) (Iraq and Kuwait Sanctions) Order 1990. It also prohibits the making of or obtaining payments under certain indemnities arising under such bonds.

This Order extends the enforcement powers under the principal Order to land transport vehicles. It also introduces minor amendments to articles 2, 3, 5, 6 and 10 of the principal Order.

Supplementary Material: UK

Bank of England

Press Notice

Press Office
Threadneedle Street
London EC2R 8AH
Telephone 01-601 4411

THE CONTROL OF GOLD, SECURITIES, PAYMENTS AND CREDITS (KUWAIT) DIRECTIONS 1990

The Bank of England, on behalf of HM Treasury, announce that authorised institutions and building societies may permit private Kuwaiti individuals to draw on their personal accounts in the UK without infringing the above Directions.

3 August 1990

EMERGENCY LAWS (RE—ENACTMENTS AND REPEALS) ACT 1964

Bank of England Notice dated 7 August 1990:   **KUWAIT**

Supplement No. 3
13 SEPTEMBER 1990

CONTRACTS OF INSURANCE

1   The purpose of this Supplement, which is issued in accordance with the powers delegated by HM Treasury, is to withdraw the permission for payments in respect of contracts of insurance (including reinsurance) to be made by payments to "Kuwaiti Accounts" in the United Kingdom. With effect from the date of this Supplement, such payments may only be made if permission for the payment or for the class of payments within which the payment falls is given on behalf of HM Treasury by the Secretary of State for Trade and Industry. Further information about the need for permission is contained in the DTI Press Notice dated 12 September 1990.

2   Accordingly, delete paragraph 10 as inserted by Supplement No. 1 and substitute the following:

"Payments ordered by or on behalf of residents of Kuwait

10(a) Any payment required by an order given by or on behalf of the government of Kuwait or a resident of Kuwait to a person subject to the directions (see paragraph 4) is prohibited except with permission. Permission will not be given for payments to meet calls under contract bonds. Nor will permission normally be given for any payment to any account held outside the United Kingdom. Subject to paragraph 10(b) below permission is hereby given for any other payment whether in sterling or in foreign currency to be made to a "Kuwaiti Account" in the United Kingdom.

(b) Payment to "Kuwaiti Accounts" in respect of contracts of insurance (including reinsurance) will require the permission of the Secretary of State for Trade and Industry."

BANK OF ENGLAND
13 SEPTEMBER 1990

EMERGENCY LAWS (RE—ENACTMENTS AND REPEALS) ACT 1964

Bank of England Notice dated 7 August 1990:   **IRAQ**

Supplement No. 3
13 SEPTEMBER 1990

CONTRACTS OF INSURANCE

1   The purpose of this Supplement, which is issued in accordance with the powers delegated by HM Treasury, is to withdraw the permission for payments in respect of contracts of insurance (including reinsurance) to be made by payments to "Iraqi Accounts" in the United Kingdom. With effect from the date of this Supplement, such payments may only be made if permission for the payment or for the class of payments within which the payment falls is given on behalf of HM Treasury by the Secretary of State for Trade and Industry. Further information about the need for permission is contained in the DTI Press Notice dated 12 September 1990.

2   Accordingly, delete paragraph 9 as inserted by Supplement No. 1 and substitute the following:

"Payments ordered by or on behalf of residents of Iraq

9(a) Any payment required by an order given by or on behalf of the government of Iraq or a resident of Iraq to a person subject to the directions (see paragraph 4) is prohibited except with permission. Permission will not be given for payments to meet calls under contract bonds. Nor will permission normally be given for any payment to any account held outside the United Kingdom. Subject to paragraph 9(b) below permission is hereby given for any other payment whether in sterling or in foreign currency to be made to a "Iraqi Account" in the United Kingdom. No payment or transfer may be made from one "Iraqi Account" to another "Iraqi Account" without permission, which will not normally be given.

(b) Payment to "Iraqi Accounts" in respect of contracts of insurance (including reinsurance) will require the permission of the Secretary of State for Trade and Industry."

BANK OF ENGLAND
13 SEPTEMBER 1990